CAN'T BUY MY LOVE

HOW ADVERTISING CHANGES THE WAY
WE THINK AND FEEL

JEAN KILBOURNE

A TOUCHSTONE BOOK
PUBLISHED BY SIMON & SCHUSTER
NEW YORK LONDON TORONTO SYDNEY SINGAPORE

TOUCHSTONE
Rockefeller Center
1230 Avenue of the Americas
New York, NY 10020

Copyright © 1999 by Jean Kilbourne

All rights reserved,
including the right of reproduction
in whole or in part in any form.
First Touchstone Edition 2000
TOUCHSTONE and colophon are registered trademarks
of Simon & Schuster, Inc.

Designed by Carla Bolte

Manufactured in the United States of America

10 9 8 7 6 5 4 3 2 1

The Library of Congress has cataloged the Free Press edition as follows:

Kilbourne, Jean.
    Deadly persuasion : why women and girls must fight the addictive
power of advertising / Jean Kilbourne.
        p.   cm.
    Includes bibliographical references and index.
        1. Women in advertising.   2. Women consumers.   I. Title.
    HF5823.K363   1999
    658.8'34'082—dc21   99-38496
                                                         CIP

ISBN 0-684-86599-8
        0-684-86600-5 (Pbk)
Previously published as *Deadly Persuasion*

IN MEMORY OF LILLIAN BRAZIER KILBOURNE (1910–1952)
AND W. WALLACE KILBOURNE (1910-1999)

AND FOR MY DAUGHTER, CLAUDIA

CONTENTS

FOREWORD

Mary Pipher

LET'S START WITH TWO WORDS: "GOLDEN ARCHES." WHAT'S THE FIRST thought that comes to your mind? I bet I know. It's the same thought that comes to everyone's mind when they hear those words. You could be a vegetarian who never watches television; you would still know. We all know. Advertising in America really, really works.

In *Deadly Persuasion,* Jean Kilbourne exposes "the United States of Advertising" as no one else has dared to before. With stories, research support, and cogent analysis, Kilbourne explores advertising's commodification of our lives, not only in America but all over the world. In Poland, where billboards with anorexic models sprout along the streets, or in Burma, where Leonardo DiCaprio beach towels hang in the markets, countries confront the glitzy perils of advertising and its bankrupt values. In a world increasingly organized around money and driven by hype, Kilbourne's book is timely and important.

In her introduction, Kilbourne writes that her whole life has led her to this book. It is the culmination of her lifelong interest in feminism, advertising, and addictions, and it is full of heart. As a young woman, Kilbourne was brilliant (with a perfect score on the verbal SAT), well educated, and ambitious. But after graduating from Wellesley, she could find only secretarial jobs or work with employers who wanted sexual favors. Eventually she created her own job deconstructing advertising. Many of us first "met" Kilbourne in her electrifying film *Killing Us Softly,* which changed forever the way we view ads about women. But later, Kilbourne expanded her analysis into many areas, such as the effect of advertising on our values, relationships, and commitment to civic life.

In this book she debunks the idea that any of us are "uninfluenced by advertising." Advertising works best precisely because we don't think it works on us. Kilbourne reports that the average American sees more than three thousand ads per day and spends more than three years of his or her life watching commercials. Their messages are inside our intimate relationships, our homes, our hearts, and our heads. She argues that our culture increasingly has adopted what John Maynard Keynes called "the values of the casino." Advertising is a key purveyor of these casino values, and it contributes mightily to a climate of denial in which, as Kilbourne points out, "relationships flounder and addictions flourish." The addict is, after all, the ideal customer; and when an addict gets well, someone loses money. Using recent mainstream advertisements, Kilbourne demonstrates how ads encourage us to objectify each other and to believe that our most significant relationships are with products. As she says, "Ads turn lovers into things and things into lovers."

Jean Kilbourne shows that the main message is that happiness comes from products. Advertisers exploit our very real human desires for connection, calmness, respect, and excitement. Every emotion is used to sell something. The cumulative effect of all these ads is to leave us romantic about objects and deeply cynical about humans, who are after all much more complicated than products. ("Who says guys are afraid of commitment? He's had the same backpack for years.") Over and over, ads' messages are that human relationships are fragile, difficult, and disappointing but products won't let us down. ("The ski instructor faded away three years ago, but the sweater didn't.") But, Kilbourne points out, "Products are only things, and no matter how much we love them, they won't love us back."

Kilbourne writes that our children are being buried alive in what David Denby calls "an avalanche of junk." Twenty years ago, kids drank twice as much milk as soda. Thanks to ads, today the reverse is true. Both alcohol and cigarette companies target young children as consumers (in ads featuring Joe Camel, Spuds Mackenzie, and the Budweiser frogs) and sell them sugary, fruit-flavored products (Mrs. Pucker's Alcoholic Orangeade and Tumblers, a 24 proof version of Jello shots). Advertisers also exploit adolescents' social anxiety and need for approval and independence to sell them crap, some of it addictive crap. ("You've got what it takes . . . Salem Spirit.")

Kilbourne's arguments are as focused and unassailable as those of a good prosecutor. Piece by piece she builds a case for an America deeply corrupted by advertisers. We are led via ads to expect transformation via products. Ads also steer us away from what really makes us happy: "meaningful work, authentic relationships, and a sense of connection with history, community, nature, and the cosmos."

Americans think we know about advertising, but we don't. Our very complacency leaves us vulnerable. And developing countries urgently require education about the true costs of advertising. They need to learn not only that all that glitters is not gold, but also that it is sometimes poison. Kilbourne is our best, most thoughtful, most compassionate teacher.

As songwriter Glen Brown wrote, we are all living in "one big town." It's a town with new billboards going up every day, with ads on our buses and on our clothing, in movies, on our phones, and in our schools. It's a company town that makes us consumers, not citizens, and where we live in demographic niches, not neighborhoods. Kilbourne is here to shout, "Look at our town. Look at what we're doing to it. If we love it, let's save it. Let's make a community plan that helps us develop into the people we can be."

Kilbourne wants to change the world, and she is not apologetic about it. She sees cynicism not as sophistication but as social apathy and even as a kind of naivete, a belief that scorning something makes one superior to it or that scorn is a substitute for social action. While Kilbourne allows that ads don't cause all our problems, she asserts that they create an environment in which bad choices are constantly reinforced. She argues that we must take back our culture and rebuild a society in which good choices are encouraged. Her book is a clarion call for a new era of social protest. I am ready to march.

CAN'TBUYMYLOVE

"A GIRL OF MANY PARTS"

The Making of an Activist

IN 1968 I SAW AN AD THAT CHANGED MY LIFE. ONE OF THE MANY MINDLESS jobs I had that year was placing ads in *The Lancet,* a medical journal. This particular one was for a birth control pill called Ovulen 21. It featured a smiling woman's head and the caption "Ovulen 21 works the way a woman thinks—by weekdays . . . not 'cycle days.'"

Inside the woman's head were seven boxes, each one a day of the week. And inside each box was a picture of that day's activity. Sunday had a roast, Monday a laundry basket, Tuesday an iron, and so forth. I realized that the ad was basically saying that women were too stupid to remember their cycles but could remember days of the week. And the days of their weeks were an endless rotation of domestic chores.

I took the ad home and put it on my refrigerator. For the next few months, I kept noticing ads that demeaned women in popular magazines as well as in *The Lancet*. Many of them ended up on my refrigerator. Some of them were outrageous. ("My boyfriend told me he loved me for my mind. I was never so insulted in my life," said a woman with a cigarette.) Many were demeaning, such as the ad for a "feminine hygiene" spray that said, "You don't sleep with teddy bears any more," implying that, although our teddy bears don't mind how we women smell, our boyfriends do. Some were shockingly violent.

I began to notice patterns and categories. I saw that women's bodies were often dismembered in ads—just legs or breasts or torsos were featured. I saw that women were often infantilized and that little girls were sexualized. ("You're a Halston woman from the very beginning," said a shampoo ad, featuring a girl of about five.) I bought a macrolens for my camera and turned the ads into slides. I wasn't sure what I was going to do with them, but I knew I wanted to preserve them. I had begun my life's work.

For over twenty years I have been lecturing all around the country on the image of women in advertising. My films based on my lectures, *Killing Us Softly* and others, have been seen by millions of people. Wherever I go, one question always comes up. "How did you get into this?" The answer is so complex that I usually brush it off and say something like, "Oh, I've long been active in the women's movement." Or, "I was a teacher and interested in media." The real answer is that my whole life led me into this.

When I was a child, I used to dream that I would find a magic potion that would make people notice me, maybe even love me—some lucky charm that would make me the center of attention. Suddenly, when I was sixteen, my dream came true. The world found me beautiful and focused its attention on me. I first realized this when, to my complete astonishment, I won a beauty contest in my hometown, a contest I had entered on a dare. Even though I was no Sophia Loren or Elizabeth Taylor, my appearance was to be the most important fact of my life—more important than my gender or my family background. My life, my

work, my choice of mates—all have been shaped primarily by the way I looked. One is not supposed to talk about this. One is never supposed to mention it. But it is true.

From the very beginning, I felt extremely ambivalent about this gift. Being stared at made me nervous, made me feel that something was terribly wrong. My mother, a beautiful woman, died of cancer when I was nine. This has remained what the poet César Vallejo calls "my silver wound, my eternal loss." I watched my mother lose her beauty and then her life within a few months. For several years after that I felt invisible—in my family, at school, in the world. My three brothers and I were each locked in our own private cocoons of grief. My father was often away on business. Sometimes I curled up in my mother's empty closet, just to be close to her scent.

One of my favorite games at that time was to walk on the ceilings. I would look into a hand mirror as I walked through my house, carefully stepping over thresholds and walking around light fixtures. This is one of the few memories I have of the years immediately following my mother's death. Indeed my world was as upside down and empty as those ceilings. I began having a nightmare that was to persist for decades. In this dream, I am buried alive. I can hear people walking on my grave, but when I open my mouth to scream for help, I am suddenly mute.

The spotlight that focused on me in mid-adolescence was shocking, scary, seductive, compelling. Having "won the lottery," I went from poverty to riches in less than a year. I never felt that it had anything to do with me. At the same time, I knew it had extraordinary value and that the dread of losing it was the ever-present dark side. As in the old fairy tales, every gift comes with a price, a curse. I was particularly haunted by the fear that any man I loved would eventually leave me for someone young when I grew old and lost my beauty. Whatever the reason, I was aware from the very beginning that my looks were not simply a blessing. It was probably this realization, more than any other, that eventually led to my work of deconstructing the image.

I rarely found myself beautiful, although sometimes I thought I might be if I were carefully groomed and polished and the light was just right. Always aware of every flaw, I felt a terrible gap between the way the world perceived me and the way I felt about myself. On the surface, I was a model child, a straight-A student. My perfect score on the verbal SAT was announced on the school's intercom, thus insuring that no boy in my high school would ever date me. Vice-president of the drama club and just about everything else, I had the lead in almost every play. My best friend, Judy, also a top student, was the daughter of the surgeon who had operated on my mother. Her family took me skiing and to their summer home in New Hampshire.

But I had another best friend. Deedee came from a troubled family. Creative, warm, and sensitive but also blond and very curvaceous, she had an undeserved reputation for being fast. She introduced me to cigarettes and Orange Blossoms (orange juice with gin). It was love at first sip. Judy and I did award-winning science projects (one year we made soap) and went sailing at the yacht club. Deedee and I smoked in the basement and listened to Elvis. This split would persist for years. I made the near-fatal mistake so many girls and women make of thinking that alcohol and cigarettes set me free, helped me express my wild self, the self that was so buried during those repressive years of the 1950s.

When I was fifteen, a boy I had a crush on stood me up for an important party.

Girl of
many
parts . . .

THE here - biggest
beauty in a
Grecian dress is a girl
of many parts.
Jean Kilbourne is a
17-year-old American
who lives in London
and recently returned
from a three-week holi-
day in Greece — hence
the dress.

I was alone at home. After a couple of hours, in a state of terror and panic, I went to my father's liquor cabinet and downed a fifth of vermouth. Later that night, in a drunken haze and really frightened about what I might do to myself, I called Judy and she and her father came to get me. I woke up the next morning with an awful headache—but also with the new and terrible knowledge that alcohol could erase pain. From then on, for almost twenty years, my most important relationship was with alcohol.

So many years later, I wish I could reach out to that girl I once was and prevent her from making that catastrophic choice. The terror she felt, so perplexing to her, is completely understandable to me now. After her mother's death, there had been no period of mourning, no permissible grieving, indeed no mention of her mother ever again. Forever after, the mere suggestion of loss and abandonment was intolerable and would send her plunging into terror and despair. She would feel that she had to get away from her emotions, to run from them. Alcohol and cigarettes seemed to be her friends, her comforters, her liberators. She had no idea they were her jailers.

I went to Wellesley College on a full scholarship, with an award for being the most promising freshman from New England. I had a grand passion for alcohol and at last the freedom to indulge it. I smoked a pack of Newports a day. I was in desperate trouble, although no one suspected it. In my senior year, I won an award that enabled me to spend a year in London working for the British Broadcasting Corporation. During the summer, I took a course at a secretarial school in order to be prepared for my job.

In Europe, I got a taste of the fast life. By day, I was a secretary in a job so boring that my cigarettes were major events in the day. I also did a bit of modeling. By night, I drank a great deal of champagne and danced at discos. I partied at Roman Polanski's apartment and dated Ringo Starr

JEAN IS
PROTESTING

and a knight of the British empire. Although I earned about twenty-eight dollars a week, Europe was cheap in those days. I was able to travel to France and Greece and to ski the Alps. I took a train to Russia with a group of French students.

I also got involved in the antiwar movement, protesting American involvement in Vietnam. One day I participated in some guerilla theater. I dressed up as Miss America in a silver lamé miniskirt and sequined top with a banner across my chest. I was joined by two male friends dressed as a businessman and a soldier. Together we marched to Prime Minister Harold Wilson's house and presented him with a gigantic draft card. If you're going to support the war, you should go fight it, we told him. There was major newspaper coverage. The London tabloids focused on me in my miniskirt. One ran a photo with the caption "Jean is protesting." My father, a retired Army colonel and a hawk, said, "Well, at least it doesn't say 'Jean is revolting.'" Looking back, I see this was my first experience with media advocacy.

I returned from Europe in 1967 and tried to find work in Boston. For the next two years, I had so many jobs I had to alphabetize my W-2 forms. In spite of my Wellesley degree and my European experience, I simply couldn't find meaningful work. The women's movement had not yet begun and women were expected to type or teach until we married.

I was still involved in the antiwar movement and spent some time standing in Harvard Square wearing a sandwich board with photographs of napalmed children on it. As with many others of my generation, this involvement led me to the women's movement. It also eventually led me into teaching, as a way to try to change the society, to be part of the solution instead of the problem (as we said in those days).

I experimented a bit with the drugs of the time (and I did inhale), but my major drugs continued to be alcohol and nicotine. Like many alcoholics, I had an enormous tolerance for alcohol. It was always amusing when men tried to get me drunk. Inevitably, they would slide under the table as I ordered another. I continued to make the dreadful mistake of thinking that alcohol was helping me combat the terrible bouts of depression I had periodically suffered from ever since my mother's death. Of course, alcohol is a depressant drug and it was burying me alive. I often thought of suicide, although I never spoke of it to anyone.

Drinking and smoking were important parts of my self-image. I thought of myself as an outlaw, a rebel (or, more often, as an alien, a freak). I was outspoken about never wanting to marry. I had an interest in sex that was not acceptable for a woman (to admit to, at least) in those days. I wore miniskirts and black leather. At the same time, I was quite shy and easily frightened. Alcohol made me bolder. I could not imagine life without it. Given my tolerance, my will, and my natural stamina, I was able to confine my drinking to the evenings and to function fairly well. In those days of widespread ignorance about alcoholism, no one would have thought I was in trouble. In fact, a doctor I once confided in looked closely at me and said, "Don't worry, honey, you're not the type to be an alcoholic."

People encouraged me to model. One day I went to New York and modeled for a world-famous fashion designer. I'd never been on a runway before and I barely knew how to move. After the show, the designer invited me back to his home, where he told me that I could have a very successful and lucrative career as a model. All I had to do was sleep with him. I went back to Boston and to my eighty-dollar-a-week job as a waitress. My depression deepened.

Through a newspaper ad, I got a job doing some ghostwriting for Al Capp. He was a very smart and funny man, but bitter. He liked my writing very much. He also wanted sex in exchange for a job. His manager called me and said, "Go to bed with him, honey—it won't kill you." I thought it might, but I was quite desperate. I loved the intellectual challenge of the work I was doing with Capp and was bored with every other job I had ever had. I was also broke. One hot August day I flew to New York with the intention of sleeping with Capp. I went to his apartment on Park Avenue. I may have even started to undress. But I couldn't do it. I left and caught a cab to the Village.

This was one of the lowest points of my life. I could rationalize that the fashion designer wouldn't hire me unless I slept with him. After all, modeling is a form of selling one's body anyway. But Capp thought I was brilliant. He thought I was a wonderful writer. But that wasn't enough. I was still going to have to put my body on the line. I was desperate. Finally I heeded the advice of a close friend and began therapy.

It was 1968. And one of my jobs was putting ads into *The Lancet*. When I saw the ad featuring the woman's head with seven boxes in it, I can't say that I understood immediately that there was a connection between that image and the fact that I was a Wellesley graduate working in a mindless job. Nor did I know the term "sexual harassment," so I wouldn't have drawn the link between this image and Capp's and the designer's treatment of me. But I did know there was something terribly wrong with the ad.

The following year I went back to school to get a master's degree in education and began teaching English at a nearby high school. That year I also fell in love with the Polish writer Jerzy Kosinski and began a relationship that was to last for several years and be one of the most important of my life. He encouraged my interest in advertising and the media and we spent many hours talking about it. To paraphrase the cigarette ad, he loved me for my mind and I was never so ecstatic in my life.

To teach about gender stereotypes, I used some of my slides of ads in my classroom. The students were very responsive. It was clear that the slides made them look at advertising and sexism in a new way. Other teachers invited me into their classrooms. I put together a whole slide show on the image of women in ad-

A New Film Presentation....

KILLING US SOFTLY:
Advertising's Image of Women

A unique analysis of one of the most powerful forces in our society.

"Jean Kilbourne's excellent presentation demonstrates that what is done to women in the imagery of advertising is a kind of violence; the female self is not simply objectified but literally disintegrates into a collection of disparate and relentlessly judged components."
Karen Durbin
Senior Editor, *The Village Voice*

vertising. I was invited to speak to larger groups. I was very afraid of public speaking, but I also really wanted to talk about this issue. Early in 1976 I gave my first lecture to a large audience, the student body at Concord Academy. I was so nervous driving there that I seriously considered driving off the road—not to kill myself, but to be incapacitated. I also considered phoning in a bomb scare. However, I showed up and gave the presentation and the students loved it.

A few months later, on the first day of spring in 1976, I stopped drinking. Although my therapist didn't know anything about alcoholism and never suspected mine, he was brilliant and extremely warm and helped me care enough about myself to want to live. I read about alcoholism and gradually understood that alcohol was the "x" in every equation of my life. I went to a support group and never picked up another drink. I was lucky that I was in the middle stages of the disease. I had lost several years, but I hadn't done terrible damage to myself or anyone else.

Almost immediately, I had new confidence and energy. Within a year I had found an agency to represent me and had begun my career as a full-time lecturer. In 1979 I made my first film, *Killing Us Softly: Advertising's Image of Women*, which is still shown throughout the world. In the late seventies I also began collecting ads for alcohol and tobacco and developed other slide shows and films. In 1983 I finally quit smoking, after many failed attempts. What finally led me to quit smoking wasn't the threat of cancer or of wrinkles or even my morning cough. What got to me was that I was giving a couple of bucks a day to an evil industry. I understood that this had nothing to do with liberation; it had to do with slavery. I decided to become a healthy rebel and to turn all that antiauthoritarian energy, which had gone into self-destructive behavior, against the real authorities, these industries that were duping and snaring so many of us.

In the eighties I also found colleagues. I had been working alone for several years. I was invited to become a visiting scholar at the Stone Center at Wellesley

College and to work with Jean Baker Miller, a woman I greatly admired. I was very interested in the work she and her colleagues were doing on the importance of relationships in women's psychological development.

I also suddenly found myself on the cutting edge of a new movement in public health. For decades the primary focus of public health had been on the host, the person with the disease (the person with cholera, the smoker, the drunk driver). In the 1980s the focus began to shift to the environment (polluted water, the price of cigarettes, lax laws on drinking and driving). Advertising, long considered trivial, began to be viewed as an important part of this environment. I was invited to speak at health and addiction conferences, to work with Surgeons General Everett Koop and Antonia Novello, and to testify for Congress. I made films on alcohol and tobacco advertising. In the 1970s I worked alone and my work was considered radical. By the end of the 1980s, I was considered a pioneer who was now part of the mainstream.

In the mid-eighties I married a man I had loved for a long time and was lucky enough to have a baby at the age of forty-four. Several years later, the week of my fiftieth birthday, my childhood fear came true when my husband abruptly left me for one of his students. My ongoing recovery from this is another important part of my story, of course. It is also related to my work, which has to do with the devaluing of relationships, the objectification of people, and addictions of all kinds. I believe there is a connection between the throwaway world of advertising and today's throwaway approach to marriage. All too often our market-driven culture locks people into adolescent fantasies of sex and relationships. And there is a connection between the constant images of instant sexual gratification and passion and the increasing burden on marriage and long-term lovers. This is only part of the story, of course, but it is a part that needs more exploration.

Terrible as that time was, it did give me a new, more deeply personal perspective on these issues. As the poet Theodore Roethke once wrote, "In a dark time, the eye begins to see." Today I am happily raising my wonderful daughter. I have good friends and work that I love. I've been sober for over twenty-three years, longer than I drank. I no longer feel split. I feel lucky and blessed. I also feel more rebellious than ever.

This book is a part of my rebellion. More important, it is an attempt to redefine rebellion, to challenge the advertisers' cynical equation of it with smoking, drinking, and impulsive sex. We are all encouraged to confuse addiction with liberation, enslavement with freedom. Our need for social and personal change and power is often co-opted and trivialized into an adolescent and self-centered kind of rebellion.

I bought this myth when I was growing up. I acted out my rebellion and my despair by nearly destroying myself with cigarettes, alcohol, and harmful relationships. I was influenced by many factors, of course, from genetic predisposition to alcoholism to the particular traumas that afflicted my family. I made my poor choices in an environment that encouraged those poor choices, partly through advertising. It was an environment in which vital information was kept from me, in part because of the influence advertisers have on editors and publishers. We all make our choices for complex reasons in a complex world. Advertising is just one part of that complex world, but it is an increasingly important and influential part.

This book is not about alcoholism or my recovery. It is part of my ongoing attempt to break through denial—the personal denial that kept me locked into addiction and hopeless relationships, but more important the cultural denial that does the same on a grander scale to so many of us. There are many sources of this cultural denial, one of which is advertising. I know it seems ridiculous to many people to give so much weight to advertising. Most people feel that advertising is fun, sexy, often silly but certainly not anything to take seriously. Other aspects of the media are serious—the violent films, the trashy talk shows, the bowdlerization of the news. But not advertising! Surely I am not suggesting that advertising drove me to alcoholism? Did a little sign hidden in an ice cube in an alcohol ad say "Get drunk, kid"?

No, of course not. Advertising doesn't cause addictions. But I will argue throughout this book that advertising, an enormously important part of our culture, contributes mightily to the climate of denial in which relationships flounder and addictions flourish. I will also argue that these two consequences are related: disconnection (loss, rejection, isolation, abuse), especially early in life, drives many people to addiction, which in turn makes authentic connection impossible. It is not a coincidence that we find ourselves at the end of the twentieth century in a time of troubled relationships and in an age of addiction.

This book is about how advertising corrupts relationships and then offers us products, both as solace and as substitutes for the intimate human connection we all long for and need. Most of us know by now that advertising often turns people into objects. Women's bodies, and men's bodies too these days, are dismembered, packaged, and used to sell everything from chain saws to chewing gum. But many people do not fully realize that there are terrible consequences when people become things. Self-image is deeply affected. The self-esteem of girls plummets as they reach adolescence partly because they cannot possibly escape the message that their bodies are objects, and imperfect objects at that. Boys learn that masculinity requires a kind of ruthlessness, even brutality. Violence becomes inevitable.

Advertising encourages us not only to objectify each other but also to feel that our most significant relationships are with the products that we buy. It turns lovers into things and things into lovers and encourages us to feel passion for our products rather than our partners. Passion for products is especially dangerous when the products are potentially addictive, because addicts do feel they are in a relationship with their substances. I used to joke that Jack Daniel's was my most constant lover. The smoker feels that the cigarette is her best friend. Advertising reinforces these beliefs, so we are twice seduced—by the ads and by the substances themselves.

Although much more attention has been paid to the cultural impact of advertising in recent years than ever before, just about everyone in America still feels personally exempt from advertising's influence. Almost everyone holds the misguided belief that advertisements don't affect *them,* don't shape their attitudes, don't help define their dreams. What I hear more than anything else, as I lecture throughout the country, is "I don't pay attention to ads . . . I just tune them out . . . they have no effect on me." Of course, I hear this most often from young men wearing Budweiser caps. In truth, we are all influenced by advertising. There is no way to tune out this much information, especially when it is carefully designed to break through the "tuning out" process.

The fact is that much of advertising's power comes from this belief that advertising does not affect us. The most effective kind of propaganda is that which is not recognized as propaganda. Because we think advertising is silly and trivial, we are less on guard, less critical, than we might otherwise be. It's all in fun, it's ridiculous. While we're laughing, sometimes sneering, the commercial does its work.

Some of the most talented and creative people in the world are dedicated to this work. Indeed, the most skillful propagandists of our time are not working for dictators, they are certainly not working exclusively for the Democratic party or the Republicans either. They are working for Foote, Cone & Belding, Ogilvy & Mather, and DDB Needham Worldwide. Their job is very specific: They are to use all of their powers of persuasion, explicit and implicit, to sell a particular product. That's all! No moral, no obligation to any other set of values. They just have to use their wits to put together a hip, funny, seductive, *persuasive* ad campaign. If they don't, another agency will take away the account. These folks are just doing their job—and maybe they're even doing us a service by giving us information about products and entertaining us while they're at it. What's the harm in that?

This book is about the harm in that—the dangerous, often enormously dangerous, side effects of advertising. Like a very potent drug, advertising is designed to do one particular job, but along the way it often has other, much broader results. Although some of this is intentional on the part of advertisers, much of it is not. Advertising often sells more than products, but advertisers generally don't care about that. If the cumulative effect of some advertising, for example, is to degrade women or to sexualize children or to increase eating disorders, surely that is not the *intent* of the advertisers. It is simply an unfortunate side effect.

Even in the case of addictive products, the aim of advertisers is to make money, not to create addicts. Unfortunately, they can't do the former without doing the latter. Indeed, the addict is the ideal consumer. Ten percent of drinkers consume over 60 percent of all the alcohol sold. These aren't the folks who are having an occasional Cabernet Sauvignon with dinner or one beer with their pizza. Advertisers spend enormous amounts of money on psychological research and understand addiction at least as well as, if not better than, any other group in the country. They use this knowledge to target children (because if you hook them early, they are yours for life), to encourage all people to consume more, in spite of often dangerous consequences for all of us, and to create a climate of denial in which all kinds of addictions flourish. This they do with full intent, as we see so clearly in the "secret" documents of the tobacco industry that have been made available to the public in recent years.

And we are all affected, not just addicts. Of course, we are all affected by the behavior of addicts, at home, at work, and in the larger society. This has become clearer to everyone as we have learned more about the terrible costs of drunk driving and secondhand smoke. But we are also affected on a deeper level. Who among us hasn't ever smoked a cigarette to suppress her anger or had a drink to get himself in the mood for sex or eaten some cake to numb the disappointment of a failed love affair or purchased a car in search of excitement or simply gone shopping as an antidote to boredom or sadness. As Neil Young sang, "I've seen the needle and the damage done, a little part of it in everyone."

One certainly doesn't have to be an alcoholic or any kind of addict to have suffered from a sense of emptiness. Our materialistic culture encourages this because people who feel empty make great consumers. The emptier we feel, the more likely we are to turn to products, especially potentially addictive products, to fill us up, to make us feel whole. Not everyone has to give up these things (although some of us do), but we all can profit from becoming more conscious of their role in our lives. They all serve to distance us from our feelings and to deflect attention from that which might really make a difference in our lives.

Addiction is the number-one health problem in America today. Many people feel that addiction is also at the root of other problems, such as crime, poverty, divorce, child abuse, and other forms of violence. Others argue that it is these problems that lead to addiction. At the very least, addiction makes these problems more serious and intractable. Certainly if young people can avoid addiction and drug and alcohol abuse, they have a fighting chance of getting through the minefields of adolescence.

And young people are at much greater risk for addiction than the rest of us. The younger people are when they start drinking or smoking or using other drugs, the more likely they are by far to abuse these drugs and to become addicted. The smoking rates for teenagers, especially African-American teenagers, are soaring. Binge drinking is at record levels, a problem in and of itself and also a major factor in other problems such as date rape, battering, and teen pregnancy.

Most of us know by now that adolescence is especially perilous for girls, who are the most likely victims of rape and battering, who are biologically more vulnerable to alcohol than boys, and who often suffer from depression and eating disorders. We also know that women and girls are especially likely to seek connection through alcohol, food, and cigarettes, partly as a response to disconnection in our human relationships. Teenage women today are engaging in far riskier health behavior in greater numbers than any prior generation. What is causing this and what can we do about it?

It's a multifaceted problem and there is no simple cause. However, it is clear that the current crisis goes way beyond individual psychological development and pathology. Indeed, it cannot be understood without recognizing that our children are growing up in a toxic cultural environment, one made more toxic by advertising. No one can escape it, just as no one can escape air pollution or pesticides in our food. And this is increasingly a worldwide phenomenon. The world is fast becoming a global marketplace controlled not by individual governments but by transnational conglomerates interested only in profit. As we Americans export our economic system and our lifestyle, we also export the addictions, diseases, and psychological problems associated with it—our hazardous cultural environment.

We cannot solve the problem of addiction without changing the environment. As the old story goes, when bodies are floating in a river downstream it is important to get ambulances to the site and get the bodies out of the river. But in the long run, it is far more important to investigate what is happening upstream, perhaps to put a fence at the edge of a cliff up there—or to stop the madman who is pushing people in.

Our children are falling into the river. Some are flinging themselves in—suicide is the third leading killer of teenagers (and probably the major killer of gay and lesbian teens). I have a daughter who is on the brink of adolescence. She is smart and kind, funny and radiant, creative and soulful (and I, of course, am completely objective), and I fear for her. I feel that I am raising her in a culture that is hostile to every single thing I want for her. I am raising her in a culture that still teaches that girls are less valuable than boys, that girls are sex objects and must be beautiful and thin in order to be successful, that women who are the victims of sexual harassment and violence asked for it, and that women are completely responsible for the success or failure of their relationships with men. At the same time that she is being raised in an environment of love and abundance, there are boys being abused or powerlessly watching their mothers being battered, or simply being socialized to repress their feelings and feel contempt for girls, who might grow up to be violent and hard, who might rape or murder her or perhaps just break her heart.

I am raising my child, in my case a child who is at genetic risk for alcoholism and other addictions, in a culture that targets her with billions of dollars worth of glamorous images of young healthy people using alcohol and tobacco, not only in ads but in films and television shows, in music—a culture that links these drugs with romance and rebellion, the two irresistible themes for adolescents (and those legions of adults who wish to remain adolescents). I am raising her in a culture that is entirely materialistic, that co-opts spiritual values and movements for social change and uses them to sell her jeans and cigarettes. I am raising her in a culture that trivializes relationships and encourages her to envy her friends and compete with them for the attention of boys.

I am also raising my daughter in an environment that will blame me should something go wrong with her. Should she become an alcoholic or commit suicide or develop an eating disorder, most of the fingers will be pointed at me. Why didn't I protect her? Why didn't I raise her differently? Parents, especially mothers, are blamed for everything that happens to our children. There is no question that parents have a great deal of responsibility and that many parents today abdicate that responsibility. However, putting all the responsibility on parents is like making us responsible for the poisoned air our children breathe. The parents on Love Canal no doubt loved their children, but they couldn't protect them. Their children were poisoned by the water they drank, by their mothers' milk.

I want my daughter to be a rebel—to defy the cultural stereotypes of "femininity." I love and value her strength and feistiness, her sexuality, her longing for independence and for authentic connection. I loathe and fear the advertisers' cynical equation of rebellion with smoking, drinking, and impulsive and impersonal sex, the way they encourage all of us to confuse addiction with liberation, enslavement with freedom. I know that the girls who go under in adolescence are almost always in the grip of one addiction or another. The saddest girls are those who choose self-destruction in the name of liberation and rebellion, who see no other way out of the terrible dilemma of having to choose between the stifling false self of the "good girl" and the more authentic self that society so often labels the "bad girl."

This book weaves together three of my lifelong interests: advertising, addiction, and feminism. Because I am dealing with the intersection of vast topics, I inevitably have to leave out a lot. I can deal only cursorily with the history of advertising and addiction, with feminist theory, with all the research that has been done on women and addictions. Most regrettably, I am writing mostly about white, middle-class, heterosexual women because these are the women in the world of advertising images. Women of color, lesbians, women with disabilities are primarily invisible in this world. This is a huge problem, of course, but one beyond the scope of this book. I believe, however, that what I have to say about women and relationships and addictions will be helpful to all women and girls—and to men and boys. Although my work has always focused on women, the cultural environment is toxic for men and boys too and I address that.

Both advertising and addiction are most profoundly about self-deception. This book is a detailed map and a cautionary guide to the immensely powerful messages projected by advertising. It is about understanding false values and illusions that damage our relationships and often lure us toward addictive behavior. My nightmare about being buried alive ended soon after I quit drinking. A few years later I dreamed that my best friend was buried alive and I rescued her. We *can* rescue ourselves, our children, each other. But the first step, as always, is to break through the denial.

I sometimes think of what I do as a kind of judo. The advertisers have an enormous amount of money and power. But we can use their weight against them. We can use their very images to educate about their real messages. We can redefine the crucial concepts—love, rebellion, sexuality, friendship, freedom—that advertising has corrupted, and take them back for our own health, power, and fulfillment.

"BUY THIS 24-YEAR-OLD AND GET ALL HIS FRIENDS ABSOLUTELY FREE"

We Are the Product

They're the ones you want.
They're the ones we've got.
They're hip.
They reinvent themselves constantly.
They search the pages of *seventeen* to create their look.
They'll skip their favorite show,
but never skip shopping.
Hip doesn't just happen.
It starts at the source: Seventeen.

seventeen

IF YOU'RE LIKE MOST PEOPLE, YOU THINK THAT ADVERTISING HAS NO INFLUENCE on you. This is what advertisers want you to believe. But, if that were true, why would companies spend over $200 billion a year on advertising? Why would they be willing to spend over $250,000 to produce an average television commercial and another $250,000 to air it? If they want to broadcast their commercial during the Super Bowl, they will gladly spend over a million dollars to produce it and over one and a half million to air it. After all, they might have the kind of success that Victoria's Secret did during the 1999 Super Bowl. When they paraded bra-and-panty-clad models across TV screens for a mere thirty seconds, one million people turned away from the game to log on to the Website promoted in the ad. No influence?

Ad agency Arnold Communications of Boston kicked off an ad campaign for a financial services group during the 1999 Super Bowl that represented eleven months of planning and twelve thousand "man-hours" of work. Thirty hours of footage were edited into a thirty-second spot. An employee flew to Los Angeles with the ad in a lead-lined bag, like a diplomat carrying state secrets or a courier with crown jewels. Why? Because the Super Bowl is one of the few sure sources of big audiences—especially male audiences, the most precious commodity for advertisers. Indeed, the Super Bowl is more about advertising than football: The four hours it takes include only about twelve minutes of actually moving the ball.

Three of the four television programs that draw the largest audiences every year are football games. And these games have coattails: twelve prime-time shows that attracted bigger male audiences in 1999 than those in the same time slots the previous year were heavily pushed during football games. No wonder the networks can sell this prized Super Bowl audience to advertisers for almost any price they want. The Oscar ceremony, known as the Super Bowl for women, is able to command one million dollars for a thirty-second spot because it can deliver over 60 percent of the nation's women to advertisers. Make no mistake: The primary purpose of the mass media is to sell audiences to advertisers. We are the product. Although people are much more sophisticated about advertising now than even a few years ago, most are still shocked to learn this.

Magazines, newspapers, and radio and television programs round us up, rather like cattle, and producers and publishers then sell us to advertisers, usually through ads placed in advertising and industry publications. "The people you want, we've got all wrapped up for you," declares *The Chicago Tribune* in an ad placed in *Advertising Age,* the major publication of the advertising industry, which pictures several people, all neatly boxed according to income level.

Although we like to think of advertising as unimportant, it is in fact the most important aspect of the mass media. It *is* the point. Advertising supports more than 60 percent of magazine and newspaper production and almost 100 percent of the electronic media. Over $40 billion a year in ad revenue is generated for television and radio and over $30 billion for magazines and newspapers. As one ABC executive said, "The network is paying affiliates to carry network commercials, not programs. What we are is a distribution system for Procter & Gamble." And the CEO of Westinghouse Electric, owner of CBS, said, "We're here to serve advertisers. That's our raison d'être."

The media know that television and radio programs are simply fillers for the space between commercials. They know that the programs that succeed are the ones that deliver the highest number of people to the advertisers. But not just any people. Advertisers are interested in people aged eighteen to forty-nine who live in or near a city. *Dr. Quinn, Medicine Woman,* a program that was number one in its time slot and immensely popular with older, more rural viewers, was canceled in 1998 because it couldn't command the higher advertising rates paid for younger, richer audiences. This is not new: the *Daily Herald,* a British newspaper with 47 million readers, double the combined readership of *The Times, The Financial Times, The Guardian,* and *The Telegraph,* folded in the 1960s because its readers were mostly elderly and working class and had little appeal to advertisers. The target audience that appeals to advertisers is becoming more narrow all the time. According to Dean Valentine, the head of United Paramount Network, most networks have abandoned the middle class and want "very chic shows that talk to affluent, urban, unmarried, huge-disposable-income 18-to-34-year-olds because the theory is, from advertisers, that the earlier you get them, the sooner you imprint the brand name."

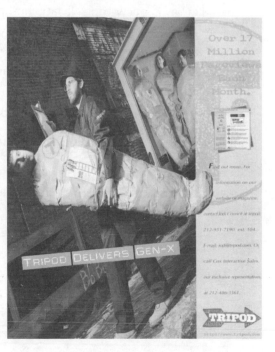

"Tripod Delivers Gen-X," proclaims a sinister ad for a Website and magazine that features a delivery man carrying a corpselike consumer wrapped from neck to toe in brown paper. Several other such "deliveries" are propped up in the truck. "We've got your customers on our target," says an ad for finan-

WHEN YOU'VE GOT THEM BY THE EARS THEIR HEARTS AND MINDS WILL FOLLOW

cial services that portrays the lower halves of two people embedded in a target. "When you've got them by the ears their hearts and minds will follow," says an ad for an entertainment group. And an ad for the newspaper *USA Today* offers the consumer's eye between a knife and a fork and says, "12 Million Served Daily." The ad explains, "Nearly six million influential readers with both eyes ingesting your message. Every day." There is no humanity, no individuality in this ad or others like it—people are simply products sold to advertisers, of value only as potential consumers.

Newspapers are more in the business of selling audiences than in the business of giving people news, especially as more and more newspapers are owned by fewer and fewer chains. They exist primarily to support local advertisers, such as car dealers, realtors, and department store owners. A full-page ad in *The New York Times* says, "A funny thing happens when people put down a newspaper. They start spending money." The ad continues, "Nothing puts people in the mood to buy like newspaper. In fact, most people consider it almost a prerequisite to any spending spree." It concludes, "Newpaper. It's the best way to close a sale." It is especially disconcerting to realize that our newspapers, even the illustrious *New York Times,* are hucksters at heart.

Once we begin to count, we see that magazines are essentially catalogs of goods, with less than half of their pages devoted to editorial content (and much of that in the service of the advertisers). An ad for a custom publishing company in *Advertising Age* promises "The next hot magazine could be the one we create exclusively for your product." And, in fact, there are magazines for everyone from dirt-bike riders to knitters to mercenary soldiers, from *Beer Connoisseur* to *Cigar Aficionado.* There are plenty of magazines for the wealthy, such as *Coastal Living* "for people who live or vacation on the coast." *Barron's* advertises itself as a way to "reach faster cars, bigger houses and longer prenuptial agreements" and promises a readership with an average household net worth of over a million.

The Internet advertisers target the wealthy too, of course. "They give you Dick," says an ad in *Advertising Age* for an Internet news network. "We give you Richard." The ad continues, "That's the Senior V.P. Richard who lives in L.A., drives a BMW and wants to buy a DVD player and a kayak." Not surprisingly, there are no magazines or Internet sites or television programs for the poor or for people on welfare. They might not be able to afford the magazines or computers but, more important, they are of no use to advertisers.

This emphasis on the affluent surely has something to do with the invisibility of the poor in our society. Since advertisers have no interest in them, they are not reflected in the media. We know so much about the rich and famous that it becomes a problem for many who seek to emulate them, but we know very little about the lifestyles of the poor and desperate. It is difficult to feel compassion for people we don't know.

Publications and programs that target minorities are also only interested in the affluent. "At $446 billion, African American buying power is more than the GNP of Switzerland," says an ad in *Advertising Age*. Another, for a "Black owned agency," implies it can "get you inside the soul of the African American consumer." "Are You Skirting a Major Market?" asks an ad for a local Florida television station picturing a Latina in a very short skirt. It concludes, "Channel 23. Because South Florida spends a lot of dinero!" An ad for *Latina* magazine says, "She's Latina. She spends more." And the Hispanic Network tells advertisers that "Hispanic families are more responsive to advertising. And ads in Spanish are 5 times more persuasive."

This persuasiveness seems pernicious in an ad placed by an advertising agency in *Advertising Age* after the 1998 reelection of George W. Bush as governor of Texas. "If you have high ambitions, hire us. He did," says the ad opposite a

full-page picture of Bush. The ad continues, "If we can create advertising that persuades Hispanic Democrats to vote Republican, we can get them to buy your product." Although most of us know that politicians are sold like beer or soap these days, it is chilling to see this bragged about in an ad.

Early in 1999 William Eisner, head of an advertising agency in Milwaukee, began a multimillion-dollar campaign designed to repackage Republican presidential candidate Steve Forbes just as he once repackaged Mrs. Paul's fishsticks. "We're trying to resuscitate brands all the time that lost their luster with consumers," said Mr. Eisner. "We're doing the same with Steve." To make the candidate look presidential, some commercials were shot in black and white with backdrops resembling the Oval Office.

Ethnic minorities will soon account for 30 percent of all consumer purchases. No wonder they are increasingly important to advertisers. Nearly half of all Fortune 1000 companies have some kind of ethnic marketing campaign. Nonetheless, minorities are still underrepresented in advertising agencies. African-Americans, who are over 10 percent of the total workforce, are only 5 percent of the advertising industry. Minorities are underrepresented in ads as well—about 87 percent of people in mainstream magazine ads are white, about 3 percent are African-American (most likely appearing as athletes or musicians), and less than 1 percent are Hispanic or Asian. As the spending power of minorities increases, so does marketing segmentation. Mass marketing aimed at a universal audience doesn't work so well in a multicultural society, but cable television, the Internet, custom publishing, and direct marketing lend themselves very well to this segmentation. The multiculturalism that we see in advertising is about money, of course, not about social justice.

The same is true for the increased visibility of gay men and lesbians in advertising. The gay media have provided the lucrative market of gay men to advertisers, such as IBM, Benetton, Johnson & Johnson, and United Airlines, for years. Hartford Financial Services Group launched a 1998 campaign aimed at gays that not only appeared in the gay media but crossed over to mainstream media. Ads picturing pairings of pink and blue cars promoted Hartford's discounts to gay and lesbian couples with the tagline, "Commitment. Bring it on."

Lesbians are still on the fringes of the gay marketing movement, probably because most women still have lower incomes than men. A male couple would be likely to have a higher joint income than a heterosexual couple, but this is not usually the case for a female couple. Nonetheless, Olivia Cruises ran an overtly lesbian commercial during the coming-out episode of *Ellen,* and Molson beer launched a commercial featuring a lesbian kiss in Canada in 1997. A Subaru print ad featured two women with the headline, "It loves camping, dogs and long-term commitment. Too bad it's only a car." And American Express ran an ad featuring a real-life lesbian couple with copy that included, "When you're ready to plan a future together, who can you trust to understand the financial challenges that gay men and lesbians face?"

Advertisers don't casually decide to target gays. They spend significant amounts of money to conduct research on the market and to find out how their products are faring. American Express spent $250,000 for research in 1997 before committing additional funds to the market. More advertisers are seeking the gay audience on the Internet, ever since a major gay-market study in 1997 found that gays are large online subscribers (51.5 percent use for gays compared with 15.8 percent for the general population).

However, many advertisers who target gay consumers still prefer to remain closeted about it, for fear of offending their heterosexual customers. More than two-thirds of gay-market advertisers contacted in 1997 by *Advertising Age* chose not to comment for an article on the topic.

The gay market is especially important to the alcohol industry. As is the case with many oppressed groups, gay people have a higher rate of alcohol abuse and alcoholism than do straight people. They have a tradition of congregating in bars, perhaps because there is nowhere else to go and feel safe. According to a corporate relations manager for Coors Brewing Company, gay consumers drink about twice as much as straight consumers—which is good news for Coors, of course. After all, heavy drinkers are the alcohol industry's best customers. Thus alcohol advertisers often target gay men and lesbians, although they have to be very careful not to alienate their macho heterosexual consumers. "For the last time, it's not a lifestyle, it's a life," says an ad for Johnnie Walker Red scotch, which ran, of course, only in gay publications. Signs of ever more closely targeted niche marketing were evident with the 1997 release by Australian brewers Lion Nathan of a "gay beer." The limited-edition label featured 1950s-style cartoons of same-sex couples and the suggestive slogan "Goes Down a Treat." And Baileys liqueur targeted lesbians with an ad featuring two feminized coffee cups and the copy, "Our limited-edition coffee cups are available nationwide, though only recognized as a set in Hawaii." Hawaii, of course, is the only state that has tried to legalize same-sex marriages.

So, the media round us up—gay and straight, male and female, African-American, white, Latino, young, and middle-aged (advertisers are not interested in old people, who usually already have brand loyalty and often have limited incomes). Then they spend a fortune on research to learn a lot about us, using techniques like polls, trends analysis, focus groups, and PRIZM, a marketing program that garners information about consumers from their ZIP codes—and that is advertised in *Advertising Age* as "the targeting tool that turns birds of a feather into sitting ducks."

Many companies these days are hiring anthropologists and psychologists to examine consumers' product choices, verbal responses, even body language for deeper meanings. They spend time in consumers' homes, listening to their conversations and exploring their closets and bathroom cabinets. Ad agency Leo Burnett's director of planning calls these techniques "getting in under the radar." Robert Deutsch, a neuroscientist and anthropologist who works for ad agency DDB Needham, likens himself to a vampire—"I suck information out of people, and they love it."

One new market research technique involves monitoring brain-wave signals to measure how "engaged" viewers are in what they are watching. According to the president of the company doing this research, "We are the only company in the industry reading people's thoughts and emotions. Someone's going to be a billionaire doing this. I think it will be us."

Through focus groups and depth interviews, psychological researchers can zero in on very specific target audiences—and their leaders. "Buy this 24-year-old and get all his friends absolutely free," proclaims an ad for MTV directed to advertisers. MTV presents itself publicly as a place for rebels and nonconformists. Behind the scenes, however, it tells potential advertisers that its viewers are lemmings who will buy whatever they are told to buy.

The MTV ad gives us a somewhat different perspective on the concept of "peer pressure." Advertisers, especially those who advertise tobacco and alcohol, are forever claiming that advertising doesn't influence anyone, that kids smoke and drink because of peer pressure. Sure, such pressure exists and is an important influence, but a lot of it is created by advertising. Kids who exert peer pressure don't drop into high schools like Martians. They are kids who tend to be leaders, whom other kids follow for good or for bad. And they themselves are mightily influenced by advertising, sometimes very deliberately as in the MTV ad. As an ad for *Seventeen* magazine, picturing a group of attractive young people, says, "Hip doesn't just happen. It starts at the source: *Seventeen.*" In the global village, the "peers" are very much the same, regardless of nationality, ethnicity, culture. In the eyes of the media, the youths of the world are becoming a single, seamless, soulless target audience—often cynically labeled "Generation X," or, for the newest wave of teens, "Generation Y." "We're helping a soft drink company reach them, even if their parents can't," says an ad for newspapers featuring a group of young people. The ad continues, "If you think authority figures have a hard time talking to Generation X, you should try being an advertiser," and goes on to suggest placing ads in the television sections of newspapers.

Of course, it's not only young people who are influenced by their peers. *Barron's* tells its advertisers, "Reach the right bird and the whole flock will follow." The MTV ad promises advertisers that young "opinion leaders" can influence what their friends eat, drink, and wear, whereas *Barron's* sells them leaders "whose simple 'yes' can legitimize a new product, trigger eight-figure purchases, and alter the flow of cash and ideas throughout the economy." Advertisers sometimes criticize my work by saying I imply that consumers are brainwashed, stupid, and easily led. Although I never say this, it often seems that the advertisers themselves describe consumers as sitting ducks.

Magazines like *Barron's* round up relatively small target audiences, but they can't compare with the precision and efficiency of direct marketing. "Score a bull's-eye with every ad" claims an ad for targeting software that promises, "We have your customers in our sights" and "can help you hit your mark every time." Continuing the analogy, the vice-chairman of a direct-marketing firm said, "Mass marketing is like defoliating Vietnam." He continued that direct marketing is more like dropping a smart bomb with pinpoint accuracy. The violent military language certainly makes it seem that marketers are waging a war against consumers. As another advertiser said, "We're in

Score A Bull's-Eye With Every Ad.

ADVO, we have your customers our sights. By utilizing ADVO rgeter, our proprietary targeting/ apping software, you will be le to identify your most important rget audience and deliver your lvertising message to them.

We can help you hit your mark every time. Call Cheryl Ives at 1-800-248-0490 and let ADVO's shared mail package **Mailbox Values** start working for you.

an era of global marketing warfare. The number one tactical weapon of the age is advertising."

Direct-marketing techniques make it possible for advertisers to customize ads for subscribers of the same magazine according to what a particular subscriber has previously bought. In 1994 the direct-marketing firm Bronner Slosberg Humphrey Inc. customized a print campaign for L.L. Bean by comparing the company's customer base to the subscription lists of about twenty national magazines. Different ads were tailored to specific customers. Thus if two *New Yorker* subscribers lived next door to each other, the same edition of the magazine could contain two different L.L. Bean ads. According to Mike Slosberg, vice-chairman of the company, "In essence, the ad becomes direct mail, and the magazine is the envelope."

Perhaps we are not surprised that magazines are only envelopes. But many of us had higher hopes for cable television and the Internet. However, these new technologies have mostly become sophisticated targeting devices. "Now you can turn your target market into a captive audience," says an ad for an Internet news and information service that features a man roped into his office chair.

"Capture your audience," says another, featuring a bunch of eyeballs dripping in a net. This ad is selling software that "allows you to track the clicks and mouse-over activities of every single user interacting with your banner ad." Another company recently launched a massive data-collection effort, with the goal of getting at least one million consumers to fill out surveys. It will use the data to deliver ads it claims can be targeted right down to the individual. "Sorry. We can't target by shoesize. YET," says an ad for Yahoo!, a very successful Internet company, which goes on to tell advertisers, "You're wondering . . . what do our 35 million registered users offer you? Well, information. A lot of it. About who they are. What they're interested in. What kind of job they hold.

eNLIVEN

capture your audience

Statistics show that 98% of the people who see your ad on the Web do exactly the same thing. Ignore it. And when you happen to launch a successful Internet campaign, current technology can't tell you why your viewers responded favorably. Enliven is a breakthrough advertising technology that lets you create fully animated, fully interactive, highly measurable Web promotions with the software tools you're already using. Enliven's server software allows you to track the clicks and mouse-over activities of every single user interacting with your banner ad. No plug-ins are required. Discover how to attract, engage and learn more about your audience on the Web. For more information, call 1-800 978-8670 today or visit www.enliven.com/aa

How old they are. Get the picture?" As a writer for *Advertising Age* said, "What was once a neutral platform for global communication and vast information gathering is now seen as a virtual playground for marketers seeking new and better ways to reach consumers."

Home pages on the World Wide Web hawk everything from potato chips to cereal to fast food—to drugs. Alcohol and tobacco companies, chafing under advertising restrictions in other media, have discovered they can find and woo young people without any problem on the Web. Indeed, children are especially vulnerable on the Internet, where advertising manipulates them, invades their privacy, and transforms them into customers without their knowledge. Although there are various initiatives pending, there are as yet no regulations against targeting children online. Marketers attract children to Websites with games and contests and then extract from them information that can be used in future sales pitches to the child and the child's family. They should be aware that this information might be misleading. My daughter recently checked the "less than $20,000" household income box because she was thinking of her allowance.

Some sites offer prizes to lure children into giving up the e-mail addresses of their friends too. Online advertising targets children as young as four in an attempt to develop "brand loyalty" as early as possible. Companies unrelated to children's products have Websites for children, such as Chevron's site, which features games, toys, and videos touting the importance of—surprise!—the oil industry. In this way, companies can create an image early on and can also gather marketing data. As one ad says to advertisers, "Beginning this August, Kidstar will be able to reach every kid on the planet. And you can, too."

The United States is one of the few industrialized nations in the world that thinks that children are legitimate targets for advertisers. Belgium, Denmark, Norway, and the Canadian province of Quebec ban all advertising to children on television and radio, and Sweden and Greece are pushing for an end to all advertising aimed at children throughout the European Union. An effort to pass similar legislation in the United States in the 1970s was squelched by a coalition of food

ONLY OUR KIDS HAVE THIS MUCH POWER OVER THEIR PARENTS.

Today's kids influence over $130 billion of their parent's spending annually. Kids also spend $8 billion of their own money. That makes these little consumers big business. Kids who watch Turner's animated programming will consume 3/4 of the products purchased across a variety of kids' categories. So if you need a lift in reaching these powerful consumers, let Turner help support your marketing efforts. TNT CARTOON NETWORK TBS

Source: 1. "Kids As Consumers" 1992 James McNeal. 2. 1991 Simmons Kid Study projected to 1993. "Barney Barney" and "Barney Rubble" are trademarks of Hanna-Barbera Productions, Inc. ©1993 Turner Broadcasting System, Inc. All Rights Reserved.

and toy companies, broadcasters, and ad agencies. Children in America appear to have value primarily as new consumers. As an ad for juvenile and infant bedding and home accessories says, "Having children is so rewarding. You get to buy childish stuff and pretend it's for them." Our public policy—or lack thereof—on every children's issue, from education to drugs to teen suicide to child abuse, leaves many to conclude that we are a nation that hates its children.

However, the media care about them. The Turner Cartoon Network tells advertisers, "Today's kids influence over $130 billion of their parent's spending annually. Kids also spend $8 billion of their own money. That makes these little consumers big business." Not only are children influencing a lot of spending in the present, they are developing brand loyalty and the beginnings of an addiction to consumption that will serve corporations well in the future. According to Mike Searles, president of Kids 'R' Us, "If you own this child at an early age, you can own this child for years to come. Companies are saying, 'Hey, I want to own the kid younger and younger.'" No wonder Levi Strauss & Co. finds it worthwhile to send a direct mailing to seven- to twelve-year-old girls to learn about them when they are starting to form brand opinions. According to the senior advertising manager, "This is more of a long-term relationship that we're trying to explore." There may not seem much harm in this until we consider that the tobacco and alcohol industries are also interested in long-term relationships beginning in childhood—and are selling products that can indeed end up "owning" people.

Advertisers are willing to spend a great deal on psychological research that will help them target children more effectively. Nintendo U.S. has a research center which interviews at least fifteen hundred children every week. Kid Connection, a unit of the advertising agency Saatchi & Saatchi, has commissioned what the company calls "psychocultural youth research" studies from cultural anthropologists and clinical psychologists. In a recent study, psychologists interviewed young people between the ages of six and twenty and then analyzed their dreams, drawings, and reactions to symbols. Meanwhile, the anthropologists spent over five hundred hours watching other children use the Internet.

Children are easily influenced. Most little children can't tell the difference between the shows and the commercials (which basically means they are smarter than the rest of us). The toys sold during children's programs are often based on characters in the programs. Recently the Center for Media Education asked the Federal Trade Commission to examine "kidola," a television marketing strategy in which toy companies promise to buy blocks of commercial time if a local broadcast station airs programs associated with their toys.

One company has initiated a program for advertisers to distribute samples, coupons, and promotional materials to a network of twenty two thousand day care centers and 2 million preschool children. The editor-in-chief of *KidStyle,* a kids' fashion magazine that made its debut in 1997, said, "It's not going to be another parenting magazine. This will be a pictorial magazine focusing on products."

Perhaps most troubling, advertising is increasingly showing up in our schools, where ads are emblazoned on school buses, scoreboards, and book covers, where corporations provide "free" material for teachers, and where many children are a captive audience for the commercials on Channel One, a marketing program that gives video equipment to desperate schools in exchange for the right to broadcast a "news" program studded with commercials to all students every morning. Channel One is hardly free, however—it is estimated that it costs taxpayers $1.8 billion in lost classroom time. But it certainly is profitable for the owners who promise advertisers "the largest teen audience around" and "the undivided attention of millions of teenagers for 12 minutes a day." Another ad for Channel One boasts, "Our relationship with 8.1 million teenagers lasts for six years [rather remarkable considering most of theirs last for . . . like six days]." Imagine the public outcry if a political or religious group offered schools an information package with ten minutes of news and two minutes of political or religious persuasion. Yet we tend to think of commercial persuasion as somehow neutral, although it certainly promotes beliefs and behavior that have significant and sometimes harmful effects on the individual, the family, the society, and the environment.

"Reach him at the office," says an ad featuring a small boy in a business suit, which continues, "His first day job is kindergarten. Modern can put your sponsored educational materials in the lesson plan." Advertisers are reaching nearly 8 million public school students each day.

Cash-strapped and underfunded schools accept this dance with the devil. And they are not alone. As many people become less and less willing to pay taxes to support public schools and other institutions and services, corporations are only too eager to pick up the slack—in exchange for a captive audience, of course. As one good corporate citizen, head of an outdoor advertising agency, suggested, "Perhaps fewer libraries would be closing their doors or reducing their services if they wrapped their buildings in tastefully done outdoor ads."

According to the Council for Aid to Education, the total amount corporations spend on "educational" programs from kindergarten through high school has increased from $5 million in 1965 to about $500 million today. The Seattle School Board recently voted to aggressively pursue advertising and corporate sponsorship. "There can be a Nike concert series and a Boeing valedictorian," said the head of the task force. We already have market-driven educational materials in our schools, such as Exxon's documentary on the beauty of the Alaskan coastline or the McDonald's Nutrition Chart and a kindergarten curriculum that teaches children to "Learn to Read through Recognizing Corporate Logos."

No wonder so many people fell for a "news item" in *Adbusters* (a Canadian magazine that critiques advertising and commercialism) about a new program called "Tattoo You Too!", which pays schools a fee in exchange for students willing to be tattooed with famous corporate logos, such as the Nike "swoosh" and the Guess question mark. Although the item was a spoof, it was believable enough to be picked up by some major media. I guess nothing about advertising seems unbelievable these days.

There are penalties for young people who resist this commercialization. In the spring of 1998 Mike Cameron, a senior at Greenbrier High School in Evans, Georgia, was suspended from school. Why? Did he bring a gun to school? Was he smoking in the boys' room? Did he assault a teacher? No. He wore a Pepsi shirt on a school-sponsored Coke day, an entire school day dedicated to an attempt to win ten thousand dollars in a national contest run by Coca-Cola.

Coke has several "partnerships" with schools around the country in which the company gives several million dollars to the school in exchange for a long-term contract giving Coke exclusive rights to school vending machines. John Bushey, an area superintendent for thirteen schools in Colorado Springs who signs his correspondence "The Coke Dude," urged school officials to "get next year's volume up to 70,000 cases" and suggested letting students buy Coke throughout the day and putting vending machines "where they are accessible all day." Twenty years ago, teens drank almost twice as much milk as soda. Today they drink twice as much soda as milk. Some data suggest this contributes to broken bones while they are still teenagers and to osteoporosis in later life.

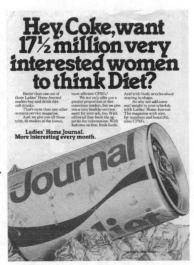

Just as children are sold to the toy industry and junk food industry by programs, video games, and films, women are sold to the diet industry by the magazines we read and the television programs we watch, almost all of which make us feel anxious about our weight. "Hey, Coke," proclaims an ad placed by *The Ladies' Home Journal*, "want 17-1/2 million very interested women to think Diet?" It goes on to promise executives of Coca-Cola a "very healthy environment for your ads." What's being sold here isn't Diet Coke—or even *The Ladies' Home Journal*. What's really being sold are the readers of *The Ladies' Home Journal*, first made to feel anxious about their weight and then delivered to the diet industry. Once there, they can be sold again—*Weight Watchers Magazine* sells its readers to the advertisers by promising that they "reward themselves with $4 billion in beauty and fashion expenditures annually."

In the same way, female drinkers are sold to the alcohol industry. As alcohol consumption has been falling in recent years, the alcohol industry has been directly targeting groups that traditionally have been lighter drinkers. One important target is women. Women's magazines are happy to cooperate.

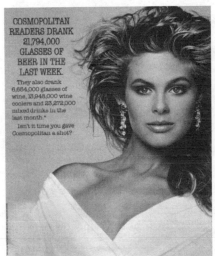

Cosmopolitan sells its readers to the alcohol industry in a trade publication ad proclaiming, "Cosmopolitan Readers Drank 21,794,000 Glasses of Beer in the Last Week." No wonder *Cosmopolitan* runs articles such as "The Beer-Drinker's Diet." It is also no surprise that Absolute vodka would "honor" *Cosmopolitan* and its founder Helen Gurley Brown in an ad (see next page) that merges all three.

Family Circle promises executives of the alcohol industry that they can deliver women who drink. "Attention Alco-

ABSOLUT GURLEY BROWN.

holic Beverage Marketing Executives," headlines their ad in *Advertising Age*. "American women make up 48% of your market. You need to reach our 16 million to earn your market share." Many people in my audiences gasp out loud at this ad. They expect this kind of thing from *Cosmopolitan*, but *Family Circle* is such a wholesome magazine! If *it* is in the business of selling women to the alcohol industry, then no magazine can be trusted. Which is, sadly, the truth (except for those very few magazines, like *Ms.* and *Consumer Reports*, which take no advertising).

Young people are also an important market for alcohol. *Sport* magazine reminds the alcohol industry that "what young money spends on drinks is a real eye-opener," and, through its ad space, *Sport* is more than willing to help. "Black people drink too much," says an ad for the Black Newspaper Network. "Too much, that is," the copy continues, "for you to ignore." "Diario Las Américas readers Pour It On," echoes an ad in *Advertising Age* for a Spanish-language newspaper sold in Florida. The truth is that African-Americans and Latinos don't drink nearly as much as Caucasians, but they represent desirable new territory for the alcohol industry. And so the African-American and Latino media hand them over.

Perhaps this wouldn't matter very much if it didn't affect the content of the media. But it does. "Uncork the black market," says an ad for *Ebony* magazine in *Advertising Age,* which promises alcohol advertisers that "nothing sells black consumers better." A few years later *Ebony* did a story on the ten most serious health problems affecting blacks—but did not include the fact that alcohol is related to nine out of the ten health problems. There were eleven alcohol ads in this same issue of *Ebony.*

Magazines, television programs, newspapers, all in the business of attracting advertisers, certainly can't afford to offend them. On the contrary, they promise their advertisers an editorial climate in which their ads will be favorably received. Corporations exert great influence on the programs they sponsor, from news to soap operas to talk shows, which in turn reflect consumerist values and become little more than advertising themselves. It becomes increasingly difficult to tell the difference between advertising and editorial content, which we need to understand in order to take advertising seriously.

Advertising's influence on media content is exerted in two major ways: via the suppression of information that would harm or "offend the sponsor" and via the inclusion of editorial content that is advertiser-friendly, that creates an environment in which the ads look good. The line between advertising and editorial content is blurred by "advertorials" (advertising disguised as editorial copy) "product placement" in television programs and feature films, and the widespread use of

UNCORK THE BLACK MARKET

Nothing sells black consumers better

"video news releases," corporate public-relations puff pieces aired by local television stations as genuine news. Up to 85 percent of the news we get is bought and paid for by corporations eager to gain positive publicity.

Although people have become used to news reporters popping up in commercials and movies (as Joan Lunden and Linda Ellerbee did in television commercials for Vaseline and Maxwell House coffee, respectively, and as almost everyone at CNN did in the movie *Contact*), many were shocked in late 1997 when retired newsman David Brinkley became the pitchman for agribusiness giant Archer Daniels Midland, a company that has been convicted of price fixing on an international scale.

In 1998 Nike's sponsorship of CBS's Olympic coverage was rewarded when the correspondents delivered the news wearing jackets emblazoned with Nike's symbolic swoosh. The president of CBS News vehemently denied that this sponsorship had anything to do with the thwarting of a follow-up to a hard-hitting investigative piece on Nike for *48 Hours*. The editor of *The San Francisco Examiner* likewise denied that Nike's cosponsorship of their big annual promotion was in any way related to the decision to kill a column by a reporter that was highly critical of Nike.

In 1996 Chrysler Corporation set off a furor by demanding in writing that magazines notify it in advance about "any and all editorial content that encompasses sexual, political, social issues or any editorial that might be construed as provocative or offensive." According to Chrysler spokesman Mike Aberlich, placing an ad is like buying a house: "You decide the neighborhood you want to be in." Fear of losing the lucrative Chrysler account led *Esquire* to kill a long story with a gay theme, already in page proofs, by accomplished author David Leavitt. Will Blythe, the magazine's literary editor, promptly quit, saying in his letter of resignation that "in effect, we're taking marching orders (albeit, indirectly) from advertisers." Of course, had Blythe not gone public, the public would never have known what happened. When we don't get the story, we don't know what we're missing.

In reaction to the Chrysler letter, the American Society of Magazine Editors and Magazine Publishers of America issued a joint statement in the fall of 1997 calling for editorial integrity and barring magazines from giving advertisers a preview of stories, photos, or tables of contents for upcoming issues. This is to their credit, of course, but it won't protect us from similar phenomena occurring: According to an article in the *Columbia Journalism Review,* in 1997 a major advertiser (unnamed in the article) warned all three newsweeklies—*Time, Newsweek,* and *U.S. News & World Report*—that it would award all of its advertising to the magazine that portrayed its company's industry in the most favorable light during the upcoming quarter.

More often than not, self-censorship by magazine editors and television producers makes such overt pressure by corporations unnecessary. According to Kurt Andersen, the former editor of *New York* magazine, "Because I worked closely and happily with the publisher at *New York,* I was aware who the big advertisers were. My antennae were turned on, and I read copy thinking, 'Is this going to cause Calvin Klein or Bergdorf big problems.'" No doubt this is what ran through the minds of the CBS executives who canceled Ed Asner's series after two large corporate advertisers—Vidal Sassoon and Kimberly-Clark—withdrew their sponsorship because of Asner's association with Medical Aid for El Salvador.

Sometimes the self-censorship involves an entire industry rather than a specific company or corporation. For example, several radio stations in the Midwest not only refused to play a commercial advocating vegetarianism in which country singer k.d. lang appeared as a spokesperson, but also banned lang's songs from the air. Clearly this kind of thinking has more serious consequences than an occasional editorial omission or favorable mention—it warps a worldview and distorts the editorial content we read and the programs we listen to and watch.

Nowhere is this more obvious than in most women's and girls' magazines, where there is a very fine line, if any, between advertising and editorial content. Most of these magazines gladly provide a climate in which ads for diet and beauty products will be looked at with interest, even with desperation. And they suffer consequences from advertisers if they fail to provide such a climate.

Gloria Steinem provides a striking example of this in her article "Sex, Lies & Advertising," in which she discusses an award-winning story on Soviet women that was featured on the cover of the November 1980 issue of *Ms.* In those days, *Ms.*, like every other woman's magazine, depended on advertising. Following that story, *Ms.* lost all hope of ever getting Revlon ads. Why? Because the Soviet women on the cover weren't wearing makeup.

More recently, the editor of *New Woman* magazine in Australia resigned after advertisers complained about the publication's use of a heavyset cover girl, even though letters had poured in from grateful readers. According to *Advertising Age International,* her departure "made clear the influence wielded by advertisers who remain convinced that only thin models spur sales of beauty products." One prevalent form of censorship in the mass media is the almost complete invisibility, the eradication, of real women's faces and bodies.

No wonder women's magazines so often have covers that feature luscious cakes and pies juxtaposed with articles about diets. "85 Ways to Lose Weight," *Woman's Day* tells us—but probably one of them isn't the "10-minute ice cream pie" on the cover. This is an invitation to pathology, fueling the paradoxical obsession with food and weight control that is one of the hallmarks of eating disorders.

It can be shocking to look at the front and back covers of magazines. Often there are ironic juxtapositions. A typical woman's magazine has a photo of some rich food on the front cover, a cheesecake covered with luscious cherries or a huge slice of apple pie with ice cream melting on top. On the back cover, there is usually a cigarette ad, often one implying that smoking will keep women thin. Inside the magazine are recipes, more photos of fattening foods, articles about dieting—and lots of advertising featuring very thin models. There usually also is at least one article about an uncommon disease or trivial health hazard, which can seem very ironic in light of the truly dangerous product being glamorized on the back cover.

In February 1999, *Family Circle* featured on its front cover a luscious photo of "gingham mini-cakes," while promoting articles entitled "New! Lose-Weight, Stay-Young Diet," "Super Foods That Act Like Medicine," and "The Healing Power of Love." On the back cover was an ad for Virginia Slims cigarettes. The same week, *For Women First* featured a chocolate cake on its cover along with one article entitled "Accelerate Fat Loss" and another promising "Breakthrough Cures" for varicose veins, cellulite, PMS, stress, tiredness, and dry skin. On the back cover, an ad for Doral cigarettes said, "Imagine getting more." *The Ladies' Home Journal* that same month offered on its cover "The Best Chocolate Cake You *Ever* Ate," along with its antidote, "Want to Lose 10 lbs? Re-program Your Body." Concern for their readers' health was reflected in two articles highlighted on the cover, "12 Symptoms You Must Not Ignore" and "De-Stressors for Really Crazy Workdays"—and then undermined by the ad for Basic cigarettes on the back cover (which added to the general confusion by picturing the pack surrounded by chocolate candies).

The diseases and health hazards warned about in the women's magazines are often ridiculous. *Woman's Day* once offered a "Special Report on Deadly Appliances," which warned us about how our appliances, such as toasters, coffeemakers, baby monitors, and nightlights, can suddenly burst into flame. Lest we think this is not a serious problem, the article tells us that in 1993, the last year for which figures were available, 80 people died and 370 were injured by these killer appliances. I don't wish to minimize any death or injury. However, on the back cover of this issue of *Woman's Day* is an advertisement for cigarettes, a product that kills over four hundred thousand people, year in and year out.

The January 1995 issue of *Redbook* warns us on the cover about all sorts of pressing problems from frizzy hair to "erotic accidents" and promotes an article entitled "If Only They'd Caught It Sooner: The Tests Even Healthy Women Need." On the back cover, as always, an ad for Virginia Slims. Needless to say, being set afire from smoking in bed (one of the leading causes of fire deaths) does not make it into the "erotic accidents" article.

An informal survey of popular women's magazines in 1996 found cover stories on some of the following health issues: skin cancer, Pap smears, leukemia, how breast cancer can be fought with a positive attitude, how breast cancer can be held off with aspirin, and the possibility that dry-cleaned clothes can cause cancer. There were cigarette ads on the back covers of all these magazines—and not a single mention inside of lung cancer and heart disease caused by smoking. In spite of increasing coverage of tobacco issues in the late 1990s, the silence in women's magazines has continued, in America and throughout the world. In my own research, I continue to find scanty coverage of smoking dangers, no feature stories on lung cancer or on smoking's role in causing many other cancers and heart disease . . . and hundreds of cigarette ads.

Dr. Holly Atkinson, a health writer for *New Woman* between 1985 and 1990, recalled that she was barred from covering smoking-related issues, and that her editor struck any reference to cigarettes in articles on topics ranging from wrinkles to cancer. When Atkinson confronted the editor, a shouting match ensued. "Holly, who do you think supports this magazine?" demanded the editor. As Helen Gurley Brown, former editor of *Cosmopolitan,* said: "Having come from the advertising world myself, I think, 'Who needs somebody you're paying millions of dollars a year to come back and bite you on the ankle?'"

It is not just women's magazines that tailor their articles to match their ads. The July 1995 issue of *Life* magazine warns us of the dangers our children face, including drugs, and asks, "How can we keep our children safe?" On the back cover is a Marlboro ad. Our children are far more likely to die from tobacco-related diseases than from any other cause, but cigarettes are not mentioned in the article.

Americans rely on the media for our health information. But this information is altered, distorted, even censored on behalf of the advertisers—advertisers for alcohol, cigarettes, junk food, diet products. We get most of our information from people who are likely to be thinking, "Is this going to cause Philip Morris or Anheuser-Busch big problems?" Of course, in recent years there has been front-page coverage of the liability suits against the tobacco industry and much discussion about antismoking legislation. However, there is still very little information about the health consequences of smoking, especially in women's magazines. The Partnership for a Drug-Free America, made up primarily of media companies dependent on advertising, basically refuses to warn children

against the dangers of alcohol and tobacco. The government is spending $195 million in 1999 on a national media campaign to dissuade adolescents from using illicit drugs, but not a penny of the appropriated tax dollars is going to warn about the dangers of smoking or drinking.

No wonder most people still don't understand that these heavily advertised drugs pose a much greater threat to our young people and kill far more Americans than all illicit drugs combined. Thirty percent of Americans still don't know that smoking shortens life expectancy, and almost 60 percent don't know it causes emphysema. There is still so much ignorance that, when I was invited recently to give a talk on tobacco advertising to students at a progressive private school outside Boston, the person extending the invitation said she was also going to invite someone from the tobacco industry to represent "the other side." I was tempted to ask her if she felt equally compelled to have a batterer on hand during a discussion of domestic violence.

The influence of these huge and powerful corporations on the media leads to a pernicious kind of censorship. The problem is exacerbated by the fact that many of these corporations own and control the media. In 1996 the Seagram Company ran a whiskey ad on an NBC affiliate in Texas, thus breaking the decades-old tradition of liquor ads not being carried on television. Although network television is leery of running liquor ads for fear of offending their beer advertisers, *Advertising Age* reported that Seagram might have a "winning card to play," since the company owns 50 percent of both the USA Network and the Sci-Fi Channel. Although both have a ban on hard-liquor advertising, a top executive for USA Network said, "If Seagram came to us with a hard-liquor ad, we'd have to look at it."

Today, Time Warner, Sony, Viacom, Disney, Bertelsmann, and News Corporation together control most publishing, music, television, film, and theme-park entertainment throughout the developed world. It is estimated that by the end of the millennium these companies will own 90 percent of the world's information, from newspapers to computer software to film to television to popular music. We may be able to change the channel, but we won't be able to change the message.

Almost everywhere we look these days, anywhere in the world, there is a message from one of these conglomerates. An ad in *Advertising Age* shows a huge picture of the earth and the headline, "Do you see the trillion dollar market?" The triumph of democracy is becoming the triumph of consumerism, as the global village is reduced to a "trillion dollar market."

"Why 6,000,000 women who used to carry a little red book now carry a little red lipstick," says an ad for *Allure,* an American beauty magazine, featuring a Chinese woman in a military uniform wearing bright red lipstick. The copy continues, "When nail polish becomes political, and fashion becomes philosophy, Allure magazine will be there." In the world of advertising the political is only personal. Six million women carrying a book of political ideas might be a movement, even a revolution. The same women, carrying lipstick, are simply red-lipped consumers. Advertisers are adept at appropriating dissent and rebellion, slickly packaging it, and then selling it right back to us.

Although the conglomerates are transnational, the culture they sell is American. Not the American culture of the past, which exported writers like Ernest Hemingway and Edgar Allan Poe, musical greats like Louis Armstrong and Marian Anderson, plays by Eugene O'Neill and Tennessee Williams, and Broadway musicals like *West Side Story.* These exports celebrated democracy, freedom, and vitality as the American way of life.

Today we export a popular culture that promotes escapism, consumerism, violence, and greed. Half the planet lusts for Cindy Crawford, lines up for blockbuster films like *Die Hard 12* with a minimum of dialogue and a maximum of violence (which travels well, needing no translation), and dances to the monotonous beat of the Backstreet Boys. *Baywatch,* a moronic television series starring Ken and Barbie, has been seen by more people in the world than any other television show in history. And at the heart of all this "entertainment" is advertising. As Simon Anholt, an English consultant specializing in global brand development, said, "The world's most powerful brand is the U.S. This is because it has Hollywood, the world's best advertising agency. For nearly a century, Hollywood has been pumping out two-hour cinema ads for Brand U.S.A., which audiences around the world flock to see." When a group of German advertising agencies placed an ad in *Advertising Age* that said, "Let's make America great again," they left no doubt about what they had in mind. The ad featured cola, jeans, burgers, cigarettes, and alcohol—an advertiser's idea of what makes America great.

Some people might wonder what's wrong with this. On the most obvious level, as multinational chains replace local stores, local products, and local character, we end up in a world in which everything looks the same and everyone is Gapped and Starbucked. Shopping malls kill vibrant downtown centers locally and create a universe of uniformity internationally. Worse, we end up in a world ruled by, in John Maynard Keynes's phrase, the values of the casino. On this deeper level, rampant commercialism undermines our physical and psychological health,

Let's make America great again.

our environment, and our civic life and creates a toxic society. Advertising corrupts us and, I will argue, promotes a dissociative state that exploits trauma and can lead to addiction. To add insult to injury, it then co-opts our attempts at resistance and rebellion.

Although it is virtually impossible to measure the influence of advertising on a culture, we can learn something by looking at cultures only recently exposed to it. In 1980 the Gwich'in tribe of Alaska got television, and therefore massive advertising, for the first time. Satellite dishes, video games, and VCRs were not far behind. Before this, the Gwich'in lived much the way their ancestors had for a thousand generations. Within ten years, the young members of the tribe were so drawn by television they no longer had time to learn ancient hunting methods, their parents' language, or their oral history. Legends told around campfires could not compete with *Beverly Hills 90210*. Beaded moccasins gave way to Nike sneakers, sled dogs to gas-powered skimobiles, and "tundra tea" to Folger's instant coffee.

Human beings used to be influenced primarily by the stories of our particular tribe or community, not by stories that are mass-produced and market-driven. As George Gerbner, one of the world's most respected researchers on the influence of the media, said, "For the first time in human history, most of the stories about people, life, and values are told not by parents, schools, churches, or others in the community who have something to tell, but by a group of distant conglomerates that have something to sell." The stories that most influence our children these days are the stories told by advertisers.

"IN YOUR FACE . . . ALL OVER THE PLACE"

Advertising Is Our Environment

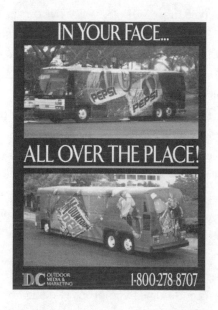

ADVERTISERS LIKE TO TELL PARENTS THAT THEY CAN ALWAYS TURN OFF THE TV to protect their kids from any of the negative impact of advertising. This is like telling us that we can protect our children from air pollution by making sure they never breathe. Advertising is our *environment*. We swim in it as fish swim in water. We cannot escape it. Unless, of course, we keep our children home from school and blindfold them whenever they are outside of the house. And never let them play with other children. Even then, advertising's messages are inside our intimate relationships, our homes, our hearts, our heads.

Advertising not only appears on radio and television, in our magazines and newspapers, but also surrounds us on billboards, on the sides of buildings, plastered on our public transportation. Buses now in many cities are transformed into facsimiles of products, so that one boards a bus masquerading as a box of Dunkin' Donuts (followed, no doubt, by a Slimfast bus). The creators of this atrocity proudly tell us in their ad in *Advertising Age*, "In your face . . . all over the place!" Indeed.

Trucks carry advertising along with products as part of a marketing strategy. "I want every truck we have on the road making folks thirsty for Bud Light," says an ad in *Advertising Age*, which refers to a truck as a "valuable moving billboard." Given that almost half of all automobile crashes are alcohol-related, it's frightening to think of people becoming thirsty for Bud Light while driving their cars. A Spanish company has paid the drivers of seventy-five cars in Madrid to turn their cars into Pall Mall cigarette packages, and hopes to expand its operation throughout Spain. Imagine cars disguised as bottles of beer zipping along our highways. If we seek to escape all this by taking a plane, we become a captive audience for in-flight promotional videos.

Ads are on the videos we rent, the shopping carts we push through stores, the apples and hot dogs we buy, the online services we use, and the navigational screens of the luxury cars we drive. A new device allows advertisers to print their messages directly onto the sand of a beach. "This is my best idea ever—5,000 imprints of Skippy Peanut Butter jars covering the beach," crowed the inventor. Added the promotion director, "I'm here looking at thousands of families with kids. If they're on the beach thinking of Skippy, that's just what we want." Their next big idea is snow imprinting at ski resorts. In England the legendary white cliffs of Dover now serve as the backdrop for a laser-projected Adidas ad. American consumers have recently joined Europeans in being offered free phone calls if they will also listen to commercials. Conversations are interrupted by brief ads, tailored to match the age and social profiles of the conversants. And beer companies have experimented with messages posted over urinals, such as "Time for more Coors" or "Put used Bud here."

The average American is exposed to at least three thousand ads every day and will spend three years of his or her life watching television commercials. Advertising makes up about 70 percent of our newspapers and 40 percent of our mail. Of course, we don't pay direct attention to very many of these ads, but we are powerfully influenced, mostly on an unconscious level, by the experience of being immersed in an advertising culture, a market-driven culture, in which all our institutions, from political to religious to educational, are increasingly for sale to the highest bidder. According to Rance Crain, editor-in-chief of *Advertising Age*, the major publication of the advertising industry, "Only eight percent of an ad's message is received by the conscious mind; the rest is worked and reworked deep within the recesses of the brain, where a product's positioning and repositioning takes shape." It is in this sense that advertising is subliminal: not in the sense of hidden messages embedded in ice cubes, but in the sense that we aren't consciously aware of what advertising is doing.

Children who used to roam their neighborhoods now often play at McDonald's. Families go to Disneyland or other theme parks instead of state and national parks—or to megamalls such as the Mall of America in Minneapolis or Grapevine Mills in Texas, which provide "shoppertainment." One of the major tourist destinations in historic Boston is the bar used in the 1980s hit television series *Cheers*. The Olympics today are at least as much about advertising as athletics. We are not far off from the world David Foster Wallace imagined in his epic novel *Infinite Jest*, in which years are sponsored by companies and named after them, giving us the Year of the Whopper and the Year of the Tucks Medicated Pad.

Commercialism has no borders. There is barely any line left between advertising and the rest of the culture. The prestigious Museum of Fine Arts in Boston puts on a huge exhibit of Herb Ritts, fashion photographer, and draws one of the largest crowds in its history. In 1998 the museum's Monet show was the most popular exhibit in the world. Museum officials were especially pleased by results of a survey showing 74 percent of visitors recognized that the show's sponsor was Fleet Financial Group, which shelled out $1.2 million to underwrite the show.

Bob Dole plays on his defeat in the presidential election in ads for Air France and Viagra, while Ed Koch, former mayor of New York City, peddles Dunkin' Donuts' bagels. Dr. Jane Goodall, doyenne of primatology, appears with her chimpanzees in an ad for Home Box Office, and Sarah Ferguson, the former duchess of York, gets a million dollars for being the official spokeswoman for Weight Watchers (with a bonus if she keeps her weight down).

Dead celebrities, such as Marilyn Monroe and Humphrey Bogart and John Wayne, are brought to life through computer magic and given digitized immortality in ads (how awful it is to see classy Fred Astaire dancing with electric brooms and hand vacs). Even worse, advertising often exploits cultural icons of rebellion and anticommercialism. Jimi Hendrix was raised from the dead by Aiwa to sell stereos, and John Lennon's haunting song "Imagine" is used by American Express. The Beatles' "Revolution," Bob Dylan's classic anthem "The Times They Are A-Changin'," and Janis Joplin's "Oh Lord, won't you buy me a Mercedes-Benz?" have all been used as advertising jingles, appealing to baby-boomers' nostalgia while completely corrupting the meaning of the songs. And the Rolling Stones, those aging rebels, have allowed Sprint to put a straight-pin through the band's tongue logo. However, when Neil Young recorded a video for his song "This Note's for You," which states that he won't sing for Pepsi or Coke and includes the lines "I don't sing for nobody/Makes me look like a joke," MTV refused to run it.

Live celebrities line up to appear in ads and people who simply appear in ads become celebrities. Today little girls constantly rate the supermodels high on their list of heroes, and most of us know them by their first names alone . . . Cindy, Elle, Naomi, Iman. Imagine—these women are *heroes* to little girls, not because of their courage or character or good deeds, but because of their perfect features and poreless skin. Models become more famous than film and television stars and rock stars, and the stars themselves often become pitchmen (and women) for a variety of products ranging from candy to cigarettes to alcohol.

Stars such as Harrison Ford, Woody Allen, Paul Newman, Whoopi Gold-berg, and Bruce Willis, who don't want to tarnish their image in the United States, gladly appear in foreign television ads and commercials. Antonio Ban-deras and Kevin Costner have pushed cars, Brad Pitt watches, Dennis Hopper

bath salts, Michael J. Fox fishing tackle, and Jennifer Aniston shampoo. In a commercial for Nippon Ham, Sylvester Stallone munched sausages at a garden party. After the success of *Titanic*, Leonardo DiCaprio was paid $4 million to play a noodle-eating detective in a Japanese commercial for credit cards. And in a commercial for Austrian Rail-ways, Arnold Schwarzenegger rebuffs a steward who offers him a drink with the

reply, "Hasta la vista, baby." Not surprisingly, he agreed to make the commercial only on the condition that the international media not be told about it. Madonna has a similar deal with Max Factor, which is paying her $6.5 million to sell cosmetics on TV, billboards, and in magazines throughout Britain, Europe, and Asia, but is prohibited from circulating photos from the ad campaign in the United States.

We are also influenced by advertising that we do not recognize as such, like the use of brand names during televised sporting events (during one ninety-minute car race, the word "Marlboro" appeared 5,933 times). In 1983 Sylvester Stallone wrote a letter to the Brown & Williamson tobacco company in which he promised to use their tobacco products in five feature films in exchange for half a million dollars. Compare this with the old days of "Brand X," the days when Julia Child covered the brand name "Pyrex" on her measuring cup!

Increasingly, films and television shows carry these hidden commercials. Often characters use certain products, the brands are prominently displayed, but the audience remains unaware that money has changed hands. New technology allows advertisers to have products digitally added to a scene, such as a Coca-Cola can on a desk or commercial billboards in the background of baseball games. At the very least, these "commercials" should be directly acknowledged in the credits. Writer and cartoonist Mark O'Donnell suggests that someday there will be tie-ins in literature as well, such as "All's Well That Ends With Pepsi," "The Old Man, Coppertone and the Sea," and "Nausea, and Periodic Discomfort Relief."

Sometimes the tie-ins are overt. Diet Coke obtained the rights to the cast of the hit series *Friends* and built a promotion around a special episode of the show that aired after the Super Bowl. In 1997 ABC and American Airlines announced a program that grants bonus miles and vacation credits to enrolled members who can correctly answer questions about shows that recently aired on the network. In the spring of 1998 product peddling on television was brought to new heights (or a new low) when a character in the hit show *Baywatch* created a line of shoes in her fashion-design class that viewers can actually buy. Stay tuned for *Shoe-watch*.

Far more important than the tie-ins, however, is the increasing influence of advertising on the form and content of films, television shows, and music videos (which aren't so much *like* ads as they *are* ads). Among other things, advertisers prefer that their products be associated with upbeat shows and films with happy endings, shows that leave people in the mood to buy. "People have become less capable of tolerating any kind of darkness or sadness," says media scholar Mark Crispin Miller. "I think it ultimately has to do with advertising, with a vision of life as a shopping trip." Steven Stark, another media critic, holds advertising responsible for a shift in television programs from glamorizing private detectives to glamorizing the police. According to Stark, "A detective show often leaves the audience with the impression that the system, police included, is corrupt and incompetent. An audience left with that message is in less mood to buy than an audience reassured, night after night, that the system works because the police are doing their job."

The cast of *Seinfeld* were the most successful hucksters in TV history, so successful that in 1994 *Advertising Age* gave their Star Presenter of the Year award to the entire cast. As Jerry Seinfeld, star of the show, said, "It is a good combination. When you're on TV in a sitcom, there's a loose reality that lends itself to doing commercials, which are also on TV. As long as you're on TV pretending to be something you're not anyway, why not do it for a commercial?" Opening an adver-

These days, kids don't want to grow up to be athletes, comedians or movie stars.

They want to be highly leveraged brands.

tising agency, one of the paths Seinfeld is reportedly now considering, wouldn't be much of a leap (not that there's anything wrong with that). No wonder Seinfeld was one of the celebrities featured in a 1999 ad placed by *Forbes* magazine in *Advertising Age* that said, "These days, kids don't want to grow up to be athletes, comedians or movie stars. They want to be highly leveraged brands." The ad continues, "The real power in America no longer belongs to the most talented celebrities. But the most marketable ones."

The 1997 James Bond film *Tomorrow Never Dies* broke new ground for global integrated film tie-ins. In an ongoing effort to raise its profile, beer marketer Heineken USA featured James Bond, portrayed by Pierce Brosnan, in point-of-purchase displays worldwide and also offered a James Bond holiday catalog of electronic devices. During one scene in the film Bond crashes a car into a Heineken truck. Other marketers with major tie-ins to the film include Heublein's Smirnoff vodka brand, Omega watches, Avis, L'Oreal, and Visa International. More recently, the 1998 hit movie *You've Got Mail* basically costarred America Online, which in turn spent millions on television and online advertising for the movie. "Warner Brothers came to us and we agreed to be as helpful as we possibly could," said an AOL spokeswoman.

And independent films are becoming as tight with Madison Avenue as are the big flicks. Although I have no evidence that it was intentional, *The Brothers McMullen* prominently featured Heineken and Budweiser beer, which was ironic given its underlying theme of the havoc wreaked by family alcoholism. According to Ted Hope, the film's producer, "We struggle with product placement all the time, and I know other producers and directors struggle with it. I actively discourage it in movies but there are times when I contradict myself."

According to Paul Speaker, director of marketing for the independent production company responsible for *Sling Blade,* the key "is not only to find opportunities to seamlessly place products, but more importantly to associate brand to the entire film relevance." In order to appear hip and cool, major clothing manufacturers, such as Dockers, Tommy Hilfiger, and Polo Ralph Lauren, are associating their products with the low-budget independent films that are usually seen as "counterculture." Hilfiger provided the wardrobe for the independent film *The Faculty* and, in exchange, the teenage actors in the film appeared in commercials for Hilfiger. Andy Hilfiger, the company's vice-president of marketing, said, "The cast is great, and they went so well with our clothing."

The music world is in the game too, as rappers launch clothing lines and designers start record labels. Maurice Malone, who designs sportswear and has a record company, says, "You can use your music videos and your artists on your label to show your clothes," and, "You can talk about your clothes in the songs and hype the name." In 1999 designer Tommy Hilfiger sponsored concert tours for the Rolling Stones, Lilith Fair, and Britney Spears. All the musicians wore Hilfiger items onstage, while ads in fashion magazines depicted staged scenes from the concerts.

Not everyone is enthusiastic about this trend. Chris Gore, publisher of the Webzine *Film Threat,* thinks that sponsorship will inevitably guide what kinds of films get made, discouraging those with less consumer-friendly content. "Think of classic movies, like *The Wizard of Oz* or *Gone With the Wind,* and the products that could have been branded with them," he said. "Not only would that date them, it would be pathetic. We're not creating classics here—this is about commerce."

In spite of the fact that we are surrounded by more advertising than ever before, most of us still ridicule the idea that we might be personally influenced by it. The ridicule is often extremely simplistic. The argument essentially is, "I'm no robot marching down to the store to do advertising's bidding and therefore advertising doesn't affect me at all." This argument was made by Jacob Sullum, a senior editor at *Reason* magazine, in an editorial in *The New York Times.* Writing about "heroin chic," the advertising fad in the mid-1990s of using models who looked like heroin addicts, Sullum says, "Like you, I've seen . . . ads featuring sallow, sullen, scrawny youths. Not once have I had an overwhelming urge to rush out and buy some heroin." He concludes from this in-depth research that all critics of advertising are portraying "people not as independent moral agents but as mindless automatons," as if there were no middle ground between rushing out to buy heroin and being completely uninfluenced by the media images that surround us—or no possibility that disaffected teens are more vulnerable than middle-aged executives. After all, Sullum is *not* the target audience for heroin chic ads.

Of course, most of us feel far superior to the kind of person who would be affected by advertising. *We* are not influenced, after all. We are skeptical, even cynical . . . but ignorant (certainly not stupid, just uninformed). Advertising is familiar, but not known. The fact that we are surrounded by it, that we can sing the jingles and identify the models and recognize the logos, doesn't mean that we are educated about it, that we understand it. As Sut Jhally says, "To not be influenced by advertising would be to live outside of culture. No human being lives outside of culture."

Advertisers want us to believe that we are not influenced by ads. As Joseph Goebbels said, "This is the secret of propaganda: Those who are to be persuaded by it should be completely immersed in the ideas of the propaganda, without ever noticing that they are being immersed in it." So the advertisers sometimes play upon our cynicism. In fact, they co-opt our cynicism and our irony just as they have co-opted our rock music, our revolutions and movements for liberation, and our concern for the environment. In a current trend that I call "anti-advertising," the advertisers flatter us by insinuating that we are far too smart to be taken in by advertising. Many of these ads spoof the whole notion of image advertising. A scotch ad tells the reader "This is a glass of Cutty Sark. If you need to see a picture of a guy in an Armani suit sitting between two fashion models drinking it before you know it's right for you, it probably isn't."

cuk advertising

And an ad for shoes says, "If you feel the need to be smarter and more articulate, read the complete works of

fcuk is a trademark of French Connection UK

Shakespeare. If you like who you are, here are your shoes." Another shoe ad, this one for sneakers, says, "Shoe buying rule number one: The image wears off after the first six miles." What a concept. By buying heavily advertised products, we can demonstrate that we are not influenced by advertising. Of course, this is not entirely new. Volkswagens were introduced in the 1960s with an anti-advertising campaign, such as the ad that pictured the car and the headline "Lemon." But such ads go a lot further these days, especially the foreign ones. A British ad for Easy jeans says, "We don't use sex to sell our jeans. We don't even screw you when you buy them." And French Connection UK gets away with a double-page spread that says "fcuk advertising."

A Sprite campaign plays on this cynicism. One commercial features teenagers partying on a beach while drinking a soft drink called Jooky. As the camera pulls back, we see that this is a fictional television commercial being watched by two teens, who open their own cans of Jooky and experience absolutely nothing. "Image is nothing. Thirst is everything," says the slogan. However, there is nothing in the ad about thirst—or taste, for that matter—or anything intrinsic to Sprite. The campaign is about nothing but image. Of course, what other way is there to sell sweetened, flavored carbonated water? If thirst is really everything, our best bet is water, and not high-priced bottled water either, such as Evian, which costs more than some champagne (no wonder that Evian backward spells "naive").

When Nike wanted to reach skateboarders, it had to overcome the fact that skateboarders are "about the most cynical bunch of consumers around" and often downright hostile to the idea of Nike entering the market. By putting a humorous spin on a powerful insight about how skateboarders want to be treated,

Nike created the "What if we treated all athletes the way we treat skateboard-ers?" campaign, which has "won over skateboarders around the country and made them believe that Nike knows them and has the guts to defend them and their sport." Who cares if this is true—what is important is that skateboarders be-lieve that it is true.

Some advertisers use what they chillingly call "viral communications" as a way to reach teenagers alienated from traditional forms of advertising. They use posters on construction sites and lampposts, sidewalk markings, and e-mail to in-filtrate youth culture and cultivate the perception that their product is hot. One marketing consultant suggests picturing the mind as a combination lock and says, "One has to know what the particular stimuli are that are the 'clicks' heard by the inner mind of the target market and then allow the target market to open the lock so it is their own 'Aha!'—their own discovery, and so their own commitment."

Some ads make fun of high-pressure tactics. "Perhaps you'd consider buying one," says an ad for Saturn, and then in brackets below, "Sorry, we didn't mean to pressure you like that." Another car ad declares, "We're not trying to sell you this car. We're just letting you know it exists." An ad for sneakers tells us that "market-ing is just hype." This is a bit like a man unbuttoning a woman's blouse, all the while telling her that she is far too smart to be seduced by the likes of him.

Cynicism is one of the worst effects of advertising. Cynicism learned from years of being exposed to marketing hype and products that never deliver the promised goods often carries over to other aspects of life. This starts early: A study of children done by researchers at Columbia University in 1975 found that heavy viewing of advertising led to cynicism, not only about advertising, but about life in general. The researchers found that "in most cultures, adolescents have had to deal with social hypocrisy and even with institutionalized lying. But today, TV advertising is stimulating *preadolescent* children to think about so-cially accepted hypocrisy. They may be too young to cope with such thoughts without permanently distorting their views of morality, society, and business." They concluded that "7- to 10-year-olds are strained by the very existence of ad-vertising directed to them." These jaded children become the young people whose mantra is "whatever," who admire people like David Letterman (who has made a career out of taking nothing seriously), whose response to almost every experience is "been there, done that," "duh," and "do ya think?" Cynicism is not criticism. It is a lot easier than criticism. In fact, easy cynicism is a kind of naivete. We need to be more critical as a culture and less cynical.

Cynicism deeply affects how we define our problems and envision their so-lutions. Many people exposed to massive doses of advertising both distrust every possible solution *and* expect a quick fix. There are no quick fixes to the problems our society faces today, but there are solutions to many of them. The first step, as always, is breaking through denial and facing the problems squarely. I believe it was James Baldwin who said, "Not everything that is faced can be changed, but nothing can be changed until it is faced." One of the things we need to face is that we and our children are indeed influenced by advertising.

Although some people, especially advertisers, continue to argue that advertis-ing simply reflects the society, advertising does a great deal more than simply re-flect cultural attitudes and values. Even some advertisers admit to this: Rance Crain of *Advertising Age* said great advertising "plays the tune rather than just dancing to the tune." Far from being a passive mirror of society, advertising is an effective and pervasive medium of influence and persuasion, and its influence is cumulative, often subtle, and primarily unconscious. Advertising performs much the same function in industrial society as myth performed in ancient and primitive societies. It is both a creator and perpetuator of the dominant attitudes, values, and ideology of the culture, the social norms and myths by which most people govern their be-havior. At the very least, advertising helps to create a climate in which certain atti-tudes and values flourish and others are not reflected at all.

Advertising is not only our physical environment, it is increasingly our spiri-tual environment as well. By definition, however, it is only interested in material-istic values. When spiritual values or religious images show up in ads, it is only to appropriate them in order to sell us something. Sometimes this is very obvious. Eternity is a perfume by Calvin Klein. Infiniti is an automobile and Hydra Zen a moisturizer. Jesus is a brand of jeans. "See the light," says an ad for wool, while a face powder ad promises "an enlightening experience" and "absolute heaven." One car is "born again" and another promises to "energize your soul." In a full-page ad in *Advertising Age*, the online service Yahoo! proclaims, "We've got 60 million followers. That's more than some religions," but goes on to assure readers, "Don't worry. We're *not* a religion." When Pope John Paul II visited Mexico City in the winter of 1999, he could have seen a smiling image of himself on bags of Sabritas, a popular brand of potato chips, or a giant street sign showing him bowing piously next to a Pepsi logo with a phrase in Spanish that reads, "Mexico Always Faithful." In the United States, he could have treated himself to pope-on-a-rope soap.

An ad for kosher hot dogs pictures the Bible beside a hot dog with the caption, "If you liked the book, you'll love the hot dog." The campaign slogan is, "We answer to a higher authority." "God bless America," says a full-page newspaper ad featuring a little boy with his hand over his heart. The copy continues, "Where else can you find one company that offers phone, cable and internet service?" And an ad for garage doors says, "The legendary architect Mies van der Rohe said, 'God is in the details.' If that's so, could these be the pearly gates?"

Sometimes the allusion to the spiritual realm is more subtle, as in the countless alcohol ads featuring the bottle surrounded by a halo of light. Indeed products are often displayed, such as jewelry shining in a store window, as if they were sacred objects. Buy this and your life will be better. Advertising co-opts our sacred symbols and sacred language in order to evoke an immediate emotional response. Neil Postman refers to this as "cultural rape" that leaves us deprived of our most meaningful images.

But advertising's co-optation of spirituality goes much deeper than this. It is commonplace these days to observe that consumerism has become the religion of our time (with advertising its holy text), but the criticism usually stops short of what is most important, what is at the heart of the comparison. Advertising and religion share a belief in transformation and transcendence, but most religions believe that this requires work and sacrifice. In the world of advertising, enlightenment is achieved instantly by purchasing material goods. As James Twitchell, author of *Adcult USA,* says, "The Jolly Green Giant, the Michelin Man, the Man from Glad, Mother Nature, Aunt Jemima, Speedy Alka-Seltzer, the White Knight, and all their otherworldly kin are descendants of the earlier gods. What separates them is that they now reside in manufactured products and that, although earlier gods were invoked by fasting, prayer, rituals, and penance, the promise of purchase calls forth their modern ilk."

Advertising constantly promotes the core belief of American culture: that we *can* re-create ourselves, transform ourselves, transcend our circumstances—but with a twist. For generations Americans believed this could be achieved if we worked hard enough, like Horatio Alger. Today the promise is that we can change our lives instantly, effortlessly—by winning the lottery, selecting the right mutual fund, having a fashion makeover, losing weight, having tighter abs, buying the right car or soft drink. It is this belief that such transformation is possible that drives us to keep dieting, to buy more stuff, to read fashion magazines that give us the same information over and over again. Cindy Crawford's makeup is carefully described as if it could transform us into her. On one level, we know it won't—after all, most of us have tried this approach many times before. But on another level, we continue to try, continue to believe that this time it will be different. This American belief that we can transform ourselves makes advertising images much more powerful than they otherwise would be.

The focus of the transformation has shifted from the soul to the body. Of course, this trivializes and cheapens authentic spirituality and transcendence. But, more important, this junk food for the soul leaves us hungry, empty, malnourished. The emphasis on instant salvation is parodied in an ad from *Adbusters* for a product called Mammon, in which a man says, "I need a belief system that serves my needs right away." The copy continues, "Dean Sachs has a mortgage, a family and an extremely demanding job. What he doesn't need is a religion that complicates his life with unreasonable ethical demands." The ad ends with the words, "Mammon: Because you deserve to enjoy life--guilt free."

As advertising becomes more and more absurd, however, it becomes increasingly difficult to parody ads. There's not much of a difference between the ad for Mammon and the real ad for cruises that says "It can take several lifetimes to reach a state of inner peace and tranquillity. Or, it can take a couple of weeks." Of course, we know that a couple of weeks on a cruise won't solve our problems, won't bring us to a state of peace and enlightenment, but it is so tempting to believe that there is some easy way to get there, some ticket we can buy.

To be one of the "elect" in today's society is to have enough money to buy luxury goods. Of course, when salvation comes via the sale, it becomes important to display these goods. Owning a Rolex would not impress anyone who didn't know how expensive it is. A Rolex ad itself says the watch was voted "most likely to be coveted." Indeed, one of adver-

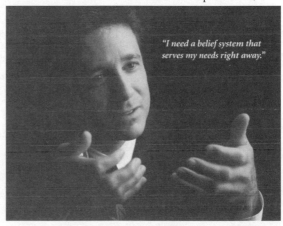

"I need a belief system that serves my needs right away."

Dean Sachs has a mortgage, a family and an extremely demanding job. What he doesn't need is a religion that complicates his life with unreasonable ethical demands.

Spiritual providers in the past have required a huge amount of commitment — single-deity clauses, compulsory goodness, and a litany of mystifying mumbo-jumbo. It's no wonder people are switching to Mammon.

Mammon isn't the biggest player in the spiritual race. But our ability to deliver on our promises is unique. And our moral flexibility unmatchable.

MAMMON *Because you deserve to enjoy life – guilt free*

tising's purposes is to create an aura for a product, so that other people will be impressed. As one marketer said recently in *Advertising Age*, "It's no fun to spend $100 on athletic shoes to wear to high school if your friends don't know how cool your shoes are."

Thus the influence of advertising goes way beyond the target audience and includes those who could never afford the product, who will simply be envious and impressed—perhaps to the point of killing someone for his sneakers or jacket, as has sometimes happened in our poverty-stricken neighborhoods. In the early 1990s the city health commissioner in Philadelphia issued a public health warning cautioning youths against wearing expensive leather jackets and jewelry, while in Milwaukee billboards depicted a chalk outline of a body and the warning, "Dress Smart and Stay Alive." Poor children in many countries knot the laces of their Nikes around their ankles to avoid having them stolen while they sleep.

Many teens fantasize that objects will somehow transform their lives, give them social standing and respect. When they wear a certain brand of sneaker or jacket, they feel, "This is important, therefore I am important." The brand gives instant status. No wonder they are willing, even eager, to spend money for clothes that advertise the brands. A *USA Today*–CNN–Gallup Poll found that 61 percent of boys and 44 percent of girls considered brand names on clothes "very important" or "somewhat important." As ten-year-old Darion Sawyer from Baltimore said, "People will tease you and talk about you, say you got on no-name shoes or say you shop at Kmart." Leydiana Reyes, an eighth-grader in Brooklyn, said, "My father always tells me I could buy two pairs of jeans for what you pay for Calvin Klein. I know that. But I still want Calvin Klein." And Danny Shirley, a fourteen-year-old in Santa Fe decked out in Tommy Hilfiger regalia, said, "Kids who wear Levi's don't really care about what they wear, I guess."

In the beginning, these labels were somewhat discreet. Today we see sweatshirts with fifteen-inch "Polo" logos stamped across the chest, jeans with four-inch "Calvin Klein" labels stitched on them, and a jacket with "Tommy Hilfiger" in five-inch letters across the back. Some of these outfits are so close to sandwich boards that I'm surprised people aren't paid to wear them. Before too long, the logo-free product probably will be the expensive rarity.

What people who wear these clothes are really buying isn't a garment, of course, but an *image*. And increasingly, an image is all that advertising has to sell. Advertising began centuries ago with signs in medieval villages. In the nineteenth century, it became more common but was still essentially designed to give people information about manufactured goods and services. Since the 1920s, advertising has provided less information about the product and focused more on the lives, especially the emotional lives, of the prospective consumers. This shift coincided, of course, with the increasing knowledge and acceptability of psychology, as well as the success of propaganda used to convince the population to support World War I.

Industrialization gave rise to the burgeoning ability of businesses to mass-produce goods. Since it was no longer certain there would be a market for the goods, it became necessary not just to mass-produce the goods but to mass-produce markets hungry for the goods. The problem became not too little candy produced but not enough candy consumed, so it became the job of the advertisers to *produce consumers.* This led to an increased use of psychological research and emotional ploys to sell products. Consumer behavior became recognized as a science in the late 1940s.

As luxury goods, prepared foods, and nonessential items have proliferated, it has become crucial to create artificial needs in order to sell unnecessary products. Was there such a thing as static cling before there were fabric softeners and sprays? An ad for a "lip renewal cream" says, "I never thought of my lips as a problem area until Andrea came up with the solution."

Most brands in a given category are essentially the same. Most shampoos are made by two or three manufacturers. Blindfolded smokers or beer-drinkers can rarely identify what brand they are smoking or drinking, including their own. Whether we know it or not, we select products primarily because of the image reflected in their advertising. Very few ads give us any real information at all. Sometimes it is impossible to tell what is being advertised. "This is an ad for the hair dryer," says one ad, featuring a woman lounging on a sofa. If we weren't told, we would never know. A joke made the rounds a while ago about a little boy who wanted a box of tampons so that he could effortlessly ride bicycles and horses, ski, and swim.

Almost all tobacco and alcohol ads are entirely image-based. Of course, when you're selling a product that kills people, it's difficult to give honest information about it. Think of all the cigarette ads that never show cigarettes or even a wisp of smoke. One of the most striking examples of image advertising is the very successful and long-running campaign for Absolut vodka. This campaign focuses on the shape of the bottle and the word "Absolut," as in "Absolut Perfec-

tion," which features the bottle with a halo. This campaign has been so successful that a coffee-table book collection of the ads published just in time for Christmas, the perfect gift for the alcoholic in your family, sold over 150,000 copies. Collecting Absolut ads is now a common pastime for elementary-school children, who swap them like baseball cards.

Adbusters magazine often parodies the Absolut ads. One such parody, headlined "Absolut Nonsense," pictures a bottle with the following copy on the label: "This superb marketing scheme has been carefully distilled for smoothness. . . . Although no one pays attention to advertising, after one year of this campaign, sales soared from 54,000 cases to 2.4 million cases." Since all vodka is essentially the same, all the campaign can sell us is image.

Even the advertisers admit to this. Carol Nathanson-Moog, an advertising psychologist, said, "More and more it seems the liquor industry has awakened to the truth. It isn't selling bottles or glasses or even liquor. It's selling fantasies." An article in *Advertising Age* went further, stating that "product image is probably the most important element in selling liquor. The trick for marketers is to project the right message in their advertisements to motivate those often motionless consumers to march down to the liquor store or bar and exchange their money for a sip of image."

"A sip of image." Just as simple films relying on crude jokes and violence are perfect for the global marketplace, since they require little translation, so is advertising that relies entirely on image. Bare breasts and phallic symbols are understood everywhere. As are the nude female buttocks featured in the Italian and German ads for similar worthless products to remedy the imaginary problem of cellulite. Unfortunately, such powerful imagery often pollutes the cultural environment. Certainly

CONTRO LA CELLULITE: CELLULASE.
E I RISULTATI TE LI PORTI DIETRO.

this is so with the Olivetti ad that ran in a Russian publication. In case the image is too subtle for some, the copy says "Fax me." Sexism in advertising, although increasingly recognized as a problem, remains an ongoing global issue.

How does all this affect us? It is very difficult to do objective research about advertising's influence because there are no comparison groups, almost no people who have not been exposed to massive doses of advertising. In addition, research that measures only one point in time does not adequately capture advertising's real effects. We need longitudinal studies, such as George Gerbner's twenty-five-year study of violence on television.

The advertising industry itself can't prove that advertising works. While claiming to its clients that it does, it simultaneously denies it to the Federal Trade Commission whenever the subject of alcohol and tobacco advertising comes up. As an editorial in *Advertising Age* once said, "A strange world it is, in which people spending millions on advertising must do their best to prove that advertising doesn't do very much!" According to Bob Wehling, senior vice-president of marketing at Procter & Gamble, "We don't have a lot of scientific studies to support our belief that advertising works. But we have seen that the power of advertising makes a significant difference."

What research can most easily prove is usually what is least important, such as advertising's influence on our choice of brands. This is the most obvious, but least significant, way that advertising affects us. There are countless examples of successful advertising campaigns, such as the Absolut campaign, that have sent sales soaring. A commercial for I Can't Believe It's Not Butter featuring a sculptress whose work comes alive in the form of romance-novel hunk Fabio

boosted sales about 17 percent. Tamagotchis—virtual pets in an egg—were intro-duced in the United States with a massive advertising campaign and earned $150 million in seven months. And Gardenburger, a veggie patty, ran a thirty-second spot during the final episode of *Seinfeld* and, within a week, sold over $2 million worth, a market share jump of 50 percent and more than the entire category sold in the same week the previous year. But advertising is more of an art than a sci-ence, and campaigns often fail. In 1998 a Miller beer campaign bombed, costing the company millions of dollars and offending a large segment of their cus-tomers. The 1989 Nissan Infiniti campaign, known as the "Rocks and Trees" cam-paign, was the first ever to introduce a car without showing it and immediately became a target for Jay Leno's monologues. And, of course, the Edsel, a car intro-duced by Ford with great fanfare in 1957, remains a universal symbol of failure.

The unintended effects of advertising are far more important and far more difficult to measure than those effects that are intended. The important question is not "Does this ad sell the product?" but rather "What else does this ad sell?" An ad for Gap khakis featuring a group of acrobatic swing dancers probably sold a lot of pants, which, of course, was the intention of the advertisers. But it also con-tributed to a rage for swing dancing. This is an innocuous example of advertis-ing's powerful unintended effects. Swing dancing is not binge drinking, after all.

Advertising often sells a great deal more than products. It sells values, im-ages, and concepts of love and sexuality, romance, success, and, perhaps most important, normalcy. To a great extent, it tells us who we are and who we should be. We are increasingly using brand names to create our identities. James Twitchell argues that the label of our shirt, the make of our car, and our favorite laundry detergent are filling the vacuum once occupied by religion, education, and our family name.

Even more important, advertising corrupts our language and thus influences our ability to think clearly. Critic and novelist George Steiner once talked with an interviewer about what he called "anti-language, that which is transcendentally annihilating of truth and meaning." Novelist Jonathan Dee, applying this concept to advertising, writes that "the harm lies not in the ad itself; the harm is in the ex-change, in the collision of ad language, ad imagery, with other sorts of language that contend with it in the public realm. When Apple reprints an old photo of Gandhi, or Heineken ends its ads with the words 'Seek the Truth,' or Winston suggests that we buy cigarettes by proposing (just under the surgeon general's warning) that 'You have to appreciate authenticity in all its forms,' or Kellogg's identifies itself with the message 'Simple is Good,' these occasions color our contact with those words and images in their other, possibly less promotional applications." The real violence of advertising, Dee concludes, is that "words can be made to mean anything, which is hard to distinguish from the idea that words mean nothing." We see the consequences of this in much of our culture, from "art" to politics, that has no content, no connection between language and conviction. Just as it is often difficult to tell what product an ad is selling, so is it difficult to determine what a politician's beliefs are (the "vision thing," as George Bush so aptly called it, albeit unintentionally) or what the subject is of a film or song or work of art. As Dee says, "The men and women who make ads are not hucksters; they are artists with nothing to say, and they have found their form." Unfortunately, their form deeply influences all the other forms of the culture. We end up expecting nothing more.

This has terrible consequences for our culture. As Richard Pollay says, "Without a reliance on words and a faith in truth, we lack the mortar for social cohesion. Without trustworthy communication, there is no communion, no community, only an aggregation of increasingly isolated individuals, alone in the mass."

Advertising creates a worldview that is based upon cynicism, dissatisfaction, and craving. The advertisers aren't evil. They are just doing their job, which is to sell a product, but the consequences, usually unintended, are often destructive to individuals, to cultures, and to the planet. In the history of the world, there has never been a propaganda effort to match that of advertising in the twentieth century. More thought, more effort, and more money go into advertising than has gone into any other campaign to change social consciousness. The story that advertising tells is that the way to be happy, to find satisfaction—and the path to political freedom, as well—is through the consumption of material objects. And the major motivating force for social change throughout the world today is this belief that happiness comes from the market.

So, advertising has a greater impact on all of us than we generally realize. The primary purpose of the mass media is to deliver us to advertisers. Much of the information that we need from the media in order to make informed choices in our lives is distorted or deleted on behalf of corporate sponsors. Advertising is an increasingly ubiquitous presence in our lives, and it sells much more than products. We delude ourselves when we say we are not influenced by advertising. And we trivialize and ignore its growing significance at our peril.

3

"BATH TISSUE IS LIKE MARRIAGE"

The Corruption of Relationships

"BATH TISSUE IS LIKE MARRIAGE," SAYS AN AD FOR CHARMIN FEATURING A smiling old couple in their kitchen. When I read this to my happily married friend Bettie on the phone, she was mystified. "But I thought what one wants most in bath tissue is to be able to flush it away," she said. From my more disillusioned point of view, I thought it might mean that you have to deal with a lot of shit. But the ad tells us: "The longer it lasts, the better it is." Although at first glance, this might seem to be a nice statement about long marriages, the comparison is ludicrous, trivializing, and ultimately odious.

The problem with advertising isn't that it creates artificial longings and needs, but that it exploits our very real and human desires. In some ways, advertisers know us better than we know ourselves, and they use this knowledge to take advantage of us. Above all, advertising promotes a corrupt and bankrupt concept of *relationship*. Most of us yearn for intimate and committed relationships that will last. We are not stupid: We know that buying a certain brand of toilet tissue, or anything else for that matter, won't bring us one inch closer to that goal. But we are surrounded by advertising that yokes our needs with products and promises us that *things* will deliver what in fact they never can. In the world of advertising, lovers are things and things are lovers. It is difficult, perhaps impossible, not to be affected by this.

We are surrounded by hundreds, thousands, of messages every day that link our deepest emotions to products, that objectify people and trivialize our most heartfelt moments and relationships. Every emotion is used to sell us something. Our wish to protect our children is leveraged to make us buy an expensive car. A long marriage simply provides the occasion for a diamond necklace. A painful reunion between a father and his estranged daughter is drawn out and dramatized to sell us a phone system. Everything in the world—nature, animals, people—is just so much stuff to be consumed or to be used to sell us something.

Even when advertisers tell us that something is priceless, they manage to put a price on it. In 1998 MasterCard had a campaign with the tagline, "There are some things money can't buy. For everything else there is MasterCard." One commercial shows a father and son at a baseball game. It places a dollar value on lots of things related to the game—tickets, snacks, an autographed baseball—but rates "real conversation with an 11-year-old" as priceless. Other commercials in the campaign also link intangible emotions with activities that cost money. The ostensible message of the commercial is that you can't put a price on what is most valuable in life . . . but the underlying message is that sure you can. You can not only put a price on it, you can put it on a credit card.

It may be that there is no other way to depict relationships when the ultimate goal is to sell products. But this apparently bottomless consumerism not only depletes the world's resources, it also depletes our inner resources. It leads

A CHILD IS THE ULTIMATE PET

JOOP! JEANS
JUST A THOUGHT.

inevitably to narcissism and solipsism. It becomes difficult even to imagine a way of relating—to ourselves, our children, our partners, our environment—that isn't objectifying and exploitive.

Children, especially babies, are sometimes used for shock value, to grab attention, as in the ads headlined "A child is the ultimate pet" and "A kiss is *not* just a kiss." The child is nothing but a fashion accessory in these ads, in one attached to a jeweled collar and leash, in the other fastened to the woman's breast like a brooch. Perhaps we should be grateful that real children are pictured— "It's a girl!" says an ad featuring a watch substituting for the fetus in an ultrasound of the womb. I guess life begins at consumption. When we really look at these ads, we see that they are shocking, outrageous. We would be horrified by images like these of our own children. But until we force ourselves to pay attention, these ads are just part of the mostly unconscious blur of images that surrounds us every day. No big deal.

Some ads hark back to the days when children were supposed to be "seen but

A kiss is *not* just a kiss.

Bisou Bisou
NOUVELLE COUTURE

not heard." "Quiet kids. How's that for a product benefit?" says an ad for a sport utility vehicle that comes with a TV/video cassette player. A commercial for a minivan features an entire family cruising along, each one but the driver wearing individual headsets and watching a movie on the overhead video screen. And a candy bar ad asks, "Kids talking too much? Give 'em a Chewy Grand Slam . . . Really, really chewy." Do we need this kind of message in a culture in which people say they spend about forty minutes each week in meaningful conversation with their children?

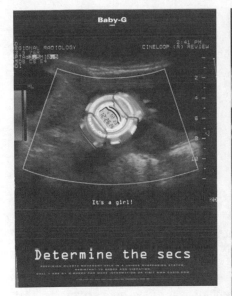

Sometimes children are portrayed as getting in the way of our pleasure. "We can get rid of the pain in your neck but not the cause of it," declares an ad for physical therapy featuring a woman dragging a little boy out of a park. Although the copy assures us, "Of course, you'd never want to get rid of the little guy," the initial impression is of shocking hostility. Of course, the creators of this ad use shock to get our attention; they intend no larger consequence. But an image of potential child abuse, in a culture in which millions of children are abused and neglected, is used to attract our attention and perhaps to make us laugh.

More often, sentimental images of children are used to evoke deep feelings of love and protectiveness, which are then connected to the product. "Can a shoe hug you like a tiny hand?" asks an ad featuring a woman cradling a child in her arms. The answer, of course, is no—but that's not what the ad implies. Whatever emotional response we might have to the image is immediately transferred to the product. We might well feel betrayed by this, but it happens so often every day that it is more likely we don't even notice (or think we don't).

Many ads that seem to be about the relationship between a parent and a child turn out to be glorifying the relationship between the parent and a product. "What makes this room so cozy?" asks an ad featuring a woman and a little girl. The little girl is behind the woman, touching her hair, but the woman is on the telephone, seemingly absorbed in her conversation, not looking at the child.

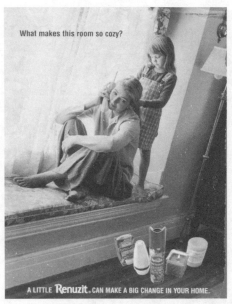

Nonetheless, the room is cozy . . . because of the air freshener. "There are some things you wouldn't trade for the world," says an ad featuring a beautiful woman wearing a fur coat and holding a child rather stiffly on her lap. The copy continues, "If you don't feel that way about your fur, why not trade it for a new one?"

A stunning example of this kind of confusion between products and people occurs in an ad featuring a girl running into the open arms of a woman, presumably her mother. The copy says, "Open your eyes. What's important is right in front of you." One hopes, expects, that what is important to this woman is her child. But no, it turns out the ad is referring to her shoes. Again, if we take time to reflect on this, the message is truly awful. The ad explicitly states that the shoes are more important than the child to

this woman. But we don't usually pay conscious attention to ads, so the message slides right by . . . into our unconscious. One ad like this wouldn't matter at all, but the constant repetition of the belief that products are more important than people has an impact.

Advertisers know that many of us, perhaps most of us, feel guilty about not spending enough time with our children. So they use this guilt to sell us watches, as if somehow telling time is related to having more of it. "Of all the things you give her, time is the most valuable," says an ad featuring a woman kissing a young girl. This is true, but how does it relate to the watch being advertised? Is this mother going to remember to spend more time with her daughter whenever she checks her watch? How many hours did she have to work to earn the money to buy the watch?

An ad picturing what we assume to be a grandfather reading to his grand-daughter says "Life's precious gifts." Again, if one were unfamiliar with advertising one might assume that one of life's precious gifts is this warm relationship. However, the ad is for little crystal knick-knacks, which somehow are supposed to be related to this cozy scene. Perhaps the child will be reminded of her closeness with her grandfather when she sees these

LIFE'S PRECIOUS GIFTS.

Magic Moments are made of simple things. A thought to share, a song to sing. Those happy times will never leave you. For Silver Crystal treasures them for ever.

SWAROVSKI
SILVER CRYSTAL

knickknacks later in life. Or perhaps the items are totems imbued with the emotions in the room. The grandfather dies, the little girl grows up and moves away, but the little knickknacks go on forever. Except, of course, we know this can't be true. We don't think about all this when we look at the ad, however. Perhaps we glance at it as we turn the page. The immediate message, unchallenged, is that the warmth between the two people is somehow related to the crystal objects flying around the room (like the floating cherubs in old religious paintings). Just as, in another ad, the camaraderie and friendship among three laughing young women are due to the Coca-Cola they are drinking. If we didn't see this kind of thing all the time, surely it would strike us as surreal.

Ads have long promised us a better relationship via a product: buy this and you will be loved. But more recently they have gone beyond that proposition to promise us a relationship with the product itself: *Buy this and it will love you.* The product is not so much the means to an end as the end itself.

Products are not only sold by celebrities; they have become celebrities. Indeed one of the functions of advertising is to make the products familiar to us. We encounter them like old friends in the shopping aisles. Look, there's Mr. Clean and Budweiser and Crest! We are proud to be associated with them. We are encouraged to identify with Coke rather than Pepsi, with Burger King rather than McDonald's, as if they were feuding families and we had to take sides. This is especially true for children, for whom personality almost literally becomes the product, whether it's Tony the Tiger, the Ninja Turtles, or My Little Pony.

Lifestyle, the ultimate self-expression of the 1990s, is available even to those on a budget. People can sleep on sheets with Ralph Lauren's name on them or decorate their houses with materials blessed by Martha Stewart and sold at K-mart. We can dine on Christian Dior dinnerware, drive a Nautica minivan, lunch at a Giorgio Armani café, and put our children to bed in Guess cribs. Clothing designer Bill Blass put his signature on Lincoln cars, but he drew the line at braces for children's teeth and coffins.

Associating a product with Ralph or Martha or Calvin gives it magic value for some consumers. We are encouraged not only to constantly buy more but to seek our identity and our fulfillment through what we buy, to express our individuality through our "choices" of products. We're a "Marlboro man" or a "Maidenform woman." "Some people are born with charisma. Others just buy it," says an ad that exploits James Dean to sell towels. Of course, there is no real magic in these products. One does not have a relationship with them or with the people whose names are branded on them, although we might believe that we do.

Many advertisers are using the Internet these days to encourage this sense of a relationship with a product or a brand. Most insidiously, cartoon pitchmen create individual "virtual relationships" with children. According to the Center for Media Education, any marketer who learns a kid's favorite color or pet or activity can harness sophisticated child psychology and interactive technology to "prey on children's vulnerabilities" and "manipulate your child in very profound ways."

As always, Calvin Klein goes further. He set up Internet addresses for the three models depicted in a campaign for his cK one perfume and encouraged consumers to write them for vivid details about their lives. The only catch is, the characters are make-believe, the life stories imaginary. According to Klein, "What you have is a new kind of intimacy that's really a paradox—people all over the world are more in touch than ever, but they're doing it one-to-one on e-mail and the Internet. When we take this new campaign to e-mail, it makes it very personal."

No wonder some people become confused about what's real and what isn't in advertising. One researcher, interviewing ninth-grade students in a school with Channel One, found that many of them believed that the people in commercials weren't paid actors. One girl, speaking about a Pepsi commercial, said, "I know that I'd be terribly disappointed if the kids in that commercial turned out to be paid actors—they're just real kids off the street, like us. . . . They just couldn't be actors, ya know?"

When we're not involved in pseudo-relationships with the models in ads, we can be falling in love with our hamburgers. "Attention: Big Mac lovers" appears on the television screen in a Burger King commercial, while a singer croons, "Who do you love? Who do you love?" and burgers and fries dance through the air. Then "Ready for a new relationship?" appears on the screen, with a heart surrounding the Burger King logo. Time to break up with McDonald's and fall in love with Burger King.

Very little in advertising is coincidental. Consider the way a six-pack of soda announces the last date the drink should be consumed. It doesn't say "drink" or "consume," but rather invites you to "enjoy," as in "Enjoy by May 30." According to Steve Chinn, director of business strategies at Saatchi & Saatchi, "It's such a simple thing, but it's a stunning difference. You feel that the people behind the brand care about you. They're using the same words you'd use for a relationship with someone you like."

The important thing, of course, is not that the people behind the brand care about us, but that we *feel* that they do. "Know the heart of the consumer, and you will own the future," says market researcher John Houlahan. Many chains, from pizza stores to moviehouses, are trying to deal with the troublesome fact that the lowest paid and least trained workers are the ones who interact with the consumers not by paying them more or training them better but by requiring them to repeat certain phrases, such as "Thank you for coming to Loew's" and "Hi, welcome to McDonald's!" This facade of friendliness is probably meant to give the illusion that these huge and impersonal chains are as homey as the neighborhood stores they drove out of business.

The research on the significance of relationships to women has not been lost on advertisers. According to market analyst Faith Popcorn, "Marketers will need to create a rich series of connections and bonds" in order to reach women. And market researcher Bernadette Tracy says that women want Websites that build relationships. "On the Internet," she writes, "if content is king, relationships are the trump card." Kraft recently announced a plan to target advertising messages so finely that two households watching the same program could see radically divergent Kraft spots. In fact, different television sets within the same household could have different spots—one for Minute Rice in the kitchen and one for Kool-Aid in the family room. "It's a one-to-one communications approach," said the Kraft executive overseeing the project. "Relationship marketing is what it's all about."

As the products (and stores and fast-food restaurants and airlines and phone companies) are portrayed as ever more intensely alive, we are encouraged to feel that we are in relationships with them, to feel passion for our products rather than our partners. "The right dress is like the right guy," says an ad featuring a couple embracing. "You love it more when you get it home." A facial care line is advertised as "the most exciting thing to happen to your face since your first kiss." "Oh my goodness!" proclaims an ad featuring a bottle of Coca-Cola. "You should've seen this one . . . tall, dark and cooler than cool. I had to pick it up." The overt eroticism of this ad is no coincidence, of course. The bottle has even worked up a sweat!

After all, it is easier and considerably safer to love a product than a person. Relationships with human beings are messy, unpredictable, often uncomfortable, sometimes dangerous. "When was the last time you felt this comfortable in a relationship?" asks an ad for sneakers. Our sneakers never have bad moods or ask

us to wash the dishes or tell us we're getting fat. Even more important, products don't betray or abandon us. "You can love it without getting your heart broken," proclaims a car ad. One certainly can't say that about loving a human being. As most of us know, love is risky, love is painful, and love without vulnerability is impossible.

A forlorn young man in a shoe ad says, "I loved Missy from next door. She moved. I loved my French teacher. She got married. I loved Betty on TV who said, 'Oop boop bee doo.' She was a cartoon. Well, at least my feet have always known true love." A similar ad features a closeup of a woman's foot in a sandal and the copy, "It is said that when the heel of the foot is caressed, it stimulates the heart. Sure beats waiting for love to come along." Clearly these two soles are meant for each other.

Taken individually, these ads are silly, sometimes funny, certainly nothing to worry about. But cumulatively they create a climate of cynicism and alienation that is poisonous to relationships. Many people end up feeling romantic about material objects yet deeply cynical about other human beings. In a society in which one of two

Who says guys are afraid of commitment? He's had the same backpack for years.

When it comes to choosing a lifelong companion, lots of guys pick one of our backpacks. Each one comes with a lifetime guarantee not to rip, tear, break, or ask for a ring.

marriages ends in divorce, we are offered constancy through our products. As one ad says, "Some people need only one man. Or one woman. Or one watch." Okay, so we can't be monogamous—at least we can be faithful to our watches. Because of the pervasiveness of this kind of advertising message, we learn from childhood that it is far safer to make a commitment to a product than to a person, far easier to be loyal to a brand. Ad after ad portrays our real lives and relationships as dull and ordinary, and commitment to human beings as something to be avoided.

"Who says guys are afraid of commitment? He's had the same backpack for years," states an ad that features photographs of a young man with several different women, but always the same backpack. The young women are the accessories, the backpack is the intimate partner. The copy assures the reader that the backpack "comes with a lifetime guarantee not to rip, tear, break, or ask for a ring." You know, people are so annoying—they want promises, permanence. Such a drag. So much easier to snuggle up with your undemanding backpack.

An ad featuring a couple cuddled up on a sofa says, "Some people just know how to live." Lest we think this refers to their relationship, the copy tells us, "Life forces you to make far too many commitments. Which is why we offer you the opportunity to live with furniture that doesn't." On closer look, the woman does

seem a bit anxious and quite desperately focused on the man, whereas he is looking straight at us with great confidence. It is commonplace today to note that many men are phobic about commitment and that women have to be more wily than ever to "snare a man." This ad illustrates this. The apartment is barely furnished. The paintings are not hung on the walls. The crate substituting for a table is so small that only one cup fits on it. The couple could be moving in or moving out. Or maybe they're not a couple at all, at least not for long. The appeal of the sofa, according to the ad, is that it comes with washable slipcovers so you "can change the look of your home with every season, or simply because you're in the mood . . . living this carefree can be very habit-forming." Carefree is one word to describe the mood of this scene. Uncommitted, insecure, tentative, uprooted are others. It's one thing to live this way, quite another to love like this.

If a guy does get roped into marriage, he can always drown his sorrows in booze. "Hang on to your spirit," says an ad for Southern Comfort, which features an anxious groom with a hangman's rope around his neck. The bride is smiling, completely oblivious to the true feelings of this moron she is so, so lucky to marry. Another ad in this campaign pictures a man accompanying a woman on a shopping expedition. In addition to being laden with packages, he has a ball and chain around his ankle.

Women are told we can adjust to fleeting, impermanent

relationships with men by focusing on our lasting relationships with products. "The ski instructor faded away 3 winters ago. At least the sweater didn't," says an ad featuring a woman alone on a beach, smiling happily in her sweater.

"Getting engaged means making a huge decision. You live with it for the rest of your life," says a smiling young woman in an ad for diamonds. She concludes, "So I decided on the solitaire." A diamond, long considered a girl's best friend, has now become her lifetime companion. We get this message again and again and again—the ring is more important than the man, the backpack more reliable than the woman. The average wedding in America today costs $17,634. If at least some of this money was spent on premarital counseling, maybe more of these marriages would succeed.

Sometimes advertisers tell us we'll find true love and commitment with the products. Other times we'll apparently settle for great sex. For decades products have been advertised as the route to passionate lovemaking. "There are times when making the right shoe decision can keep you up all night," says an ad featuring a couple embracing on a balcony. Are they going to have terrific sex all night long because of the shoes she's wearing? Are they going to have sex with the shoes? Where can I get a pair? If those shoes don't do the trick, one can always try the sandals pictured in another ad with the copy, "The pair you wear to rekindle

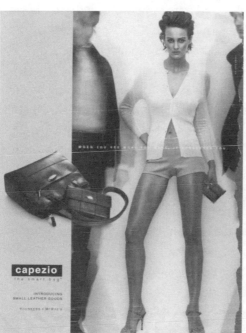

your marriage . . . will also look stunning at the maternity ward." "If these can't put a little romance in your life, maybe you need a dating service," declares an ad for . . . slipcovers. I can see ads claiming that perfume will lead to passionate sex, maybe even shoes, but slipcovers?

These days, however, we are often offered a sexual relationship with the products themselves. "When you see what you want, it possesses you," says an ad featuring an extremely "sexy" woman, standing with her legs apart, clutching a small leather

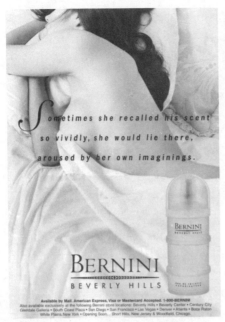

Sometimes she recalled his scent so vividly, she would lie there, aroused by her own imaginings.

BERNINI

BERNINI
BEVERLY HILLS

Available by Mail. American Express, Visa or Mastercard Accepted. 1-800-BERNINI
Also available exclusively at the following Bernini store locations: Beverly Hills • Beverly Center • Century City
Glendale Galleria • South Coast Plaza • San Diego • San Francisco • Las Vegas • Denver • Atlanta • Boca Raton
White Plains,New York • Opening Soon... Short Hills, New Jersey & Woodfield, Chicago.

purse. The attraction between the woman and the little purse seems to be mutually intense. In a watch ad, we are promised "goose bumps as well as the time." In a Bernini perfume ad, it looks as if the product is specially designed for the woman "aroused by her own imaginings." We don't need people at all, either present or implied.

In a recent television commercial, a man is snoring in bed while the woman beside him tosses and turns and hugs her pillow and a song called "Dreamin'" plays in the background. A female voiceover says, "Put some excitement back into your life." What is the ad for? Marriage counseling? French ticklers? No. It turns out what the woman longs for is new sheets.

In another commercial, a heavy woman dances with a man, while a woman's voice sings, "I never felt like I fit in 'til you curved around my curves. My body feels so right when you caress my skin. It's hard to tell where you end and I begin. I know you'll never stray. Just keep holding me each day." My first thought is that it's nice to see a heavy woman portrayed as attractive in a commercial. Next I wonder what the ad is for—perhaps perfume? Not a diet product, I hope. But it turns out that the woman's relationship is with her lingerie. It is her bra with the stay-free straps that will hold her and never stray. I suppose we should be grateful that she isn't dancing with her bra. Maybe she became aroused on a shopping spree at J.C. Penney and will end the evening by having sex not on but with her sheets.

Alas, even relationships with products can sour, at least according to the ad for stereo speakers that asks, "Will you still respect your speakers in the morning?" It certainly looks as if the guy on the bed took the promise of advertising too literally and actually slept with the speaker. No wonder he's so depressed. The speaker's probably not in great shape either. The man might have had a better time if he'd taken the risk of relating to a human being.

In the topsy-turvy world of advertising, we are told to expect that our lovers will be distracted by their possessions, that we will end up in competition with products for our partners' attention—and losing. "I remember when he couldn't keep his hands off me," says a frustrated woman wearing sexy lingerie as her lover plays a video game. The copy continues, "He used to play all night with me. Hot action, fantasy games . . . you name it. Now he says his NEO.GEO gives him more, plus major league sports, ninja warriors, and flame throwing enemies. Can you do that? he asks. . . . I scream but he doesn't hear me."

This woman seems to have the right lingerie. Perhaps she needs to change her hair color. After all, Clairol Ultress offers such shades as "Super Bowl? What Super Bowl? Blonde," and "Make Him Drop the Remote Control Red." The truth is many women do feel

abandoned by men who compulsively watch sports, play video games, or surf the Internet (or will do almost anything to avoid having to talk). Ads that imply we could make our mates more responsive to us by changing our hair color increase our sense of self-blame and trivialize the agonizing loneliness of the disconnection.

At the same time that relationships are increasingly trivialized in the popular culture, some theorists are discovering that they are even more important in our lives than has been traditionally recognized. Although most of us know, of course, that relationships are central in our lives, it is only recently that psychological theory has truly understood this. Traditional psychoanalytic and developmental theories start with the notion that healthy development is based on a person *disconnecting* from relationships, beginning with his or her parents (especially, of course, the mother). These theories, based on studies of males but assumed to apply to females as well, focus on a goal of autonomy, separation, and development of the independent individual and emphasize self and work rather than intimacy and love. Of course, this focus seems entirely "natural" in a culture that values rugged individualism and independence above all else.

Jean Baker Miller, author of the classic *Toward a New Psychology of Women,* and her colleagues at the Stone Center at Wellesley College have done groundbreaking work on the nature and importance of relationships, of connection, especially for women. Their theory, originally called self-in-relation theory, shifts the emphasis from separation to the "relational" self as the basis for growth and development. A fundamental tenet of their work is a recognition that an inner sense of connection to others is a central organizing feature in women's psychological development. For individuals to develop in a healthy direction, Dr. Miller says, they must engage in relationships that foster growth, empowerment, and empathy. This is important for men too, of course, as well as women. But boys are still rigidly socialized in a way that makes authentic intimacy difficult. This depresses men and sometimes makes them violent, and it also depresses women who are blamed for failing to make successful relationships with these depressed, violent, and inaccessible men.

Sometimes relational theory is dismissed as "difference feminism" by people who mistakenly see it as a claim that women are innately superior to or different from men. In fact, Miller never suggests that women's relational orientation is innate, nor does she idealize women or relationships. Indeed she recognizes and discusses some of the problems that result from this emphasis on relationships in women's lives, especially when the relationships are not mutual.

According to Miller, mutuality is the key to healthy connections—both people in a relationship must have an impact and be able to grow. Such growth-fostering connections promote *zest and vitality, empowerment to act,* greater *knowledge of self and others,* an increased *sense of self-worth,* and a *desire for more connection.* These outcomes are what we all long for and what we need. Sadly, the very nature of our culture makes it extremely difficult for relationships to flourish. And even more sadly, advertising (and a market-driven culture) co-opts the desirable outcomes of real connection. Advertising promises us that products can deliver what, in fact, we can only get through healthy interpersonal relationships:

Zest and vitality. Ads often promise that products will make us feel more alive, will help us to experience life more intensely. Ad after ad links drinking a soda with risky and exciting adventures like sky-diving or tells us that shaving with a certain lotion is "up there with your peak experiences." In the world of advertising, Zest is literally a soap and "Happy" a perfume (and New Freedom is a maxipad, Wonder a bread, Good Sense a teabag, and Serenity a diaper).

Everywhere we look, we are offered false excitement, pseudo-intensity. Not only does this inevitably disappoint us, it also contributes to the general feeling in

the culture that every moment of our lives should be exciting, fun, that sex should always be passionate and intense, education ceaselessly entertaining, that anything less is bo—ring.

Empowerment to act. Ads also promise us that products will give us courage, will empower us to act. "Just do it," Nike ads tell us, as if putting on high-priced sneakers will help us achieve our goals. "Everybody's afraid," another ad tells us. "People in leather just don't look like they are." All we need is the right outfit and we can overcome our fears and triumph. Empowerment is almost always defined in advertising as power over other people (such as those people who are too stupid to cover up their fear with a leather jacket) rather than the ability to act for others as well as oneself.

Knowledge and clarity of self and others. Ads constantly tell us that products can help us find our identity, can make us unique, can help us understand ourselves and each other better. An ad for accessories from Emporio Armani says, "The big items say what you do. But the little details say who you are." "Define yourself," says an ad for pantyhose, which continues, "If you are what you wear, wear what you are." And Calvin Klein tells us, "be good. be bad. just be," as if somehow his perfume had something to do with our core identity, indeed was more important in defining us than our morality.

Just as enlightenment comes without hard work in the world of advertising, perhaps via a cruise, so does self-knowledge. Lexus offers us "personal empowerment without the long boring seminar." "Fulfilling your dreams is better than having them analyzed," says a travel ad, while another ad promises an herbal tea that "works approximately six years faster than psychotherapy."

Ads also promise that products will lead instantly to better communication. "The woman who claims men hide their feelings never gave a man a diamond," one ad tells us. Is there a woman alive who doesn't think men hide their feelings? Is it all because we haven't given them diamonds? Men are socialized to hide their feelings, at enormous cost to themselves as well as to women. This ad trivializes the power of cultural conditioning and places the blame squarely on the shoulders of the woman who just doesn't get how simple it is to change all this with the right gift. Many women do believe that we could get our men to open up if we could just find the right words, the right combination to the lock—in other words, if we just tried harder and were better women.

At the same time that most of us yearn for better communication and deeper relationships, men are encouraged to be distant (strong and silent) and women are exhorted to be mysterious—surefire ways to make real intimacy impossible. "You've known her for years, yet she still remains a mystery," an ad says. Because the woman in the ad is beautiful, we know this is a compliment. Of course, women are mysterious to men in the same way that Asians are "inscrutable" to Westerners. A group perceived as subordinate has to pay very close attention to the dominant group for its very survival, whereas the opposite isn't true.

Sense of self-worth. One of the central messages of advertising is that products will enhance our sense of self-worth. "And I'm worth it," say Cybill Shepherd, Heather Locklear, and others in the endlessly irritating ads for l'Oreal hair products, which tell us we can demonstrate our self-worth by spending a little more on hair coloring. More recently, these ads feature children claiming their worth and therefore their right to expensive hair products. We don't have to do anything but buy the right products in order to experience this sense of self-worth. "You're worth it," says an ad for beer, which continues "(And even if you're not)."

Advertising interprets self-worth to mean valuing one's self more than anyone else and being absorbed with oneself to the almost complete exclusion of others. "And so my fellow women ask not what you can do for everyone else's happiness but what you can do for your own," says a Reebok ad featuring a group of powerful women on Rollerblades. "We are hedonists and we want what feels good," says another ad for an overpriced sneaker.

Desire for more connection. And finally, the consumer culture always attempts to instill in us a longing for more of a given product (especially if that product is potentially addictive), more goods and services, more money—rather than a longing for more authentic connection with the people in our lives. An ad featuring a beautiful woman caressing some bracelets says, "Just exactly how much do you want someone to like you?" "In this icy world, gold warms her heart," says another jewelry ad, this one featuring a couple in a strangely dispassionate embrace. They're not looking at each other, they don't look happy, but she is wearing gold jewelry, so all must be well. We know the codes of advertising:

When we see an image of a heartfelt connection between people, we understand that it has a commercial purpose.

The desire for more connection is trivialized in a clever commercial that features a woman at a restaurant table talking to someone across from her who is off-camera. "You know," she says, "we've been together awhile and I've been thinking . . . I'm missing something from our relationship." At this point, the camera pulls back and we see that she is talking to a credit card perched on a chair. She continues, "I think it's best if we make a clean break." A voiceover says, "Expect more from your credit card," and goes on to advertise the Discover Platinum card. The woman calls to the waiter, "Check, please," and then says to the credit card, "Oh, you'll get this, right?"

This corruption of relationships in advertising is taking place at a time of great trouble for real relationships, as indicated by the increasing rate of divorce, the breakdown of our civic life, the rate of domestic violence, and the neglect and abuse of children. Half of all marriages in America now end in divorce, and demographers forecast that two-thirds of recent first marriages will fail. Although it is only one measure of failure, of course, this rate of divorce is tragic, especially for children. Marriages are falling apart because of individual failures, to be sure, but also because our culture is hostile to marriage, commitment, delayed gratification, and families. Rest easy—I am not blaming advertising for the divorce rate in this country. However, it is part of a cultural climate that discourages successful long-term relationships. Advertising, a key component of our consumerist culture, constantly exhorts us to be in a never-ending state of excitement, never to tolerate boredom or disappointment, to focus on ourselves, never to delay gratification, to believe that passionate sex is more important than anything else in life, and always to trade in old things for new. These messages are a kind of blueprint for how to destroy an intimate relationship.

How are we supposed to understand that all long-term relationships go through periods of anger, boredom, disillusionment, that aridity inevitably replaces ardor from time to time? How many people leave marriages for more passionate pastures, never learning that relationships require work, patience, tolerance, compassion (all the things that are so often ridiculed or trivialized in ads)? In a culture that surrounds us with images of lust and romance and very few models of long-term love, most of us grow up totally unprepared for life after infatuation. Actor Charlie Sheen unfortunately reflected a fairly common attitude when he said about his recent failed marriage, "You buy a car, it breaks down,

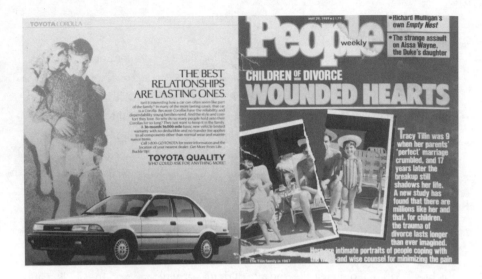

what are you going to do? Get rid of it." As the Coke ad says, "The same applies to relationships: if it's not the real thing, move on, honey."

A few years ago *People* magazine carried on its cover the headline "Children of Divorce: Wounded Hearts" and a photograph of a family ripped in two. The inside story claimed that the trauma of divorce for children lasts longer than ever imagined. On the back cover, a Toyota ad featured a shadowy couple embracing beside a car. The headline for the ad was "The best relationships are lasting ones." It clearly referred to the couple's relationship with the car, not with each other. Inside the magazine, an ad for Coca-Cola featured an empty glass with a lipstick imprint on it and the caption, "The end of a brief but meaningful relationship."

In the world of advertising, lovers grow cold, spouses grow old, children grow up and away—but possessions stay with us and never change. Of course, seeking the outcomes of a healthy relationship through products cannot work. For one thing, the possessions can never deliver the promised goods. They can't make us happy or loved or less alone or safe. If we believe they can, we are doomed to disappointment. It simply is not true, as an ad for Waterford crystal tells us, that "in a room with a thing of beauty, you are never truly alone." Because products are only *things*. No matter how much we love them, they will never love us back.

4

"CAN AN ENGINE PUMP THE VALVES IN YOUR HEART?"

Crazy for Cars

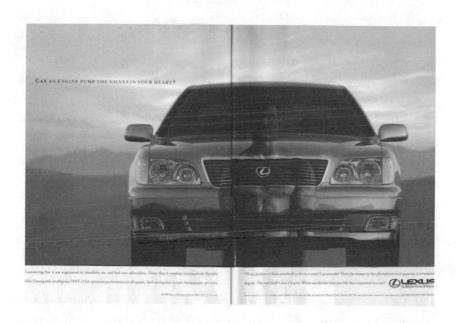

NOWHERE IS IT CLEARER THAT ADVERTISING ENCOURAGES US TO FEEL WE ARE in a relationship with our products than in car advertising. "Rekindle the romance," says a newspaper ad for a Jaguar. "Young, breathtaking beauty seeks sophisticated, self-assured individual who likes long drives and lasting relationships." Romance and rebellion are, broadly speaking, the two main themes. The romantic ads tell us the car will make us feel sexy and safe and loved, that it will give us passion and security in a world that is both humdrum and dangerous, and sometimes that it will substitute for human relationships. The rebellious ads emphasize how the car will make us feel tough, in control, free. "Goats understand your need to climb mountains," says an ad for a Toyota truck. "At least, male goats do."

The automobile is the basis for our economy. One-third of the land in our cities is devoted to cars, and Americans spend more money on driving each year than we do on health, education, or food. Although we are only 5 percent of the world's population, we generate 50 percent of the world's vehicle mileage and use 40 percent of the oil being produced in the world.

No wonder car advertising is such big business. As an ad in *Advertising Age* tells us, "Automotive marketers are what's behind $12.8 billion in media spending every year." The top three automakers spend about six billion dollars a year on advertising, so much in fact that most major magazines have sales offices in Detroit. And "relationship marketing," in which companies use data from customers to increase loyalty and profits, is gaining momentum in the auto industry. Jeep runs an annual weekend event for owners in Colorado called Camp Jeep, which features speakers, entertainment, and children's activities. Attendees fill out questionnaires, which allow Jeep to create a database. Carmakers used to leave relationship-building to dealers, but now, according to auto consultant David Kalmus, "They realize they can profit by it, so they're paying attention to it."

Just as the car companies want us to think of ourselves as part of their big happy families, they also encourage us to think of our cars as family members. "It has its mother's eyes, its father's stature and its brother's appetite for mischief," says an ad for a new Jaguar. "It's not a family car. It's family," a Mazda ad declares, while a Toyota ad introduces a new make of car with the copy, "The new family member with a great set of genes."

As is often the case in the world of advertising, however, the product is more important than the people. In a strange perversion of a typical family scene, a commercial for Toyota's Tacoma pickup truck features a man showing home movies . . . of his truck's achievements. As the camera shifts, we see that his audience is the photo of a magazine model taped to a chair.

"If anybody should ask, go ahead and show them your pride and joy," says a Honda ad. We assume the ad is referring to the children in the photo in the wallet. But no, it's the car. Of course, children are so much trouble compared to cars.

If anybody should ask, go ahead and show them your pride and joy. The Civic 4-Door. HONDA

"Chances are their teeth will need more work than your Lumina," another ad tells us. It continues, "Being a parent isn't easy or cheap. So it's got to be a relief to drive a car that could need a lot less attention than your children's teeth." Of course, it might be better still to skip the children altogether and just have a nicer car. In a way that is what a Chevrolet ad suggests: An out-of-focus photo of a woman holding a baby is juxtaposed with a clear shot of the car, while the headline says, "Don't spend the next six years wondering if you did the right thing." The ad absurdly compares the decision to have a baby with the decision to buy a car and suggests that the car is a clearer choice. After all, it comes with a warranty.

In ad after ad, we are told that buying a car is like falling in love and getting married. "We don't sell cars," a Lexus ad tells us, "We merely facilitate love connections." And an ad for Mercedes-Benz begins, "Buying a car is like getting married. It's a good idea to get to know the family first," while an ad for Acura promises "communication between road and driver that would make even a marriage counselor happy."

A Toyota Paseo ad pictures the car with the headline "Makes a better first impression than your last date." The copy continues, "Finding the 'right' one isn't always easy. You want to be comfortable, have similar tastes and at the same time find it easy to be yourself. Choosing the right car isn't much different." Another ad in the same campaign features a woman standing very happily next to her car, with the copy "Stylish. Responsive. Fun. If it were a man you'd marry it." (Let's not even touch the idea of marrying someone because he's stylish and fun.) The ad continues, "Let's face it, there are a lot of similarities when it comes to choosing a car and a mate. While this may seem surprising to some, even more surprising is that in today's society the chances for a lasting relationship just may be greater with a car. . . . Drive the new Paseo. Fall in love." And a 1999 Toyota commercial begins with the camera caressing a car while a woman's sexy voice says, "If a car has its own personality, you'd want it to be soft but strong, frugal, and worthy of your respect." As we see closeups of headlights and cup-holders, the woman continues, "It should remember the little things that are important to you and be reasonable always. Like a best friend, it should be there for you every day."

"Hannah fell in love yesterday," says an ad for Ford Mustang. "Which came as a big surprise to her boyfriend, Rick. But that's the way it's been since '64. Mustang = Love. It's hard to explain. Hannah says it's the spirit. Whatever it is, she loves her new Mustang. Oh, and whatshisname too." It is probably true that our chances for a lasting relationship are greater with our cars than our partners—but surely the solution can't be to fall in love with our cars, to depend on them rather than on each other.

Indeed, the ads tell us our cars are more likely to be true-blue and loyal than our mates. A Honda ad pictures a snazzy red car with the following sentences above it: "It's not you, it's me. I need more space. I'm just going through a stage. I can't go out with one person now. I need a break. I'm not ready for a commitment. Can we just be friends?" The copy below the car says, "Lots of significant others. One car." And a Mazda ad with the tagline "A change from your high maintenance relationships" says, "European good looks. Athletic. Stable. Strong, silent type. Sounds like a good personals ad. Difference is, it's true."

It's not you, it's me. **I need more space.**
I'm just going through a stage.
I can't go out with one person now.
I need a break.
I'm not ready for a commitment.
Can we just be friends?

Lots of significant others. One car. Make it a good one. The Civic Coupe.

Simplify.

Given the nature of the product, it makes sense that car advertisers mostly sell long-term commitment. Sometimes, however, they offer the automotive equivalent of a one-night stand. Since the beginning, cars have been advertised as a way to impress and seduce women. (As one ad says, "It's not a car. It's an aphrodisiac.") For several years, the car itself has been featured as the driver's passionate lover (in the words of one ad, "What happens when you cross sheet metal and desire"). "Deny yourself an obvious love affair?" asks an Audi ad, featuring a picture of the car. "Didn't you read *Romeo & Juliet*?"

Until recently the car was always symbolized as a woman. A Toyota Celica is described as having "vivacious curves, a shimmering body and . . . striking good looks." And Mercedes-Benz ran an ad featuring a photo of Marilyn Monroe's face, with the Mercedes-Benz symbol replacing her famous mole. No words were necessary. It was clear from the image that the car and the sex goddess were somehow one and the same. Sales increased by 35 percent. Vespa, the Italian motorcycle, also exploited Monroe in an ad entitled "Marilyn Vespoe," which features the motorcyle on pink satin sheets.

Glamour

This is taken a step further in a newspaper ad for Autique stores in which the car is a nude woman "accessorized" with automobile parts, such as tires and headlights. The objectification of the woman is particularly chilling in this ad, as she is barely human. There is also implicit violence in the metal chain around her neck, her extreme passivity, the blood-red background. Once again, lovers are things and things are lovers.

Of course, this has been going on a long time. Ever since Vance Packard wrote *The Hidden Persuaders,* we've known that cars are often men's symbolic mistresses. Sometimes the copy for car ads reads like pornography. A Subaru ad from the 1970s, headlined "Like a Spirited Woman Who Yearns to Be Tamed," says, "Sleek. Agile. The sculptured lines of the one-piece body invite you in. . . . Go to her. . . . Surround yourself with the lushness of her interior appointments. . . . Now. Turn her on. . . ."

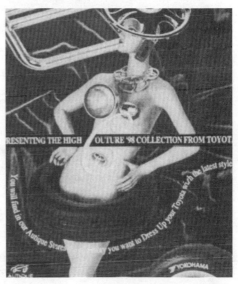

These days there's more equal opportunity for objectification, so while Mercury suggests we "think of it as a steel bikini," a BMW is advertised with the headline "Imagine Hercules in a steel tuxedo." And a tire ad tells us that "the most potent versions come equipped with Pirelli tires." Robyn Meredith suggests that Detroit's metal

has had a sex change operation and describes the Dodge Durango as follows: "Muscles seem to ripple under its shiny sheet metal, causing its fenders to bulge. Its hood is lifted above the brawn, like the short neck of a wrestler rising from beefy trapezius muscles." Nissan's Pathfinder was nicknamed the "hardbody," and designers described the "triceps" around each wheel. Some think the change is due to more women buying cars, others that people have come to think of their cars as bodyguards in a dangerous world.

An ad for the Oldsmobile Intrigue features a woman looking in her compact mirror at a car parked not coincidentally outside a hotel. The copy says, "Intrigued? A quick glance. You immediately notice the catlike eyes, the muscular lines. . . . You stare, knowing that only when you drive it will all its secrets be told." This ad is really amazing when we pay attention to it. The woman seemingly is putting on lipstick to prepare for her encounter with a *car,* a car that will appraise her with "catlike eyes." A car with "muscular lines" that is about to reveal secrets to her when she slips inside and starts to drive it. As is usually the case in advertising, the woman is preparing herself to be looked at, to be the object of

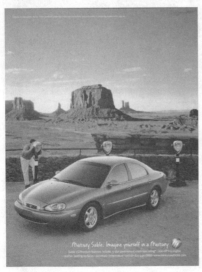

the male gaze. In a Mercury ad, the man is the gazer and the car the object of his affection (or at least his obsessive attention), as he ignores the gorgeous landscape behind him and turns the binoculars toward the car.

Countless ads today offer the car not only as a sex symbol, for women as well as for men, but as a substitute for sex. Chevrolet promises that "after Lumina satisfies what you need, it quickly responds to what you want." And an Infiniti ad asks, "What makes you happy? . . . Is it the sparkle in a lover's smile? . . . Or the warmth of a kiss goodnight? . . . But could it be a car?" "Is it wrong to be in love with a car?"

asks an ad for the Honda Accord. It continues, "There's no reason to hide your true feelings. The deep, consuming passion you may now be experiencing for the 1999 Accord Coupe is perfectly normal. After all, who could blame you for giving in to the seductive powers of this sleek, sexy automobile?"

A television commercial, shot in black and white, begins with the words on-screen, "How to build a lasting relationship." Immediately we see a closeup of a car and hear racy music in the background. More words appear onscreen, inter-spersed with more closeup shots of the car: "Instant attraction," "Ooh, that first touch" (hand on the gearshift), "Your heart races" (closeup of the speedometer), "And then . . . bam!" (foot on the gas pedal). The car zips along the road, through the countryside, and through the inevitable tunnel (to paraphrase Freud, sometimes a car is just a car, but a tunnel in a car ad is never just a tun-nel). The commercial ends with the words, "You'll never want to look at another car again."

"Dim the lights, put on some music, and it's just you and 280 horses," says a Lincoln ad, promising "the perfect setting for an intimate meeting between you, your favorite road and the 280 horses of the Lincoln Mark VIII luxury coupe." And a BMW ad says, "If you do shiver, it'll be from excitement." Exactly what are these ads promising? What is the nature of the intimate meeting? Are we sup-posed literally to be turned on by the experience of driving these cars (or simply being inside them)? Is it progress that both men and women can now experience the thrill of having sex with their cars? Will people go parking by themselves be-fore long? I can picture cars lined up by a beach on a moonlit night, the drivers in ecstasy, each one alone.

Sometimes straight sex isn't enough. "People who drive the Bravada are into leather," says one ad. Lest one think I am reading too much into this, the sentence is highlighted in red and the copy concludes, "People who drive the Bravada are basically into everything except letting someone else drive." If this were a "per-sonals ad," would there be any doubt? As another ad, this one for the Toyota Camry, says, "Any more leather might arouse suspicions."

At least one woman's magazine has identified the problem of "Autoeroti-cism: When His Car Excites Him More Than You Do." Given that the magazine is *Cosmopolitan*, it not surprisingly suggests as a remedy: "Perfume the bedroom with an auto air freshener. Attach fuzzy dice, like tassels, to your breasts. Tie him to the bed with jumper cables and whisper that your battery needs a charge too." At least *Cosmo* is bringing the attention back to human beings—it's no doubt better to turn your lover into a car than your car into a lover. There remains the possibility of intimacy.

Sometimes people are no longer necessary at all. The passionate relationship is between the car and the sky or the car and the road. "Hugs the road. Kisses the sky," says a Mitsubishi ad, while an Oldsmobile ad tells us, "While some cars can hug the road, very few can actually seduce it." One of the most erotic ads I've ever seen is a 1999 television commercial for BMW. It begins with a sensuous closeup of a car driving along a road. There is no sound but music, and the ad is shot in black and white with a split screen. We see that the car is a convertible and that a man is driving. As the car goes around a curve, the word "Hug" appears on the screen. Next there is a closeup of the wheel against the road and the word "Kiss" appears. And then "Caress." In the climax of the commercial, so to speak, the car whooshes through a dark tunnel, while "The driver loves the car" appears on the screen. Next we see "The car loves the road." And then "The car loves the driver." The message continues to change— "The driver loves the car," and so forth. The commercial is so sexy, I longed for a cigarette ad afterward.

A Lexus campaign, similarly but less breathtakingly, describes sexy encounters between the car and asphalt, the car and a bridge, and so forth. In the print version, the road curves beautifully into the hills and the headline says, "Hug me." The copy continues, "The road is calling. It's a siren song from a sliver of asphalt that crosses the Mississippi. . . . The road is stretched before you. How will you embrace it?"

This Lexus campaign also epitomizes the theme of control and competition. One commercial begins with the road breathing, heaving, while a German-accented creepy voice says, "Hi, I'm Autobahn, lord of the highways. Do you think you have what it takes to tame me? Hmm? Do you? Try me. I dare you." The camera caresses the curves of the road and approaches a dark tunnel with a light at the end. A Lexus roars into view. The announcer says, "The all-new ES300. The road is calling. Answer it." As the car zooms away, the road says with an eerie laugh, "Come back. I let you win that time." In a world in which we so often feel powerless, how seductive is this promise of overpowering, not just other drivers but the road itself. We may be locked into our dull jobs, our mortgage payments, our disappointing spouses and needy children, but we become rulers of the world when we get into our cars.

Certainly the craze for sport utility vehicles has something to do with this need to feel more powerful and more secure in a time of widespread worries about corporate downsizing, family breakups, and crime. According to Nissan's president of North American design, "There's a feeling, 'When I'm in this car, I'm in command of my future.' Home and work have not been symbols of stability." One auto design and marketing consultant thinks men buy the rugged vehicles to compensate for loss of masculine power and women buy them to flaunt the power they've achieved. Conversely, sociology professor Pepper Schwartz describes the image projected by minivans as "I've no fangs left, I've been declawed."

Certainly that's the image portrayed in a Mitsubishi commercial that opens in a health club. A group of handsome, muscular men are pumping iron. A woman announces over the loudspeaker, "The owner of a tan minivan—you left your lights on." The camera zooms around the zoom . . . no one makes a move. The announcer repeats her message. Again, no one moves. The camera stops on a guy who looks sheepish. No way is he going to admit to owning the dreaded feminized minivan. The commercial switches to a scene of a Mitsubishi SUV roaring across the landscape. Real men drive SUVs.

Sales for these light trucks nearly quadrupled between 1992 and 1998. Suddenly in the mid-1990s people found they must have automobiles designed for the desert and the jungle and clothing meant for Arctic expeditions just to get to the mall. Sometimes it seems as if *everyone* has fallen for the advertising image of the lone soul conquering the wilderness. And make no mistake: The wilderness is to be conquered. Nature, often personified as female, is dangerous. As one SUV ad says, "She will freeze you, she will burn you, she will try to blow you away." One ad after another tells us that the best way to relate to nature is to run over it (or, more symbolically, her).

We drive vehicles made for off-road adventures to the supermarket, where we shop in clothing designed to keep us alive in a blizzard on a mountaintop. Talk about virtual reality. Ads for SUVs almost always show the vehicle perched on a mountaintop or barreling over rocky terrain and then equate this with courage. "Goodbye yellow striped road," says one (and we all know what it means to have a yellow stripe). "To go off-road, you've gotta have backbone," says another. "Tread softly and carry a big V-8," says yet another. Such advertising has an impact. One marketing consultant says, "People will argue SUVs are bought for functionality and utility. But our focus groups state the overriding reason is image."

Are there consequences to any of this? The 13 percent of SUVs that are used off-road cause a disastrous combination of soil erosion and compaction, killing

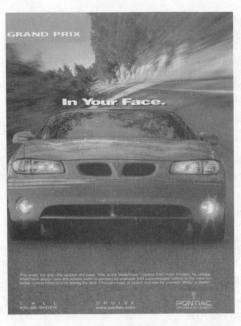

plants and destroying animal habitats. In addition, advertising that encourages us to personify and identify with our cars may well affect our driving behavior. More people die in automobile crashes than from homicide, yet many people are resistant to prevention measures such as seat belts and lower speed limits that are guaranteed to save lives, because they feel "controlled" by such measures. Risky driving without consequences is as common in advertising and throughout the media as is risky sex. Surely an ad like the one for a Grand Prix featuring a closeup of the front of the car and the tagline "In your face" doesn't help.

Sport utility vehicles are especially dangerous . . . to people in cars. So dangerous that they are sometimes referred to as Somebody's Under the Vehicle. The three-ton vehicles are a serious threat to smaller cars. When cars and SUVs collide, the person in the car is four times more likely to die than the person in the truck. And if a car is hit in the side, that brings the odds to twenty-seven to one. At the moment, the drivers of SUVs tend to be older, married, and therefore safer drivers. However, there is likely to be increasing trouble when these drivers sell their expensive toys to reckless youths and heavy drinkers who have high accident rates and can seldom afford new cars. Sport utility vehicles are three times more likely to roll over during crashes than are passenger cars (and two-thirds of all spinal injuries in crashes occur when vehicles roll over). SUV drivers are two and a half times more likely to die in a rollover crash than car drivers.

In spite of all this, the trend is definitely toward bigger SUVs and even big-cab pickup trucks. In 1998, Americans bought more vans, pickup trucks, and SUVs than they did cars. The 2000 Ford Excursion, which weighs two thousand pounds more than the Chevrolet Suburban and gets around ten miles per gallon, is dubbed the Ford Valdez by those who are appalled by its creation and threat to the earth.

We seem increasingly territorial when in our cars. A 1997 study in the *Journal of Applied Social Psychology* of behavior in parking lots found that a person who normally takes about thirty-two seconds to vacate a parking space will take thirty-nine seconds if another driver is waiting, and forty-three seconds if that driver beeps. The study also found that male drivers will pull out of parking spaces more quickly for expensive prestige cars, whereas women don't care. An editorial about this study concluded, "Perhaps a man, having served more time as ancient hunter and hunted, sees an Infiniti as lion and a station wagon as hyena. A woman figures they're all animals."

In 1996 a study by the American Automobile Association reported that violence by hostile drivers had increased by 51 percent since 1990. Most aggressive drivers were men (mostly between the ages of eighteen and twenty-six); about 4 percent were women. Calling the problem at least as dangerous as drunken driving, the article suggested promoting "socially responsible driving" and avoiding confrontations with aggressive drivers. Since then the media have focused extensively on the growing problem of "road rage," which one pundit called "a cultural illness rooted in our hectic, hostile way of life." According to the National Highway Traffic Safety Administration, violent, aggressive driving contributes to two-thirds of all traffic deaths.

People sometimes feel exempt from the laws of civilized behavior in their cars and thus wield them in a way they would wield no other "weapon." Ads that encourage drivers to break the rules certainly contribute to this attitude. "The engineers of the Pontiac Grand Am see no shame in gutsy driving. Only in timid cars," declares one such ad. The copy continues, "If you're not exactly the shy type on the road, you belong in a Pontiac Grand Am. Because . . . it suits your driving style to a 'T.' As in 'tough.' Not as in 'tame.' " And an Audi ad says, "Why push the envelope when you can shred it?"

A 1997 Lexus campaign, introduced just before Halloween, looks like an ad for a slasher film. In one version, the car emerges, as if from flames, from a forest of bare, blackened trees against an orange sky. The copy, in the script of witchcraft and alluding to Shakespeare's *Macbeth*, says:

> *Distant thunder, cold as stone,*
> *a V8 screams down from its throne.*
> *One by one, each car succumbs.*
> *Something wicked*
> *This way comes.*

Additional copy describes the car as "a fixture of intimidation" that "seethes within . . . the fiercest, fastest automatic sedan in the world." The slogan for this car from hell? "Faster, sleeker, meaner." Of course, this is overkill, so to speak, intended to be funny, ironic, at least on one level. But do we need advertising like this when people are literally killing each other with their cars?

Ad critic Bob Garfield apparently thinks so. He gave the campaign a rave in his column, saying that "the listless, vanilla Lexus is finally imbued with a fearsome character with which to battle the brawny German competition." Garfield presumably is personifying German cars such as BMW and Mercedes-Benz as the enemy, the competition. It may be precisely this personification of cars that leads to the extreme sensitivity to insult that some drivers feel.

Car ads often encourage this overidentification of owners with their automobiles. "Infiniti. Own one and you'll understand," says an ad featuring a woman asleep outdoors in a sleeping bag, while her car resides inside a spacious tent. Many ads encourage us to feel that the car has a soul as well as a personality. "Born again," says a Toyota ad for used cars. And Chrysler tells us, in an ad picturing a car, "They say the soul lives on. And it does."

"If they made a movie about your life, who would you want to star as your car?" asks an ad for BMW. "You and your M3 are locked in an embrace with the road. Cut to a close-up of your gaping jaw as you feel the power of its engine. . . . The two of you ride off into the sunset." Who among us would want a movie about our life to end with us going off into the sunset, alone in our car?

Some ads go even further. The car is no longer a close companion or a lover. It becomes the self. "Can an engine pump the valves in your heart?" asks an ad for Lexus, which features a man's body superimposed on the front of a car. "When was the last time you felt this connected to a car?" the ad concludes. Another ad in the campaign features the interior of the car, with a man's hand and arm becoming the gearshift. The copy says, "The symmetry is uncanny. It has a heart. . . . You have a heart. It has a conscience. . . . You have a conscience. . . . It's not simply a car you drive, it's one that gets under your skin."

The television version of the campaign goes even further. The man's hand merges with the gearshift and then the steering wheel, his skin becomes leather, while the voiceover says, "Its beauty will draw you in. Its new engine will pump the valves of your heart. And the line that separates man from machine will disappear . . . completely. . . . You've never felt so connected to a car."

A woman paints her toenails—with silver metallic touch-up paint for a Honda. A British ad for Pirelli tires features Olympic athlete Carl Lewis running over mountains and leaping over rooftops. Toward the end, we see a closeup of

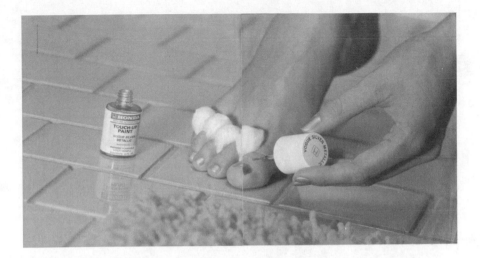

his feet and his soles are treaded rubber, like tires. "Power is nothing without control," the announcer tells us.

Do we want the line that separates man from machine to disappear? If a man feels that the car engine is his heart, that the tires are his feet, and that "power is nothing without control," no wonder he overreacts to "disrespectful" or "threatening" moves from another driver.

As always, taken individually, the car ads are funny, silly, exciting, sometimes breathtakingly clever, and seemingly insignificant. However, they have a cumulative direction and a cumulative impact. As is the case with many other products, the car in commercials has gone from being a symbol of power to the actual source of power (the engine that pumps the valves in our hearts), from a symbol of sex to an actual lover, from a conduit to relationships to the important relationship itself, and from a prized possession to the very emblem of oneself. The car ads are an important part of a world in which things are becoming ever more, and people ever less, important.

5

"PLEASE, PLEASE, YOU'RE DRIVING ME WILD"

Falling in Love with Food

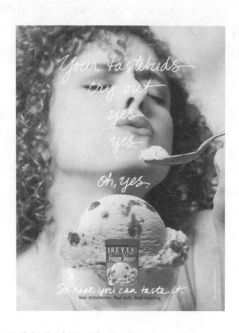

WHILE MEN ARE ENCOURAGED TO FALL IN LOVE WITH THEIR CARS, WOMEN are more often invited to have a romance, indeed an erotic experience, with something even closer to home, something that truly does pump the valves of our hearts—the food we eat. And the consequences become even more severe as we enter into the territory of compulsivity and addiction.

Women have always been closely linked with food—with its gathering, preparation, and serving. We're called peaches, tomatoes, pieces of meat, dishes . . . honey, sugar, sweetie. Beautiful women, especially those who accompany playboys and older men, are "arm candy." And increasingly, as with ads for cars and other products, the thing becomes the lover, as in the ad in a Thai publication featuring two scoops of ice cream as a woman's breasts.

Food is intertwined with love throughout our culture. We give chocolates on Valentine's Day. We say that we are "starved for affection." We think of certain foods, such as custard, ice cream, and maca- roni and cheese, as "comfort foods." In infancy and

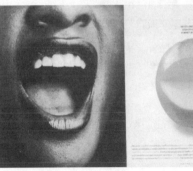

early childhood, food was a major way we were connected to some- one else, the most important way that we were nurtured. Many of us had caregivers who used food as a reward or a punishment. Others suffered terrible trauma in child- hood and learned to use food for solace and escape. No wonder feeding ourselves can sometimes be an attempt to re-create some sense of wholeness and connection. No wonder it is so easy to confuse food and love.

Food has long been advertised as a way for women both to demonstrate our love and to insure its requital. Countless television commercials feature a woman trying to get her husband and children to love her or just to pay attention to her via the cakes and breakfast cereals and muffins she serves them. "Bake a Com- stock pie," one ad says, "they'll love you for it." Instant oatmeal "warms your heart and soul," a print ad tells us, "like a hug that lasts all day." "Awesome Mom" is the tagline for an ad featuring a little boy smiling widely, obviously delighted to find prepackaged junk food in his lunchbox. "Skip the Zip on my little girl's sandwich and give up one of her bear hugs? Not in her lifetime," says a mother hugging her daughter in a mayonnaise ad. The implication, of course, is that the child won't hug her mother unless she gets the right kind of mayonnaise on her sandwich. As always, the heartfelt connection, the warm relationship is simply a device to sell something—and even our children's love for us is contingent upon our buying the right product.

Very few ads feature women being given food by men or even by other women. More often, when a woman is being fed, she is feeding herself. A television commercial for candy features a series of vignettes in which what a woman does for others (such as making a costume for her daughter) is ignored and unappreciated. At the end of each vignette, the woman pops a piece of candy in her mouth and says, "I thank me very much with Andy's Candies." Another commercial featuring a woman feeding herself candy has the tagline "From you to you."

In many of these commercials, the woman is not only rewarding herself, she also is coping with her disappointment at being unappreciated. Advertisers often offer food as a way to repress anger, resentment, and hurt feelings. "What to do for dinner after a long day of eating your words and swallowing your pride" says an ad for frozen chicken. "Got a big mouth?" asks an ad for caramel candies, "Put a soft chewy in it." "Not satisfied with your payday?" asks an ad for Payday candy bars. "Try ours." And an ice cream ad featuring a young woman walking her dog says, "He never called. So Ben and I went out for a pint of Frusen Glädjé. Ben's better-looking anyway." Another ad features the empty foil wrappings of twelve pieces of candy with statements beneath them, from "I didn't sleep late" to "I didn't call him" to "I didn't buy it," "I didn't put off the laundry," "I didn't get upset" to "I didn't skip gym," ending with "He called."

It is interesting that the ad includes so many ways that people escape from difficulties with relationships (shopping, sleeping, watching television) and yet encourages one of the most common escape routes of all, overeating. I am especially struck by "I didn't get upset." Sometimes getting upset is the healthiest and most appropriate response. Certainly it is better to get upset than to numb one's feelings with an overdose of chocolate. Better for us, that is—not better for candy manufacturers. No wonder they run ads like the one that says, "Whatever mood you're in, you're always in the mood for chocolate."

A 1995 Häagen-Dazs ad features a large spoon dipping into a pint of ice cream and the copy, "Your fiance agreed to have a big wedding. *Have a Häagen-Dazs.* He wants to have it in a Sports Bar. *Have some more.*" Again the message to women is clear. When your man upsets you, don't make trouble, don't argue, just eat something—or have a drink or a tranquilizer or a cigarette. "At least one thing in your day will go smoothly," says an ad for a candy bar. Sadly, many

women do eat compulsively in an attempt to assuage loneliness and disappointment within relationships (from the past as well as in the present). Family therapist Jill Harkaway says, "When you are lonely, you can't count on people, but you
can count on your refrigerator, or the nearby 7-Eleven not to let you down." Of
course, this fails to address the real problems, thus insuring continued feelings of
isolation and alienation, while breeding eating disorders.

Advertisers spend a lot of money on psychological research. They know that
many people, especially women, use food to help us deal with loneliness and disappointment and also as a way to connect. The ads play on this. "You know that
empty feeling you have when you're watching what you eat?" asks a four-page ad
featuring an empty dessert bowl on the first page. "Start filling up," the ad continues on the next two pages, which picture a variety of sugar-free puddings. A
1999 Burger King commercial features flashes of food and the Burger King logo
while Leslie Gore's old hit "It's My Party" plays in the background— "it's my party
and I'll cry if I want to." The final caption reads "Stop crying and start eating" and
the burger disappears in three large bites.

Advertisers especially offer food as a way to relate romantically and sexually.
A television commercial for a pasta sauce features a couple eating and gazing intensely at each other while "I don't know why I love you like I do" plays in the
background. "In the mood for something really intense?" asks the sexy female
voiceover. The couple feed each other while the words "Unexpected . . . Intense
. . . Bold" appear onscreen. In the last shot, the woman is suggestively licking the
man's finger while the voiceover says, "You're gonna love it." And an ad for a
frozen mousse dessert features Dr. Ruth Westheimer, America's sexual guru, dig-
ging in and advising the reader, "Achieving mutual satisfaction is easy. Just share
some Mousse du Jour."

One of my favorite ads of all time ran in the early 1980s in many women's
magazines. It showed a closeup of a woman's face. She was smiling very seductively and the copy said, "Whatever you're giving him tonight, he'll enjoy it more
with rice." As I said to my audiences at the time, "I don't think I'm particularly
naive, but I haven't figured out what the hell you do with rice." "Maybe it's wild
rice," someone suggested. Another woman called out, "Let's just hope it isn't
Minute Rice." The 1990s version of using sex to sell rice is much more explicit, of
course: an ad for Uncle Ben's rice shows a woman feeding a man a forkful of rice
by candlelight. The copy says, "Passion Lesson #13. From now on every night
would be different . . . filled with endless variety."

One of the most erotic commercials I have ever seen is a British óne (no doubt too racy for America) that features a man and a woman making love while feeding each other something. Because the commercial is shot with infrared film, we see only their shapes and intense patterns of red and yellow and blue. "Make Yourself Comfortable" is playing on the record player. They lick some substance off each other's bodies, while an elderly man below bangs on the ceiling with a broomstick, shouting "Mr. Rogers" (thus playing on the British slang "to roger," meaning to have intercourse, and also implying that the man is single and that this is a tryst, not a marriage). At the very end of the commercial we see that the couple's erotic toy is a pint of Häagen-Dazs ice cream. "Dedicated to pleasure" is the slogan.

This campaign ran in print too, with erotic black and white photographs by French photographer Jeanloup Sieff. In just a few months after the campaign broke in upscale magazines such as *Tatler* and *Vogue*, sales of Häagen-Dazs in Great Britain rose 400 percent. This spectacular success indicates that advertisers do indeed sometimes know what they are doing.

Of course, we are not stupid. We don't for a minute believe that we're actually going to improve our relationships with ice cream or pasta sauce. But these ads do contribute to a cultural climate in which relationships are constantly trivialized and we are encouraged to connect via consumption. An obsession with food interferes with real relationships just as any other obsession does, yet food advertising often normalizes and glamorizes such an obsession.

We are not only offered connection via the product, we are offered connection *with* the product. Food becomes the lover. "Rich, impeccable taste and *not an ounce of fat.* Wow, if only I could find a guy like that," says a woman holding a candy bar. "Looking for a light cheesy relationship?" asks an ad for macaroni and cheese, which concludes with a shot of the package and the copy, "Oh, baby, where have you been all my life?" And another ad features an extreme closeup of potatoes with the headline, "Potatoes that get more oohs and aahs than a supermodel." This ad ran in women's magazines and clearly targets women, so the promise is that the woman can distract her husband's attention from supermodels by cooking the right food.

Men are sometimes also targeted, however, with the message that food is love. In a commercial broadcast on Valentine's Day, romantic music plays as we see a couple coming out of the Tunnel of Love at an amusement park, embracing passionately. A voiceover says, "Can you put a price on love?" As the next boat comes out of the tunnel, carrying a man alone, eating a large hamburger, the voiceover continues, "You betcha—if the object of your affection is a McDonald's Big Mac!" The man seems delirious with happiness as he eats his burger, and the voiceover gives some details about the price and says, "Taste that makes you swoon. Or, if you're a two-timer, get cozy with two Big Mac sandwiches. But hurry—your love may be eternal but these prices aren't." The commercial ends with the old man who is running the ride looking with envy at the man with the burger while saying to his helper, "Where does one find such love?"

However, women and girls are targeted far more often. A television commercial broadcast during *Sabrina, the Teenage Witch,* a show popular with teenage girls, features a woman reading a book by a window. "You are my destiny, you share my reverie, you're more than life can be" plays in the background. The woman takes a bite of a cookie and fantasizes a handsome man on a white horse coming to her, riding his horse into her house. "Ah," a female voiceover says, "the new moister than ever devil's food cookie from SnackWell." The man reaches for the cookie and the woman turns him into a frog. "Passion, desire, devotion?" says the voiceover while the words appear on screen. "Nah, it goes way beyond that." This is funny, of course, but it also normalizes an obsession with food that takes precedence over human connection.

Another television commercial goes even further. It begins with an extreme closeup of the peaks and swirls of frosting on a cake. A woman's voice passionately says, "Oh, my love." A man's voice says, "Huh?" and the woman replies, "Not you—the frosting!" With increasing excitement, she continues, "It's calling my name!" and the man replies, "Janet?" The woman cries out, "I'm yours!" as a male voiceover says, "Give in to the rich and creamy temptation of Betty Crocker frosting." As one of the peaks of the frosting peaks, so to speak, and then droops, the woman says, in a voice rich with satisfaction, "That was great." As is often the case, this ad is very funny and seemingly harmless. But also, as is often the case, it is frightful upon reflection. A human relationship is trivialized and ignored ("Not you—the frosting!") while someone connects passionately with a product. Imagine if this were an ad for alcohol ("Not you—the bourbon!"). Perhaps we'd understand how sad and alienating it is.

"I had a dream about salad dressing. Is that weird?" asks a woman lifting a lettuce leaf to her mouth. Of course it's weird! A Cool Whip ad shows a manicured hand plunging a strawberry into whipped cream and the caption, "Go skinny dippin'." And an ad for frozen yogurt features a closeup of a woman's face in what looks like sexual ecstasy and the copy, "Vanilla so pure it sends chills down your spine and back up again." Another version of the ad shows the same ecstatic face and the copy, "Your tastebuds cry out yes yes. Oh, yes." Shades of Molly Bloom!

Certainly food can be an important part of loving ourselves and others. It can be comforting as well as nourishing and indeed it can be sexy. When a friend of mine told her husband on the phone that she had just eaten a persimmon, he said, "You had sex without me!" Who can forget the erotic feasting scene in the film *Tom Jones,* the characters looking hungrily at each other, grease glistening on their lips, while ripping meat from bones? This scene, which shocked many people back in 1963, would be tame compared to many food advertisements today.

Often food is shot in extreme closeup and is very sensually inviting. "Bet this little lite will turn you on," says an ad that features a very suggestive closeup of

the inside of a candy bar. Another ad featuring a Fudgsicle oozing its chocolate filling is headlined, "Introducing our deep, dark secret," and an ad for a cereal bar says, "Trapped inside this wholesome rolled oats crust is a sultry little French pastry struggling to get out."

A hilarious ad for sour cream features a baked potato begging for the sour cream's touch, "Please . . . please . . . you're driving me wild." Another baked potato is brought to ecstasy by a bottle of tabasco sauce (named "The Exciter"). Indeed there were a series of ads featuring tabasco sauce as a stud. At the end of what must have been a wild night in the kitchen, the bottle is on its side, empty, and the copy says, "A good time was had by all." These ads are powerful examples of the wit, humor, and sheer cleverness one sometimes finds in advertising. There is no harm and indeed much delight in them individually, but their cumulative impact is another story.

Add your own dash at the table.

Just what is this cumulative impact? What's the problem? For one thing, when food is sex, eating becomes a moral issue—and thinness becomes the equivalent of virginity. The "good girl" today is the thin girl, the one who keeps her appetite for food (and power, sex, and equality) under control. "I'm a girl who just can't say no. I insist on dessert," proclaims a thin woman in an ad for a sugar-free gelatin. It used to be that women who couldn't say no were talking about something other than food. Women were supposed to control their sexual appetites. Now we're

supposed to control our appetite for food. If a woman comes back from a weekend and says she was "bad," we assume she broke her diet, not that she did something interesting sexually. The ménage à trois we are made to feel ashamed of is with Ben and Jerry.

"Pizza without guilt," declares an ad featuring a heavyset woman tied up to keep her from eating regular pizza. Weight Watchers ads feature extreme close-ups of rich foods and the slogan, "Total indulgence. Zero guilt." As if women should feel guilty about eating!

In the old days, bad girls got pregnant. These days they get fat—and are more scorned, shamed, and despised than ever before. Prejudice against fat people, especially against fat women, is one of the few remaining prejudices that is socially acceptable. This strikes fear into the hearts of most women, who are terrified of inspiring revulsion and ridicule. And this contributes mightily, of course, to the obsession with thinness that has gripped our culture for many years, with devastating consequences for many women and girls.

A television commercial for ice cream features actor Bernadette Peters in slinky pajamas in her kitchen at night. "I love being naughty," she says in her little-girl voice, "especially when I can get away with it. Like with Breyer's light ice cream. It has less fat so I can indulge in sinful fudge . . . real vanilla." Her voice is rising as she becomes more excited and builds to an orgasmic crescendo— "Mmmm, pure true taste!" Almost out of breath, she slides down the refrigerator

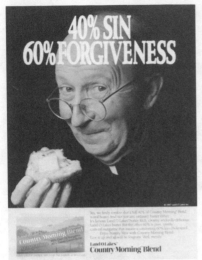

Land O Lakes
Country Morning Blend

door, saying, "I feel like I'm cheating, but I'm not . . . what a shame."

This moral tone shows up again and again, often with religious connotations. A rich chocolate sundae is labeled "Temptation" on one side of a page. On the other is the "Salvation," a low-calorie shake. "40% Sin 60% Forgiveness," proclaims an ad featuring a priest eating a blend of butter and margarine. And an ad for pork, touting its leanness, says, "We lead you to temptation but deliver you from evil."

However, unlike traditional religious morality in which one has to suffer, to do penance in order to be saved, we are offered products that will allow us to sin without consequence. Just as advertising constantly offers us sex without the burdens and responsibilities of a relationship, it offers us the pleasure of consuming rich foods without having to "pay the price." Now that we have birth control, to eliminate the "sin" of pregnancy but not the joy of sex, all we need is girth control, to eliminate the "sin" of obesity but not the joy of overeating. It doesn't matter if we are "guilty" as long as we don't look it. If we can remain thin by taking laxatives or diet pills or chugging artificially sweetened colas and eating low-fat ice cream rather than exercising moderately and eating healthfully or joining a recovery program, so much the better. In fact, bulimia is the ultimate solution.

Another problematic aspect of the cumulative impact of food advertising is that many ads normalize and glamorize harmful and often dangerous attitudes toward food and eating. And we suffer drastically as a culture from the negative consequences of these attitudes. About eighty million Americans are clinically obese, and nearly three out of four are overweight. Indeed, in a culture seemingly obsessed with thinness and fitness, Americans are fatter than ever and fatter than people in most other cultures. Eight million Americans suffer from an eating disorder and as many as 10 percent of all college-age women are bulimic. Eating disorders are the third most common chronic illness among females. In fact, they are so common it really is misleading to refer to them as "disorders." More accurately, they are a common way that women cope with the difficulties in their lives and with the cultural contradictions involving food and eating. Few of us aren't touched by some kind of problem with food (not to mention the thirty million at risk for hunger and malnutrition).

There are many reasons for these problems, ranging from the decrease in physical education in our schools to our use of the automobile to the development of the TV remote control to fear of crime, which keeps people indoors, often in front of the television set with its blaring litany of commercials for junk food and diet products. American children see over ten thousand commercials for food on television each year. Ninety-five percent are for four food groups: soft drinks, candy, fast food, and sugar-coated cereal. There's a lot of money at stake: Americans spend an estimated $14 billion a year on snack foods, $15 billion on chocolate, and $86 billion on fast food restaurants.

The commercials are only one part of the problem, but they are a significant part. Just as alcohol ads teach us that drinking leads inevitably to good times, great sex, athletic prowess, and success, without any risks or negative consequences whatsoever, so do the food ads associate eating and overeating with only good things. The negative consequences are obliterated. Indeed, in order to maximize their profits, the junk food and the diet industries need to normalize and glamorize disordered and destructive attitudes toward food and eating.

One of the clearest examples of this is the advertising campaigns for Häagen-Dazs ice cream over a period of several years. In 1990 "Enter the state of Häagen-Dazs" was the slogan for this popular ice cream. The ads featured blissful men and women eating Häagen-Dazs. Sometimes the container was empty, but the people seemed calm and happy, somewhat smug, maybe even slightly stoned. The focus was on the smiling person in the ad, not the product, and the ad was in full color.

In 1991 a new Häagen-Dazs campaign featured ghostly black-and-white photographs of people with copy inscribed over their faces. In one a man is saying, "Maybe I'm a bit of a perfectionist. My CD's are in alphabetical order. . . . Yet everytime I have Häagen-Dazs I seem to lose control. . . . Each creamy

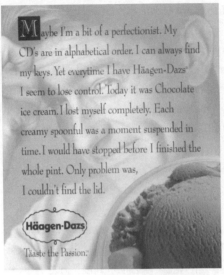

Maybe I'm a bit of a perfectionist. My CD's are in alphabetical order. I can always find my keys. Yet everytime I have Häagen-Dazs® I seem to lose control. Today it was Chocolate ice cream. I lost myself completely. Each creamy spoonful was a moment suspended in time. I would have stopped before I finished the whole pint. Only problem was, I couldn't find the lid.

(Häagen-Dazs)

Täaste the Passion.®

spoonful was a moment suspended in time. I would have stopped before I finished the whole pint. Only problem was, I couldn't find the lid."

In another, a woman says, "I pride myself on my level-headed approach to life. . . . But all it takes is one smooth taste of Häagen-Dazs Strawberry ice cream and I find myself letting go. . . . I must do something about this Häagen-Dazs passion. Maybe I could organize it, structure it or control it . . . tomorrow." The campaign slogan is "Täaste the Passion." What an invitation to binge this is! People who feel too controlled in their lives, with too few avenues to real passion, often turn to food or other potentially addictive products as a way to loosen up, to relax. This campaign normalizes and legitimizes this process.

By 1992 there were no longer people in the ads at all, simply a large photograph of the pint of ice cream, with copy beginning in small letters and gradually growing larger and larger. "Wow have you seen it? Another outrageous Exträas ice cream from Häagen-Dazs. . . . Oh my gosh! Luscious fudge chunks too. Give me the entire pint of Cookie Dough Dynamo!"

WOW HAVE YOU SEEN IT! ANOTHER OUTRAGEOUS EXTRÄAS ICE CREAM FROM HÄAGEN-DAZS. IT'S UNBELIEVABLE! MOIST AND CHEWY COOKIE DOUGH STUFFED INTO CREAMY VANILLA ICE CREAM. OH MY GOSH! LUSCIOUS FUDGE CHUNKS TOO. GIVE ME THE ENTIRE PINT OF COOKIE DOUGH DYNAMO!

NEW Häagen-Dazs EXTRÄAS Cookie Dough Dynamo

HÄAGEN-DAZS. IT'S BETTER THAN ANYTHING.

These few years of Häagen-Dazs advertising perfectly illustrate the progression of addiction. The first ad features a woman nibbling on an ice cream bar, somewhat spaced-out but still in control. In the second, a man talks about losing control and unintentionally finishing a pint. In the third, someone is shouting "I need it" and "Give me the entire pint." Granted, this is not heroin we're talking about. But compulsive overeaters will certainly say that their addiction rules and ruins their lives as completely as any other.

Although addiction to food is often trivialized, it is in fact a major problem for many women and men. People who binge on food and overeat compulsively say this has the same effect on their minds and lives as does addiction to alcohol and other drugs. They experience the terror of loss of control, diminished self-esteem, damaged relationships, and even such consequences as hangovers and blackouts. In *Make the Connection,* her best-selling book about overcoming a lifelong eating problem, Oprah Winfrey writes about a binge she had when all she could find in her kitchen was salt, Tabasco sauce, starch, maple syrup, and frozen hot dog buns. "Quickly I turned the oven on broil, threw the buns in to thaw out, and even before they could, I grabbed the syrup and smeared it over the partly burnt, partly frozen buns. Looking back, I see no difference between myself and a junkie, scrambling for a needle and whatever dope might be around. Food was my drug."

There are those who question whether food can be truly addictive. They believe that compulsive overeaters simply lack willpower. Some people still feel this way about alcoholics, although there is much more evidence these days that alcoholism is a disease. Scientists increasingly are discovering physiological and biochemical bases for eating disorders just as for alcoholism. A 1999 study, published in the American Medical Association's *Archives of General Psychiatry,* found that bulimia springs at least in part from a chemical malfunction in the brain resulting in low levels of serotonin, a mood-and-appetite-regulating chemical.

These days many people are cross-addicted. In fact, it is rare to find someone with a single addiction. Most alcoholics are addicted to other drugs too, especially nicotine. Women often wash their tranquilizers down with alcohol or become addicted to amphetamines in an attempt to control their obsession with food. The frequency of eating disorders is significantly higher in alcoholic women than in the general population. Many women with eating disorders come from alcoholic homes. Current research indicates that alcoholism and eating disorders often occur together but are transmitted independently in families. Whatever the origins, it is clear that neither alcoholism nor eating disorders are linked with any character weaknesses.

Advertisers are clearly aware of the psychology of food addiction and compulsive overeating. Since food addicts spend a lot of money on food, it is to the advertisers' advantage to make their obsessive and addictive attitudes seem normal and appropriate. An ad featuring a suggestive closeup of a candy bar says, "What you do in the dark is nobody else's business." Compulsive eaters almost always binge alone and feel terribly ashamed. This ad is clearly meant both to tempt and

What you do in the dark is nobody else's business.

Milky Way DARK

Pure pleasure in the dark.

© Mars Incorporated 1996

to assuage guilt feelings, to help the eater rationalize his or her behavior, to create the climate of denial so essential for addictions to flourish.

A 1998 SnackWell's campaign cuts right to the heart of the matter by openly declaring that eating cookies will boost a woman's self-esteem. The commercials show scenes of women in warm family embraces while a voiceover says that eating SnackWell's isn't about feeding yourself but "feeding your self-esteem," "treating yourself well," and "fulfilling yourself." Even Bob Garfield of *Advertising Age* responded to this campaign with "Women of America, feel better about yourselves: Pig out on crap!" He continues, "Feeling a bit down on yourself? Have a cookie. Career stagnating and love life not working out? Have 28 cookies. Suicidal depression? Get the caramel-filled one, melt it in a spoon and inject it directly into your vein." Eating to feel better about oneself is not a healthy idea—it is a symptom of a problem.

A recent candy commercial further illustrates this normalization of problematic attitudes. The commercial begins with a middle-aged man seated in an armchair, holding a piece of candy in his hand. He says, "What a combination— crunchy Werther's toffee and delicious milk chocolate. . .mmm." The scene switches to a beautiful young blond woman standing beside her car. She is holding a bag of the candy and says, "I keep one bag in the car, one in my desk, one in the living room, and one next to my bed." Hoarding the supply is one of the signs of addiction. Although alcoholics are best known for this (hiding bottles in toilet tanks and linen closets), most addicts do it. Surely a woman who can't be far from her stash of candy has got a problem.

The next scene in the commercial features a man in a suit holding up one piece of candy, almost as if it were a cigar, and saying, "Now that's where there's quality." Next we see a middle-aged woman pouring the candy into a dish in her kitchen. She says, "Nothing but the best for my guests." Next, a woman in a slinky black dress is seated in an armchair beside a blazing fire. A bag of chocolates is cuddled up against her. She slowly unwraps one piece and pops it in her mouth, saying suggestively, "It's going to be a *nice* evening." At this point, we see a closeup of a bowl of candy and a male voiceover touts its virtues. The commercial ends with another attractive young blond woman, sitting barefoot on a bench outdoors and holding a bag of the candy. Pulling one from the bag, she says, giggling, "I start on them right after breakfast."

This commercial normalizes some potentially dangerous attitudes toward food in some rather subtle ways. The women in trouble—the two young blondes and the woman by the fireplace—are sandwiched between people with more healthful attitudes. These three women are holding the entire bag of candy, whereas the men are holding only one piece and the middle-aged woman is pouring the candy into a bowl to serve to others. The first troubled woman is hoarding her supply, the second is seemingly preparing for a binge, and the third is rationalizing eating the candy all day long, beginning in the morning.

Thus, women with disordered attitudes toward food, women who seem to be compulsive eaters, are presented as normal, desirable, and even especially attractive. Why would the candy manufacturers want to do this? Because the compulsive eaters, obviously, are going to spend a great deal more on the candy than are the people who eat it infrequently, a piece or two at a time. No matter what a company is selling, the heavy user is their best customer. Thus, it is always in their best interest to normalize and encourage heavy use, even if that might have destructive or even deadly consequences.

Obsession with food is also presented as normal and even as attractive in an ad for sugar-free pudding that features a pretty young woman with a spoonful of pudding in her mouth and the headline, "Dessert? It's always on the tip of my tongue." The copy continues, "Really. I mean, if I'm not eating dessert, I'm talking about it. If I'm not talking about it, I'm eating it. And I'm always thinking about it. . . . It's just always on my mind." Like the women who obsess about candy, this young woman has a problem.

And, as is always the case in the world of advertising, the solution to her problem is a product, in this case a diet product. The ad promises her, as almost all the diet ads do, that she can have her pudding and eat it too. How odd this is, when we think about it. Here we are surrounded by all these tempting, luscious ads for food. We are told, on the one hand, give in, reward yourself, indulge. But, on the other hand, we (especially women) are told that we must be thin, indeed that there is no greater sin than being fat.

It might seem strange that there are so many ads for diet products interspersed with ads for rich foods. It might seem stranger still that it is often so difficult to tell the difference between the junk food ads and the diet ads. However, this is not strange at all. The tempting food ads do not contradict the message of the diet culture. They are an integral part of it. The junk food industry and the diet industry depend on each other.

In order to be profitable, both these industries require that people be hooked on unhealthy and mostly unsatisfying food, high in fat and sugar. In addition, the diet industry depends upon a rigid cultural mandate for women to be thin. If we ate and took pleasure in basically healthy food and were physically active, if we recognized that bodies come in many different sizes and shapes, and we did not consider it necessary for women to be bone-thin to be attractive—the junk food industry would lose a great deal of money and there would be no diet industry.

The success of the diet industry primarily depends on women being dissatisfied with their bodies. Many people say that advertising simply reflects the soci-

ety. But certainly the body images of women that advertising reflects today are as distorted as the reflections in a funhouse mirror. Since advertising cashes in on women's body-hatred and distorted self-images, it sometimes deliberately promotes such distortion. A yogurt ad says, "How to go from seeing yourself like this. . .to seeing yourself like this," and portrays the "before" image with a pear. In fact, it is perfectly normal for a woman to be pear-shaped. Many more women have pear-shaped bodies than have the V-shaped bodies of the models, but we don't see them in the media. Instead, we get the message that this shape is unacceptable.

The use of body doubles in films and commercials makes it even less likely that we'll see real women's bodies. A photograph of Julia Roberts and Richard Gere that was widely used to advertise the hit film *Pretty Woman* featured Julia Roberts's head but not her body. Apparently, even *her* body wasn't good enough or thin enough to be in the ad. A body double was also used for Roberts when she was nude or partially nude in the film. This is common practice in the industry. Not surprisingly, at least 85 percent of body doubles have breast implants.

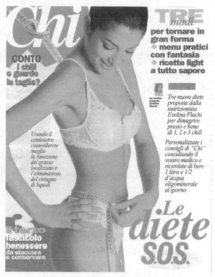

Unfortunately, the obsession with thinness is becoming a problem throughout the developed world. "Le diete S.O.S.," the title of an article featured on the cover of an Italian magazine, is understood in many languages. Italy used to be a country where voluptuous women could still feel desirable, but the model on the cover shown measuring her waist is extremely thin by any standards.

The dieter, even more than the addict, is the ideal consumer. She (most dieters are women) will spend a lot on food and then spend even more to lose weight—and the cycle never stops. Sales of low-fat frozen yogurt soar, but so do sales of high-fat premium ice cream. The diet industry, which includes diet drugs and other products, diet workshops and books, health spas, and more, has tripled in recent years, increasing from a $10 billion to a $36 billion-a-year industry. No one loses, especially the dieter (although she doesn't win either).

Some research indicates that thin people do live longer than overweight people. Some people have latched on to this as proof that we needn't worry about people dieting—in fact, we should worry more if they don't diet. The truth, however, is that fatness is related to the obsession with thinness. Chronic dieting is part of the generally bad eating and exercise habits that make so many Americans overweight and unhealthy. Although being thin is good for one's heart, dieting is bad for everyone.

The fat-free products we consume in great quantities are often bad for us. We eat them instead of eating healthy foods, drinking Coke and Pepsi instead of water, lunching on low-fat cold cuts instead of grains and vegetables and snacking on cholesterol-free cookies instead of fruit. We welcome artificial sweeteners and fake fats, even if they have unpleasant or unhealthy side effects. Olestra, the latest fake fat, not only removes some fat-soluble vitamins from the body, it also sometimes causes bloating, diarrhea, and cramping, as well as what is referred to as "rectal leakage."

Sometimes the ads themselves acknowledge the dangers of dieting. As is typical of advertising, however, the solution is not to stop the dangerous practice: The solution is another product. One ad for yogurt features a very young, very thin woman, and the headline "A body like this could be missing out on a lot." The ad acknowledges that the dieting required to keep this teenager so thin is robbing her body of necessary minerals and vitamins. Similarly, another ad reminds us that dieting damages skin tone. The solution, as always, is the product, a skin cream. Neither ad questions the practice of dieting.

An ad featuring a beautiful blonde says, "Christina is a 5'10", 125 lb. fashion model of Scandinavian heritage. Everyone thinks she has the most marvelous bone structure. She doesn't. She is on her way to osteoporosis." The copy continues, "Her cheekbones are to die for, but not her vertebrae. Too many diets and too little calcium have left her bone density below average. If she doesn't do something, she'll shrink. Her spine will compact. Her clothes won't fit. Looking up at the sky will be impossible." The solution to this impending catastrophe? Certainly

There are 3 billion women who don't look like supermodels and only 8 who do.

love your body   THE BODY SHOP

not for Christina to stop dieting. Rather, she simply should take calcium supplements. Maybe she should just buy a periscope so she can continue to see the sky.

Christina is five feet ten inches tall and weighs 125 pounds! She is a genetic freak. It's hard not to be a dieter when this is the ideal body type reflected throughout the media and the consequences for not having it are so extreme. Ninety-five percent of all women are excluded from this ideal, which is virtually unattainable by most women, yet it is *they* who feel abnormal and deviant. As an ad for the Body Shop, featuring a voluptuous Barbie-type doll, says, "There are 3 billion women who don't look like supermodels and only 8 who do." As a result, more than half the adult women in the United States are currently dieting, and over three-fourths of normal-weight American women think they are "too fat."

Certainly this delusion comes at least in part from the media images that surround us. Yesterday's sex symbols by today's standards would be considered fat: Betty Grable, Jane Russell, Marilyn Monroe—or just the pretty young woman on the beach featured on a cover of *Life* magazine in 1970. To be sure, there are some large women today, such as Rosie O'Donnell, the plus-size model Emme, and Delta Burke, who are very successful. However, it has been estimated that twenty years ago the average model weighed 8 percent less than the average woman; today she weighs 23 percent less.

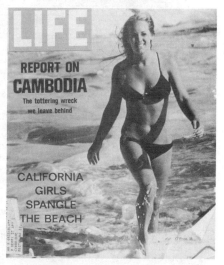

Ironically, what is considered sexy today is a look that almost totally suppresses female secondary sexual characteristics, such as large breasts and hips. Thinness is related to decreased fertility and sexuality in women. Indeed, many of the ultrathin models have ceased to menstruate. Chronic dieting is damaging to one's health and upsets the body's natural metabolism. In 1997 the drug combination of fenfluramine and phentermine, known as fen/phen, was pulled off the market by the FDA because of a high incidence of heart problems among patients who take it. Not surprisingly, research has also found that dieters often experience a temporary drop in mental abilities and thus have less energy to focus on tasks other than controlling their food.

Although the dangers of dieting are sometimes mentioned in women's maga-

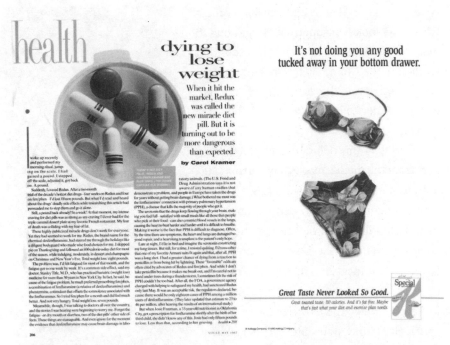

zines, the warning is certainly diminished, if not entirely negated, by the ads surrounding the articles. The May 1997 issue of *Vogue* contained an article about the dangers of diet pills called "Dying to Lose Weight." However, on the opposite page is an ad for Special K, a low-calorie cereal, featuring a tiny bikini and the tagline, "It's not doing you any good tucked away in your bottom drawer." To Kellogg's credit, it completely revamped the Special K campaign in 1998 and ran ads and commercials that explicitly challenged the emphasis on thinness and uniformity. The funniest was a commercial featuring several men sitting around talking about their bodies in the way that women often do— "Do these jeans make my butt look big?" and "I have to face it—I have my mother's thighs." The commercial made it obvious how absurd this kind of conversation is and how different are the cultural expectations for women and men. Unfortunately, commercials like this are very few and far between.

In addition to all the psychic and physical damage the diet products do, they don't even fulfill their purpose, at least not for long. Ninety-five percent of dieters are even fatter after five years of dieting than before they began. This information, if widely disseminated throughout the mass media, could be as damaging to corporate profits as is the information that cigarette smoking causes lung cancer. It is no surprise that, in both cases, there is widespread distortion and suppression of such information. Indeed, the only thing that could destroy the diet industry faster than the truth about the failure rates of diets would be a diet that did work.

A Weight Watchers ad features a Boston cream pie, oozing its creamy filling, and the caption, "Feel free to act on impulse." Why would Weight Watchers, of all companies, use such tempting images? Because it is, after all, in Weight Watchers' best interest for its customers to fail, to relapse, to have to return again and again. If people really lost weight and kept it off, Weight Watchers and other such programs would quickly go out of business.

Food ads are often funny, clever, highly entertaining. But food that is heavily advertised is seldom nourishing and rarely deeply satisfying. Often it is sold in a way that exploits and trivializes our very basic human need for love and connection. It is wonderful to celebrate food, to delight in it. Food can nourish us and bring us joy . . . but it cannot love us, it cannot fill us up emotionally. If we turn to food as a substitute for human connection, we turn away from that which could fill up the emptiness we sometimes feel inside—authentic, mutual, satisfying relationships with other human beings. And when people use food as a way to numb painful feelings, to cope with a sense of inner emptiness, and as a substitute for human relationships, for living fully, many of them end up with eating problems that can destroy them and that certainly, ironically, destroy any pleasure they might get from food.

"THE MORE YOU SUBTRACT, THE MORE YOU ADD"

Cutting Girls Down to Size

The more you subtract, the more you add.

A|X
ARMANI EXCHANGE
http://www.ArmaniExchange.com

WHEN I WAS SIXTEEN, LIKE ALMOST EVERYONE ELSE IN THE WORLD, I FELL wildly in love for the first time. My feelings were so intense that now, decades later, I still dream about him from time to time. He was good for me in every way, but I also began a sinister love affair around the same time, one that nearly consumed me—my love affair with alcohol and cigarettes. As adults in a toxic culture, some of us fall in love with cars or chocolate cake or, more dangerously, drugs. But, just as we are more vulnerable to the glory and heartbreak of romantic love than we will ever be again, at no time are we more vulnerable to the seductive power of advertising and of addiction than we are in adolescence.

Adolescents are new and inexperienced consumers—and such prime targets. They are in the process of learning their values and roles and developing their self-concepts. Most teenagers are sensitive to peer pressure and find it difficult to resist or even to question the dominant cultural messages perpetuated and reinforced by the media. Mass communication has made possible a kind of national peer pressure that erodes private and individual values and standards, as well as community values and standards. As Margaret Mead once said, today our children are not brought up by parents, they are brought up by the mass media.

Advertisers are aware of their role and do not hesitate to take advantage of the insecurities and anxieties of young people, usually in the guise of offering solutions. A cigarette provides a symbol of independence. A pair of designer jeans or sneakers convey status. The right perfume or beer resolves doubts about femininity or masculinity. All young people are vulnerable to these messages and adolescence is a difficult time for most people, perhaps especially these days. According to the Carnegie Corporation, "Nearly half of all American adolescents are at high or moderate risk of seriously damaging their life chances." But there is a particular kind of suffering in our culture that afflicts girls.

As most of us know so well by now, when a girl enters adolescence, she faces a series of losses—loss of self-confidence, loss of a sense of efficacy and ambition, and the loss of her "voice," the sense of being a unique and powerful self that she had in childhood. Girls who were active, confident, feisty at the ages of eight and nine and ten often become hesitant, insecure, self-doubting at eleven. Their self-esteem plummets. As Carol Gilligan, Mary Pipher and other social critics and psychologists have pointed out in recent years, adolescent girls in America are afflicted with a range of problems, including low self-esteem, eating disorders, binge drinking, date rape and other dating violence, teen pregnancy, and a rise in cigarette smoking. Teenage women today are engaging in far riskier health behavior in greater numbers than any prior generation.

The gap between boys and girls is closing, but this is not always for the best. According to a 1990 status report by a consortium of universities and research centers, girls have closed the gap with boys in math performance and are coming close in science. But they are also now smoking, drinking, and using drugs as often as boys their own age. And, although girls are not nearly as violent as boys, they are committing more crimes than ever before and are far more often physically attacking each other.

It is important to understand that these problems go way beyond individual psychological development and pathology. Even girls who are raised in loving homes by supportive parents grow up in a toxic cultural environment, at risk for self-mutilation, eating disorders, and addictions. The culture, both reflected and reinforced by advertising, urges girls to adopt a false self, to bury alive their real selves, to become "feminine," which means to be nice and kind and sweet, to compete with other girls for the attention of boys, and to value romantic relationships with boys above all else. Girls are put into a terrible double bind. They are supposed to repress their power, their anger, their exuberance and be simply "nice," although they also eventually must compete with men in the business world and be successful. They must be overtly sexy and attractive but essentially passive and virginal. It is not surprising that most girls experience this time as painful and confusing, especially if they are unconscious of these conflicting demands.

Of course, it is impossible to speak accurately of girls as a monolithic group. The socialization that emphasizes passivity and compliance does not apply to many African-American and Jewish girls, who are often encouraged to be assertive and outspoken, and working-class girls are usually not expected to be stars in the business world. Far from protecting these girls from eating disorders and other problems, these differences more often mean that the problems remain hidden or undiagnosed and the girls are even less likely to get help. Eating problems affect girls from African-American, Asian, Native American, Hispanic, and Latino families and from every socioeconomic background. The racism and classism that these girls experience exacerbate their problems. Sexism is by no means the only trauma they face.

We've learned a lot in recent years about the pressures on girls and the resulting problems. So much that some people think it is time to stop talking about it—maybe to focus on boys or just move on. It's important to remember that this discussion of the problems of adolescent girls is very recent. In 1980, not a single chapter in the *Handbook on Adolescent Psychology* was devoted to girls. As with other fields in psychology, the research was done on boys and assumed to apply to girls as well. The research on girls and the discussion of their issues is long overdue and far from complete.

Of course, we must continue to pay attention to the problems of boys, as well. Two books published recently address these problems. In *Raising Cain: Protecting the Emotional Life of Boys,* Daniel Kindlon and Michael Thompson examine the "culture of cruelty" that boys live in and the "tyranny of toughness" that oppresses them. In *Real Boys: Rescuing Our Sons from the Myths of Boyhood,* psychologist William Pollock examines the ways that boys manifest their social and emotional disconnection through anger and violence. We've seen the tragic results of this in the school shootings, all by angry and alienated boys.

The truth is that the problems of boys and girls are related, and not only because girls are often the victims of these angry, violent boys and the men they become. The "emotional illiteracy" of men, as Kindlon and Thompson call it, harms boys and girls, men and women. Most of us understand that the cultural environment plays a powerful role in creating these problems. But we still have a lot to learn about the precise nature of this role—and what we can do about it. How can we resist these destructive messages and images? The first step, as always, is to become as conscious of them as possible, to deconstruct them. Although I am very sympathetic to the harm done to boys by our cultural environment, the focus of my work has always been on girls and women.

Girls try to make sense of the contradictory expectations of themselves in a culture dominated by advertising. Advertising is one of the most potent messengers in a culture that can be toxic for girls' self-esteem. Indeed, if we looked only at advertising images, this would be a bleak world for females. Girls are extremely desirable to advertisers because they are new consumers, are beginning to have significant disposable income, and are developing brand loyalty that might last a lifetime. Teenage girls spend over $4 billion annually on cosmetics alone.

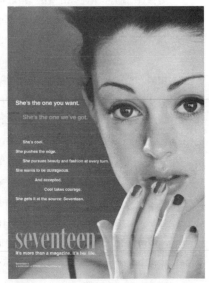

Seventeen, a magazine aimed at girls about twelve to fifteen, sells these girls to advertisers in an ad that says, "She's the one you want. She's the one we've got." The copy continues, "She pursues beauty and fashion at every turn" and concludes with, "It's more than a magazine. It's her life." In another similar ad, *Seventeen* refers to itself as a girl's "Bible." Many girls read magazines like this and take the advice seriously. Regardless of the intent of the advertisers, what are the messages that girls are getting? What are they told?

Primarily girls are told by advertisers that what is most important about them is their perfume, their clothing, their bodies, their beauty. Their "essence" is their underwear. "He says the first thing he noticed about you is your great personality," says an ad featuring a very young woman in tight jeans. The copy continues, "He lies." "If this is your idea of a great catch," says an ad for a cosmetic kit from a teen magazine featuring a cute boy, "this is your tackle box." Even very little girls are offered makeup and toys like Special Night Barbie, which shows them how to dress up for a night out. Girls of all ages get the message that they must be flawlessly beautiful and, above all these days, they must be thin.

Even more destructively, they get the message that this is possible, that, with enough effort and self-sacrifice, they can achieve this ideal. Thus many girls spend enormous amounts of time and energy attempting to achieve something that is not only trivial but also completely unattainable. The glossy images of flawlessly beautiful and extremely thin women that surround us would not have the impact they do if we did not live in a culture that encourages us to believe we can and should remake our bodies into perfect commodities. These images play into the American belief of transformation and ever-new possibilities, no longer via hard work but via the purchase of the right products. As Anne Becker has pointed out, this belief is by no means universal. People in many other cultures may admire a particular body shape without seeking to emulate it. In the Western world, however, "the anxiety of nonrecognition ('I don't fit in') faced by the majority of spectators is more often translated into identifications ('I want to be like that') and attempts at self-alteration than into rage."

Women are especially vulnerable because our bodies have been objectified and commodified for so long. And young women are the most vulnerable, especially those who have experienced early deprivation, sexual abuse, family violence, or other trauma. Cultivating a thinner body offers some hope of control and success to a young woman with a poor self-image and overwhelming personal problems that have no easy solutions.

Although troubled young women are especially vulnerable, these messages affect all girls. A researcher at Brigham and Women's Hospital in Boston found that the more frequently girls read magazines, the more likely they were to diet and to feel that magazines influence their ideal body shape. Nearly half reported wanting to lose weight because of a magazine picture (but only 29 percent were actually overweight). Studies at Stanford University and the University of Massachusetts found that about 70 percent of college women say they feel worse about their own looks after reading women's magazines. Another study, this one of 350 young men and women, found that a preoccupation with one's appearance takes a toll on mental health. Women scored much higher than men on what the researchers called "self-objectification." This tendency to view one's body from the outside in—regarding physical attractiveness, sex appeal, measurements, and weight as more central to one's physical identity than health, strength, energy level, coordination, or fitness—has many harmful effects, including diminished mental performance, increased feelings of shame and anxiety, depression, sexual dysfunction, and the development of eating disorders.

Why does body image matter?

These images of women seem to affect men most strikingly by influencing how they judge the real women in their lives. Male college students who viewed just one episode of *Charlie's Angels,* the hit television show of the 1970s that featured three beautiful women, were harsher in their evaluations of the attractiveness of potential dates than were males who had not seen the episode. In another study, male college students shown centerfolds from *Playboy* and *Penthouse* were more likely to find their own girlfriends less sexually attractive.

Adolescent girls are especially vulnerable to the obsession with thinness, for many reasons. One is the ominous peer pressure on young people. Adolescence is a time of such self-consciousness and terror of shame and humiliation. Boys are shamed for being too small, too "weak," too soft, too sensitive. And girls are shamed for being too sexual, too loud, too boisterous, too big (in any sense of the word), having too hearty an appetite. Many young women have told me that their boyfriends wanted them to lose weight. One said that her boyfriend had threatened to leave her if she didn't lose five pounds. "Why don't you leave him," I asked, "and lose 160?"

The situation is very different for men. The double standard is reflected in an ad for a low-fat pizza: "He eats a brownie . . . you eat a rice cake. He eats a

HE EATS A BROWNIE...YOU EAT A RICE CAKE.

HE EATS A JUICY BURGER...YOU EAT A LOW FAT ENTREE.

HE EATS PIZZA...**YOU** EAT PIZZA.

FINALLY, LIFE IS FAIR.

Now you can eat what you want to eat. Pizza that's loaded with real cheese. A killer sauce. And 90% fat free. Tombstone Light Pizza. Finally.

juicy burger . . . you eat a low fat entree. He eats pizza . . . you eat pizza. Finally, life is fair." Although some men develop eating problems, the predominant cultural message remains that a hearty appetite and a large size is desirable in a man, but not so in a woman.

Indeed, a 1997 television campaign targets ravenous teenage boys by offering Taco Bell as the remedy for hunger (and also linking eating with sex via the slogan "Want some?"). One commercial features a fat guy who loses his composure when he realizes his refrigerator is empty. In another, two quite heavy guys have dozed off in front of a television set and are awakened by hunger pangs, which only Taco Bell can satisfy. It is impossible to imagine this campaign aimed at teenage girls.

Normal physiological changes during adolescence result in increased body fat for women. If these normal changes are considered undesirable by the culture (and by parents and peers), this can lead to chronic anxiety and concern about weight control in young women. A ten-year-old girl wrote to New Moon, a feminist magazine for girls, "I was at the beach and was in my bathing suit. I have kind of fat legs, and my uncle told me I had fat legs in front of all my cousins and my cousins' friends. I was so embarrassed, I went up to my room and shut the door. When I went downstairs again, everyone started teasing me." Young women are even encouraged to worry about small fluctuations in their weight. "Sometimes what you wear to dinner may depend on what you eat for breakfast," says an ad for cereal that pictures a slinky black dress. In truth, daily and weekly and monthly fluctuations in weight are perfectly normal.

The obsession starts early. Some studies have found that from 40 to 80 percent of fourth-grade girls are dieting. Today at least one-third of twelve- to thirteen-year-old girls are actively trying to lose weight, by dieting, vomiting, using laxatives, or taking diet pills. One survey found that 63 percent of high-school girls were on diets, compared with only 16 percent of men. And a survey in Massachusetts found that the single largest group of high-school students considering or attempting suicide are girls who feel they are overweight. Imagine. Girls made to feel so terrible about themselves that they would rather be dead than fat. This wouldn't be happening, of course, if it weren't for our last "socially acceptable" prejudice—weightism. Fat children are ostracized and ridiculed from the moment they enter school, and fat adults, women in particular, are subjected to public contempt and scorn. This strikes terror into the hearts of all women, many of whom, unfortunately, identify with the oppressor and become vicious to themselves and each other.

No wonder it is hard to find a woman, especially a young woman, in America today who has a truly healthy attitude toward her body and toward food. Just as the disease of alcoholism is the extreme end of a continuum that includes a wide range of alcohol use and abuse, so are bulimia and anorexia the extreme results of an obsession with eating and weight control that grips many young women with serious and potentially very dangerous results. Although eating problems are often thought to result from vanity, the truth is that they, like other addictions and compulsive behavior, usually have deeper roots—not only genetic predisposition and biochemical vulnerabilities, but also childhood sexual abuse.

Advertising doesn't cause eating problems, of course, any more than it causes alcoholism. Anorexia in particular is a disease with a complicated etiology, and media images probably don't play a major role. However, these images certainly contribute to the body-hatred so many young women feel and to some of the resulting eating problems, which range from bulimia to compulsive overeating to simply being obsessed with controlling one's appetite. Advertising does promote abusive and abnormal attitudes about eating, drinking, and thinness. It thus provides fertile soil for these obsessions to take root in and creates a climate of denial in which these diseases flourish.

The influence of the media is strikingly illustrated in a recent study that found a sharp rise in eating disorders among young women in Fiji soon after the introduction of television to the culture. Before television was available, there was little talk of dieting in Fiji. "You've gained weight" was a traditional compliment and "going thin" the sign of a problem. In 1995 television came to the island. Within three years, the number of teenagers at risk for eating disorders more than doubled, 74 percent of the teens in the study said they felt "too big or too fat," and 62 percent said they had dieted in the past month. Of course, this doesn't prove a direct causal link between television and eating disorders. Fiji is a culture in transition in many ways. However, it seems more than coincidental that the Fiji girls who were heavy viewers of television were 50 percent more likely to describe themselves as fat and 30 percent more likely to diet than those girls who watched television less frequently. As Ellen Goodman says, "The big success story of our entertainment industry is our ability to export insecurity: We can make any woman anywhere feel perfectly rotten about her shape."

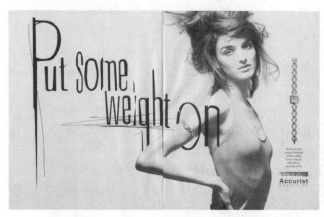

Being obsessed about one's weight is made to seem normal and even appealing in ads for unrelated products, such as a scotch ad that features a very thin and pretty young woman looking in a mirror while her boyfriend observes her. The copy, addressed to him, says, "Listen, if you can handle 'Honey, do I look fat?' you can handle this." These two are so intimate that she can share her deepest fears with him—and he can respond by chuckling at her adorable vulnerability and knocking back another scotch. And everyone who sees the ad gets the message that it is perfectly normal for all young women, including thin and attractive ones, to worry about their weight.

"Put some weight on," says a British ad featuring an extremely thin young woman—but the ad is referring to her watch. She is so thin she can wear the watch on her upper arm—and this is supposed to be a good thing.

Not all of this is intentional on the part of the advertisers, of course. A great deal of it *is* based on research and *is* intended to arouse anxiety and affect women's self-esteem. But some of it reflects the unconscious attitudes and beliefs of the individual advertisers, as well as what Carl Jung referred to as the "collective unconscious." Advertisers are members of the culture too and have been as thoroughly conditioned as anyone else. The magazines and the ads deliberately *create* and intensify anxiety about weight because it is so profitable. On a deeper level, however, they *reflect* cultural concerns and conflicts about women's power. Real freedom for women would change the very basis of our male-dominated society. It is not surprising that many men (and women, to be sure) fear this.

"The more you subtract, the more you add," says an ad that ran in several women's and teen magazines in 1997. Surprisingly, it is an ad for clothing, not for a diet product. Overtly, it is a statement about minimalism in fashion. However, the fact that the girl in the ad is very young and very thin reinforces another message, a message that an adolescent girl constantly gets from advertising and throughout the popular culture, the message that she should diminish herself, she should be *less* than she is.

On the most obvious and familiar level, this refers to her body. However, the loss, the subtraction, the cutting down to size also refers to her sense of her self, her sexuality, her need for authentic connection, and her longing for power and freedom. I certainly don't think that the creators of this particular ad had all this in mind. They're simply selling expensive clothing in an unoriginal way, by using a very young and very thin woman—and an unfortunate tagline. It wouldn't be important at all were there not so many other ads that reinforce this message and did it not coincide with a cultural crisis taking place now for adolescent girls.

"We cut Judy down to size," says an ad for a health club. "Soon, you'll both be taking up less space," says an ad for a collapsible treadmill, referring both to the product and to the young woman exercising on it. *The obsession with thinness is most deeply about cutting girls and women down to size.* It is only a symbol, albeit a very powerful and destructive one, of tremendous fear of female power. Powerful women are seen by many people (women as well as men) as inherently destructive and dangerous. Some argue that it is men's awareness of just how powerful women can be that has created the attempts to keep women small. Indeed, thinness as an ideal has always accompanied periods of greater freedom for women—as soon as we got the vote, boyish flapper bodies came into vogue. No wonder there is such pressure on young women today to be thin, to shrink, to be like little girls, not to take up too much space, literally or figuratively.

At the same time there is relentless pressure on women to be small, there is also pressure on us to succeed, to achieve, to "have it all." We can be successful as long as we stay "feminine" (i.e., powerless enough not to be truly threatening). One way to do this is to present an image of fragility, to look like a waif. This demonstrates that one is both in control and still very "feminine." One of the many double binds tormenting young women today is the need to be both sophisticated and accomplished, yet also delicate and childlike. Again, this applies mostly to middle- to upper-class white women.

The changing roles and greater opportunities for women promised by the women's movement are trivialized, reduced to the private search for the slimmest body. In one commercial, three skinny young women dance and sing about the "taste of freedom." They are feeling free because they can now eat bread, thanks to a low-calorie version. A commercial for a fast-food chain features a very slim young woman who announces, "I have a license to eat." The salad bar and lighter fare have given her freedom to eat (as if eating for women were a privilege rather than a need). "Free yourself," says ad after ad for diet products.

You can never be too rich or too thin, girls are told. This mass delusion sells a lot of products. It also causes enormous suffering, involving girls in false quests for power and control, while deflecting attention and energy from that which might really empower them. "A declaration of independence," proclaims an ad for perfume that features an emaciated model, but in fact the quest for a body as thin as the model's becomes a prison for many women and girls.

The quest for independence can be a problem too if it leads girls to deny the importance of and need for interpersonal relationships. Girls and young women today are encouraged by the culture to achieve a very "masculine" kind of autonomy and independence, one that excludes interdependence, mutuality, and connection with others. Catherine Steiner-Adair suggests that perhaps eating disorders emerge at adolescence because it is at this point that "females experience themselves to be at a crossroads in their lives where they must shift from a relational approach to life to an autonomous one, a shift that can represent an intolerable loss when independence is associated with isolation." In this sense, she sees eating disorders as political statements, a kind of hunger strike: "Girls with eating disorders have a heightened, albeit confused, grasp of the dangerous imbalance of the culture's values, which they cannot articulate in the face of the culture's abject denial of their adolescent intuitive truth, so they tell their story with their bodies."

Most of us know by now about the damage done to girls by the tyranny of the ideal image, weightism, and the obsession with thinness. But girls get other messages too that "cut them down to size" more subtly. In ad after ad girls are urged to be "barely there"—beautiful but silent. Of course, girls are not just influenced by images of other girls. They are even more powerfully attuned to images of women, because they learn from these images what is expected of them, what they are to become. And they see these images again and again in the magazines they read, even those magazines designed for teenagers, and in the commercials they watch.

"Make a statement without saying a word," says an ad for perfume. And indeed this is one of the primary messages of the culture to adolescent girls. "The silence of a look can reveal more than words," says another perfume ad, this one featuring a woman lying on her back. "More than words can say," says yet another perfume ad, and a clothing ad says, "Classic is speaking your mind (without saying a word)." An ad for lipstick says, "Watch your mouth, young lady," while one for nail polish says, "Let your fingers do the talking," and one for hairspray

promises "hair that speaks volumes." In another ad, a young woman's turtleneck is pulled over her mouth. And an ad for a movie soundtrack features a chilling image of a young woman with her lips sewn together.

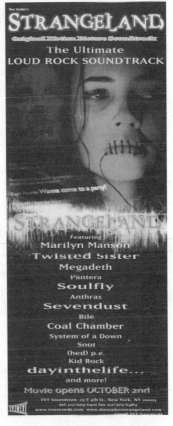

It is not only the girls themselves who see these images, of course. Their parents and teachers and doctors see them and they influence their sense of how girls should be. A 1999 study done at the University of Michigan found that, beginning in preschool, girls are told to be quiet much more often than boys. Although boys were much noisier than girls, the girls were told to speak softly or to use a "nicer" voice about three times more often. Girls were encouraged to be quiet, small, and physically constrained. The researcher concluded that one of the consequences of this socialization is that girls grow into women afraid to speak up for themselves or to use their voices to protect themselves from a variety of dangers.

A television commercial features a very young woman lying on a bed, giggling, silly. Suddenly a male

hand comes forward. His finger touches her lips and she becomes silent, her face blank. Another commercial features a very young woman, shot in black and white but with colored contact lenses. She never speaks but she touches her face and her hair as a female voiceover says, "Your eyes don't just see, they also speak.... Your eyes can say a lot, but they don't have to shout. They can speak softly. Let your eyes be heard ... without making a sound." The commercial ends with the young woman putting her finger in her mouth.

"Score high on nonverbal skills," says a clothing ad featuring a young African-American woman, while an ad for mascara tells young women to "make up your own language." And an Italian ad features a very thin young woman in an elegant coat sitting on a window seat. The copy says, "This woman is silent. This coat talks." Girls, seeing these images of women, are encouraged to be silent, mysterious, not to talk too much or too loudly. In many different ways, they are told "the more you subtract, the more you add." In this kind of climate, a Buffalo jeans ad featuring a young woman screaming, "I don't have to scream for attention but I do," can seem like an improvement—until we notice that she's really getting attention by unbuttoning her blouse to her navel. This is typical of the mixed messages so many ads and other forms of the media give girls. The young woman seems fierce and powerful, but she's really exposed, vulnerable.

The January 1998 cover of *Seventeen* highlights an article, "Do you talk too much?" On the back cover is an ad for Express mascara, which promises "high voltage volume instantly!" As if the way that girls can express themselves and turn up the volume is via their mascara. Is this harmless wordplay, or is it a sophisticated and clever marketing ploy based on research about the silencing of girls, deliberately designed to attract them with the promise of at least some form of self-

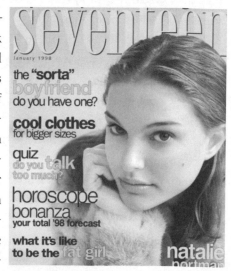

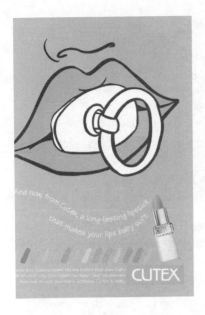

expression? Advertisers certainly spend a lot of money on psychological research and focus groups. I would expect these groups to reveal, among other things, that teenage girls are angry but reticent. Certainly the cumulative effect of these images and words urging girls to express themselves only through their bodies and through products is serious and harmful.

Many ads feature girls and young women in very passive poses, limp, doll-like, sometimes acting like little girls, playing with dolls and wearing bows in their hair. One ad uses a pacifier to sell lipstick and another the image of a baby to sell BabyDoll Blush Highlight. "Lolita seems to be a comeback kid," says a fashion layout featuring a woman wearing a ridiculous hairstyle and a baby-doll dress, standing with shoulders slumped and feet apart. In women's and teen magazines it is virtually impossible to tell the fashion layouts from the ads. Indeed, they exist to support each other.

As Erving Goffman pointed out in *Gender Advertisements*, we learn a great deal about the disparate power of males and females simply through the body language and poses of advertising. Women, especially young women, are generally subservient to men in ads, through both size and position. Sometimes it is as blatant as the woman serving as a footrest in the ad for Think Skateboards.

Other times, it is more subtle but quite striking (once one becomes aware of it). The double-paged spread for Calvin Klein's clothing for kids conveys a world of information about the relative power of boys and girls. One of the boys seems

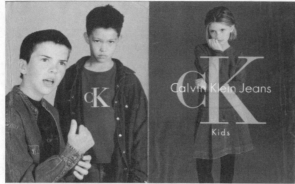

to be in the act of speaking, expressing himself, while the girl has her hand over her mouth. Boys are generally shown in ads as active, rambunctious, while girls are more often passive and focused on their appearance. The exception to the rule involves African-American children, male and female, who are often shown in advertising as passive observers of their white playmates.

That these stereotypes continue, in spite of all the recent focus on the harm done to girls by enforced passivity, is evident in the most casual glance at parents' magazines. In the ads in the March 1999 issues of *Child* and *Parents,* all of the boys are active and all of the girls are passive. In *Child,* a boy plays on the jungle gym in one ad, while in another, a girl stands quietly, looking down, holding some flowers. In *Parents,* a boy rides a bike, full of excitement, while a girl is happy about having put on lipstick. It's hard to believe that this is 1999 and not 1959. The more things change, the more they stay the same.

Girls are often shown as playful clowns in ads, perpetuating the attitude that girls and women are childish and cannot be taken seriously, whereas even very young men are generally portrayed as secure, powerful, and serious. People in control of their lives stand upright, alert, and ready to meet the world. In contrast, females often appear off-balance, insecure, and weak. Often our body parts are bent, conveying unpreparedness, submissiveness, and appeasement. We exhibit

what Goffman terms "licensed withdrawal"—seeming to be psychologically removed, disoriented, defenseless, spaced out.

Females touch people and things delicately, we caress, whereas males grip, clench, and grasp. We cover our faces with our hair or our hands, conveying shame or embarrassment. And, no matter what happens, we keep on smiling.

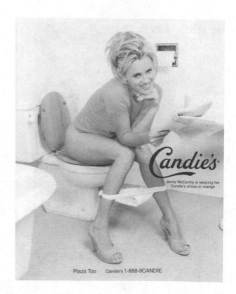

"Just smiling the bothers away," as one ad says. This ad is particularly disturbing because the model is a young African-American woman, a member of a group that has long been encouraged to just keep smiling, no matter what. She's even wearing a kerchief, like Aunt Jemima. The cultural fear of angry women is intensified dramatically when the women are African-American.

An extreme example of the shaming and trivialization of girls and women is a recent little trend of ads featuring young women sitting on the toilet, such as the shoe ad with popular MTV star Jenny McCarthy (although the ad offended a lot

of people, it also boosted sales of Candies shoes by 19 percent). Unfortunately, this phenomenon is not restricted to the United States. An Italian ad for sneakers and a British one for a magazine use the same image. Such pictures are especially humiliating to self-conscious teenagers.

Girls and young women are often presented as blank and fragile. Floating in space, adrift in a snowstorm. A Valentino clothing ad perhaps unwittingly illustrates the tragedy of adolescence for girls. It features a very young woman with her head seemingly enclosed in a glass bubble labeled "Love." Some ads and fashion layouts picture girls as mermaids or underwater as if they were drowning—or lying on the ground as if washed up to shore, such as the Versace makeup ad picturing a young girl caught up in fishing nets, rope, and seashells. An ad for vodka features a woman in the water and the copy, "In a past life I was a mermaid who fell in love with an ancient mariner. I pulled him into the sea to be my husband. I didn't know he couldn't breathe underwater." Of course, she can't breathe underwater either.

Breathe underwater. As girls come of age sexually, the culture gives them impossibly contradictory messages. As the *Seventeen* ad says, "She wants to be outrageous. And accepted." Advertising slogans such as "because innocence is sexier than you think," "Purity, yes. Innocence never," and "nothing so sensual was ever so innocent" place them in a double bind. "Only something so pure could inspire such unspeakable passion," declares an ad for Jovan musk that features a white flower. Somehow girls are supposed to be both innocent and seductive, virginal and experienced, all at the same time. As they quickly learn, this is tricky.

Females have long been divided into virgins and whores, of course. What is new is that girls are now supposed to embody both within themselves. This is symbolic of the central contradiction of the culture—we must work hard and pro-

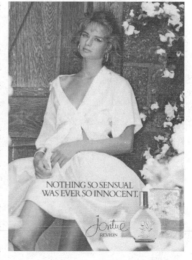

duce and achieve success and yet, at the same time, we are encouraged to live impulsively, spend a lot of money, and be constantly and immediately gratified. This tension is reflected in our attitudes toward many things, including sex and eating. Girls are promised fulfillment both through being thin and through eating rich foods, just as they are promised fulfillment through being innocent and virginal and through wild and impulsive sex.

Young people, boys and girls, are surrounded by messages urging them to be sexually active. Teachers report a steady escalation

YOU CAN LEARN MORE ABOUT
ANATOMY AFTER SCHOOL.

of sex talk among children, starting in *preschool,* as our children are prematurely exposed to a barrage of sexual information and misinformation through advertising, television shows, music, and films. "You can learn more about anatomy after school," says an ad for jeans, which manages to trivialize sex, relationships, and education all in one sentence.

The consequences of all this sexual pressure on children are frightening. The average age of first sexual intercourse is about sixteen for girls and fifteen for boys. Far more disturbing is the fact that seven in ten girls who had sex before the age of fourteen and six in ten of those who had sex before the age of fifteen report having sex involuntarily. One of every ten girls under the age of twenty becomes pregnant in the United States each year, more than in any other industrialized country in the world: twice as high as in England and Wales, France and Canada, and nine times as high as in the Netherlands or Japan. And as many as one in six sexually active adolescents has a sexually transmitted disease.

Of course, advertising and the media are not solely to blame for these appalling statistics. But they are the leading source of sex education in the nation

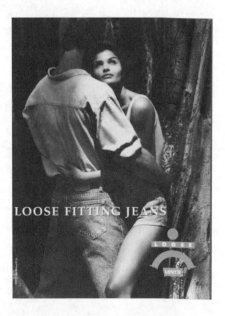

LOOSE FITTING JEANS

and they create a climate which encourages a very cavalier attitude toward sex. The typical teenage viewer who watches an average of three to five hours of television a day sees a minimum of two thousand sexual acts per year on television alone. There is also abundant sexual activity, of course, in music videos, books, movies, cartoons, video games, and song lyrics aimed at teenagers, almost all of it portraying sexual behavior as consequence-free and much of it

Wayne Maser/Visages

exploiting women's bodies and glamorizing sexual violence. Magazines targeting girls and young women are filled with ads and articles on how to be beautiful and sexy and appealing to boys—all in service of the advertisers, of course, who sell their wares on almost every page. "How Smart Girls Flirt," "Sex to Write Home About," "15 Ways Sex Makes You Prettier," and "Are You Good in Bed?" are some of the cover stories for a teen magazine called *Jane*.

At the same time, there is rarely any accurate information about sex (the networks still refuse to run condom ads) and certainly never any emphasis on relationships or intimacy (there is hardly time in thirty seconds for the sexual encounter, let alone any development of character!). We have to fight to get sex education into our schools, and the government refuses to fund any program that doesn't insist on abstinence as the only choice suitable for young people (how quickly people forget their own adolescence). Young people learn in school and in church that sex can hurt or kill them, but not that it can bring pleasure, joy, and connection. How can they learn to say "Yes!" in a loving and responsible way?

It is difficult to do the kind of research that would prove the effects of the media on sexual attitudes and behavior—because of the perceived sensitivity of sex as a topic and because of the difficulty in finding a comparison group. However, the few existing studies consistently point to a relationship between exposure to sexual content and sexual beliefs, attitudes, and behavior. Two studies have found correlations between watching higher doses of "sexy" television and early initiation of sexual intercourse, and studies of adolescents have found that heavy television viewing is predictive of negative attitudes toward virginity. In general, key communication theories and years of research on other kinds of communications effects, such as the effect of violent images, suggest that we are indeed affected by the ubiquitous, graphic, and consequence-free depictions of sexual behavior that surround us in all forms of the mass media.

Jane Brown and her colleagues concluded from their years of research that the mass media are important sex educators for American teenagers. Other potential educators, such as parents, schools, and churches, are doing an inadequate job, and even if that were to change dramatically, the media would remain compelling teachers. Brown faults media portrayals for avoiding the "three C's"—commitment, contraceptives, and consequences—and concludes, "It is little wonder that adolescents find the sexual world a difficult and often confusing place and that they engage in early and unprotected sexual intercourse with multiple partners."

The emphasis for girls and women is always on being desirable, not on experiencing desire. Girls who want to be sexually *active* instead of simply being the objects of male desire are given only one model to follow, that of exploitive male sexuality. It seems that advertisers can't conceive of a kind of power that isn't manipulative and exploitive or a way that women can be actively sexual without being like traditional men.

Women who are "powerful" in advertising are uncommitted. They treat men like sex objects: "If I want a man to see my bra, I take him home," says an androgynous young woman. They are elusive and distant: "She is the first woman who refused to take your phone calls," says one ad. As if it were a good thing to be rude and inconsiderate. Why should any of us, male or female, be interested in someone who won't take our phone calls, who either cares so little for us or is so manipulative?

Mostly though, girls are not supposed to have sexual agency. They are supposed to be passive, swept away, overpowered. "See where it takes you," says a perfume ad featuring a couple passionately embracing. "Unleash your fantasies," says another. "A force of nature." This contributes to the strange and damaging concept of the "good girl" as the one who is swept away, unprepared for sex, versus the "bad girl" as the one who plans for sex, uses contraception, and is generally responsible. A young woman can manage to have sex and yet in some sense maintain her virginity by being "out of control," drunk, or deep in denial about the entire experience.

No wonder most teenage pregnancies occur when one or both parties is drunk. Alcohol and other mind-altering drugs permit sexual activity at the same time that they allow denial. One is almost literally not there. The next day one has an excuse. I was drunk, I was swept away. I did not choose this experience.

In adolescence girls are told that they have to give up much of what they *know* about relationships and intimacy if they want to attract men. Most tragically, they are told they have to give up each other. The truth is that one of the most powerful antidotes to destructive cultural messages is close and supportive female friendships. But girls are often encouraged by the culture to sacrifice their relationships with each other and to enter into hostile competi-

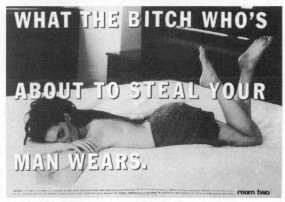

tion for the attention of boys and men. "What the bitch who's about to steal your man wears," says one ad. And many ads feature young women fighting or glaring at each other.

Of course, some girls do resist and rebel. Some are encouraged (by someone—a loving parent, a supportive teacher) to see the cultural contradictions clearly and to break free in a healthy and positive way. Others rebel in ways that damage themselves. A young woman seems to have only two choices: She can bury her sexual self, be a "good girl," give in to what Carol Gilligan terms "the tyranny of nice and kind" (and numb the pain by overeating or starving or cutting herself or drinking heavily). Or she can become a rebel—flaunt her sexuality, seduce inappropriate partners, smoke, drink flamboyantly, use other drugs. Both of these responses are self-destructive, but they begin as an attempt to survive, not to self-destruct.

Many girls become women who split themselves in two and do both—have a double life, a secret life—a good girl in public, out of control in private. A feminist in public, involved in an abusive relationship or lost in sadomasochistic fantasies in private. A lawyer by day, a barfly by night. Raiding the refrigerator or drinking themselves into a stupor alone in their kitchens at night, after the children are in bed, the laundry done. Doing well in school, but smoking in order to have a sexier, cooler image. Being sexual only when drunk.

There are few healthy alternatives for girls who want to truly rebel against restrictive gender roles and stereotypes. The recent emphasis on girl power has led to some real advances for girls and young women, especially in the arenas of music and sports. But it is as often co-opted and trivialized. The Indigo Girls are good and true, but it is the Spice Girls who rule. Magazines like *New Moon, Hues,* and *Teen Voices* offer a real alternative to the glitzy, boy-crazy, appearance-obsessed teen magazines on the newsstands, but they have to struggle for funds since they take no advertising. There are some good zines and Websites for girls on the Internet but there are also countless sites that degrade and endanger them. And Barbie continues to rake in two billion dollars a year and will soon have a postal stamp in her honor—while a doll called "Happy to be me," similar to Barbie but much more realistic and down to earth, was available for a couple of years in the mid-1990s (I bought one for my daughter) and then vanished from sight. Of course, Barbie's makers have succumbed to pressure somewhat and have remade her with a thicker waist, smaller breasts, and slimmer hips. As a result, according to Anthony Cortese, she has already lost her waitressing job at Hooter's and her boyfriend Ken has told her that he wants to start seeing other dolls.

Girls who want to escape the stereotypes are viewed with glee by advertisers, who rush to offer them, as always, power via products. The emphasis in the ads is always on their sexuality, which is exploited to sell them makeup and clothes and shoes. "Lil' Kim is wearing lunch box in black," says a shoe ad featur-

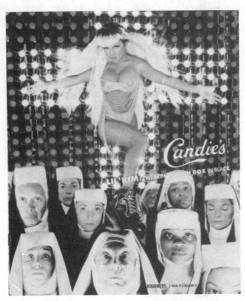

ing a bikini-clad young woman in a platinum wig stepping over a group of nuns—the ultimate bad girl, I guess, but also the ultimate sex object. A demon woman sells a perfume called Hypnotic Poison. A trio of extremely thin African-American women brandish hair appliances and products as if they were weapons—and the brand is 911. A cosmetics company has a line of products called "Bad Gal." In one ad, eyeliner is shown in cartoon version as a girl, who is holding a dog saying, "grrrr," surely a reference to "grrrrls," a symbol these days of "girl power" (as in

cybergrrrl.com, the popular Website for girls and young women). Unfortunately, girl power doesn't mean much if girls don't have the tools to achieve it. Without reproductive freedom and freedom from violence, girl power is nothing but a marketing slogan.

So, for all the attention paid to girls in recent years, what girls are offered mostly by the popular culture is a superficial toughness, an "attitude," exemplified by smoking, drinking, and engaging in casual sex—all behaviors that harm themselves. In 1990 Virginia Slims offered girls a T-shirt that said, "Sugar and spice and everything nice? Get real." In 1997 Winston used the same theme in an ad featuring a tough young woman shooting pool and saying, "I'm not all sugar & spice. And neither are my smokes." As if the alternative to the feminine stereotype was sarcasm and toughness, and as if smoking was somehow an expression of one's authentic self ("get real").

Of course, the readers and viewers of these ads don't take them literally. But we do take them in—another grain of sand in a slowly accumulating and vast sandpile. If we entirely enter the world of ads, imagine them to be real for a moment, we find that the sandpile has completely closed us in, and there's only one escape route—buy something. "Get the power," says an ad featuring a woman showing off her biceps. "The power to clean anything," the ad continues. "Hey girls, you've got the power of control" says an ad for . . . hairspray. "The possibilities are endless" (clothing). "Never lose control" (hairspray again). "You never had this much control when you were on your own" (hair gel). "Exceptional character" (a watch). "An enlightening experience" (face powder). "Inner strength" (vitamins). "Only Victoria's Secret could make control so sensual" (girdles). "Stronger longer" (shampoo). Of course, the empowerment, the enlightenment, is as impossible to get through products as is anything else—love, security, romance, passion. On one level, we know this. On another, we keep buying and hoping—and buying.

Other ads go further and offer products as a way to rebel, to be a real individual. "Live outside the lines," says a clothing ad featuring a young woman walk-

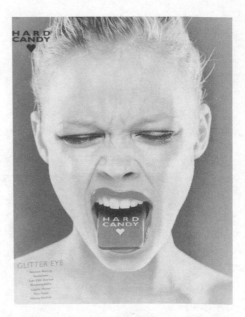

ing out of a men's room. This kind of rebellion isn't going to rock the world. And, no surprise, the young woman is very thin and conventionally pretty. Another pretty young woman sells a brand of jeans called "Revolt." "Don't just change . . . revolt," says the copy, but the young woman is passive, slight, her eyes averted.

"Think for yourself," says yet another hollow-cheeked young woman, demonstrating her individuality via an expensive and fashionable sweater. "Be amazing" (cosmetics). "Inside every woman is a star" (clothing). "If you're going to create electricity, use it" (watches). "If you let your spirit out, where would it go" (perfume). These women are all perfect examples of conventional "femininity," as is the young woman in a Halston perfume ad that says, "And when she was bad she wore Halston." What kind of "bad" is this?

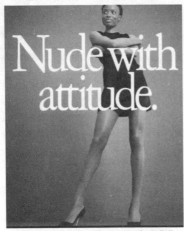

Wear nothing on your legs but sheer, luxurious silkiness. Very see through. Very subtle. Very Hanes.

HANES SILK REFLECTIONS® SHEER.

"Nude with attitude" feature an African-American woman in a powerful pose, completely undercut by the brevity of her dress and the focus on her long legs. Her "attitude" is nothing to fear—she's just another sex object. Good thing, given the fear many people have of powerful African-American women.

The British ad "For girls with plenty of balls" is insulting in ways too numerous to count, beginning with the equation of strength and courage and fiery passion with testicles. What this ad offers girls is body lotion.

Some ads do feature women who seem really angry and rebellious, but the final message is always the same. "Today, I indulge my dark side," says an ad featuring a fierce young woman tearing at what seems to be a net. "Got a problem with that?" The slogan is "be extraordinary not ordinary." The product that promises to free this girl from the net that imprisons her? Black nail polish.

Nail polish. Such a trivial solution to such an enormous dilemma. But such triviality and superficiality is common in advertising. How could it be otherwise? The solution to any problem always has to be a product. Change, transformation, is thus inevitably shallow and moronic, rather than meaningful and transcendent. These days, self-improvement seems to have more to do with calories than with character, with abdomens than with absolutes, with nail polish than with ethics.

It has not always been so. Joan Jacobs Brumberg describes this vividly in *The Body Project: An Intimate History of American Girls:*

When girls in the nineteenth century thought about ways to improve themselves, they almost always focused on their internal character and how it was reflected in outward behavior. In 1892, the personal agenda of an adolescent diarist read: "Resolved, not to talk about myself or feelings. To think before speaking. To work seriously. . . . To be dignified. Interest myself more in others."

A century later, in the 1990s, American girls think very differently. In a New Year's resolution written in 1982, a girl wrote: "I will try to make myself better in every way I possibly can with the help of my budget and baby-sitting money. I will lose weight, get new lenses, already got new haircut, good makeup, new clothes and accessories."

Not that girls didn't have plenty of problems in the nineteenth century. But surely by now we should have come much further. This relentless trivialization of a girl's hopes and dreams, her expectations for herself, cuts to the quick of her soul. Just as she is entering womanhood, eager to spread her wings, to become truly sexually *active,* empowered, independent—the culture moves in to *cut her down to size.*

Black nail polish isn't going to help. But it probably won't hurt either. What hurts are some of the other products offered to girls as a way to rebel and to cope—especially our deadliest drugs, alcohol and nicotine. These drugs are cynically and deliberately offered by advertisers to girls as a way to numb the pain of disconnection, to maintain the illusion of some kind of relationship, to be more appealing to men, to be both "liberated" and "feminine," and, perhaps most tragically, to subvert their rebellious spirits, the very spark within that could, if not co-opted, empower them to change their lives.

7

"FORGET THE RULES! ENJOY THE WINE"

Alcohol and Rebellion

THE NUMBER-ONE ILLEGAL DRUG IN AMERICA IS . . . BEER. BECAUSE BEER IS the drug of choice for young people. Although we hear a lot about marijuana, cocaine, and heroin, the truth is our children are at much greater risk from alcohol than from these other drugs. A 1999 study found that almost 8 percent of nine-year-olds are already drinking beer. Fifteen percent of eighth-graders and 30 percent of twelfth-graders are binge drinkers, which means they've had five or more drinks at one sitting within the past two weeks. In college, the percentage of binge drinkers rises to 45 percent.

What are the risks of this drinking? One risk is death. Alcohol is the leading killer of young people in America—because it is a major factor in the three main causes of death for people between the ages of fifteen and twenty-four, which are automobile crashes, homicide, and suicide. Alcohol is also linked with over half of all violent crimes, domestic violence, rape, and child abuse.

Another risk is addiction. The younger people are when they start to drink, the greater the risk of addiction, by far. People who start drinking by the age of fifteen are four times more likely to become addicted than those who wait until they are twenty-one. According to Dr. Bernadine Healey, "Exposure of the adolescent brain to alcohol appears to predispose a person to alcohol abuse and alcoholism in later life." Now this is bad news for most of us, but it's good news for the alcohol industry. Just as the tobacco industry and the food industry depend on addicts for their profits, so does the alcohol industry.

Ten percent of drinkers consume over 60 percent of all the alcohol sold. At least one in ten drinkers is an alcoholic. You don't have to be a mathematical genius to figure out that the alcoholic is the alcohol industry's best customer. Although the industry says it wants people to drink "responsibly," the truth is that so-called responsible drinking would put it out of business. As August Busch III, the CEO of Anheuser Busch, said in the company's annual report, "Every action taken by your company's management is guided by one overriding objective—enhancing shareholder value." In plain language, this means to sell as much beer as possible. Of course, this is true for any business—but when the product is alcohol, there are often tragic consequences.

If alcoholics were to stop drinking entirely, the industry would lose over half its profits. In fact, if every adult American drank at the "safe" level according to federal guidelines, which is no more than one drink a day for a woman and two drinks a day for a man, alcohol industry sales would be cut by about 80 percent. As one researcher said, "Though problem-free drinking does exist for great numbers of people, it is at such picayune levels that it would sustain only a fraction of the present alcoholic beverage industry."

It is not only alcoholics who are doing the heavy drinking—and causing the resulting problems. Thomas Greenfield of the Alcohol Research Group pooled extensive data from the United States and Canada that provided a disturbing picture of the drinking practices of young adults. Overall, the data show that 43 percent of all alcohol consumed is consumed hazardously (defined, as is binge drinking, as five or more drinks in a single sitting). However, among young adults (defined as from eighteen to thirty-nine), nearly 80 percent is consumed hazardously. Some of these people are alcoholics, of course, but many are not. Indeed it is the heavy drinkers who are not alcoholic who cause the most problems in the society, simply because there are so many more of them.

Obviously, the young people who are consuming five or more drinks in a sitting (and often causing terrible problems for themselves and the people around them) are extremely desirable to the alcohol industry. The ones who are or become alcoholic are even more desirable. The top 2.5 percent of drinkers average nine drinks a day and consume a third of all alcohol sold. Sixty-three percent of this group is eighteen to twenty-nine years old (although they make up just 27 percent of the total population). Just as the tobacco industry needs to get kids addicted in order to be sure of a fresh supply of addicts, so does the alcohol industry. Sometimes these industries are one and the same. Philip Morris, maker of Virginia Slims and Marlboros, also owns Miller beer, the number-two beer in the country. Both the alcohol and tobacco industries are in the business of recruiting new users. Of course, this means targeting children. Hook them early and they are yours for life. These young people spend a lot of money in the present on alcohol too: According to the U.S. Department of Health and Human Services, junior and senior high-school students drink over a billion cans of beer a year, spending almost $500 million.

This drink has been rated for mature audiences only.

Dewar's

What's the best way to appeal to young people? One way, of course, is to present the product as strictly for adults—as in the so-called moderation messages of the alcohol and tobacco industries. Don't drink or smoke, they say—that's for *grown-ups* (a great way to make sure kids *never* touch the stuff!). Another ploy is to use cute little animals and cartoon characters—like Spuds MacKenzie and the Budweiser frogs, lizards, and dalmatians.

Joe Camel has been sent out to pasture, but Budweiser's lethal creatures are still very much with us. Children also find these advertising icons on shirts, hats, mugs, stuffed animals, and other paraphernalia.

Budweiser, the King of Drugs, is the most widely used and widely advertised beer by far. Anheuser-Busch, the largest brewer in the world and the maker of Budweiser, supplies almost one-fourth of all the alcohol that Americans consume and spends over a quarter of a billion dollars a year on advertising and promotion. Of course, they deny that this advertising attracts young people. According to one vice-president, "We do not target our advertising toward young people. Period." A look at some of their ads reveals a different story.

Anheuser-Busch has used many different animals in its campaigns over the years, beginning with Clydesdale horses. As one Anheuser-Busch marketing executive said, "Fifty years ago, Clydesdales were just horses. Now it is impossible for people to see them and not think of Budweiser." The horses have been followed by ants, alligators, penguins, frogs, lizards, and the bull terrier Spuds MacKenzie. These images are especially alluring to children, because most children have a special affinity with animals. They have *relationships* with creatures, becoming deeply attached to stuffed animals and cartoon characters as well as to real ones.

The Budweiser frogs are especially appealing to children. Introduced during the 1995 Super Bowl to an audience of more than 40 million viewers, a fair share of whom were under the legal drinking age, this campaign featured three frogs chirping Bud-weis-er. One critic described it as "nothing but a phonics lesson for five-year-olds." The frogs have been criticized by a slew of consumer advocate groups and health associations such as the American Academy of Pediatrics and the American Public Health Association, which claim the ads deliberately target children and are the alcohol industry's version of Joe Camel. Frank and Louie, the sardonic lizards who have taken over the frogs' job, have also taken over their number-one spot in children's hearts and minds.

Anheuser-Busch also designs products with special appeal to children. According to *Supermarket News*, longneck bottles of Bud Ice and Bud Ice Light will

soon be coming with Bud Icicles, colored flavors to be added to the beer. The flavors, clearly intended for grown-ups, include Dooby-Dooby Doo, Kiss My Ice, and Loose Juice. Maybe next Bud will have Barney, dancing and singing, "I love you, you love me, grab a Bud and let's party."

Of course, Bud is not alone. Most brewers target young people. A 1994 Coors promotion featured people dressed as beer cans dancing in public places and liquor stores. They seemed to be as appealing to children as Mickey Mouse at Disneyland. As one liquor store owner said, "The dancing can from Coors was one of the best [point-of-sale materials], little kids were dragging their parents into the store to see it." An ad placed by Coors in a trade publication said, "Not since disco has there been so much money to be made in shaking cans."

All the major brewers have been involved in the campaign to turn Halloween into what a Coors executive calls "a beer-guzzling holiday." "Miller Thriller," says one ad, featuring an assortment of monsters offering beer cans. "I want your Bud," says a vampire in a Budweiser ad. According to a Coors' marketing executive, "We invented Halloween and we intend to keep it."

Do these ads affect children? Children certainly notice them: the Budweiser frog campaign is the most popular of all among children over the age of six—more popular than commercials for McDonald's, Pepsi, or Nike. According to a

1996 survey by the Center on Alcohol Advertising, almost as many children between the ages of nine and eleven know that frogs say "Budweiser" (73 percent) as know that Bugs Bunny says "What's up, Doc?" (80 percent). Laurie Leiber, the center's director, said, "After a single year of advertising, the Budweiser frogs have assumed a friendly place in our children's psyches between Bugs Bunny and Smokey the Bear."

A survey of eight- to twelve-year-olds in Washington, D.C., found that students could name more brands of beer than they could U.S. presidents. And a 1998 study, conducted by the ad agency Campbell Mithun Esty, found that most children liked the Budweiser lizard ads better than ads for Barbie (of course, this might not be such a bad thing). The advertising industry claims that the appeal of these ads to children is unintentional. As Bob Garfield, ad reviewer for *Advertising Age*, says, "Advertising is not a rifle; it is a shotgun, and any campaign featuring outdoor boards of a cartoon animal inevitably will catch children in its spray." In a different column, however, Garfield also acknowledges that a cartoon is "all it takes to be irresistible to children."

I don't think the alcohol industry wants little children to drink. However, they do want them to have positive associations with alcohol, and with specific brands of alcohol, long before they start to drink. This is a basic function of advertising. A 1919 article in *Printer's Ink,* an advertising industry publication, makes this explicit: "It requires much brain work and close study to advertise to children in the best way to sell them things that childhood craves, such as toys, but this is nothing compared to the selling of products they cannot have until they are grown up—to make boys and girls want things now they couldn't have and shouldn't have for five, ten or twenty years. Some advertisers see little sense in spending money advertising 'grown-up goods' to children; many, however, have found out the wisdom and profit in doing it." Using the example of automobile advertising, the article stresses the importance of getting a particular brand name to replace the general category of "automobile" early in a child's life. If the advertiser waits until the child has grown up, it is too late: "The waxlike mind would be crisscrossed by other names; the soil would have other seeds beside his and it would be a continual struggle for supremacy. First impressions are strong—which is particularly true of advertised goods." Many years later, an editorial in *Advertising Age* reached the same conclusion: "Quite clearly, the company that has not bothered to create a favorable attitude toward its product *before* the potential customer goes shopping hasn't much of a chance of snaring the bulk of potential buyers."

Could this be any less true for alcohol than for other products? After all, the average age at which American children start to drink these days is twelve. It's almost never too soon to reach them. It's an investment in the future. As one marketing executive said about the importance of developing brand loyalty in a college student, "If he turns out to be a big drinker, the beer company has bought itself an annuity."

Although it is difficult, if not impossible, to measure the exact influence of advertising, various research studies have shown that alcohol advertising shapes young adolescents' attitudes and intentions about alcohol and creates an unconscious presumption in favor of drinking. This unconscious presumption is extremely important. According to the *Seventh Special Report to the U.S. Congress on Alcohol and Health,* "People can acquire expectancies about alcohol long before they take their first drink and these early expectancies are strong predictors of drinking behavior in adolescence as well as of alcohol dependence in adulthood." Although behavior reflecting the impact of alcohol advertising may not occur for months or years after exposure, it is obviously very important for the alcohol industry to get 'em while they're young.

So the brewers broadcast their ads on cable television during youth viewing hours, and on shows such as *Beavis and Butthead,* whose audiences are predominantly underage. Despite their denials, leading brewers have run commercials on MTV during time periods when half or more of the audience was below the legal drinking age. Both Budweiser and Miller, along with makers of distilled spirits, sponsor the "extreme" sports that especially appeal to young people, such as snowboarding, mountain biking, and in-line skating, and sell sports paraphernalia with the brand logo through marketing campaigns like Budweiser's "Buy the Beer, Get the Gear." According to a Jose Cuervo tequila spokesperson, "It's essential to our brand image to sponsor the boldest, most surprising stuff because our audience is young and rebellious and that's how they know us."

The alcohol industry also reaches young people via magazines such as *Spin* and *Allure,* with almost half of their readers under twenty-one, and via flashy Websites on the Internet. In 1998 the Center for Media Education found that 82 percent of beer Websites and 72 percent of distilled spirits sites used techniques that are particularly attractive to underage audiences (compared with only 10 percent of wine sites). At Absolutvodka.com, Web surfers are greeted by a drum-beating rhythm. As they move their cursors, video clips featuring trendy rock bands appear and the sound level booms. At the site for Captain Morgan's rum, visitors can watch a comedy show. Cuervo tequila offers a cartoon rodent starring in an animated game, while the Miller beer site offers a monthly magazine focused on fashion, music, and sports. These sites are often called up by searches for "games," "entertainment," "music," "contests," and "Halloween." Children trying to learn more about "frogs" on the Internet could conceivably find themselves at the Budweiser site, where animated frogs like to "hang on the beach with a hot babe, a cold Bud and . . . the Kama Sutra."

In recent years the alcohol industry has developed several new products that seem expressly designed for young people. This trend began with the introduction in 1984 of wine coolers—very sweet, carbonated wine drinks that were marketed as if they were soft drinks. They are often positioned as alternatives to nonalcoholic beverages rather than as alternatives to other forms of alcohol. As one wine cooler ad said, "Sick of soft drinks? Here's Thirst Aid." Unlike beer and hard liquor, one doesn't have to develop a taste for them. According to *Advertising Age*, "One might say that this product, due to its sweet, cold and refreshing nature, appeals to the 'Pepsi generation.' " Wine coolers quickly became an over $2-billion-a-year industry. Junior and senior high-school students drink over 35 percent of all the wine coolers sold in the United States.

This success led to products targeting kids that mixed alcohol with ice cream, milk, Jell-O, popsicles, and punch, among other things. This marketing strategy began in Britain, where alcoholic "soft drinks" called Hooper's Hooch Alcoholic Lemonade, Cola Lips Alcoholic Cola, and Mrs. Pucker's Alcoholic Orangeade have found great success with young people. In 1995 the Royal College of Physicians issued a report condemning this "cynical marketing ploy to encourage young people to drink" and calling alcohol "ten times more dangerous to the health of young people than illicit drugs."

It didn't take long for the United States and other countries to catch up. "The hottest new drink trend," proclaims an ad in a trade publication for Slushies, drinks that mix alcohol and fruit slush. Tumblers is a twenty-four-proof version of Jell-O shots and Tooters are thirty-proof, neon-colored shots packaged together in test tubes. And tequila aficionados can buy lollipops complete with real worms inside. In 1996 T.G.I. Friday's, the restaurant chain, introduced small bottles of drinks made by Heublein containing 15 to 20 percent alcohol, with cartoons on the label and names such as Butter Ball, Oatmeal Cookie, and Lemon Drop. The chain claimed these products were aimed at men over thirty. In the beginning, advertising was limited to in-store displays and samples passed out at rock concerts.

Blenders, an ice cream product laced with alcohol and liqueurs sold in little cups for ninety-nine cents, is referred to by its makers as an "adult dessert." Flavors include Strawberry Shortcake, Chocolate Monkey, and Rootbeer Float. The label features the silhouette of a small child with a line drawn through it, which certainly should keep kids away. A full-page ad for Tattoo, by Jim Beam Brands, offers "the new shot sensation that leaves more than a great taste in

your mouth." The product, which is 30 percent alcohol, comes in three flavors—lemon, berry, and red licorice—and colors the drinker's tongue. Promotional merchandise includes T-shirts and temporary tattoos.

Moo and Super Milch are flavored milk drinks with an alcohol content of 5 percent, sold in supermarkets as well as in liquor stores. Liquor Pops, a popsicle with an alcohol content of 6 percent, went on sale in Australia early in 1999, in spite of protests from parent and church groups. And Australian company Candyco is test-marketing a product called Candy Shots, a 28 percent alcohol vodka-based drink that comes in flavors like banana, marshmallow, chocolate, and caramel. The drink's advertising poster depicts a bottle filled with candy. The alcohol industry sometimes refers to such products as "entry-level" drinks.

The distilled spirits industry wants its share of the youth market too, of course, but it has a hard time competing with the beer industry. One of its ploys is to offer hard liquor as the grown-up drink, what one "graduates" to after one's childish beer-drinking days. "You thought girls were yucky once too," says an ad for Dewar's scotch. Of course, most boys become interested in girls long before they reach the legal drinking age. "Your taste in music isn't

the only thing changing," says another ad in this campaign, featuring a photo of a heavy metal musician guaranteed to get the attention of very young men. Another ad offers the scotch in more explicit competition with beer, with a photo of an attractive young couple and the headline, "Now that you understand splitting a 6-pack under the bleachers is no longer considered a date."

Other distilled spirits ads also use images that will catch the attention of young people, such as a Captain Morgan rum ad featuring a cartoon pirate and young people with bright red beards and mustaches sketched on their faces. Peachtree suggests that their liqueur "jazzes ginger ale" and Bacardi promises to "spice things up around here" by replacing the predictable beer.

In addition to targeting young people in general, the alcohol industry also specifically targets young members of minority groups. A Budweiser ad features a man with "k.o.b," standing for King of Beers, designed on his head in the style often favored by young African-Americans. These young men are especially targeted by the makers of malt liquor, which is usually promoted in a forty-ounce size with the promise of a higher alcohol content and thus more bang for the

buck. Rapper King Tee sings in one commercial, "I usually drink it when I'm out just clowning, me and the home boys, you know, be like downing it . . . I grab me a forty when I want to act a fool." Phat Boy, a malt liquor sold in forty-ounce bottles, is advertised to young urban African-American men with the slogan, "The new malt liquor with an attitude."

In 1997 protests by public health advocates led McKenzie River, makers of St. Ides, to discontinue their latest product, Special Brew Freeze and Squeeze, a frozen fruit-flavored drink with 6 percent alcohol content, meant to be placed in supermarket freezers next to ice cream and popsicles, predominantly in African-American urban communities—where alcohol abuse is the leading health and safety problem. Although African-Americans drink less per capita than whites, poverty and poor health contribute to disproportionately high rates of alcohol-related disease.

The alcohol industry is also very interested in college students, who tend to drink more than their peers who don't go to college. For decades alcohol has been wreaking havoc on college campuses, with little attention paid. When I started lecturing on alcohol advertising on college campuses in the 1970s, the brewers ruled. Budweiser, Miller, and Coors had booths at all the conferences attended by college students and gave out free beer and posters. At one convention I attended, young women in short shorts roller-skated through the convention hall, offering free beer to students. I was on one campus where the administration sponsored a chug-a-lug contest and on several where the only beverage available at the reception following my lecture was alcohol.

Many ads and posters, especially those for Spring Break, quite explicitly promoted binge drinking and outrageous behavior. "The elephant is now wild on campus," said a malt liquor ad, while a poster for Stroh's beer depicted a goofy-looking guy stacking beer cans while saying to his mother on the phone, "Yeah, Mom. . . . I'm studying all about the pyramids." "Freshmen wait for the weekend to have a Michelob," said another beer ad. "Seniors know better." The truth is that seniors drink less than freshmen, because heavy drinking is a behavior one tends to outgrow (unless one is addicted, of course).

Even as late as 1989, Miller inserted into college newspapers, throughout the country, a sixteen-page "comic-book" about the adventures of a college student on spring break named Van Go-Go. From early in the morning until late at night, Van Go-Go drank beer, partied, and "scammed babes." Many students, upset by this campaign because of the exploitation of women and because it was so moronic, protested, and Miller eventually withdrew the campaign and apologized. However, it is clear that Miller wanted college students to think of Van Go-Go's drinking as normal.

"Yeah mom...I'm studying all about the pyramids!"

Stroh's

In fact, he was drinking in a very high-risk way and was likely to die from acute alcohol poisoning . . . but, on the other hand, he was spending a fortune on beer.

College students spend $4 billion a year on alcohol, more money than they spend on books. And they drink more than their noncollege peers. No wonder they are so attractive to alcohol advertisers. And no wonder drinking causes so many problems for them. Over half of all cases of violent crime, including rape, on college campuses are alcohol related, as is almost all of the vandalism. Almost all of these crimes are committed by men. The young women who are drinking heavily are more likely to be the victims of assault and to harm themselves. Of students in college in America today, the same percentage will eventually die from alcohol-related causes as will get advanced degrees.

According to Henry Wechsler of the Harvard School of Public Health, although fewer college students are consuming alcohol, those who do drink are consuming more than ever before. In his 1997 study he found that the percentage of students who reported drinking to "get drunk" had increased from 39.4 percent in 1993 to 52.3 percent. Increased drunkenness leads to more problems, of course, both for the drinkers and for those around them.

Binge drinking on college campuses has been front-page news recently, in the wake of several tragic deaths. The coverage began with the death of Scott Krueger, an MIT student who died after having twenty-four drinks in one night as part of a fraternity hazing. Five students died on the morning of their graduation from the University of North Carolina, where students partied with deadly amounts of alcohol. Virginia Tech's Mindy Somers fell out of a dormitory window while intoxicated, and Leslie Baltz, a University of Virginia senior, died after falling down a flight of stairs. Bradley McCue, a junior at Michigan State University, celebrated his twenty-first birthday by drinking twenty-four shots in ninety minutes and died later that night. In February of 1999, Nicholas Armstrong was beaten to death while he slept off a bender in his fraternity house. Jeremiah Wilkerson, the young man responsible, shot himself, apparently as soon as he sobered up and realized what he had done.

In 1988, after football star Don Rogers and college basketball sensation Len Bias died within a week of each other from cocaine overdoses, the president of the United States declared "war" on illegal drugs and Congress soon agreed to a $1 billion media blitz commanded by a retired general, drug czar Barry McCaffrey. There were at least thirty-four alcohol-related deaths on college campuses in 1998, which only hints at the number of students injured, assaulted, or raped be-

cause they or someone else drank too much. But the government didn't declare war on booze. Instead, the secretary of health and human services asked colleges to adopt voluntary restrictions on alcohol advertising.

Because of increasing scrutiny and the change in the drinking age from eighteen to twenty-one, the alcohol industry has become more subtle in its direct targeting of college students. But their clever, youth-oriented commercials and promotions still reach college students, of course, who often decorate their dorms and fraternity houses with Absolut ads and beer posters. And local bars promote heavy drinking through ads in student newspapers saying such things as "Why wet your whistle when you can drown it?" and offering "Chug-a-mug $1.25 liter drafts!" "$1 Kamikazes all night long," and "Bucket o'liquor $3!"

The brewers also have a lock on sports and on the music that appeals to young people. They sponsor rock concerts and have popular musicians play in their commercials. This can be ironic when the musicians get sober. Eric Clapton is a recovering alcoholic, who once said, "Alcoholism stunted my growth, both musically and in a human way. My ability to deal with close relationships is severely limited by the fact that I spent all my formative years completely anesthetized." But far more young people will have seen Clapton in the Michelob commercials than will ever see that quotation.

Until quite recently, most of the heavy drinking done on college campuses and elsewhere was done by men. But young women are catching up—with tragic consequences. Adolescent females are significantly more at risk for becoming dependent on alcohol than are women in any other age group. This, of course, makes them important targets for alcohol advertisers. In the early 1960s about 7 percent of the new female users of alcohol were between the ages of ten and fourteen. By the early 1990s, the figure had increased to 31 percent.

Young women are drinking more heavily than ever before and are suffering terrible consequences. Females have less gastric alcohol dehydrogenase, an enzyme that digests alcohol in the stomach, than males do, so alcohol passes more quickly into the bloodstream. Thus females tend to get drunk faster, become addicted more quickly, and develop diseases related to alcohol abuse sooner than males. In addition to sharing the risks of addiction and early death with men, young women who drink heavily are more likely than their nondrinking counterparts to be the victims of rape and sexual assault and to have unwanted pregnancies. Those who become alcoholic are far more stigmatized than their male counterparts.

There is great debate about whether alcoholics share any personality traits. Most knowledgeable people think they don't. However, some research indicates that the personality traits that influence high-risk drinking choices that can lead to alcoholism include gregariousness, impulsiveness, and rebelliousness. Certainly the advertisers, who spend billions of dollars on psychological research to identify their best customers and who understand alcoholics very well, appeal to these traits again and again in their advertising. Rebelliousness, more than any other trait, shows up in both the research and the ads. It is also, of course, a trait associated with adolescence—however, with very different parameters and consequences for females than for males.

Alcohol advertisers must walk a fine line. They want to appeal to our idealized images of ourselves, especially when we are young, as courageous rebels and free spirits, so they create ads such as the one for rum which features some half-dressed people on a tropical beach and the copy, "THERE'S A PART OF YOUR BRAIN that thinks clothes are overrated and loves to beat on drums and is not afraid of the IRS. . . . It relaxes with a cool Mount Gay on the rocks." Beneath the name of the rum is the slogan "The Primitive Spirit Refined."

The primitive spirit. Cuervo Gold uses the slogan "Untamed Spirit" and calls itself "the only shot guaranteed to release your inner lizard." I guess your inner lizard is presumed to be friendly. And a new beer called Bad Frog, introduced in 1998, features on the label, and in its advertising campaign, a frog raising its middle finger, with accompanying slogans such as "He just don't care" and "An amphibian with an attitude."

But the advertisers have to avoid the dark side of rebelliousness, the aspects that are antisocial, even criminal, and that most of us know are dreadfully linked with alcohol. We must see ourselves as independent and successful individuals, never as isolated losers. This is especially true for men, who are far more likely than women to become involved in violent crime when drunk (women are more likely to be victimized). According to the Justice Department, alcohol is a factor in nearly 40 percent of violent crimes.

The crimes committed when alcohol is involved are often especially heinous. The young men who beat Matthew Shepard to death were homophobic, to be sure, but they were also extremely drunk, as were the racist thugs who dragged James Byrd to his death behind their pickup truck. Alcohol is by no means the cause of these atrocities, just as it is not the cause of rape and battering, but it is often gasoline on the fire of racism, sexism, and homophobia, as well as a convenient excuse for the perpetrators of such violence (in their own minds, as well as to the world).

In order to appeal to rebellious young people, especially young men, alcohol advertisers must link their product with defiance and assertiveness, but they must avoid reminding us of the link between alcohol and criminal violence. So they joke about aggression, as in a Southern Comfort ad featuring a tough guy sitting on a porch holding his pet alligator and the tagline "Next door they used to have a poodle." According to the slogan, "Southerners have their own rules." They create ads, such as one featuring a handsome scowling man on a motorcycle above the caption "A little uncivilized." And they also put subtle pressure on the media not to make the links between alcohol and violent crime or to report that the majority of our nation's prisoners are alcoholic or very heavy drinkers. A little uncivilized, indeed.

Sometimes violence is overtly portrayed in alcohol ads, as in the "Absolut Psycho" ad—but again in a way that is meant to be funny, just another ultra-hip cultural reference from Absolut, not a reminder that a woman was brutally stabbed to death in the shower in the film *Psycho*.

The only exception to this silence in advertising on the subject of alcohol and criminality that I've ever seen is a Coors Light commercial that features prisoners on a chain gang. An old man says, as images of mountains and a beautiful woman go by, "I've seen a place they call the Rockies, a place covered in snow as pure as the song of an angel. I've seen a place where the mountains rise up and call to you, 'Run free and far.' " There is a pause and then one of the other prisoners says, "Tell us again, old man." Given that alcohol and other drugs are involved in over half of all crimes, the chances are great that alcohol brought many of these prisoners to the chain gang, but they are still deluding themselves that it is a route to freedom.

A campaign for Molson Ice Beer walks the fine line between wildness and antisocial behavior. In one commercial, a wolf howls and a man's voice says, "Tonight feels kind of weird, but it's a good weird. I can feel it in my bones. This is not going to be your run-of-the-mill, laundry-doing, pizza-eating kind of night. I will not be exercising tonight or philosophizing or organizing. Tonight I'm going to look for women who look like trouble and I'm going to flirt with them heavily, because tonight I'm not just drinking beer—I'm gulping life. I'm going to eat the night alive. What are you going to do?"

In another commercial in the same campaign, the man says, "I've got a plan for tonight and the plan is to have no plan at all. Maybe I'll send my left brain on vacation for a while and maybe I'll let my soul be the boss. Maybe I'll go to a party uninvited." Of course, men who go out at night with no plans and crash parties often are not so welcome.

This promise that alcohol will liberate our wild selves is especially seductive for women. The definition of a "good girl" is so narrow, so repressive, so completely asexual and passive, no wonder so many would opt to be "bad" instead.

But the social sanctions against "bad girls" remain terrifying. For all the talk about liberation and equality, overtly sexual women are still called tramps and sluts. This is especially true if they drink. So the wildness portrayed in the ads is attenuated. Men are going to "eat the night alive"—in a Zima ad, women are advised to "Laugh at inappropriate times." Another ad in the same Zima campaign suggests that women "spend time with people you actually like." This would be a daring act only for someone who was suffering from terminal niceness. "Forget the rules! Enjoy the wine," says an ad featuring a young woman kicking up her heels. But it turns out the only rule she's breaking is about the correct wine to drink with certain foods.

Throughout advertising and the popular culture we get the message that rebellious men are sexy and desirable, but rebellious women are not. Although it is fine for women to be feisty in a cute, spunky way, it is not at all fine for a woman to truly break the rules. She can pierce her tongue or her navel, but God forbid that she stops shaving her legs. She can smoke cigars or get a little high, but heaven help her if she becomes an alcoholic.

Indeed the first word most people think of when they hear the phrase "alcoholic woman" is "promiscuous." The truth is that alcoholic women are not especially promiscuous. They are, however, very likely to have been the victims of sexual violence, both as children and adults. The alcoholic woman, acting in the very same way as the alcoholic man, is despised. I once heard a man, at a support group for alcoholics, talk about being very drunk and waking up in a motel with two women he didn't know. The crowd laughed. Imagine the reaction if a woman told a story of waking up with two male strangers.

I often do an exercise in my workshops and seminars in which I call out the words "alcoholic woman" and ask people to respond spontaneously, to free-associate. I write the words on a blackboard. Always they are the same. Promiscuous, loose, tramp, slut, dirty, irresponsible, bad mother, pig, worthless. I ask the audience to choose the ones that apply only to women and they boil down to two descriptions: promiscuous and bad mother. As Marian Sandmaier says in her groundbreaking book *The Invisible Alcoholics,* these are the two worst things a woman can be accused of—to be indiscriminately sexual and to stop caring for men and children. The culture demonizes such women—alcoholics, prostitutes and now "welfare mothers." They are the witches of our time, and their fate is a warning to the rest of us.

In ad after ad, film after film, alcohol (and cigarettes) are used as shorthand to convey to men that a woman is loose, wild, sexy. An ad for E-Z rolling papers features a sultry woman with a drink in one hand and a cigarette in the other. "The lady's E-Z," the headline says. "Two strikes against her," says an ad for vitamins, which features a woman smoking and drinking.

However, these ads are for products other than alcohol and cigarettes. Alcohol advertisers have to be more careful. They want to attract men to the promise of seduction and sexual adventure and attract women to the promise of release

from inhibitions and societal restraints without frightening women or portraying them as sluts. They often portray women as sexual and untamed but not too wild.

Slogans aimed at men, such as "The party animal" and "Be off the wall" are considered too raw and crude for women. Indeed it is hard to imagine an alcohol advertiser advising a woman to "be off the wall." And I'd be stunned by a commercial that portrayed a woman going out into the night with no plans, perhaps crashing a party or flirting heavily with men who looked like trouble. If she did, the culture tells us she'd be asking for whatever happened to her. Rather, a woman looks out seductively, holding a glass of cognac, and says, "But Santa, naughty *is* nice." This reminds me of the Mayflower Madam's comment, when she was arrested for running a high-class prostitution service, "I wasn't bad. I was naughty."

An ad featuring a beautiful Nordic woman says, "If Inge Nielsen were a drink, she'd be Akvavit." The copy continues, "Don't let that innocent look deceive you. There's passion close to the surface; a hint of spice and mystery; a breath-taking zest and liveliness." Aha . . . she's not bad, she's lively. "If you never tried one, it would be a sin," claims an ad for a drink called a "Black Angel." It continues, "Being good has never been so easy. . . . But remember to take it easy; you wouldn't want to lose your halo."

A 1999 television commercial for Finlandia vodka directed by Spike Lee conveys a very similar message. The spot features a confessional scene. A hot-blooded temptress confesses her sins, one of which is drinking vodka. The priest remarks that even he sometimes drinks vodka. The woman asks which vodka. When he names Finlandia, the sinner reveals herself as an angel and says, "My Child, that is not a sin."

"A new way to gin" is the slogan for Tanqueray Malacca Gin in an ad featur-

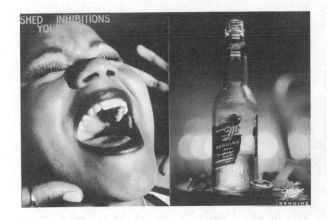

ing two sexy African-American women, described in the copy as "divine ladies." And the woman in another ad who is slipping her phone number into a man's pants isn't a slut, she's simply "Mist behavin'." Drinking will liberate your wild, sexual self, these ads imply, but you'll still be a good girl, even a "divine lady."

It's no coincidence these women are African-American. "Shed your inhibitions," shouts another African-American woman in a beer ad. I doubt advertisers would ever use a white woman in quite this way. As we all know,

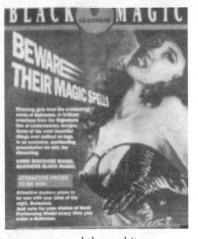

one stereotype of African-Americans is that they are more sexual than whites, so the image is more "acceptable." In fact, it probably suggests to white women (and men) that the drink can give them the legendary sexual prowess of African-Americans.

When women in alcohol ads are portrayed as dangerous, it is because they are witches or sorceresses, not because they are really threatening. "Beware their magic spells," says a Guinness poster in Malaysia, featuring a very voluptuous woman. "Make heavy objects fly across the room. Men," says a liqueur ad that portrays a wild eye and the slogan "Princess of Darkness." And a beautiful dark-haired woman stares out from a Pernod ad above the slogan "Dangerously Delicious."

A Strega (Italian for "witch") liqueur campaign features a beautiful woman with a black panther on her lap and the slogan "Spend some time with a Little

VAMP IT!

Witch tonight." Yet another ad features a woman as a vampire, but it is clear from her dress and her pose that it is not a man's blood that she is likely to suck.

All of these ads, of course, target and appeal to grown women, and men too, but they are also inevitably irresistible to many girls, who long to have this kind of sexual power and sophistication and who are trying desperately to conform to the cultural mandate that they be both sensual and innocent, experienced and virginal (a trick requiring magic, if ever there was one). They know it is good to be considered a little wild and sexy, in a cute and impish way, but unspeakably terrible to really cross the line. They see all the time what happens to the girls who are labeled sluts, the girls who are raped, the girls whom even other girls viciously turn on.

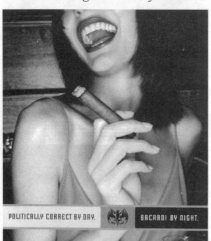

POLITICALLY CORRECT BY DAY.   BACARDI BY NIGHT.

A Bacardi rum campaign promises them that they can have it all: They can be "Banker by day. Bacardi by night" as one ad says, featuring the torso of a young woman with a pierced navel. Another ad in the campaign features a young woman smoking a cigar and laughing uproariously, with the tagline "Politically correct by day. Bacardi by night." This ad accomplishes many things for Bacardi. It trivializes the terrible health consequences of smoking and drinking for women by describing the opposition as mere political correctness. It promises young women that alcohol will liberate them, especially sexually (the woman is wearing a very low-cut red dress, after all). And it encourages and normalizes personality change via drinking, one of the symptoms of alcoholism.

The alcohol industry, like the tobacco industry, has been targeting women with the theme of liberation for many years. An ad in the mid-1970s featured a beautiful but tough-looking woman seemingly alone in a bar or restaurant and the copy, "Isn't it time you knew an exciting drink to order?—instead of taking a man's suggestion." Around the same time, Chivas Regal ran an ad with a woman's beautifully manicured hand reaching for the bottle on the shelf and the copy, "Now that you're bringing home the bacon, don't forget the Chivas." More recently, Miller ran a series of ads featuring women rodeo riders and the headline "American Rodeo Riders and Their Beer." And a campaign for rum featured women in nontraditional athletic gear and the slogan "Break tradition."

More often these days, the woman is liberated but adorable, girlish, not tough like many of the women in cigarette ads. A 1997 Miller beer commercial features a closeup of a dartboard and, one after another, three darts hitting the center to increasing gasps from the unseen audience. Then there's a giggle and a female voice says, "I swear I've never played this before." It is understood that she is in the bar, she's drinking beer, she's even winning at darts. She can do anything a man can do . . . but she's cute, unthreatening. "Rivals by day, Bacardi by night," says yet another ad in the Bacardi campaign. In this one, a woman wearing a very low-cut red dress, her breasts exposed, is pulling on a laughing man's tie. Again, she may be trying to compete with him by day—but at night she's just another sex object.

Heavy drinking is seen by the culture as something that makes both men and women more masculine. Therefore, it is considered somewhat desirable for men but repellent for women. A man who drinks heavily is often lionized, considered more virile. He is seen as someone "larger than life," with hearty appetites, robust and vigorous. This creates a further challenge for advertisers who wish to target women. They can and do offer alcohol to men as a way to be more manly ("Not every man can handle Metaxa," says one ad), but they can't suggest that drinking heavily will make women more feminine.

However, they can imply that drinking will give a woman some of men's power and privilege without detracting from her femininity. Thus they often use male symbols, such as cigars, in alcohol ads but only in the hands of stereotypically feminine and beautiful women. A recent campaign for Jim Beam bourbon advises women (and occasionally men) to "Get in touch with your masculine side." In one of these ads a woman smokes a cigar, in another she flicks a lighter, and in a third she stands by a refrigerator and drinks milk from the carton. The ads work only because all of the woman are conventionally beautiful, usually wearing lots of lipstick and dark nail polish. Imagine if they were butch instead of femme.

Expect the Best...

Drink the Finest.

TEQUILA
CAZADORES.
100% Blue Agave

In a Cazadores tequila ad, in addition to the cigar, the woman seems to be wearing a man's shirt . . . but it is way too big for her and is sexily slipping off her shoulders. She's playing with symbols of power, but they don't really fit her. Not to worry!

In a Remy Martin cognac ad, the woman seems to be releasing fiery sexual passion via her cigar. The figure in the fire looks like a centaur, holding a spear. The woman's short hair and broad shoulders contribute to an impression of strength and masculinity, but her heavy makeup and slinky dress contradict this. This ad evokes a more complicated reaction than the others, however, partly because this person could in fact be a man.

Alcohol advertisers sometimes use transsexuals in their ads—or men made up to look like women. The waterskier in a Smirnoff ad is a well-known British transsexual. Perhaps advertisers do this not only because these people are beautiful, but because it adds to the sense of androgyny, the promise of liberation and power, and the spice of rebellion. And because it is trendy these days, in certain circles, to be cool about bisexuality, transvestism, and transsexualism. Indeed the famous transvestite RuPaul is a popular model.

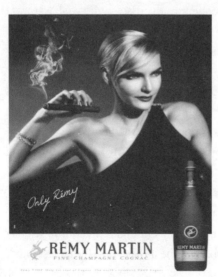

Only Rémy

RÉMY MARTIN
FINE CHAMPAGNE COGNAC

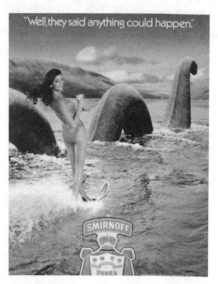

"Well, they said anything could happen."

SMIRNOFF

Consider a cartoon-style vodka ad showing a confident-looking woman holding a drink and saying, "Three things you should know, Love. The name's Mel. The drink's Tanqueray Sterling Vodka. And how unreasonable I can be if you forget the first two." It's no coincidence that she has short hair and a name that could be male or female.

A twist on the gender-bender theme is found in a three-page ad for Seagram's that ran in the 1997 swimsuit issue of *Sports Illustrated*. On the back cover is a pair of stereotypically shapely (and shaved) legs. But the fold-from-the-spine page opens to reveal the limbs are attached to a male beach bum. The tagline: "You either have it or you don't." And a gin ad featuring the ubiquitous Mr. Jenkins says, "Mr. Jenkins informs the brunch crowd that his zesty 'Tanqueray Red Snapper' was the original 'Bloody Mary.' And that the waitress was originally a man." We can have it all indeed.

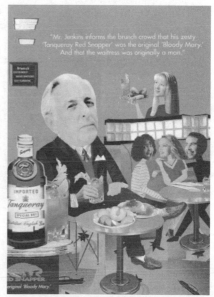

Several researchers have identified shame at having failed at the gender expectations of being female as an important issue for female alcoholics. One response to this shame is to mythologize it. I'm not only a bad girl—I am the baddest. I'm a rebel, an outlaw. I'm deeper, more complex, more interesting than ordinary women. The rules don't apply to me.

Looking back on my own life, I can see now that I thought I was a *really* bad girl, a bad seed. There was a terrible gap, an abyss, between my image and my essence, and smoking and drinking helped me feel more integrated. The self who smoked and drank always seemed more real to me, more true, than the one who turned in careful homework assignments and kept a tidy house. There were complex contradictions about this in my psyche. On the one hand, I felt bad because I believed, as most children do, that I was somehow responsible for my mother's death (if I had been a better girl, she wouldn't have abandoned me). On the other hand, I think I knew somehow that the roles for women were terribly restrictive and that I would have to sacrifice my sexuality and my authenticity in order to be "feminine." So I was both terribly wrong and terribly right.

In truth, alcoholic women are more likely than nonalcoholic women to chafe against rigid sex roles, to be androgynous. Many theorists believe that gender socialization is another primary factor (along with early trauma) in the development of alcoholism and other addictions among women. The women most vulnerable to addiction are those who feel most keenly the conflict between their true selves and the societal definition of the "good girl." This conflict is intensely painful and addictions help numb the pain. According to researcher F. B. Parker, "Alcoholism represents the ransom a woman pays for her emancipation."

This is hinted at in a 1991 ad that ran in almost all the major women's magazines. Juxtaposed with the titles of articles typical of these magazines, such as "Body Hair Horror," "How to Stop Your Body from Aging," "Blast Jiggly Hips and Thighs," and "Fixing Every Flaw," was a bottle of Michelob and and the headline,

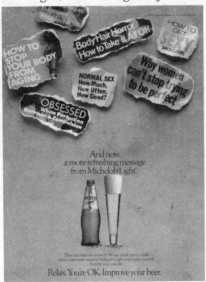

"And now, a more refreshing message from Michelob Light." The copy continues, "They say improve yourself. We say crack open a cold, clean, extremely smooth Michelob Light and enjoy yourself. Just the way you are. Relax. You're OK. Improve your beer."

I suppose on the surface this could seem like progress—telling women to ignore all these terrible exhortations. But on a deeper level the ad is simply reminding us of them—and then offering the beer as a way to cope, maybe even as a way to think of oneself as rebelling against these edicts. Another more recent and much more subtle ad pictures a woman with a list of descriptive nouns superimposed on her face, many of them contradictory ("optimist" and "pessimist," for example). "Appropriately complex" is the tagline, which is meant to refer to the woman and to the cognac being advertised. Perhaps the drink will help her resolve some of these contradictions, will enable her to pull herself together, so to speak.

Addiction is in some sense a logical response to powerlessness and rigid gender stereotypes. These stereotypes harm everyone—the girls who are denied access to their powerful selves and the boys who are denied access to their emotional selves—and, on some level, we all know it. Some people resist more than others. Some succeed, others go under.

It is not surprising that many girls and young women turn to alcohol and that alcohol advertisers target them. In the beginning, alcohol can seem to help a girl deal with the cultural contradictions, to give her some kind of connection she can count on, even if it is only the illusion of connection, to numb the pain of losing her real self, and to serve as an acceptable substitute for true rebellion.

There is also another product that is presented in advertising as absolutely perfect for a girl who wants to rebel without taking any real risks (except to her own health), who wants to escape from the trap of being a "good girl" without taking the punishment meted out to "bad girls," who wants to seem liberated without being stigmatized as a feminist, who wants to stay thin, and who, throughout all of it, needs a way to repress her rage at what is being done to her. That product is a cigarette.

8

"WHAT YOU'RE LOOKING FOR"

Rage and Rebellion in Cigarette Advertising

OF ALL THE LIES THAT ADVERTISING TELLS US, THE ONES TOLD IN CIGARETTE ads are the most lethal. Sometimes the pernicious effects of advertising are unintended, but this is certainly not the case with cigarette advertising. The tobacco industry is in the business of getting *children* addicted to nicotine. It has to get three thousand children to start smoking every day simply to replace those smokers who die or quit (in the United States alone). Why children? Because 90 percent of all smokers start smoking before they are eighteen years old and 60 percent start before high school. Almost all smokers start in their teens (or earlier) and the age of initiation has been dropping steadily, especially among girls. Today about one-third of high-school-aged adolescents in the United States smoke or use spit tobacco, and the numbers are rising, especially for African-American teens.

If you don't start smoking when you are very young, the chances are you will never start. Very few people wake up one morning at the age of twenty-two or twenty-seven and say to themselves, "I have a good idea. I think I'll take up the deadliest, most addictive product of all." And no one in midlife says, "I think I'll try something to make me look older." *Children* smoke because they want to feel more grown-up, more powerful. Teenagers smoke mostly because they want to rebel, to feel cool. They start for these reasons and then most of them become addicted, because nicotine is the most addictive drug of all. The tobacco industry wants us to think of smoking as an "adult custom." The truth is that it is an addiction that begins in childhood, a "pediatric disease."

What are the consequences for these three thousand children who become regular smokers every day? Seventy percent will regret their decision to smoke and will try to quit while still in their teens. Very few will succeed. Joseph Califano, Jr., former secretary of health, education and welfare, said, "Virtually all will be sicker than the rest of the population, most will never quit, and more than a third face early death as a consequence of their addiction." Tobacco advertisers deliberately seduce children with a promise of power, sex appeal, sophistication, and rebellion, but what they are really selling them is shortness of breath, yellow teeth, wrinkles and, quite possibly, emphysema, heart disease, and lung cancer. A 1999 study found that smoking in the teenage years causes permanent genetic changes in the lungs and forever increases the risk of lung cancer, even if the smoker quits.

Almost nothing good can truthfully be said about cigarettes. Highly addictive, the damage they do to health has been documented by over sixty thousand research studies. Cigarettes kill more Americans each year than alcohol, cocaine, heroin, fires, car crashes, homicide, suicide, and AIDS *combined.* Indeed, smoking is the single largest preventable cause of death in America (and, according to former surgeon general C. Everett Koop, the most important public health issue of our time). Yet we sell cigarettes in pharmacies, we sell them in candy stores to children. Over one thousand people die every day due to cigarette-related diseases, in the United States alone. In the twentieth century, tobacco has killed more people than war. Based on current trends, by the year 2030, the worldwide death toll will rise to ten million per year, with 70 percent occurring in developing countries.

Unlike other potentially dangerous products such as alcohol, there is no such thing as moderate, low-risk use of tobacco. Indeed tobacco is the only product advertised that is lethal *when used as intended*. There is abundant evidence that cigarette smoke is also harmful to nonsmokers, especially to children. Smoking is also heavily implicated in lost productivity and fire deaths and damage. The World Bank has estimated that the use of tobacco results in a global net loss of $200 billion each year. These costs include direct medical care costs for tobacco-related illnesses, absenteeism from work, fire losses, reduced productivity, and forgone income due to early mortality.

In spite of these appalling statistics, smoking has been promoted for decades by the most massive marketing campaign ever dedicated to a single product. While spending over five billion dollars a year in the United States alone on advertising and promotion, the tobacco industry ironically denies that this advertising has any effect. It insists that it does not target nonsmokers or young people and that the whole point of all that advertising is simply to get smokers to switch brands. Only 10 percent of the nation's fifty-five million smokers switch brands every year. It is obvious that the tobacco industry needs to aggressively recruit new smokers to replace those who die or quit. When you're selling a product that kills people, you've got a problem. Your best customers die.

Nowhere is the distorted perspective of advertising, a perspective that manages to screen out almost all unpleasant reality except the strictly personal (such as bad breath, facial hair, and fat), more obvious than in the cigarette ads. The contradictions abound. Macho men apparently owe their freedom and independence, indeed their very masculinity, to their Marlboros, although the evidence is clear that cigarettes are linked with impotence, lower testosterone count, and sterility.

In fact, Marlboros began as a cigarette designed for women. It came with a red tip so the smoker's lipstick wouldn't show, and the slogan was "Cherry tips to match your ruby lips." It didn't take long for Philip Morris, makers of Marlboro, to realize that this wasn't a good idea. A woman will most often freely use a product designed for men, but God forbid that a man would ever use a product designed for women. How many men smoke Virginia Slims? The group with higher status rarely wants to use a product designed for a lower-status group. So in 1956 Marlboro was repositioned as the ultimate man's cigarette, with the image of the cowboy. This campaign has been phenomenally successful. Almost one-third of American smokers smoke Marlboros, the most heavily advertised cigarette in the world, and the Marlboro Man was recently named by *Advertising Age* as the top advertising icon of the century. At least one writer for the magazine mentioned the irony of a "supposed symbol of rugged independence" really being a "symbol of enslavement to an addictive drug."

People start smoking and become addicted for many reasons, of course, and no one suggests that tobacco advertising is the primary one. However, cigarette advertising aggressively targets those very people most vulnerable to nicotine addiction. And it promotes a climate of denial. It is difficult for children to take health warnings seriously when they are surrounded by billboards of cartoon characters smoking, when the hottest (and coolest) celebrities light up in films and television programs and concerts, when the magazines in their homes are filled with colourful ads for cigarettes. A 1999 study found that more than two-thirds of the fifty G-rated animated films released by major studios during the past sixty years portray alcohol or tobacco use without any clear messages of negative health effects. Current research suggests that tobacco advertising has two major effects: It creates the perception that more people smoke than actually do and it makes smoking look cool. It seems that the rest of the media help further these perceptions.

One of the most successful campaigns in the history of advertising was the one for Camel cigarettes that ran from 1988 until 1997. Just about everyone remembers this campaign, which featured a cartoon camel doing lots of "cool" things, like playing in a rock band, shooting pool, and riding a motorcycle. This camel, known as Old Joe, is now as recognizable to six-year-olds as is Mickey Mouse. One-third of all three-year-olds can link him with cigarettes.

Before the advent of this campaign, Camels did not especially appeal to young people. Of smokers under the age of eighteen, less than 1 percent smoked Camels. Soon after the introduction of Joe Camel, the percentage of teen smokers who smoked Camels sky-rocketed to 33 percent. This certainly says something about the power of advertising. The fact that the campaign was finally abolished after years of citizen activism against it says something also about the power of protest. Alas, the campaign was abolished only in the United States. Old Joe continues to entice children in other countries around the world.

Eighty-six percent of all teenage smokers smoke one of the three most heavily advertised brands—Camels, Marlboros, or Newports. As further evidence of the influence of advertising, 70 percent of young African-American smokers smoke Newports, the third-most-advertised brand overall and the number-one brand advertised to African-Americans. Almost all of these teenagers would vehemently deny that advertising had any influence on their "choice," but the statistics speak for themselves.

Recent research also supports this. Several studies have demonstrated an association between exposure to cigarette advertising and adolescent smoking behavior, while others have shown that young people smoke the most heavily advertised brands. According to one of these studies, tobacco advertising and promotion influence teenagers' decision to begin smoking significantly more than does peer pressure. The same team of researchers found that sudden rises in adolescent smoking coincided with large-scale cigarette promotional campaigns. According to John Pierce, the lead author of the studies, "It is not that children see an ad and immediately start to smoke, but seeing the ads and handling the cigarette packs and the promotional gifts lessens their resistance, weakens their resolve, so that later on they will be somewhat more willing to accept a cigarette from a peer when it is offered." Pierce conducted a longitudinal study that conclusively demonstrated that over a third of all youthful experimentation with cigarettes is directly attributable to cigarette advertising and promotions.

The tobacco industry claims these studies are rigged, of course, and that advertising has no effect on young people. Even advertisers scoff at this preposterous claim. In one poll, 71 percent of advertising executives said they think cigarette advertising increases youth smoking and nearly 80 percent approved of advertising restrictions to reduce its effect on kids and teenagers. According to Rance Crain in an editorial in *Advertising Age*, "Cigarette people maintain peer pressure is the culprit in getting kids to start smoking and that advertising has little effect. That's like saying cosmetic ads have no effect on girls too young to put on lipstick."

The late Emerson Foote, founder of Foote, Cone & Belding and former chairman of the board of McCann-Erickson, one of the world's largest advertising agencies, said of the industry's claims that its advertising only affects brand-switching, "I don't think anyone really believes this. . . . I suspect that creating a positive climate of social acceptability for smoking, which encourages new smokers to join the market, is of greater importance to the industry. . . . In recent years, the cigarette industry has been artfully maintaining that cigarette advertising has nothing to do with total sales. Take my word for it, this is complete and utter nonsense." Bob Garfield of *Advertising Age* goes further: "Watch any child when a cartoon image comes on TV; it's a moth to flame. And R.J. Reynolds knows it, and has always known it, and when they start mouthing their line about smoking as an 'adult decision,' may they choke on their lying tongues."

The tobacco industry has spent a fortune on research designed to understand the psychology involved in getting young people to smoke. This research has found that people in their early and mid-teens are beginning to shape their self-image, to differentiate themselves from their parents and other adults, and that cigarette advertising can exploit this natural need by offering a destructive manner of rebellion as an alternative to more constructive varieties, such as outrageous music, fashion, and politics. It is important to get children while they are young "so that the habit may become an integral part of the image of themselves. . . . The temptation must be pressed just as the sense of self is forming, just as the child is facing the world at large for the first time, or it will not take hold."

The evidence against cigarette advertising is compelling enough that about thirty countries, including those of the European Union, have banned all tobacco advertising and sponsorships. A survey conducted by the American Cancer Society found that countries that severely restricted tobacco promotion experienced the greatest annual declines in tobacco consumption.

After years of banding together, there finally has been a break in the stone wall of the tobacco industry. In 1997 the Liggett Group, the smallest of the five major tobacco companies, defected from the rest of the industry by admitting that nicotine is addictive, that smoking causes cancer, and that the industry targets young people. Tobacco industry documents, brought to light by whistle-blowers and by product liability suits against the industry, certainly support these allegations. Knowing that teenagers are particularly susceptible to peer pressure, the industry creates the illusion of peer acceptance in its ads. As one R.J. Reynolds document says, "Overall, Camel advertising will be directed toward using peer acceptance/influence to provide the motivation for target smokers to select Camel." The document continues that Camel advertising will create "the perception that Camel smokers are non-conformist, self-confident and project a cool attitude, which is admired by their peers. . . . Aspiration to be perceived as a cool member of the in-group is one of the strongest influences affecting the be-havior of younger adult smokers."

One series documents Brown & Williamson Company's efforts to attract youth smokers with sweet-flavored cigarettes, including some with a cola-like taste. The company also considered tobacco-based lollipops, cotton candy, and fruit roll-ups. "It's a well-known fact that teenagers like sweet products. Honey might be considered," says one memo (which is titled "Project Kestrel," after a small bird of prey). And one of the most chilling documents records a study in which Philip Morris researchers tracked "hyperkinetic" grade-schoolers to deter-mine if such children would become cigarette smokers. According to the report, "We wonder whether such children may not eventually become cigarette smok-ers in their teenage years as they discover the advantage of self-stimulation via nicotine. We have already collaborated with a local school system in identifying some such children in third grade."

Of course, the industry targets children. How could they not? As an R. J. Reynolds memo says, "the 14 to 24 age group . . . represents tomorrow's cigarette business." "The base of our business is the high-school student," says a memo from a Lorillard executive. And a Philip Morris report says, "Today's teenager is tomorrow's potential regular customer." This can seem innocuous enough until one remembers that almost half of the tobacco industry's "regular customers" die prematurely from cigarette-related diseases.

The evidence is clear that all this targeted advertising does indeed influence children. *In 1968 Virginia Slims was introduced by Philip Morris. In the following six years, the number of girls ages twelve to eighteen who smoked more than doubled.* There followed a proliferation of cigarettes designed exclusively for women, such as More, Now (which exploitively had the same name as the acronym for the National Organization for Women), Max, Eve, Satin, and Misty. By 1979, magazine tobacco advertisements targeting women equaled those tar-geted to men. These advertisements offered and continue to offer smoking to young women as a way to rebel and be cool, of course, but also as a way to control both their emotions and their weight. And, of course, advertisements offer cigarettes to everyone as a powerful symbol of sexuality.

Many ads also offer cigarettes to women as a symbol of emancipation and freedom. The co-optation of women's liberation by the tobacco industry began in 1929 when Edward Bernays, the "father of public relations," was hired by George Washington Hill, the president of American Tobacco, to promote cigarette smoking by women. Hill reportedly said, "It will be like opening a new gold mine right in our front yard." Bernays did an excellent job. He persuaded some debutantes to march in the Easter Parade in New York City and to smoke Lucky Strikes, asserting that their cigarettes were "torches of freedom." This was reported as news, rather than as an advertising campaign.

Bernays did not *create* the link between cigarette smoking and emancipation for women, but he certainly exploited it. The cigarette was a symbol of liberation and independence for women in the 1920s for many political and cultural reasons. However, advertising did a great deal to legitimize, normalize, and promote this connection. In 1929 Lucky Strike ran a preposterous ad headlined "An ancient prejudice has been removed," which compared prejudice against women to prejudice against smoking. The copy said, "Today, legally, politically and socially, womanhood stands in her true light. AMERICAN INTELLIGENCE has cast aside the ancient prejudice that held her to be inferior," and continued, "Gone is that ancient prejudice against cigarettes."

Women took up smoking in greater and greater numbers. Today 25 million American women and one out of every four girls under the age of eighteen smoke. The highest rates are among whites and Native Americans, and the lowest are among African-Americans and Asians. Lesbian and bisexual rates are almost double those of the general population. Given all the billboards and tennis tournaments and fashion catalogs and other ploys designed to glamorize smoking by women, it is hard to imagine that less than a century ago it was taboo.

The insidious link between cigarette smoking and liberation and independence that Bernays promoted and exploited reached its nadir in the Virginia Slims campaign with its trivializing slogan, "You've come a long way, baby." This equation between liberation and addiction, between freedom and enslavement to tobacco, is particularly ironic, given that nicotine is the most addictive drug of all.

The truth about cigarette smoking is that most smokers wish they could quit. A whole new industry has been founded on the fact that this is often extremely difficult. Surely any intelligent person looking at the barrage of ads for nicotine patches and nicotine chewing gum (one of which promises to relieve "the agony of quitting") must conclude that smoking is more about enslavement than free will. According to tobacco industry documents, tobacco companies used coercion and economic intimidation to muffle aggressive antismoking messages by the makers of cessation products. And, of course, the ads (and the tobacco industry in its public-relations campaign) continue to tell us that smoking is a symbol of our freedom, of our right to choose. This is an example of the Big Lie—if you tell an outrageous lie often enough and powerfully enough, many people will come to believe it or at least tacitly to accept it as true.

The only equality with men the advent of women's smoking has given us is that we now are getting lung cancer at the same rate. In the past twenty years, lung cancer in women has increased nationwide by more than 400 percent, surpassing breast cancer as the leading cancer killer of women. In fact, as is the case with alcohol, smoking seems to exact a heavier toll on women than on men. Smoking only a few cigarettes a day can permanently stunt lung development in girls, whereas boys are less affected. Premature wrinkling and aging of the skin due to smoking also affects women more than men. Smoking increases a woman's chance of heart disease two to six times, her chance of lung cancer two to six times, and doubles her chances of cervical cancer. One can only consider cigarette smoking liberating if one considers death the ultimate freedom.

I was thirteen when I had my first cigarette. My friend Deedee smoked and I thought she looked very cool and mature. I was lonely and depressed. Although I did very well in school, I felt awkward and self-conscious (like every other thirteen-year-old!), dressed badly, and had very low self-esteem. I was almost completely numb from the effort it took not to feel how much I missed my mother.

"In grief the world becomes poor and empty," wrote Freud in *Mourning and Melancholia*. Cigarettes seemed to help fill the emptiness I felt. I choked on my first few cigarettes, of course, but I also liked the way they made me feel—high and calm at the same time.

I also thought smoking improved my image. I got straight As on my report card throughout my school years and many of my peers thought of me as a goody-two-shoes. I wanted them to see that I had a wild and rebellious streak, that I wasn't as straight-arrow as I seemed. I had absorbed the message of the culture that girls who smoked were wild and sexy and I wanted that image for myself. At the same time, I was frightened by my sexual feelings and by the way boys were beginning to respond to me. I felt more confident with a cigarette in my hand and it also helped me to avoid being touched or kissed.

I didn't become addicted to cigarettes because of advertising. However, I became addicted in a climate in which cigarette smoking was constantly glamorized (in films and television programs as well as in ads) and was assumed to be safe and socially desirable. In addition, I became addicted when there were no health warnings of any kind, partly because of the influence of the tobacco industry on the medical world (in those days, the American Medical Association owned tobacco stocks) and on the media. There were no programs in school—indeed many of my teachers smoked. I was thirteen years old, genetically at risk for both nicotine and alcohol addiction, and dangerously depressed. Was I responsible for my addiction? I don't think so. However, I certainly was responsible for quitting once I learned the truth.

It is not at all unusual that depression led me to cigarettes. A heavy smoker is as much as four times more likely than normal to have a history of major depression. One 1997 study found that teenage smokers were twice as likely as nonsmokers to suffer from depression and another that teenage smokers were twice as likely to report a suicide attempt. Studies suggest that a genetic makeup that raises the risk of depression may also raise the risk of nicotine addiction. Depressed smokers also find it harder to quit than average. These days, as more and more people quit smoking, those who start and who are unable to quit are increasingly those who are depressed. One middle-school girl, a participant in a series of roundtable discussions run by the Commission for a Healthy New York, said, "Smoke fills you up when you feel empty inside." And a woman in an unhappy marriage said, "Smoking helped to dampen things down. When it got to the stage when I couldn't bear it any longer, I found if I lit up a cigarette it helped to get me over the next five minutes. It gave me enough breathing space to stop the endless crying, and carry on with whatever had to be done."

Worldwide cross-cultural studies reveal that depression and anxiety disorders are two to three times more common in women than in men. This seems to be increasingly true for young women. A 1997 nationwide survey of college freshmen found that one in eight freshmen women reported frequently feeling depressed, contrasted with one in ten a decade ago.

Women are also more likely than men to use cigarettes, food, alcohol, and other drugs to deal with stress and depression and negative feelings, such as anxiety, nervousness, and especially anger. Depressed women are also more likely than depressed men to eat, smoke, and blame themselves, whereas men are more likely to become aggressive, to isolate, or to engage in sexual behavior.

Some studies indicate that women experience greater anxiety than men when they attempt to quit and seem to have a higher rate of relapse. Although this could be at least partially due to weight gain or premenstrual stress, several researchers, including myself, believe that it is women's use of cigarettes to cope with negative feelings, especially anger, that makes it easier for women both to start smoking and to relapse. This theory is supported by the fact that women are more likely to relapse in situations involving negative emotions, such as anger and stress, whereas men relapse more often in positive situations such as social events.

According to Dr. Teresa Bernardez of Michigan State University, "Anger and the attempts to eradicate it are responsible for most of the symptoms and dysfunctional behaviors that women present nowadays: from depression to inhibition of action and creativity, from apathy to disturbances in sexual behavior." She and many other therapists agree that powerful social and psychological forces combine to keep women from expressing anger and even from admitting that they feel it.

An angry woman is still often considered terribly unfeminine and undesirable. She is likely to be labeled "strident" or "bitchy," terms never applied to angry men. Since anger is one of the great taboos for women, we learn to repress anger, and usually to turn it against the self. This process occurs with all oppressed people and has been well-documented. Anyone who has been abused in childhood—sexually, physically, or emotionally—is bound to feel enormous rage, although it may not be conscious.

What to do with all that rage (or, if it has been thoroughly repressed, all that depression)? Why not have a cigarette or another piece of cake? Perhaps one of the reasons it is so difficult for women to quit smoking is that smoking becomes so inextricably linked with suppressed anger. "Stifle yourself," Archie Bunker used to say to his wife Edith whenever she got upset or angry. What better way to stifle oneself than to stuff a cigarette or some food into one's mouth? It is one of the few things one can do with all that anger and frustration that is socially acceptable for women.

Women who are doubly or triply oppressed (by their color, socioeconomic status, educational level, or sexual orientation) have higher rates of depression than do middle- to upper-middle-class heterosexual white women) and are even more likely to use cigarettes to deal with negative emotions. When people are overwhelmed by poverty, violence, and crime, it is understandably difficult for them to take the long-term health risks of smoking seriously. In *Straight, No Chaser: How I Became a Grown-up Black Woman,* Jill Nelson writes about the rage that results from being black and female in a culture that despises both: "We turn our rage inward and wreak it on ourselves; we drink too much, eat too much, inhale drugs in an effort to beat back the pain and rage."

As Nelson says, suppressed anger also plays an important role in alcoholism and in eating disorders. Jennifer, a fourteen-year-old anorexic, said, "Well, my anorexia is where I put my feelings . . . especially the angry ones." And Bone, the abused girl in Dorothy Allison's powerful novel *Bastard Out of Carolina,* says, "It was hunger I felt then, raw and terrible, a shaking deep down inside me, as if my rage had used up everything I had ever eaten."

A study reported by British researcher Bobbie Jacobson in her groundbreaking 1982 book *The Ladykillers: Why Smoking Is a Feminist Issue* found that women smoked more when they felt "uncomfortable or upset about something" or when they were "angry, ashamed or embarrassed about something" or when they wanted to "take their mind off cares and worries." Canadian researcher Lorraine Greaves found that many women smoked in order to blunt their emotional responses, to quell and suppress both feelings and comments. Some of the women described "sucking back their anger."

An article called "Why Smoking is a Real Drag" in the January 1998 issue of *Teen* magazine begins with the story of a girl named Lauren who had a huge fight with her best friend on a Saturday night:

Lauren was pissed. She slammed the phone down, headed out the front door, sat on the front steps—and lit a cigarette. "It calms me down and helps me think," Lauren says of her smoking habit. "After I had a cigarette, I was able to go back inside, call my friend and work everything out. If I hadn't had one, I probably would have called her back and yelled and screamed, and it would have been a horrible night. Having a cigarette helps me control my emotions. My problems are still there, but the tension is gone."

So a cigarette saved Lauren's Saturday night. But at what price? Addiction to a drug that can cause cancer and heart disease. In other words, kills.

This strikes me as a mixed message at best (not surprising, of course, given the dependence of the media on the goodwill of the tobacco industry). I can't help thinking that, if I were a teenager, saving a friendship in the here and now would be worth a whole lot more than avoiding cancer and heart disease in forty or fifty years.

Cigarette advertisers have long been aware of the fact that women are especially likely to use smoking as a way to regulate our moods and cope with negative feelings. A 1949 Lucky Strike ad says, "Smoke a Lucky to feel your level best," and continues, "Luckies' fine tobacco picks you up when you're low . . . and calms you down when you're tense." (The model in the ad is Janet Sackman, seventeen years old at the time, who was urged by tobacco executives to smoke in order to be more "real" in the ad. She became addicted. Years later she developed throat cancer and lung cancer and had to have her voice box removed. Today she is an admirable and compelling figure in the anti-tobacco-industry movement.)

When Junior's fighting rates a scold . . .

Why be Irritated ?
Light an Old Gold

You'll like the luxe friendly extras Old Gold gives you for greater smoking pleasure! First, moisture-guarding Apple "Honey"™ —for luxurious freshness. Then world-renowned tobaccos—blended with exacting care. Add that perfect touch—imported Latakia tobacco—for sure delivery of flavor . . . and lastly the crisp whiteness of superfine cigarette paper made from virgin pure flax! Good reasons for going around with Old Gold—starting today!

A 1951 Marlboro ad features a worried-looking baby saying, "Before you scold me, Mom . . . maybe you'd better light up a Marlboro." Another ad from the 1950s features a woman clearly at her wit's end being handed a cigarette by her husband. The copy says, "When Junior's fighting rates a scold . . . Why be irritated? Light an Old Gold." Women have long been encouraged by men, their doctors as well as their husbands and boyfriends, to use drugs to deal with negative feelings, to "calm down." Cigarettes offer a small, controllable sense of comfort while warding off a potentially dangerous outburst of emotion.

"I get enough bull at work. I don't need to smoke it," says a young woman in one of the ads in Winston's "No Bull" campaign. "I'm a damn good waitress," says another young woman in a Winston ad, "If you want an actress, go see a movie." The lower one's socioeconomic level, the more likely one is to smoke, so these women may well get a lot of bull at work. However, the solution, according to this campaign is to have a cigarette rather than to confront their bosses or take some constructive action (such as joining a union or going back to school and getting a better job). People in these kinds of jobs don't smoke because they are stupid, however. They smoke to relieve the tedium of the work, to be doing one small thing seemingly for themselves. I've had many jobs so soul-crushingly boring that cigarette breaks were the highlight of my day. As Barbara Ehrenreich said, "I don't know why the antismoking crusaders have never grasped the element of defiant self-nurturance that makes the habit so endearing to its victims—as if, in the American workplace, the only thing people have to call their own is the tumors they are nourishing and the spare moments they devote to feeding them."

Some of the "antismoking crusaders" may not have grasped this, but the tobacco industry certainly has. It has known for a long time that cigarettes are often used as a way to deal with boredom at work, a way to add a little pseudo-excitement to one's life. In the 1930s a cigarette ad featuring a woman interrupting her knitting by pulling a cigarette from a Chesterfield pack said:

> To knit and spin was not much fun
> When 'twas my sole employment
> But now I smoke these Chesterfields
> And find it real enjoyment

"Five more smokes for the long working day," proclaims a Marlboro ad. One of Satin's slogans was "Don't let anything ever be ordinary." "Flavor happens," says an ad for Merit. The copy continues, "Nothing's happening. You're bored. You try a Merit Ultra Light. WHOA! You're getting real flavor from an ultra low tar cigarette! You light up another Merit. WHAT THE? It happens again."

Nicotine is quite an amazing drug because it perks one up in times of boredom and calms one down in times of stress. Most smokers use cigarettes both to relax and to cope with crises. Stress is related to powerlessness, to feeling that one has little or no control. Thus the most stressful jobs are those in which people

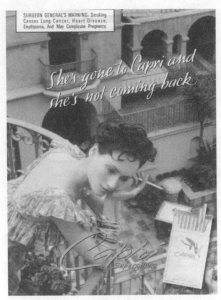

have the least power. Nurses are far more stressed than doctors (and far more likely to smoke). Secretaries are usually more stressed than their bosses. It is no coincidence that people in low-level jobs, people who are or feel powerless, are much more likely to smoke than those with high-level, high-income jobs.

One of the most stressful and at the same time most tedious jobs of all is to be at home with small children. There are great rewards as well, but anyone who is honest must admit that there are times of feeling anxious, bored, and almost completely out of control. People in these situations, almost always women, are often desperate for personal time, for "space."

And many cigarette ads offer them just this. "It's a few minutes of your own" was the slogan for Eve cigarettes in the early 1990s. "Peace & Quiet," says one of the ads in a Benson & Hedges campaign, which features a cigarette curled up on a couch. "She's gone to Capri and she's not coming back," says a cigarette campaign targeting women (perhaps a rare example of truth in advertising). The addiction becomes a place one can escape to, clearly alluding to the mind-altering properties of the drug.

Given that the tobacco industry knows that smokers, especially women, use cigarettes to cope with stress and anger, wouldn't it be brilliant of them to design a cigarette campaign that seems to offer freedom and liberation to women but that in fact, on an unconscious level, triggers depression and anger—and then offers the cigarette as the solution? This is exactly what the long-running Virginia Slims campaign has done.

For years this campaign usually featured a slim happy young woman in the foreground and a sepia-toned, pseudo-antique photograph in the background depicting those dark, dismal days when women were oppressed—back before we had our own cigarette. In a subtle way, however, the ads remind us that things really haven't changed that much. Although the model seemingly is proclaiming that she is liberated, her pose, dress, makeup, and demeanor are always stereotypically feminine in a "cute," strictly ornamental way. There is never a hint of any real freedom from traditional roles and limitations. The model is never shown doing *anything* but laughing, holding a cigarette, and wearing stylish clothes. She is never working or in any way demonstrating her liberation and independence. And she's still a "baby."

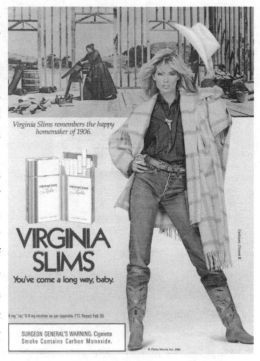

Virginia Slims remembers the happy homemaker of 1906.

VIRGINIA SLIMS

You've come a long way, baby.

SURGEON GENERAL'S WARNING: Cigarette Smoke Contains Carbon Monoxide.

In one of the old photographs, a woman, certainly overweight by today's standards, is building a home. The copy says, "Virginia Slims remembers the happy homemaker of 1906." It is ironic that it is the benighted woman of the past who is working at "a man's job," whereas the liberated modern woman is doing nothing but holding her cigarette.

Even more telling, the old photographs depict a world that seems long ago on the surface—but is disturbingly the same when examined more closely. "Equal pay for equal work," an ad tells us, and we laugh at the old photograph of the man patting both his wife's and his dog's heads. Yet women still don't get equal pay for equal work—and nowhere near equal pay for comparable work. The more things change, the more they stay the same. What effect does this have? I think it reminds us, *on an unconscious level,* that we have not come such a long way, after all. This is depressing. This arouses anxiety. Perhaps it makes us reach for the comfort of our cigarettes.

Another way that many of the Virginia Slims ads arouse anxiety is by portraying violence against women. Although always presented as a joke, the violence is not really so funny when one pays attention to it. One ad features an old photograph of a woman being hit by a figure in a clock tower and the caption, "In 1903 Naomi Fett couldn't understand why more women didn't sneak cigarettes in the Emperor's clock. A moment later it struck her."

Women are dragged behind horses, shot from rockets. Often they are in literal bondage. These are caricatures, meant to be funny, but too close to the reality of many women to be really funny. The ads feature scenes of humiliation, aban-

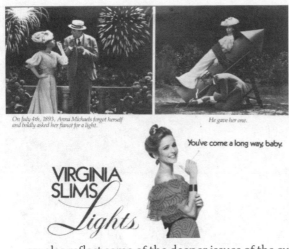

On July 4th, 1893, Anna Michaels forgot herself and boldly asked her fiancé for a light.

He gave her one.

You've come a long way, baby.

VIRGINIA SLIMS *Lights*

donment, subordination, very real themes still in many women's lives—but always as jokes.

Certainly the cigarette advertisers, like the food and diet product advertisers who also spend billions on psychological research, are aware of suppressed anger in women and deliberately play upon it in their advertising. The advertisers also reflect some of the deeper issues of the culture regarding power and freedom for women. It is difficult, if not impossible, to know how much is conscious and calculated. However, another cigarette campaign seems to do very much the same thing as the Virginia Slims campaign—to turn an anxiety-producing situation, especially for women, into a joke. For years a Newport campaign featured young men and women in playful caricatures of essentially violent situations. I first noticed this about twenty years ago and was astonished when I looked at the ads one after another. The campaign has obviously been very successful—similar ads continue to run and Newport is one of the top cigarette brands.

Many of the ads are shockingly violent, especially when seen as a group.

Newport Lights

Alive with pleasure!
Newport pleasure comes to low-tar menthols

SURGEON GENERAL'S WARNING: Quitting Smoking Now Greatly Reduces Serious Risks to Your Health.

Women are buried in snow, stuffed into boxes, thrown over men's shoulders, tied to poles, hit with snowballs, bells, a barrel of leaves, cymbals, buckets of water, and pillows. In one ad, a woman seems to be on fire. In another, a woman is seated on a basketball, about to fall onto hard pavement. Another features a woman about to be submerged in icy water, her face an odd mix of joy and terror. Perhaps the strangest one of all features a woman in a yoke, such as is used on oxen.

In others, women are teased, made to seem weak and inferior, ridiculous. A man derisively laughs while testing the biceps of a woman ludicrously dressed in a man's football jersey. An-

other man howls with laughter as a woman wears fishing pants far too big for her and awkwardly carries a fishing pole (try as a woman might to wear the pants and have a penis, she just can't get it right). A woman on her knees grabs onto a man who is skiing (she just doesn't have the right equipment—the right pole, to be exact). Another woman grabs a man on skates. In one ad a woman's head is covered with a paper bag and in another she is hobbled and blindfolded in a sleeping bag.

Occasionally, other cigarette ads play on the theme of violence against women. An ad for Camels advises young men at the beach to "Run into the water, grab someone and drag her back to shore as if you've saved her from drowning. The more she kicks and screams, the better."

While women are threatened with violence, men are sometimes portrayed as fools. One Virginia Slims ad says, "A deck of cards where the only men are jokers? How appropriate." When psychologist Judith Jordan asked a group of women what they most feared from men, the women replied, "That they will hurt us." When men were asked the same question about women, they replied, "That they will laugh at us." There's a world of difference, of course, between being hurt and being ridiculed, but either one can arouse anxiety—which, in turn, can make smokers reach for their cigarettes.

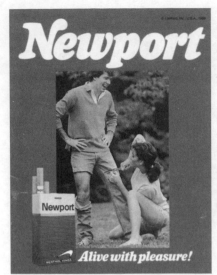

Alive with pleasure!

Newport targets men as well as women, of course, so the ads sometimes trigger male anxiety. Several ads show men, often African-American men, in ludicrous positions. In one such ad, the man has the head of a jackass. In another, he has the body of a fat woman in a tutu. In yet another, two men are dancing in hula skirts. As is often the case, the quickest way to ridicule a man is to present him as a woman. A man with balloons or socks stuffed into his shirt is seen as hilarious—not so a woman with a balloon stuffed in her pants.

Sometimes the woman is presented as potentially threatening. In one a woman is cutting a man's pants into shorts, the scissors precariously close to his crotch. In another, she is shaving him, the razor poised against his throat. In yet another, she seems to be executing him with her hair drier, blowing his brains out. Thus the Newport campaign, like the Virginia Slims campaign, arouses unconscious anger and anxiety and offers the cigarette as a solution.

As audiences have become more sophisticated, cigarette ads have become more subtle. For a couple of years after Virginia Slims stopped using the old photographs, their ads featured a thin, beautiful young woman confidently asserting herself. "Management with style . . . obviously my strong suit," says one. "What do you call a take-charge woman? How 'bout boss?" says another. A woman perched on a motorcycle says, "I don't necessarily want to run the world, but I wouldn't mind taking it for a ride."

A few of the ads use the beautiful women to downplay the importance of looks. "Beauty without brains is just window dressing," says one, featuring two beautiful women (one wearing glasses, however, such an original way to indicate that a woman is intelligent) and a mannequin. "Judge me on looks? You're just scratching the surface," says another.

Of course, it is not surprising that advertisers would use beautiful, independent, confident women to sell their products. What's the problem? The problem is the dissonance between the image in the ads and the reality of many female smokers' lives—and the implicit promise that smoking will somehow resolve this dissonance. A typical woman smoker is young (or became addicted while very young), depressed, and stuck in a dead-end job or life and perhaps in a violent relationship as well. She is far from taking the world for a ride. Cigarettes won't help, to say the least.

The Commission for a Healthy New York study found that girls saw smoking not only as a way to deal with nervousness, to control appetite, and to look older, but also as a way to create a tougher image and to rebel against a boyfriend. Certainly cigarettes give a girl a tougher image. A cigarette (or a cigar these days) is an instant symbol in many films and situations to indicate that a

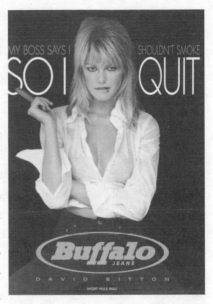

woman is strong-willed and defiant. An ad for Buffalo jeans features a beautiful young woman holding a cigar. The copy says, "My boss says I shouldn't smoke so I quit." The implication, of course, is that she refused to be told what to do and quit her job. She seems quite arrogant, but she is biting her lip and her breasts are almost completely exposed. Her posture is also extremely defensive. She is more vulnerable than she appears at first glance.

Perhaps the girls most susceptible to addiction are the ones who are really least tough, most vulnerable, feeling most in need of a tougher image for protection. Especially for adolescents, the tough talk, the callous image, almost always signals a terror of vulnerability within. The high-school dropout, the teenager being sexually abused at home, the pregnant teenager, the child of alcoholic and nicotine-addicted parents, the young woman being battered by her boyfriend or harassed by young men at school—all are at great risk for smoking. How appealing the Virginia Slims message must be—"A woman's place is any place her feet will take her" and "I always take the driver's seat. That way I'm never taken for a ride."

Other cigarette brands often offer a similar message. "Here's to women

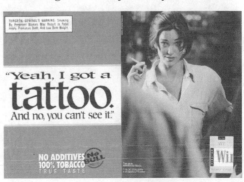

who can light their own cigarette," says a Winston ad. As if this is all it takes for a woman, especially an African-American woman, such as the one in the ad, to be powerful. "Yeah, I got a tattoo," says a young woman in another Winston ad. "And no, you can't see it." She sounds tough but she looks quite vulnerable and the man standing very close to her (we see only his out-of-focus broad shoulder) is potentially threatening.

Girls and women are likely to be dominated by the men in their lives—by their lovers and the men they work for. Rather than offering models of healthy intimacy and mutual respect, advertising usually normalizes and eroticizes this domination. Lack of communication and an edge of hostility between women and men are also normalized. "To us, 'open' communication means when we're talking, your eyes are open," says a young woman in one Virginia Slims ad. "When we ask for your honest opinion," says another, "you should know this is a trick question." And, in yet another, an African-American woman throws back her head and laughs, while saying "Just because we laugh at your stories doesn't mean we believe 'em for a second."

We are often encouraged to have sexual adventures with men who are bad for us. Forget the sensitive men— "We love a man who cries, just not more than we do," says a Virginia Slims ad, which quite obviously ridicules the man who cries. "You're looking at my feminine side," says a muscular man with a girlie tattoo on his biceps. Fall for the men who mistreat us, abuse us, objectify and disap-

We love a man who cries... just not more than we do.

VIRGINIA SLIMS
It's a _woman_
thing.

point us. "Some men are like chocolates," says a Virginia Slims ad. "We know we shouldn't but occasionally we just can't help ourselves." Of course, this is the voice of denial, no matter what the addiction—whether it be to dangerous men, alcohol, chocolates, or cigarettes.

The voice of denial tells us that we are in control of our addictions. Adolescent girls in particular want to believe that they are controlling their cigarettes rather than that their cigarettes are controlling them, and cigarette ads generally perpetuate this delusion. In most of the Virginia Slims ads, young women seem

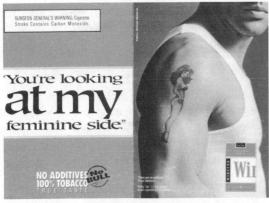

to be completely in charge. They have nothing to fear from men. They are feisty and sassy. They know exactly what they are doing. "A kiss is the only part of romance I go into with my eyes closed," declares one woman who seems to be literally bowling over a man. In fact, they sometimes objectify and use men. "There's nothing wrong with putting a man first as long as you enjoy the view," says one woman coolly. "What's the first thing we look for in a guy?" asks an ad featuring two women ogling a young man in tight jeans. "A really great . . . um . . . personality."

They don't even have to fear rejection and abandonment. "This is what we call redecorating," says a furious woman ripping up a man's photograph. "It takes time to get over a breakup," says a woman snuggling in a man's arms. "Fortunately a new boyfriend can cut that time in half." And, these ads imply, your cigarettes can help too.

These young women call the shots. "Who says you can't make the first move?" says one ad. "Hey, if anyone tries to rein you in, just say whoa," says an African-American woman, sitting on a fence, literally head and shoulders above her boyfriend. "Pretty in pink doesn't make you a pushover," says another. And yet another features a woman leading her man by the hand and the copy, "Lead the way? Yeah . . . even in 3-inch heels." The men are all laughing, compliant, completely unthreatening. How cool these women are, how supremely confident.

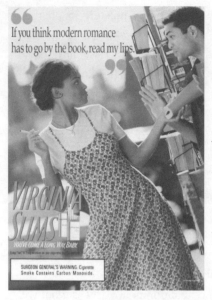

And what rage there is, just below the surface. "The real reason we bring you with us to the beach is so we have some place to put the car keys," says one woman. "Sit and wait for a phone call? Forget that number," says another, carrying a red motorcycle helmet. "If you think modern romance has to go by the book, read my lips," says an African-American woman while defiantly pushing a book into a man's chest. "Who cares who wears the pants," says a tough-looking young woman while pointing her middle finger at us.

Ads for other brands also offer women cigarettes as a way to safely ridicule or express hostility to men. A 1999 Camel ad features a young woman sticking pins into a male doll while her two friends look on approvingly. Two young women in a convertible in a Winston ad laugh uproariously at a balding man on a motorcycle next to them. "Old men should stick to hitting on old women," says the ad. Another ad in this campaign features a woman sitting beside a man with her hand over her face and the copy, "I wanted a light, not his life story."

Many of the Virginia Slims ads feature women who are giving advice to men on how to behave. "When we ask 'Is that what you're wearing?' we're actually hoping it's not," says one particularly insulting version of this theme. Others feature extreme closeups of women's faces and copy that says, "If you give us flow-

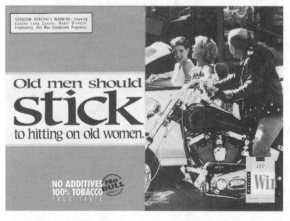

ers, never tell us what a great deal you got on them," "If it slices, dices or scrubs, it's hardly ever the gift we've always wanted," "If we liked being called 'Sweetie Pie,' we'd change our names," and "Three words of advice when giving us a gift: save the receipt."

However, some of the advice given is edgier, more defensive. "To us, 'I'll call you' means tomorrow, not sometime before the next century," says a woman in a bathtub, wearing bubbles and a tight smile. Others are seemingly in response to critical comments that men sometimes make about women's appearance. "'What did you do to your hair?' is not our idea of a compliment," says one. Another features a woman painting her fingernails green and the copy, "The correct answer to the question, 'Does this look stupid on me?' is 'No.'"

Rather than being angry or depressed by these comments, as most real women would be, the confident women in the ads are cool and sassy. The campaign actually plays upon the anxiety that most women feel about how attractive their boyfriends and men in general will find them. We worry about looking fat and silly. Fashion is so often ridiculous that we have reason to fear looking stupid. We have the little surveyor in our head constantly criticizing us. In this campaign Virginia Slims encourages us to knock him out with a cigarette.

The campaign is also meant as a rebellious response by young women to those who criticize their smoking. I can paint my nails green, shave my head, and smoke cigarettes—whatever the hell I feel like doing, so there!

Many cigarette ads present smoking as a symbol of women's liberation while subtly arousing feelings of anger, humiliation, and anxiety. The cigarette is the "friend" who alleviates the feelings. The cigarette allegedly helps the woman to control her feelings and thus to be like the supremely cool and confident woman in the ads. Smoking, like dieting, is offered to women as a way of being in control. However, since few if any women can be like the models and since the cigarette does not *really* bestow confidence and control, the overall effect of these ads is to reinforce a feeling of personal failure while *seemingly* addressing positive aspirations.

In many ways, cigarette ads offer smoking to girls and young women as a way to control their emotions. They also offer cigarettes as a way to control weight. A primary reason that many girls start smoking and women do not quit is their terror of gaining weight. Cigarette advertising has played upon this fear for a long time. In 1928 a Lucky Strike ad said, "To keep a slender figure, no one can deny . . . Reach for a Lucky instead of a sweet." It is interesting to note how plump the model looks by today's standards.

The tobacco industry probably couldn't get away with such an overt message today. However, the advertisers can use extremely thin models and copy that almost always includes such words as "slim" and "slender," such as "There's

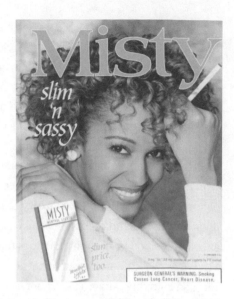

no slimmer way to smoke" and "The slimmest slim in town" (Capri), "Very slim price" and "Slim Lights" (Newport). "Slim 'n sassy," says the ad for Misty, thus promising girls and young women both thinness and independence with their cigarettes.

Sometimes cigarette ads have directly linked the cigarette with food. Most bizarre of all was a campaign for Kent in the early 1980s that literally put the pack or carton of cigarettes into a sandwich, a drink, a blender, a can of sardines, a box of candy, or an oyster shell and used the slogan, "The low tar that won't leave you hungry for taste." Newport links cigarettes with food in some of its ads too. Often a young man is eating something enormous (a huge sandwich, a stack of pancakes) while a young woman looks on. As always, a hearty appetite is considered a good thing for a man but is something to be controlled by a woman. While he eats a banana split, she gets to wistfully lick a spoon and perhaps to smoke a Newport.

Virginia Slims has played on the theme of weight control in many ways. In 1989 Superslims were introduced with the slogan "Fat smoke is history." In 1990 the campaign featured photographs distorted to make the models seem extremely thin and elongated, as if in a fun-house mirror. And in 1994 Virginia Slims directly advertised the cigarette as a diet aid in an ad featuring a thin woman waving away a plate of food, while holding a cigarette. The copy says, "If I ran the world, calories wouldn't count." The implication is clear that calories do count and that girls and women should use cigarettes to resist the temptation of eating.

More recently, in the face of extensive criticism of tobacco advertising, the link with weight control has been a bit more subtle. It is still clearly made, however, in ads such as one in which a young woman says, "When we're wearing a bathing suit, there's no such thing as constructive criticism." Note how this normalizes female anxiety about our bodies, our weight. The woman in the ad is young, thin, and beautiful, and yet she feels anxious about being seen in a bathing suit. How are we mortals supposed to feel?

Virginia Slims cigarettes initially were marketed as "slimmer, longer, not like those fat cigarettes men smoke." In addition to the promise of weight control, this language is quite clearly sexual. Overcoming "penis envy" certainly seems to be part of the Virginia Slims message. In one ad, the model tauntingly says, "He said, 'A slims that's even longer?' I said, Jealous?" This even brought protests from advertisers. *Advertising Age* published a letter from a copywriter that said, "Here's my vote for the new year's first bad ad. Get a load of the expression on the model's face and the little bit of subtle dialog, then tell me that Philip Morris hasn't hit a new low in the battle of the sexes."

As psychologist Karen Horney pointed out in her critique of Freudian theory in the 1920s, it wasn't the actual penis that women envied and wanted, it was the power that the penis represents. Virginia Slims tells women that by bringing this phallic object, even longer than a man's, to our lips, we can take on some of men's power. We won't even need men any more. We'll be independent, self-sufficient.

Of course, there is nothing new about using sexual innuendo to sell ciga-

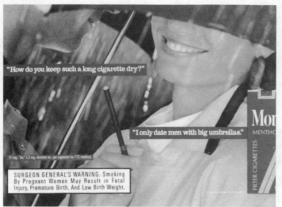

rettes. "It's what's up front that counts" was once the slogan for Tareyton. "I don't judge my cigarette by its length," announced a stern-faced man in a Winston ad from the 1970s. "Who says length doesn't matter?" confides one woman to another in a recent ad for Eve Lights.

In the late 1980s More had a campaign featuring a man and a woman in extreme closeup flirtatiously discussing her long cigarette. "Why such a long cigarette?" he asks her and she replies, "I like to stretch things out." "Is it hard to smoke a cigarette that long," he asks in another ad, and she replies, "Only if you're in a hurry." In the most blatant of them all, he says, "How do you keep such a long cigarette dry?" and she responds, "I only date men with big umbrellas."

Phallic imagery as well as sexual innuendo is often used in cigarette ads. A Salem ad features a man being pushed on a cart by two women, with the slogan "You've got what it takes." Nestled between the man's legs are two bottles, each one pointing at one of the women. More recently, another Salem ad features a woman's hand caressing a champagne bottle as it pops its cork.

One doesn't have to search for exotic subliminal images. Joe Camel is perhaps the most blatant phallic symbol in the history of advertising. I sometimes

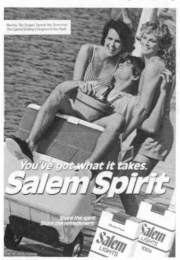

refer to him in my lectures as the rare Australian Dick-Faced Camel. Richard Pollay, curator of the Advertising Archives at the University of British Columbia, has also commented on Joe's extraordinarily well-hung nose and refers to him as Genital Joe.

Why would R. J. Reynolds use such an image? Because it is offering power to children, especially to boys. The ads contain all kinds of icons of power, such as motorcycles, ships, airplanes, usually thrusting into the air. Everything is erect! Joe's phallic face underscores the message: smoke this brand of cigarettes and

you will be a man, you will be powerful. Perhaps young girls get the message that smoking will give them some of the power held by men, the same message Virginia Slims is giving them.

Or perhaps girls and young women are amused by Joe Camel. Elizabeth Hirschman, a marketing professor at Rutgers University, wrote:

> How many times have we—in our female-chauvinist, male-degrading minds—thought that a particular man, or occasionally even men in general, were indeed *pricks* (or in Yiddish terms: *schmucks* with ears). Here, in full-color spreads pasted across billboards, double-trucking through magazines and newspapers, peering down from supermarket cigarette counters, is proof-positive that we were right! Thus, although young men may think it is arousing to have their private parts on public display, dressed up in various costumes, women see these same images as poetic justice: men are dicks!

Countless cigarette ads feature men with fishing poles between their legs, jackhammers, tree trunks, telephone poles. Newport had an entire campaign based on phallic images so blatant that they were often hilarious. A man and woman hug with some gigantic balloons between them. A woman feeds a man a huge icicle or marshmallows from a long stick . . . or squirts wine into his mouth from a winebag. A woman jumps over an ejaculating fire hydrant. This campaign would appeal to both men and women. Both are promised exciting sex and phallic power via the cigarette. It is quite possible that these ads are also playing on men's fears of being inadequate, of not measuring up. In this case, their effect on

men would be similar to the effect of the Virginia Slims ads on women: They would create anxiety and offer the cigarette to alleviate it.

The subliminal phallic images are silly, sometimes hilarious. But they make clear the intent of the advertisers, which is to addict people to a lethal product in whatever way necessary, including promising power to the most powerless people in our society—children, especially children at risk. And many young people, influenced by these images whether they know it or not, fall for this promise. According to a Philip Morris document, "Smoking a cigarette for the beginner is a symbolic act. . . . 'I am no longer my mother's child, I'm tough, I am an adventurer,

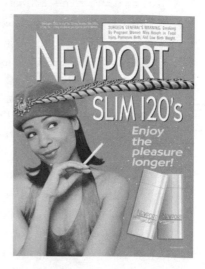

I'm not square.' . . . As the force from the psychological symbolism subsides, the pharmacological effect takes over to sustain the habit." In plain language, the child becomes addicted.

The irony, of course, is that cigarettes, like alcohol, are linked with impotence. Indeed, smokers are 50 percent more likely to suffer from impotence than nonsmokers. A 1959 tobacco industry study concluded that it is "not strength but weakness of the masculine component" that is "more frequent in the heavier smokers." Thus, it is very important for advertisers to make smokers *feel* like virile cowboys. In addition, smoking itself is increasingly linked with symbolic impotence in our society, as the powerful people quit and our most vulnerable children become addicted. No wonder it is more important than ever for the tobacco industry to promise potency to these powerless children and addicted adults. But what a travesty this is—not only does the product not deliver the promised potency, it actually depletes it, in ways ranging from literal impotence to social liability and ostracism to illness and death.

In addition to offering potency on an unconscious level, ads also very directly offer cigarettes to young people as a way to be more powerful. A major theme in cigarette advertising is that smoking is a brave and gutsy thing to do. Many ads feature risky activities, such as hang-gliding, auto-racing, and parasailing. Be a daredevil, be a rebel, the ads seem to say. "Some people still surf without a net," says an ad for Winston featuring a surfboard in a convertible. Many young smokers are rebellious and are also likely to be sensation-seekers. It is no coincidence that tobacco companies are the leading sponsors of events that appeal to risk-taking and rebellious teenagers, such as motorcycle, dirt bike, and hot rod races, rodeos, and ballooning.

The tobacco industry also appeals to rebellious teenagers in other ways. They promote the cigarette itself as an emblem of independence and nonconformity. The smoker is portrayed as the man (or woman) who dares to defy public opinion, to stand on his or her own. "No compromise" declares one campaign for Winston. "Buck the system," says an ad for low-priced Buck cigarettes. Triumph had a whole campaign in which Triumph smokers symbolically gave the world the finger. More recently, Doral ran an ad in *TV Guide*, a magazine seen by millions of young people, which features a dog

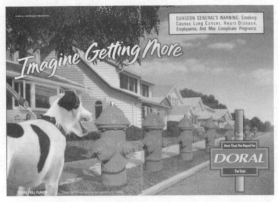

staring at a row of fire hydrants. "Imagine getting more" is the tagline, but "Piss on the world" might be more accurate.

Teenage girls, who identify smoking with independence and rebellion, are especially vulnerable to this pitch. Young men in cigarette ads are far more likely than young women to be physically daring, to be engaged in a dangerous sport or activity. Young women are pictured as daring when they act tough or defy conventional feminine stereotypes or wear outrageous clothing. "Go wild," says a Virginia Slims ad. And just how are young women supposed to demonstrate this wildness? "Call for our new catalog," says the ad. Capri had a campaign in the early 1990s featuring a series of young women flaunting their cigarettes while the headlines said "A taste for the UNconventional," "A taste for the outspoken," "A taste for the daring," and so forth.

Young women are also considered daring and wild when they are overtly sexual. "Light my Lucky," a series of very young, very defiant-looking women told us in the mid-1980s. "The power of now," says a German ad, for a brand of cigarette called West, featuring two tough young women who look like prostitutes.

"What you're looking for," is the tagline for a Camel campaign in the late 1990s. Some of the ads picture very seductive young women. A concurrent Kool campaign running in magazines and on billboards features various sexy young women whose attention is drawn away from the oblivious men with them to another man who is holding a lit cigarette (we see only his hand). "B Kool" is the tagline. These campaigns appeal to both boys and girls, with their promise of seduction and sexual adventure.

In a Winston ad, a young woman looks defiantly at the reader and declares, "My buns might not be steel, but my butt's all tobacco." Here she seems to be a tough cookie who is bravely defying the cultural demand for perfection in women's bodies and yet she is rebelling in a stereotypical "female" way—by harming herself. This ad is reminiscent of the Michelob ad that urges young women to ignore the demands of the fashion magazines for physical perfection and to "relax and enjoy your beer."

Another ad in the Winston campaign features an attractive young woman pushing her way into the men's room. "My patience is gone," she explains, "and so are the additives in my smokes." She, and all the other "daring" young women, are, of course, basically tithing to the tobacco men, who profit mightily from their "rebellion."

Unfortunately, the negative focus on smoking in recent years only increases its allure for rebellious young people. They are attracted to an activity that is both hazardous to health and socially unacceptable. It is difficult to dissuade people by emphasizing the dangerousness of a product, when that very danger is a large part of the appeal. Thus smokers in the United States today are more likely than ever to be especially rebellious and even "deviant."

The tobacco industry often attempts to glamorize this deviance. The Camel campaign that followed the demise of Joe Camel features scenes of outrageous behavior, such as a maid flicking ashes over an abusive rich woman's dinner and phony "warnings" under the heading "Viewer Discretion Advised," such as IR for Idle Rich and PA for Premeditated Ashing.

These ads are clearly meant to satirize the concern about Joe Camel and about the hazards of smoking in general and to encourage people to take the whole issue more lightly. Indeed the campaign itself gives the finger to antismoking activists by clearly appealing to kids every bit as effectively and cynically as did Joe Camel.

Winston goes several steps further in its campaign of the late 1990s. "Finally a butt worth kissing," proclaims one of the ads in this campaign, not only in mag-

azines but on billboards for all to see. The most amazing example is an ad that ran in youth-oriented magazines such as *Rolling Stone* that features a man with his head literally up his butt. "Still smoking additives?" says the irrelevant copy. What is the point of this campaign? It's meant to appeal to young smokers who relish the idea of being deviant, rebellious, even offensive. According to media critic Mark Crispin Miller, cigarette ads in general these days "offer none of the idyllic and escapist scenes that filled the advertising prior to the '80s. Instead, the pitch is nasty and divisive, appealing to the worst impulses of those who smoke or who might start to smoke." He argues that cigarette ads often portray the smoker as a threatening, aggressive figure whose power derives

from the cruel domination of the other. Nowhere is this more evident than in the Winston ad featuring a dominatrix with a whip saying, "When I say no additives, I mean no additives."

A long-running Benson & Hedges

ad glamorizes deviance in a much less heavy-handed way by poking fun at efforts to restrict smoking in public. "Have you noticed the welcome mat is hardly ever out for smokers?" asks an ad featuring attractive young people smoking together on a rooftop. "For a great smoke, make yourself at home."

Ever wonder why she's holding a light?
For a great smoke, take a few liberties.

Finally, a welcome sign for people who smoke
Call 1-800-494-5444 for more information

Sometimes the ads picture smokers in social situations, other times at work, such as the ad featuring people sitting at desks outside on office window ledges and the copy, "Have you noticed finding a place to smoke is the hardest part of your job? For a great smoke, put in for a window office." Another ad in the campaign features young people riding on top of a train. "These days commuters can't climb aboard with a cigarette. For Benson & Hedges, travel the scenic route." Whatever the case the smokers are always very attractive and seem to be having lots of fun.

The link with freedom is made most explicit in the Benson & Hedges ad featuring smokers sitting on top of the Statue of Liberty. "Ever wonder why she's holding a light?" asks the copy. "For a great smoke, take a few liberties."

The tobacco industry is attempting to get even more mileage from this image by portraying public health advocates as antismoking fanatics who want to tell everybody else what to do (what R.J. Reynolds refers to as the "Lifestyle Police") and setting us against the courageous, independent, free-thinking smoker. The billions of dollars the industry has poured into advertising campaigns equating smoking with freedom have had an extra dividend: Critics of smoking are seen as enemies of freedom. For several years the tobacco industry has been running a very expensive public-relations campaign that equates smoking with freedom and the criticism of smoking with totalitarianism.

Perhaps the most outrageous example of this campaign was Philip Morris's use of the Bill of Rights to promote smoking. They enlisted politicians, actors, and even a former American POW in their ads. The POW, Everett Alvarez, says,

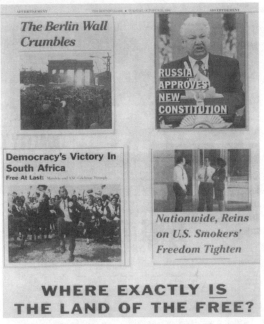

The Berlin Wall Crumbles

RUSSIA APPROVES NEW CONSTITUTION

Democracy's Victory In South Africa
Free At Last:

Nationwide, Reins on U.S. Smokers' Freedom Tighten

WHERE EXACTLY IS THE LAND OF THE FREE?

"You'll never know how sweet freedom can be unless you've lost it for eight and a half years." Thus Philip Morris is associated with freedom and the anti-tobacco-industry forces are associated with America's enemies, such as the North Vietnamese.

R.J. Reynolds Tobacco Company used the same ploy in a full-page newspaper ad featuring photos of the Berlin Wall collapsing, Russia approving the new constitution, and the African National Congress celebrating victory in South Africa juxtaposed with a photo of some people forced to smoke outside their office building and the ludicrous headline, "Where exactly *is* the land of the free?" Once again the people fighting for public health are identified with the enemy—with communists and the creators of apartheid. These ads also undermine the government. Indeed the tobacco industry has played a major role in the burgeoning hostility of Americans to their own government. Although it is not the whole story, of course, it is no coincidence that Bill Clinton is the first president in U.S. history who has taken on the tobacco industry and that Ken Starr is a tobacco industry lawyer.

Consider a full-page ad run in virtually every newspaper in the country that featured a solemn woman saying, "The smell of cigarette smoke annoys me, but not as much as the government telling me what to do." In ad after ad like this, the industry tries to turn a public health issue into a political issue. Imagine this approach about some other public health issue, such as the immunization program for children or alcohol-impaired driving. Imagine a woman in an ad saying, "The death of small children annoys me, but . . ." Or "Drunk drivers annoy me, but . . ." The use of the word "annoys" trivializes the whole issue. Cigarette smoke is not an annoyance—it is a *proven killer,* of nonsmokers as well as smokers.

The alcohol industry also often takes an antigovernment stance, as in an Absolute ad headlined "Absolut DC," which features the familiar bottle all wrapped up in red tape. It is very much to the alcohol and tobacco industries' advantage to have a noninterventionist government and a cynical and apathetic citizenry. Both industries, in their advertising, not only ridicule the government, they promote apathy. "Scientists predict global warming," says a beer ad featuring a six-pack. "Miller says no problem." Don't worry about the destruction of the environment . . . just have another beer or six.

"Make the world a brighter place," says a Virginia Slims ad featuring three women sitting on a snowbank, but the ad suggests no way to do this other than via the glow of one's cigarette. Meantime, Philip Morris's (maker of Virginia Slims) way to make the world a brighter place is to addict more women and girls all over the globe. Its international sales have quadrupled in the past decade. Worldwide today, 47 percent of men smoke compared to only 12 percent of women. In developing countries, between 2 and 10 percent of women smoke compared with 25 to 30 percent in developed countries. Two out of the top three global tobacco companies are American, and they are aggressively targeting women and girls in developing countries with slick advertising promising emancipation, power, and slimness with every puff. They sponsor tours by female pop stars, fashion shows, and other promotions. One year after the entry of American tobacco companies into Korea, smoking rates among female teenagers increased from less than 2 percent to nearly 9 percent. "Camel Planet," says an ad in a Polish youth-oriented magazine, which reads, "The Earth is ours. You have no alternative. Either you come to us or we come to you." Mark Palmer, the U.S. ambassador to Hungary, said, "[The United States and its allies] worked for 45 years to get the communists out. And when we did, the Marlboro Man rode into town to claim the victory."

Is it far-fetched and "paranoid" to suspect such cynical and deliberate manipulation? I am not at all suggesting that women are offered cigarettes in the way that Native Americans were offered alcohol or the Chinese opium, as a conscious attempt on the part of those in power to demoralize and destroy them. However, there are some similarities in the results. For all the talk about freedom and liberation, the truth is that addiction of any kind makes women more passive and far less likely to rebel in any meaningful way. When people are drunk or stoned or high, they don't usually have the energy or the focus to make serious changes in their situation as individuals, let alone as a group. As Barbara Gordon said in *I'm Dancing as Fast as I Can,* the harrowing account of her Valium addiction, "As long as I took the pills, I had been incapable of feeling the anger necessary to make changes in my life."

Addiction hinders a woman's search for equality and power in many ways, not least by defusing the anger and frustration necessary to fuel it. As one former smoker in the New York roundtable discussions said, "Smoking was a release. When things bothered me, I would have a cigarette to avoid dealing with them. Now I don't have the release, so I tend to deal with problems head on." Certainly this is far better than the conclusion drawn by the young woman who used cigarettes to control her anger in a *Teen* article: "My problems are still there, but the tension is gone." As Sue Delaney said in her book *Women Smokers Can Quit: A Different Approach,* "Sometimes we smoke when it would be better to speak. Sometimes we smoke when it would be better to act."

Girls and women are encouraged to use cigarettes and alcohol to cope with anger and depression and to repress their authentic rebelliousness, all the while deluding themselves that they are being genuinely defiant. The girls and women most likely to smoke, the rebels, the risk-takers, the "bad girls," are the very ones most likely to change the system if they had direct access to their energy and their rage. If they were to stop smoking, not only would many lives be saved, but we might also gain access to some of the collective energy presently stifled and defused by cigarettes. This in turn could bring about true liberation for women— and ultimately greater freedom for men too—rather than the illusory liberation offered in the cigarette ads. As Jill Nelson, writing about the rage of African-American women, says, "Mostly, this happens individually, when one woman has reached her end, has had enough of violence, or dishonesty, or being demonized, or being invisible, and breaks out, goes off. It is a powerful thing when this happens. Imagine how much power we'd have if we could figure out how to do this collectively."

9

"THE DREAM BEGINS AS SOON AS YOU OPEN THE DOOR"

Advertising an Addictive Mind-Set

THE DREAM BEGINS
AS SOON AS YOU OPEN THE DOOR.

2 door or 4 door. On-road or off-road. Front-wheel or full-time 4-wheel drive. 4-wheel independent suspension for tight, twisty roads. Fully caffeinated engine. Tons of people space and cargo space. See-above-traffic visibility. In other words, there's never been a vehicle like this before. Not even in your wildest dreams. The RAV4. It's out there.

TOYOTA RAV4
I love what you do for me

LONG BEFORE A GIRL OR A BOY PICKS UP A CIGARETTE OR A BEER, HE OR SHE
has been primed by advertising to expect transformation via a product. From infancy on, we get a seductive and incessant message from ads—products are magical, can fulfill our dreams. "The dream begins as soon as you open the door," says

217

Take me to the water.

a car ad. Imagine if this were an ad for alcohol ("the dream begins as soon as you open the bottle") or cigarettes ("the dream begins as soon as you open the pack") or heroin ("the dream begins as soon as you put in the needle"). Perhaps we would understand what a dangerous message this is.

The landscape of advertising is often deliberately dreamlike, surreal. In an ad for bottled water, a businessman rides the rapids down an escalator, while the faceless masses ride up, paying no attention. A 1997 commercial for Levi jeans features a cowboy driving through the desert in a 1971 Impala filled with stuffed animals. He strolls into a seedy roadhouse with two plush dinosaurs. He hops on a bus. Cut to the bus stopping in New York, and a young woman disembarking—wearing Levi's and holding one of the dinosaurs. The director of the commercial calls it "dream logic." One could also call it "drug logic," since it mimics the altered consciousness of a drug-induced state.

Food is often offered as a way to enter into a dreamworld ("Drift into a chocolate daydream," says an ad for flavored coffee) and indeed into heaven it-

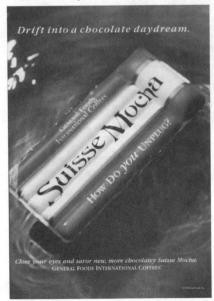

Drift into a chocolate daydream.

Close your eyes and savor new, more chocolatey Suisse Mocha.
GENERAL FOODS INTERNATIONAL COFFEES

self. A yogurt ad claims that the product will "take you to paradise." Another ad, featuring a luscious closeup of a bagel and cream cheese, says, "Find heaven where you least expect it." And an ad for grapefruit juice features an "Actual photo of woman in nirvana."

Women are especially encouraged to reach for food to find peace, an oasis in our hectic days. In an ad for cheese, a woman dreamily says, "Some people journey to distant mountains to replenish their creativity. I prefer a short trip to the dairy case." And an ad for chocolate candy pictures a woman lying on a sofa, with a faraway look in her eyes and a Dove bar in her hands, and the tagline "Let the world pass you by." None of this is coincidental, of course, since advertisers know that food is commonly used, especially by women, to escape from problems. Ads like these, deceptive to be sure but innocuous enough one at a time, cumulatively legitimize and normalize this unhealthy and risky use of food. They also inevitably lead to disappointment since no food will transport us to paradise (although chocolate comes close).

Other products are also offered to women as a way magically to transport ourselves into a state of bliss. "Intoxicate your senses," says an ad for bath products, while other ads promise a soft drink to "refresh your body and soul," a shampoo to "soothe the soul of your hair," and an herbal tea to "satisfy the soul." Now there is certainly nothing wrong with women being encouraged to relax in a nice hot bath. But there is something wrong with the promise that any product is going to soothe our souls.

No product promises entry into the dreamworld more often or more dangerously than alcohol. "Fairy tales can come true," says a vermouth ad, which features the liquor in a glass slipper. An ad featuring an ice cream soda glass with a colorful straw in it and an ice cream scoop beside it announces "The Bailey's Dream Shake." Although most ads are misleading, it is one thing to promise fulfillment of dreams via a car or a perfume, quite another via a powerfully mind-altering drug, which is in fact used by many to escape from reality and responsibilities.

In addition to the literal promises of a dreamworld, alcohol ads often use the kind of verbal and visual puns that occur in dreams. "They were anxious to try that new white wine," features a courtroom scene with the wine on trial. "Tossing back a little J&B," pictures a fisherman throwing the letters J&B into a lake. Such surrealistic imagery is common. "Follow your own plans and dreams take on dimensions," says an ad for scotch featuring a young man walking through a Daliesque landscape. A very strange photo of some people in an open field approaching a rock with a staircase inside has the tagline, "Welcome to the state of Courvoisier." Beer commercials feature giant ants and talking penguins and frogs that chant the

THEY WERE ANXIOUS TO TRY THAT NEW WHITE WINE.

LIBAIO

SEEN IN ALL THE RIGHT PLACES.

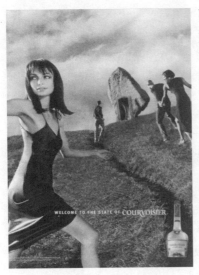

WELCOME TO THE STATE OF COURVOISIER

brand name. Such ads attract attention, especially the attention of young people, and they give the brands a certain cachet of newness, hipness, originality.

Countless ads offer alcohol as a route to paradise or paradise itself. "Paradise found," says one. "Escape to the islands," says another. "Now available in bottles," says a wine cooler ad, featuring a palm tree leaning into a brilliant tropical sunset. "Your own special island" certainly seems to be recommending solitary drinking, a sure sign of trouble with alcohol. There is room for only one glass on the tray. This ad also features a magic bottle, which remains filled and unopened, even though the drink has been poured. An alcoholic's paradise indeed. And yet also an alcoholic's hell. Almost all alcoholics experience intense feelings of isolation, alienation, and loneliness. Most make the tragic mistake of believing that the alcohol alleviates these feelings rather than exacerbating them. The ads take that symptom and turn it around, just as the alcoholic does. You are not isolated and alone: You're on your own special island.

In another version of paradise, this time in a beer commercial, three young men on a beach are watching three beautiful young women walk by. One of the young men holds up the beer can as if it were a remote control and "rewinds" the scene, causing the women to walk by again and again. On the most obvious level, of course, this commercial objectifies women and trivializes the dreams of young men. But it also powerfully reinforces the idea that alcohol is a magic potion that can make our dreams come true. And this has serious consequences. Heavy drinkers tend to believe that alcohol is a "magic elixir" that will enhance their pleasure, sexual performance, and social competence. Teenage alcohol abusers expect more positive effects from alcohol than do their nonabusing peers.

Your own special island.

We've brought a very special rum to the Mainland. And at a very palatable price. Old St. Croix. The Virgin Rum from the Virgin Islands. Light, flavorful and once enjoyed only by a fortunate few who lived on the island. Tonight, it's yours to enjoy. Welcome to the islands!

OLD ST. CROIX

Where do these expectations come from? At the least these ads reinforce them and perhaps even instill them in very young people. "Absolut Magic," promises the vodka ad. This is Absolute Intention on the part of the alcohol advertisers, who know very well that their profits depend upon creating a new market of heavy drinkers.

Again and again we are told that products can give us energy, power, sex appeal, magnetism. "Get your hands on the newest source of energy," says an ad for . . . gloves (which are emitting so much energy they seem radioactive). This ad is merely stupid. But ads with a similar message about addictive products are far more seriously misleading, because these products deplete our energy and rob us of power. You would never guess it from the advertising, however. "Alive with pleasure!" says a cigarette ad, which certainly beats "Dead with cancer!" as a slogan.

We are primed from birth to believe that magical products can make our lives extraordinary. A commercial for the breakfast drink Tang opens with a weary-looking kid who drinks a glass of Tang and suddenly finds himself in a wildly colorful kitchen with orangutans jumping on the counters. "Tang . . . it's a kick in a glass," says the voiceover. What a message this is to little children—this drink can transform you. How could they possibly tell the difference between this and the beer commercials? And if they do believe this, even on an unconscious level, how do they feel when they drink the drink and nothing happens? Does the disappointment set them up for something less innocuous than Tang?

One way to look at drug use is as an attempt to bridge the gap between the constant hype and false promises of advertising and the inevitable disappointment that results when one seeks real gratification from products. At least drugs deliver the goods temporarily—they truly do alter our consciousness.

"A kick in a glass." The very language of advertising to children is often drug language. A campaign called "Craving" advertises a sugary cereal by showing a cute little monster that, according to the advertisers, represents "every kid's uncontrollable craving for sweet and crunchy Honeycomb." An "uncontrollable craving" for anything is a symptom of addiction. An ad for Diet Coke featuring a young woman going wild on a balcony talks about the "heightened sense of reality" associated with the product. In recent years there has been an explosion of new brands of soft drinks called energy drinks or extreme beverages, which contain megadoses of caffeine and are sometimes laced with exotic additives such as ginseng and guarana berries. The "kick in the glass" is not always just advertising hyperbole, since these products really do contain drugs.

Jolt is advertised as "America's most powerful cola" in a television commercial that features a kid with his eyes bulging out. Surge, a citrus soft drink with a blast of caffeine made by the Coca-Cola Company, uses the slogans "Feed the Rush" and "Fully Loaded Summer." Krank2o says "Water with caffeine, lots of caffeine." It is probably no coincidence that crank is the street nickname for methamphetamines. Another brand, XTC, advertised as "a carbonated slap in the face," alludes to the illegal hallucinogenic "ecstasy." Red Bull promises to "give you wings," and GoGo says, "It'll blow your mind." Other brands are Hype, Boost, Guts, Zapped, and RC Edge "Maximum Power" cola. Coca-Cola and Pepsi alone spend over $500 million a year pushing their caffeinated liquid candy with increasingly powerful imagery (while the National Cancer Institute spends less than $1 million on programs encouraging people to eat more fruits and vegetables).

Very young children are enticed by these ads, some of which feature cartoon

characters, such as a rhinoceros, a dinosaur, and a turtle. Heavily caffeinated Mountain Dew, the fastest-growing soft drink in the country, is more than twice as popular as other soft drinks among children younger than six. Its television commercials feature young people sky-diving, bungee-jumping, and engaged in other risky activities. A 1999 Mountain Dew commercial shows skateboarders racing across the roof of a New York skyscraper.

Surge, rush, loaded, blow your mind? The double meaning of these words certainly isn't lost on children, nor is it unintended by advertisers. According to Michael Bainbridge, a brand identity consultant, "There's sort of this need for sensory overload. People are looking for total stimulation in all walks of life, and beverages are one way to get that." Tom Pirko, a beverage consultant, said "Teens are looking for a turn-on that doesn't put them in jail. They want more stimulation."

A turn-on that doesn't put them in jail? How about Kentucky Hemp Beer, a brew made from hemp seed, that is advertised as "Undetectable to police dogs"? The ad sets the bottle of beer, which has a cartoon horse on the label, against a psychedelic background.

Where does this need for sensory overload and more and more stimulation come from, if not from being constantly overstimulated from birth? Advertising deliberately offers us escape into a colorful, exciting, endlessly passionate world—not only via the products being sold but via the very pace of advertising itself, the beat, the colors, the thrills. How can our real lives and real relationships not seem dull by comparison? It isn't only the goods that tantalize us, it is this dreamworld.

But the dreamworld and all the images of magical transformation are not sufficient to influence us in and of themselves. They probably wouldn't matter very much if they didn't connect with the core belief of American culture—that we *can* re-create ourselves, transform ourselves, indeed we should. Advertising has reshaped this into a belief that we can do it all effortlessly if we just use the right products. The underlying assumption is that life should be easy and painless. We shouldn't have to work too hard at our jobs or our relationships. We shouldn't have to struggle to alter our moods or have a good time. This belief in instant transformation is at the heart of addiction. If I drink this, I'll be sexier, wittier. If I smoke this, I'll be calmer, more sophisticated. If I eat this, I'll feel safe and comforted. This product, this substance, will change me, will change my life. And, in spite of all the evidence, this time it will be different.

Of course, to be susceptible to these messages, we must also believe that our lives need changing, that they are not at all okay the way they are. Both addictions and advertising offer us the promise of a much more exciting and glamorous and colorful life, instantly, via a substance or product. They offer us escape, not only from pain but also from boredom and the horror of being ordinary in a culture that equates that with failure. Advertising for many products, not just addictive ones, often reinforces and normalizes the addict's belief that life is dull and unpleasant and needs to be escaped. As the campaign for the television channel Showtime says, "Sometimes being somewhere else is the best place to be."

Adulthood and responsibility are often equated in ads with boredom and terrifying ordinariness. "Oh no, you're becoming your parents," says an ad for a minivan. "Before the spouse, the house, the kids, you get one chance," declares another car ad, which continues, "There's something you should do before life hits you in the knees with ten bags of groceries and the need for a garden hose." "Postpone adulthood," says yet another car commercial.

Living fully in the present is one of the keys to a happy life (as well as to successful recovery from addiction). However, in the dreamworld of advertising, living in the present means that we can put down our burdens, our responsibilities, and become children again—usually spoiled, narcissistic children used to instant gratification, endless recess, no restraints. An ad featuring a hot red

sportscar says, "Why wait to enjoy your second childhood when you can still enjoy your first?" Another features a sedan in the midst of a playground and the copy, "The need for recess hasn't changed. Just the toys." Yet another car ad says, "Not since you lived with Mom and Dad have you gotten so much for so little." And a Jeep ad, drawing a direct connection between driving the Jeep and swinging in a tire swing, promises "to make your off-road dreams a reality." We never have to grow up. We can drive these cars right to never-never-land.

According to child psychiatrist and author Robert Coles, America has entered a second adolescence with the following characteristics: grandiosity and a sense of invulnerability, heightened self-absorption, ironic detachment and defensiveness, and a preoccupation with appearance and sex. Media critic Steven Stark adds "defiant, oppositional anger" to the list. Most of these are characteristics of addiction as well, and many addicts in recovery feel that their addictions "froze" them in adolescence and that they must now grow up for the first time.

There is clearly nothing desirable in the world of advertising about growing up. An ad for a truck says, "About the only thing it has in common with the typical 50-year-old is the spare tire." Fifty is still young these days. Most of us at fifty are much wiser than we were at thirty and we still have another twenty-five or thirty years to go. But we get the constant message that it is all over for us. This is demoralizing for all of us, men and women, young and old—we learn to dread the natural process of growing older and we feel terribly devalued as we age.

Again and again advertising depicts adulthood as a drag, our real lives as monotonous, gray, our relationships as boring and obligatory, our jobs meaningless. According to an alcohol ad, the "perfect week" is "Saturday, Sunday, Saturday, Sunday, Saturday, Sunday, Holiday." Advertising presumes that our work, although often stressful, is basically tedious. How are children to learn about the joys and rewards that can result from responsibility and commitment and hard work?

As one ad says, "We go from our safe little dwelling areas to our climate controlled office cubicle thingys where we spend our days staring at computers and talking to each other in the binary language of ones and zeroes. No wonder we're all going nuts." The solution? "We need the sun and the wind and the smell of trees and flowers." It certainly seems true that one of the reasons we're going nuts is that we're so disconnected from nature and the natural. This ad, however, is selling us a car—the chief destroyer of our natural environment. There is a de-

nial going on in this ad that mirrors the denial of addiction.

Reality is boring, the ads tell us, so we should escape whenever we can and always seek instant gratification. A commercial for Pepsi's new drink Josta features a grandfather telling his grandson that when he was his age his peers encouraged him to chase women, stay out all night, and party. He then says he resisted the impulse—and has been sorry ever since. Josta's slogan is "Better do the good stuff now." So, children get the message early on that it is better to do the good stuff now and, furthermore, that the "good stuff" is to chase women, stay out all night, and party. How ready they are then for a campaign such as Beefeater gin's "Live a little," which features young people partying hard to ward off dread of a dismal future. "Imagine dying without ever having said, 'shaken, not stirred,'" says one ad in this campaign, featuring a beautiful young woman at a bar. On the other hand, imagine dying without ever having gotten so drunk that you throw up on your shoes or sleep with someone you despise or wrap your car around a tree.

Again and again ads promise that alcohol will help us break the chains of ordinary life and wearisome responsibility. Sometimes I think that what alcoholics are most afraid of is being ordinary. Most of us seek in alcohol not only surcease from pain but also some kind of transcendent experience. In the beginning, we think we've found it. As William James said, "However we view things otherwise, under the influence they seem more utterly what they are, more 'utterly utter' than when we are sober." The state of drunkenness, according to James, "expands, unites and says 'Yes'" in contrast to the diminished "no" of sobriety. The alcohol advertisers are aware of this belief and they promise continued excitement and transcendence. Drinking is described as a way to "escape the ordinary," to "defy mediocrity." Alcohol is described as "The Impossible Cream," "The Present Perfect," and "Splendor in the Glass." A beer commercial tells us to "Reach for what's out there" and to "grab for all the gusto you can" (as if a product that numbs us can help us live more intensely).

Occasionally the promised transcendence is divine. Carl Jung described a craving for alcohol as "the equivalent, on a low level, of the spiritual thirst of our being for wholeness." Certainly many alcoholics seek a spiritual experience in alcohol, some perfect connection. Another word for alcohol is "spirits." "Absolut Grail," says the vodka ad, featuring a knight's hand reaching for the drink. Indeed the experience of drunkenness does involve a loss of self, a merging with the alcohol, that is a kind of perversion of a transcendent spiritual experience. This is played on in the many ads in which people are swimming in the alcohol, partying inside the bottle, or sometimes even living inside the bottle.

We are all susceptible to this incessant message that our lives are not exciting enough. It is hard not to feel that we are missing out on something—that everyone else is having more passionate sex (and far more often), more fun, more joy. But addicts are particularly susceptible to this message because many of us have a diminished capacity for joy. Some research indicates that we may have lower levels than nonaddicts of dopamine and serotonin, natural chemicals in the brain that regulate feelings of well-being, sadness, pleasure, and elation. It may be more difficult for us to experience euphoria or even a normal sense of well-being. Alcoholics often say that alcohol makes them feel "normal," not high.

Many addicts need to experience things very intensely in order to feel anything at all. Although the stereotype of the male heavy drinker is of someone larger than life, a creature of hearty appetites, in truth he is far more likely to be suffering from depression. Most alcoholics also suffer from the tragic illusion, promoted heavily and with full intent by the advertising, that what pleasure and gusto we do experience comes from alcohol. Thus the ads that promise that alcohol will bring us joy, will bring magical pleasure into our lives, are especially and intentionally seductive to alcoholics and potential alcoholics.

"Just add Bacardi," says an ad in which a splash of Bacardi rum transforms a walrus on an ice floe into one wearing sunglasses on a colorful tropical beach. Scores of ads show alcohol turning a black and white scene into blazing color, such as another ad in the Bacardi campaign that turns penguins into brilliant flamingos. "Day is grey," says an ad for Black & White scotch, but "The night is Black & White." When I was drinking, I, like most other alcoholics, believed that life without alcohol was gray and humdrum and two-dimensional, an Arctic tundra, but that alcohol flooded it with color and sensation and emotion.

Alcohol ads present a clear choice: fun and excitement with alcohol, or monotony and dreariness without it. "Saturday 2:17 PM," says an ad featuring a man and two women drinking vodka and playing cards on the beach. "You could be home cataloguing your CD collection." Of course, you also could be home playing with your children or writing a poem or meditating or taking a long walk with a friend. But these activities contribute nothing to a corporation's bottom line.

In the beginning, alcohol and other drugs and addictions work. They do make us feel better, sometimes "normal" for the very first time. Initially they seem to add excitement to our lives. The great irony is that there is nothing more monotonous, more routine, more ultimately boring than being an addict. The addict's world becomes more and more constricted, centered only on the drug or substance or activity. I used to look out my kitchen window at night, after I'd had a few drinks, and watch a traffic light turn from red to green to red and think "Is this all there is?" At the very same time, I was convinced that alcohol made my life exciting. This ability to hold two paradoxical beliefs in one's mind is the essence of denial.

All addictions depend on denial. Denial isn't lying (although that often comes with the territory). Denial is being able to hold contradictory beliefs in one's mind simultaneously. It is seeing the evidence of one's addiction everywhere and still believing that one is "in control." "I can quit anytime," is the self-deluding mantra of the addict.

In the strictest scientific sense, addiction is a state in which three criteria—dependence (physical and psychological), tolerance, and withdrawal—all exist. In the past several years, it has often been defined more broadly as the persistent compulsive use of a substance (or an activity such as gambling or work or sex) with harmful consequences for the user and other people. It is increasingly clear that most addictions, including those activities, have a biochemical component and genetic predisposition. Although we are not at all sure yet what causes addiction, there are no doubt many neurotransmitters and other brain chemicals involved, as well as cultural, environmental, and psychological factors.

All kinds of behavior are labeled addictive these days, from jogging to drinking lattes, but this trivializes the devastation caused by serious addictions. At the same time, it remains difficult for most people to accept the concept of addictions such as sex addiction, work addiction, and gambling addiction that are very real and very destructive to individuals, families, and the society as a whole. As James Royce said, "A common reward center that mediates euphoria may be the clue to cross-addiction and to the similarity with other compulsive behaviors."

Advertising doesn't cause addiction. But it does encourage people to experiment with drugs at an early age, thus placing them at greater risk for addiction. In addition to everything else, of course, the constant barrage of advertising for pain-relievers and headache remedies and other over-the-counter drugs teaches us that pain and other unpleasant states are avoidable through drugs. Many drugs are packaged and promoted to appeal to children, such as Gassy Gators, Better Bear Pops, and Kids-Eeze bubble gum. Although it is undoubtedly helpful for children's medicine to taste better, there is a problem when medicine masquerades as candy.

Since the Food and Drug Administration loosened restraints on prescription drug advertising in 1997, there has been an explosion of drug ads. The pharmaceutical industry now spends over a billion dollars a year on advertising aimed at consumers, often using celebrity endorsers such as high-profile athletes. "Have you discovered the pain relief that lies behind this door?" says an ad for an analgesic featuring a closeup of a pharmacy door. And a campaign for another analgesic says, "Life got tougher. We got stronger." As Lily Tomlin says, "Reality is for people who can't handle drugs."

Advertising also encourages compulsion, greed, and a belief in transformation via substances and goods. Perhaps most important, advertising creates a climate of denial in which addictions flourish. It creates this climate of denial, a climate in which harmful and compulsive attitudes toward the product (or activity, in the case of sex and gambling, for example) pass as normal, not only for the addict, but also for all those around him or her—family members, coworkers, doctors. This is absolutely essential because the makers of addictive products must prevent addicts from being confronted and perhaps forced into recovery. *Every time an addict recovers, someone loses money, whether it's the pusher on the corner or the pushers in the boardrooms. This is the bottom line.*

The makers of addictive products prosper when a community or culture colludes with the addict's version of reality. On most college campuses, for example, about 40 percent of the students are binge drinkers. However, the majority of students, if surveyed, believe that 80 or 90 percent of their fellow students are binge drinkers. This belief in and of itself makes it more likely that more students will tolerate the hazardous drinking of others and perhaps will drink more hazardously themselves. It also, of course, makes it far less likely that those students in serious trouble with alcohol will be identified and treated. By the same token, in a culture where almost everyone eats junk food, those who are eating it compulsively can pass for normal and avoid detection. And if promiscuous sex for men is glorified, as it is in this culture, then male sex addicts can end up lionized rather than treated, and the man who ditches his wife of thirty years for a trophy

wife the age of his daughter is seen as a winner rather than as a cad.

No wonder advertising often normalizes disordered attitudes and even symptoms of addiction. The most obvious example is obsession. Alcohol, cigarettes, food, sex are at the center of the ads just as they are at the center of the addict's life. The ads imply, for example, that alcohol is an appropriate adjunct to almost every activity, from making love to white-water canoeing. They also rationalize drinking at any time and for any reason, just as the alcoholic does. "A full day of shopping?" asks an ad for scotch, "Now that calls for a drink." Another features a bottle of champagne on ice with the tagline "The meter maid actually bought your story." I recently passed two billboards within a block of each other. The first offered beer as a reward and celebration because "Life is good." The second offered tequila as a consolation because "Life is harsh." Whatever one's state of mind, whatever one's circumstances, ads tell us that the appropriate response is to drink. Alcoholics are all too eager to believe this.

The wine industry has recently begun a campaign designed to deflate its

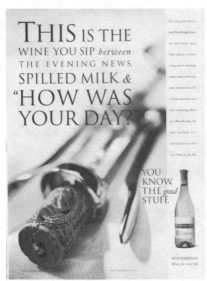

special-occasion-only image. One commercial says, "You're actually home watching TV? This is a special occasion." A print ad says, "It is well to remember that there are five reasons for drinking: the arrival of a friend; one's present or future thirst; the excellence of the wine; or any other reason." And an ad aimed at the woman at home, alone except for her children says, "This is the wine you sip between the evening news, spilled milk, & 'How was your day?'" Another in the same campaign says, "The while-you-set-the-table wine that usually gets invited to dinner," and describes the product as "a wine you drink just about every day." Of course, drinking alone "just about every day" is both a sign of and a route to trouble with alcohol—but in this campaign it is presented as just another innocuous part of one's daily routine. The beer commercials that are indistinguishable from soft-drink commercials have a similar effect. This isn't a drug, they seem to say, this is a harmless beverage that you can indulge in any time without consequences.

Progression is also one of the hallmarks of addiction. Most people begin the addictive process gradually—one or two drinks, a few cigarettes a day, a dish of ice cream, a joint, one hit of cocaine. Gradually they need more of the substance in order to achieve the same effect. Eventually they feel they cannot live without it and it becomes the center of their lives.

A classic example of normalizing progression occurred in a national beer campaign several years ago. In the late 1970s the slogan for Michelob was "Holidays were made for Michelob." A year or so later it became "Weekends were made for Michelob." It must have been apparent to the makers of Michelob that they would not make nearly enough money if people only drank their product on weekends, so the next slogan was "Put a little weekend in your week." Eventually the slogan became "The night belongs to Michelob." There is a world of difference between having a beer on a special occasion and feeling that your night belongs to alcohol. The Michelob campaign deliberately normalizes a potentially dangerous and destructive process. Perhaps the next slogan will be "Put a little Michelob in your morning."

Thus alcohol ads tell the alcoholic and those around him or her, as well as impressionable young people, that it is all right, indeed splendid, to be obsessed with alcohol, to consume large quantities on a daily basis and to have it be a part of all one's activities. At the same time, all signs of trouble and any hint of addiction are erased. Every instance of use seems spontaneous, unique. Bottles are magically unopened even when drinks have been poured. There is no drunkenness, only high spirits. There are never any negative consequences. The denial is unchallenged, indeed reinforced.

Ads for nonaddictive products can reinforce denial too. A 1998 Levi's campaign features "real" teenagers revealing some personal anecdote or fragment of philosophy. One speaks of early morning surfing that makes him late for school. A musician brags about hooking up with two groupies in a ménage à trois. And another, when his father jokingly suggests that the neighbors think he is a gay drug user, says, "Dad, they don't know that I'm gay . . . I mean, they don't know

that I do drugs." According to ad reviewer Bob Garfield, "In the name of relating to teenagers and setting itself apart from adult authority, Levi Strauss is glamorizing a checklist of disturbing, self-destructive behaviors," such as illegal drug use and reckless sex in the age of AIDS.

Signs of trouble with alcohol, even symptoms of alcoholism, are sometimes joked about, trivialized and normalized in ads. This is especially disturbing when the ads are obviously targeting young people. "How a night out with the guys became a long weekend," says an ad for tequila that clearly normalizes and glamorizes binge drinking. Another ad in the same campaign has a similar message: "To them it was a holiday party, to their neighbors a reason to move."

A shocking campaign for Malibu rum targets young people with messages that normalize blackouts as well as binge drinking, encouraging them to "Blame it on Malibu." The ads feature young people partying in the Caribbean with headlines such as, "You're going to call your boyfriend back home. As soon as you can remember his name," and, "You're 262 days late for work." A blackout is a period of time while drinking which the drinker is never able to recall, in spite of being conscious at the time. Blackouts are very serious signs of trouble with alcohol. And, of course, many terrible things occur when drinkers are in blackouts, such as automobile crashes and especially heinous rapes, child abuse, and domestic violence. People coming out of blackouts are far more likely to find themselves in a bloody car wreck than on a tropical beach, just as girls who use alcohol to give themselves permission to be sexual are more likely to encounter rape than romance, pregnancy than passion.

Alcohol is related to parties, good times,

celebrations, and fun, but it is also related to murder, suicide, unemployment, and child abuse, and these connections are never made in the ads. Of course, one would not expect them to be. The advertisers are selling their product and it is their job to erase any negative aspect as well as to enhance or invent the positive ones. However, when the product is the nation's most destructive drug, the consequences go far beyond product sales. The alcohol industry spends over two billion dollars a year promoting its product, a product that is undeniably used in a low-risk way and with pleasure by many people but that is also undeniably a problem for many, with dreadful consequences for the entire society. Certainly it is not only the alcoholic who suffers. According to a recent Gallup survey, one out of three Americans today says that alcohol has been the cause of trouble in his or her family. Countless others are the victims of alcohol-related accidents and crimes. Everyone is affected by the economic and psychological costs.

Of course, alcoholism is not the only addiction. Millions of people are also addicted to other drugs, including nicotine, and to overeating, gambling, sex, and other activities, and most addicts are cross-addicted. Many people consider addiction our society's major problem. As I have said repeatedly, advertising doesn't cause addictions. But it does create a climate of denial and it contributes mightily to a belief in the quick fix, instant gratification, the dreamworld, and escape from all pain and boredom. All of this is part of what addicts believe and what we hope for when we reach for our particular substance.

But there is something else going on too, at a much deeper level. We don't reach for our drugs just for escape or transcendence or relief from pain. We reach for them in the hope of making a *connection*. Addiction begins with the hope that something "out there" can instantly fill up the emptiness inside. Advertising is all about this false hope.

Above all, addiction is a romance, a love affair—a relationship that goes terribly wrong. Advertising most contributes to the addictive mindset by trivializing human relationships and encouraging us to feel that we are in relationships with our products, especially with those products that are addictive. This not only disappoints us. It also diverts attention from what would really satisfy us and make us happy—meaningful work, authentic relationships, and a sense of connection with history, community, nature, and the cosmos. We end up looking for love in all the wrong places—which could be the very definition of addiction.

10

"IN LIFE THERE ARE MANY LOVES, BUT ONLY ONE GRANDE PASSION"

Addiction as a Relationship

"DO YOU LOVE BEER?" A SMOOTH MALE VOICE ASKS, WHILE THE CAMERA lovingly caresses a foaming glass of beer. "If you could have only one thing in your refrigerator, what would it be? . . . How many different languages can you order beer in? . . . Have you ever spent twenty minutes in the beer aisle? . . . Do you love beer?" This is one in a series of commercials for Sam Adams beer that ask different versions of the same question.

A very powerful 1997 commercial gives the alcoholic's answer to this question. The opening shot is of beer pouring from a tap. A man in his bedroom, looking haggard and anxious, hung over, looks into the mirror and sees an image of Guinness. On the soundtrack we hear the old Platters hit, "My prayer is to linger with you, at the end of the day, in a dream that's divine."

The man hears the ocean roar, looks up at a skylight, and sees the image of Guinness again. He looks at an aquarium and sees the image again. He goes outdoors and sees the image in a puddle. He is in a bar, everything in slow motion, welcomed warmly by friends. A woman looks at him very intensely, but he raises his glass of Guinness, which completely obscures her face. He licks his lips and focuses entirely on the drink. This commercial completely captures the alcoholic's intense focus on his drug—the man sees the bottle everywhere, his drink obliterates the face of the woman looking at him. She is of no importance—only the bottle is real to him.

Advertisers spend an enormous amount of money on psychological research. As the chairman of one advertising agency says, "If you want to get into people's wallets, first you have to get into their lives." As a result, they understand addiction very well. Soon after I began my study of alcohol advertising, I realized with horror that alcohol advertisers understand alcoholism perhaps better than any other group in the country. And they use this knowledge to keep people in denial.

The addict's powerful belief that the substance is a friend or lover is constantly reinforced by advertising. In alcohol ads, the bottle itself is sometimes portrayed as the friend or family member. "Bring our family home for the holidays," says a Michelob ad, in which the beer bottles are dressed up as Santa Claus. Another describes a bottle of vodka as "The perfect summer guest." A sign outside a bar at Chicago's O'Hare Airport says, "Why wait at the gate? Your Bud's at the bar." Bud Light takes this theme one step further in an ad featuring two women engrossed in conversation over bottles of

Bring our family home for the holidays.
Celebrate the season with your family and ours.
Serve Michelob, Michelob Light, and Michelob Classic Dark.
Very special beers for a very special time.

beer, with the copy, "Is the best thing about sharing a secret who you share it with or what you share it over?"

Dogs often appear in alcohol ads as a symbol of "man's best friend." A gorgeous Irish setter is pictured in a Johnnie Walker Red ad above the headline, "It's funny how often the comforts of home include Red." A cognac ad, featuring a bloodhound sleeping by the fire, declares "You've been working like one for years, it's time you threw yourself a bone," and a Saint Bernard with a bottle of Chivas Regal around his neck appears above the copy, "It's enough to make you want to get lost." A beer called "Red Dog" uses a picture of a bulldog and the slogan "Be your own dog." More recently, a Miller Lite commercial shows people playing with a puppy and announcing that the beer is "Man's Other Best Friend." The message is clear: Alcohol is loyal and steadfast, just like your dog. Alcohol will never let you down. Alcohol is always there when you need it.

Cigarettes are also often portrayed as friends, companions. Anthropomorphic cigarettes star in a campaign for Benson & Hedges. "Sitting and talking" features two cigarettes on a porch swing. This pitch is especially effective with women because we are socialized to see ourselves in a relational context. Many cigarette ads feature women together, often just talking, with the cigarette as the symbolic bond between them. Sometimes there is deliberate ambiguity about whether the most important relationship is with the friend or the cigarette, as in a Virginia Slims ad featuring two women together with the copy, "The best part about taking a break is who you take it with."

Cigarettes are also used by women, and sometimes by men as well, to facilitate relationships in other ways. They can defuse tense situations or hide anxiety. There is a whole lexicon of smoking as a facilitator for sexual activity, ranging from the man handing a lit cigarette to a woman to her blowing the smoke suggestively in his direction to the two of them sharing a cigarette in the bedroom following their lovemaking.

Even more than a friendship, addiction is a romance—a romance that inevitably goes sour, but that is amazingly intense. As Lou Reed sang in a song called "Heroin," "It's my life and it's my wife." "Your Basic Romance" says a cigarette ad, while another, headlined "Moonlight and romance," features two cigarettes touching by the light of the moon. And an ad for More features the cigarette leaning against a personal ad that says, "Wanted. Tall dark stranger for long lasting relationship. Good looks, great taste a must. Signed, Eagerly Seeking Smoking Satisfaction." The long brown cigarette is, of course, the "tall dark

stranger." And the tobacco industry certainly hopes that the relationship will be long-lasting.

A liqueur ad features a loving couple and the headline "The romance never goes out of some marriages." But it turns out the true marriage is of Benedictine and Brandy, the ingredients of the liqueur. "The result is what every marriage should be—unvarying delight. That's why when there is romance in your soul, there should be B and B in your glass." Alcoholics are far more likely than nonalcoholics to be divorced, but maybe that's because they weren't drinking B and B. And smokers are 53 percent more likely to have been divorced than nonsmokers. An important part of the denial so necessary to maintain alcoholism or any other addiction is the belief that one's alcohol use isn't affecting one's relationships. The truth, of course, is that addictions shatter relationships. Ads like the one for B and B help support the denial and go one step further by telling us that alcohol is, in fact, an enhancement to relationships.

"In life there are many loves. But only one Grande Passion," says an ad featuring a couple in a passionate embrace. Is the passion enhanced by the liqueur or is the passion for the liqueur? For many years I described my drinking as a love affair, joking that Jack Daniels was my most constant lover. When I said this at my lectures or my support group meetings, there were always nods of recognition. Caroline Knapp used this idea as the central metaphor of her memoir about her recovery from alcoholism, *Drinking: A Love Story,* which begins, "It happened this way: I fell in love and then, because the love was ruining everything I cared about, I had to fall out." And Margaret Bullitt-Jonas titled her book about recovering from an eating disorder *Holy Hunger: A Memoir of Desire.*

I can remember loving the names of drinks, from sloe gin fizzes to Manhattans. I loved the look of bottles glowing like jewels in the mirror of a bar—ruby, amber, emerald, topaz. I loved the paraphernalia of drinking—the cherries and olives, the translucent slices of lemon, the salt on the rim of the glass, the frost on the shotglass waiting for the syrupy Stolichnaya straight from the freezer.

Even now, over twenty years since my last drink, if I suddenly catch a glimpse of Jack Daniels on a shelf or in someone's shopping cart, it's a bit like running into an old lover—a lover who was dangerous and destructive, but who completely captured my heart. "You Don't Own Me" was my theme song in high school, a reflection of how frightened I was by intimate relationships, but the truth is that, for many crucial years thereafter, alcohol owned me, heart and soul.

I loved the way alcohol made me feel, the coziness and warmth, the lifting of care. I remember how the first sip of alcohol felt so warm, every time. The glowing feeling in my solar plexus grew more intense as I got high. I felt embraced by alcohol, felt safely enclosed in a little cave of amber light. When I was with another person, I often mistook that little cave for intimacy. The rest of the world went away.

I've been struck since by how many ads re-create the glow, the cave of amber light. There is often a golden halo around the bottle or around the drink itself. A cognac ad features two men, perhaps a father and son, embracing. The copy says, "If you've ever come in from the cold, you already know the feeling of Cognac Hennessy." The two men are in black and white, but the label and the glasses of cognac are a rich, deep amber. The alcohol ads not only promise intimacy, they promise spectacular intimacy, a closeness one has never experienced before. The men in the cognac ad were perhaps estranged, they were out in the cold. Now they are inside the circle of warmth, and alcohol has brought them there. For many years I believed, as most alcoholics do, that only alcohol could take me into that circle. Without it, I was outside, alone. It frightens me still to realize how deeply alcohol advertisers understand the precise nature of the addiction and how deliberately and destructively they use their knowledge.

It is one thing when advertisers exploit people's longing for relationship and connection to sell us shoes or shampoo or even cars. It is quite another when they exploit it to sell us an addictive product. As we saw earlier, some of the ways that products seem to meet Jean Baker Miller's terms for a growth-enhancing connection—increased sense of zest, empowerment to act, greater clarity and self-knowledge, a greater sense of self-worth, and a desire for more connection—are funny and clever and seemingly harmless. It's a great deal more sinister when the products are potentially addictive. We're not likely really to believe that shampoo is going to improve our sex lives, for example, but we might well believe that champagne will.

It is especially sinister for women because so much of our drinking is connected with our relationships with other people. This begins in childhood when problems in relationships, such as early separation from a parent or sexual abuse, predict a greater likelihood of alcoholism. Later in life a loss or impairment of a close relationship, such as divorce or having a partner with whom we feel unable to talk, often influences women drinkers to drink more heavily. And many women drink in an attempt to facilitate relationships, to reduce sexual inhibition, and to be able to speak more openly, especially when angry or upset. Perhaps we are especially vulnerable to the advertising messages that promise us a relationship with an addictive product.

In the beginning, most addictions seem to fill us with *zest and vitality* and advertising often plays on this. "Alive with pleasure" and "Fire it up!" say the cigarette ads, while a beer ad proclaims, "Grab for all the gusto you can," as if a product that eventually numbs many of us could help us live more intensely. "Pursue your passion and new possibilities will awaken," claims an ad for Scotch. A gin ad features a man blissfully swimming in a sea of alcohol, with the caption "Innervigoration." Since gin is a clear drink, a huge lemon slice provides the glow, the amber light.

We feel *empowered to act* by our addictions, often foolishly or rebelliously. "Yes, I can!" say a cigarette ad. "Anything can happen," claims a campaign for tequila, featuring young happy people in glamorous outdoor settings. Yet the ads promise us that the only results of such impulsiveness will be adventure and romance. What happens in the ads, of course, is always wonderful—picnics on the beach at sunset, hang-gliding. Even though most of us know, on some level, that the surprises that accompany drinking are not usually so pleasant, the ads are still seductive.

In a commercial for Zima, a malt-based alcohol, a young woman sits at an airport bar, her flight to Minneapolis delayed. The bartender pours her a Zima, she takes a sip, she hears the announcement of a flight to Paris, and she spontaneously departs for the City of Light (fortunately, she must have had her passport on hand). The Zima is her magic carpet.

The promise always is that the surprise will be happy—a flight to Paris as opposed to a car crash, falling in love rather than being raped on a date, winning the lottery as opposed to getting AIDS from unprotected drunken sex. Or, less dramatically, picnicking on a beach at sunset rather than throwing up at midnight, being the life of the party as opposed to insulting the host.

"Your night is about to take an unexpected twist," promises an ad for gin. One is supposed to think of adventure, not embarrassment, certainly not catastrophe.

Alcohol gives us the illusion of *clarity.* "In vino veritas," we are told. Alcohol sometimes loosens our tongues so we can speak the truth, but for alcoholics it far

more often makes us project our grief and self-hatred onto those closest to us. Through a combination of denial and projection, alcoholism prevents us from seeing the truth about ourselves or our loved ones. And yet sometimes alcohol is very directly advertised as a way to achieve clarity. A scotch ad headlined "Vision" continues, "Seeing clearly is the first step towards acting decisively," as if the drink would contribute to this.

As always, the mythology presented in the alcohol ads is exactly the opposite of the truth about alcohol. Again and again, alcohol is advertised as a way to enhance communication. One ad says, "If the world's biggest problem is a lack of communication, might we suggest a corner table and a fine scotch." Another, featuring a young couple walking together, promises "the art of conversation" along with the cognac.

With enough alcohol, the ads tell us, conversation can be dispensed with altogether: "You must be reading my mind" is the caption over a picture of another young couple walking arm in arm on a cobblestone street, beneath golden gaslights.

"Can the generation gap be bridged?" asks another ad, which concludes that perhaps the right kind of scotch can bridge it. Of course, the truth is that alcohol is far more likely to widen gaps between people than to bridge them.

"I love you, man," says a son to his father while the two are fishing in a very successful Bud Light commercial. However, it turns out he just wants his father's beer and his father snaps back, "You're not getting my Bud Light."

"We sat, my father and I, and indulged in fine cigars and the taste of Pinch. Then we did something we rarely do. We talked," says a scotch ad, one of many in which advertisers offer alcohol as a route to intimacy. The promise of better communication between parents and children is particularly ironic given the devastating effects of parental alcoholism on children and families. Alcohol is involved in over half of all cases of domestic violence and child abuse, and alcoholic families are usually marked by denial and silence (interrupted in many families by emotional and physical explosions, but not by communication). Yet the bottle often represents home itself, as in a Smirnoff vodka campaign with the slogans,

"Home is where you find it," and, "Isn't it funny how so many of the places we find Smirnoff feel like home?" "Home improvement," claims an ad for Bacardi rum, while a beer ad tells us that "a man's beer is his castle." Indeed. Almost any child of an alcoholic would find the Absolut ad featuring every window and door of a house in the shape of a bottle an unintentionally ironic picture of the huge and destructive role that alcohol so often plays in families. More accurate, albeit unintentionally, is a rum ad that says, "The dark taste that eclipses everything."

ABSOLUT WELCOME.

Any kind of addiction gets in the way of communication, mostly because the addict is so focused on the substance. A woman in an ice cream ad says, "I was talking to my boyfriend as I unwrapped my Häagen-Dazs Vanilla Almond Bar. Slowly his voice started to drift away. Completely consumed, I carefully licked the thick Belgian chocolate off. Then I immersed myself in the creamy center. Of all the wonderful things I can say about Häagen-Dazs, I can't say it's great for conversation."

Of course, food and drink can be wonderful for conversation. It somehow seems easier to have intimate conversations while sharing something to eat or drink, a glass of wine, a caffe latte, a good meal. I remember the taste of the chicory in the coffee and the powdered sugar on the beignet as I talked with a friend in New Orleans, a few years after I got sober, about my childhood. "You must have thought you were a bad person," she said and, at that moment, I realized that I had thought that for a long, long time but I no longer did. I realized, as I savored the rich taste of the coffee and the southern sun warm on my skin and the compassionate perceptiveness of my friend, that I was happier than I had ever expected to be.

However a glass of wine might enhance a conversation, a bottle of wine will make it at best difficult to recall. When the food or the alcohol or any addictive substance becomes the focal point, relationships inevitably suffer. Countless children grow up with parents whose attention is tragically diverted by an addiction.

Through the miracle of denial, alcohol seems to increase our *sense of self-worth,* but in fact it mires us more deeply in our self-hatred. "Love thyself," says an ad for scotch, one of many ads offering alcohol as a reward, a gift for oneself.

"I.O. ME" declares a billboard ad for whiskey. Ads often offer us alcohol and food as richly deserved rewards, whatever the occasion. It takes an enormous amount of energy to maintain the kind of denial necessary to protect an alcoholic from his or her self-loathing. It is so painful to face the deep belief that one is worthless, unlovable, that many alcoholics, especially male alcoholics, seek refuge in grandiosity—which is, after all, a form of self-hatred. The alcohol advertisers know this—and play on it in ad after ad.

Finally, what is addiction if not a *desire for more connection?* Unfortunately, it is a connection that makes human connection and real intimacy difficult, if not impossible. "More . . . more . . . more . . . gin taste," one ad declares. More gin taste simply means more gin, of course. "More" is even the name of a cigarette brand. "Absolut Attraction," says an ad featuring a cocktail glass leaning toward a bottle of vodka. People are not even present and yet the ad still implies a promise of greater connection.

Most often, the intimate connection that the alcohol ads offer is a sexual experience. Countless ads feature couples passionately embracing, with suggestive copy such as, "May all your screwdrivers be Harvey Wallbangers," "Wild things happen in the 'oui' hours," and, "Is it proper to Boodle before the guests arrive?" "If the French can do this with a kiss . . . ," asks an ad featuring a man passionately kissing a woman's neck, "imagine what they can do with a vodka!" Given that the vodka is called Grey Goose, I hate to think.

"May all your screwdrivers be Harvey Wallbangers."

That's how true believers in vodka and orange juice toast each other. Because, thanks to Galliano, a Harvey Wallbanger is more than just a gold-plated screwdriver. It's the party drink of the decade, the taste that's sweeping the country. Proving how Galliano can add new life to the most familiar combinations.

Make your next drink with a friend or friends a Harvey Wallbanger party. Somebody brings

Liquore Galliano. You take it from there: Fill tall glass with ice cubes. Fill 3/4 full with orange juice. Add 1 oz. vodka. Stir. Float 1/2 oz. Liquore Galliano on top.

LIQUORE GALLIANO

Of course, alcohol has long been advertised to men as a way to seduce women. An ad for Cherry Kijafa from the 1970s features a virginal young woman dressed entirely in white and the headline "Put a little cherry in your life." Such double entendres abound, ranging from a cocktail called "Sex on the Beach" to an ad featuring a young man dressed as a fencer declaring, "I'm as sure of myself on each thrust as I am when choosing my scotch." In a series of suggestive print and television ads in the 1980s, Billy Dee Williams promised that Colt 45 malt liquor "works every time." Years later a radio ad, also for malt liquor and also targeting young African-American men, said, "Grab a six-pack

and get your girl in the mood quicker. Get your jimmy thicker with St. Ides malt liquor." Imagine—our kids are growing up in this kind of environment and some people think it's enough to tell them to "just say no" to sex. "Get your jimmy thicker" but keep it in your pants?

An extremely erotic 1999 ad for Kahlua pictures a milkmaid lasciviously pouring milk all over her leg. Her head is tossed back and her eyes closed, as if she were in the throes of orgasm. The goosebumps on her leg are obvious as is the erect state of her exposed nipple. "Anything goes" is the tagline.

Using sex to sell alcohol certainly isn't new. What is new in recent years is the promise in alcohol ads of a sexual relationship with the alcohol itself. No longer a means to an end, the drink has become the end. "You never forget your first girl" is the slogan for St. Pauli Girl's beer. "Just one sip of St. Pauli Girl's rich, imported taste is the start of a beautiful relationship." "Pilsner is a type of beer," says an ad featuring a beautiful young woman, "kind of like Rebecca is a type of woman." The ad concludes that it would be great to meet either one in a bar.

"Six Appeal" is the slogan for an ad that features a six-pack of beer and the copy, "The next time you make eye contact with a six-pack of Cold-Filtered Miller Genuine Draft Longnecks, go ahead and pick one up. You won't be disappointed!" In a 1998 Bud commercial, a group of women are standing in a bar and, nodding toward some leering guys, talk about how men think about "it" every eight seconds. But it turns out that the guys are ogling bottles of Bud. An Absolut ad features the top part of a woman's leg clad in a black silk stocking with a garter

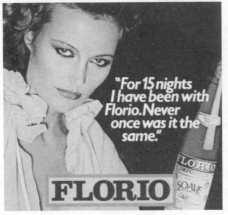

in the familiar shape of the Absolut bottle. This focus on one part of the female body, this dismemberment, is common in ads for many products, but especially so for alcohol. The image draws men in, but there is no person, not even a whole body, to distract them from the focus of the ad, the bottle.

Women are increasingly encouraged to think of the bottle as a lover too. "If your man won't pour, I will," says an ad for cognac which features the bottle rakishly leaning toward the woman. Another ad pictures a bottle of whisky in a drawstring pouch with the tagline "Smooth operator." In an ad for an Italian wine called Florio, a beautiful and sultry woman says, "For 15 nights I have been with Florio. Never once was it the same." This reminds me of a joke I used to make about my drinking years—that perhaps I had had the same conversation every night over and over again and just didn't know it!

In the early 1980s Campari ran a series of ads featuring celebrities such as Geraldine Chaplin and Jill St. John talking lasciviously about their "first time." "There are so many different ways to enjoy it," Chaplin says. "Once I even tried it on the rocks. But I wouldn't recommend that for beginners." The sophomoric campaign used the slogans, "The first time is never the best," and, "You'll never forget your first time." One of the ironies of this campaign is that alcoholics usually do remember their first drink and often romanticize it. For this reason, there's a saying among alcoholics that we should remember our last drunk, not our first drink.

A rawer version of the sexualization of the product was a campaign for the subtly named Two Fingers tequila. Every ad in the campaign featured an older man caressing a beautiful younger woman and saying such things as, "This woman, she is like my tequila. Smooth, but with a lot of spirit," and, "Señor, making good tequila is like looking for a good woman." One of the ads further describes the woman as "the only other love Two Fingers had besides his tequila." Given their age difference, it seems that Two Fingers spent most of his life in love with tequila.

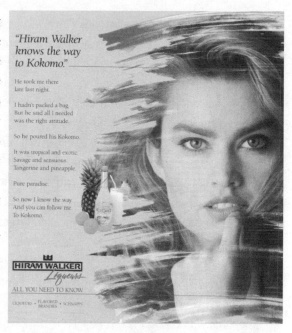

A strange campaign for Hiram Walker liqueurs personifies the product in a series of ads. In one a beautiful young woman says, "Hiram Walker knows the way to Kokomo." She continues, "He took me there late last night. I hadn't packed a bag. But he said all I needed was the right attitude." Another ad in the campaign features a fairly distraught young man saying, "Who is this Hiram Walker guy anyway?" He goes on to say, "My girlfriend couldn't stop talking about him. 'He's spirited . . . and sophisticated . . . and fun. Everything a man should be!' I said, 'Listen, it's him or me. Make up your mind.' She said, 'I want you both.'" The young man ends up having some Hiram Walker, saying, "If you can't beat him, join him." Sadly, this is an attitude many people adopt when dealing with alcoholics.

In this case, the man is introduced to the drink by the woman. Usually, in life and in advertising, it is the other way around. Women and girls are usually introduced to alcohol and other drugs by their boyfriends, who generally are older and more experienced. Women often use the drugs to please their men, to have a common activity, or simply to make the relationship bearable.

The advertisers sometimes encourage women to drink in order to keep company with drinking men. "Share the secret of Cristal," says a beautiful woman. The copy continues, "The Colombians kept it to themselves. Men mostly drank it straight. I thought it was pretty tough stuff 'til the night I met him in Miami and he persuaded me to try CRISTAL & O.J. on ice. Very nice!" Often, as in this ad, the man is urged to drink the product straight while the woman is encouraged to cut it with juice, orange juice in this case, or soda (a more "feminine" approach).

The increasing sexualization of alcohol in ads parallels the progression of the disease of alcoholism, in which alcohol plays a more and more important role. Alcohol is used initially by many people as an attempt to increase confidence, especially sexual confidence, and for some a drink or two can lead to greater relaxation and less inhibition (although intoxication usually reduces sexual responsiveness). For the alcoholic, however, alcohol eventually becomes the most important thing in life and makes other relationships, including sexual relationships, more difficult, if not impossible. Thus, the ads move from a soft-core promise of sexual adventure and fulfillment with a partner to a more hard-core guarantee of sexual fulfillment without the trouble of a relationship with a human being. Alcohol becomes the beloved. And when alcohol is the beloved, relationships with people—with lovers, children, friends—suffer terribly.

One of the most chilling commercials I've ever seen is a 1999 one for Michelob. It opens with an African-American man and woman in bed, clearly just after making love. A fire is blazing and romantic music is playing. "Baby, do you love me?" the woman asks. "Of course I do," the man replies. "What do you love about me most?" she asks. The man looks thoughtful, "Well, Michelob, I love you more than life itself." "What did you call me?" the woman asks indignantly. "I called you Theresa," he replies. "No, you did not," she says, leaping from the bed, "You just called me Michelob. I'm outta here." "Wait, wait," the man says. "What?" she asks. "While you're up," the man says, "could you get me a Michelob?" On the surface, this commercial is intended to be funny, of course. But on a deeper level, and I believe intentionally on the part of the advertisers, it is meant to normalize and trivialize a symptom of alcoholism. The terrible truth is that alcoholics do love alcohol more than the people in their lives and indeed more than life itself.

The Black Velvet campaign of the late 1970s and early 1980s featured a beautiful blonde wearing a sexy black velvet outfit seductively inviting the viewer to "Feel the Velvet" or "Touch the Velvet" or "Try Black Velvet on this weekend." A few years ago, a product called Nude Beer went further and featured a bikini-topped model on the label. The bikini top could be scratched off, revealing her bare breasts. Even then, however, although the woman was a symbol of the alcohol, the focus was still on her.

In recent years, women's bodies in alcohol ads are often turned into bottles of alcohol, as in a Tanqueray gin ad in which the label is branded on the woman's stomach. A beer ad shows cases of Miller Lite stacked (so to speak) on a beach, with the headline "The perfect 36–24–36." There are women in bikinis in the

The perfect tan.

Tanqueray.' A singular experience.

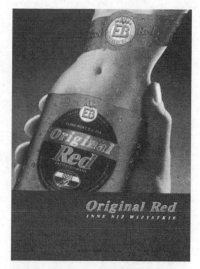

Original Red
INNE NIŻ WSZYSTKIE

background, but clearly the headline refers to the numbers of cans of beer. "The best little can in Texas" pictures a close-up of a woman's derriere with a beer can held up against it. In these cases, the woman is the intermediary. Sometimes the bottle literally becomes the woman, as in an Original Red ad. At least in these ads, a real woman is present to some degree, although objectified and dismembered. In many alcohol ads these days, the woman is completely dispensed with and the bottle itself is sexualized. A college poster advertising beer features a glass of beer and the caption, "Great head, good body."

"Italy's classics have always had great shapes," declares an ad spotlighting a curvaceous bottle of an Italian liqueur. "Not exactly for the bourbon virgin," says an ad for Knob Creek bourbon featuring an extreme closeup of the bottle with an emphasis on the word "pro" within "proof" (this campaign was so successful, it increased sales by 55 percent). "You'd even know us in the nude," says an ad for scotch, which features a man's hand suggestively peeling back the label from the bottle. Again, the promise is that the alcohol alone will provide a fulfilling relationship, even a sexual relationship—nothing else is necessary.

The popular Absolut campaign has several ads in which the bottle is sexualized, including "Absolut Centerfold," which features the bottle

ITALY'S CLASSICS HAVE ALWAYS
HAD GREAT SHAPES.

without its label, and "Absolut Marilyn," in which the bottle symbolizes Marilyn Monroe in her famous dance above the grating.

"A few insights into the dreams of men,"says an ad that features four cartoon men dreaming of a bottle of whiskey. "Yes, men dream in color" is the caption above the first man, referring to a drawing of the bottle in a colorful velvet sack. "The average male only remembers 62 % of his dreams," is above the second man and the bottle is one-third gone. "5% of all men have a recurring nightmare" is the caption for a picture of an empty bottle. "Every man gets aroused at least once per night," depicts a case of whiskey. Women don't exist in this ad, even in the dreams of men. Preoccupation with alcohol is one of the signs of alcoholism. Some alcoholics don't drink all that much, but all alcoholics think about drinking a lot of the time. This ad, in its funny, lighthearted way, normalizes this preoccupation. But the truth is that people who are preoccupied with alcohol create nightmares for themselves and others.

Sometimes it is the drink that is sexualized rather than the bottle. "Peachtree excites soda," proclaims a liqueur ad. A series of ads for Seagram's Extra Dry Gin

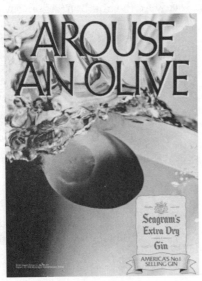

features extreme closeups of the gin in a glass with an olive, a piece of lemon, and a cherry with the bold headlines, "Arouse an olive," "Tease a twist," "Unleash a lime," and "It's enough to make a cherry blush."

Even the cork sometimes gets into the act, as in a liqueur ad featuring a phallic cork and the words "It's not a stopper. It's a starter." Such suggestiveness might seem silly and trivial or unconscious, as perhaps it sometimes is. However, given the money and energy that advertisers spend on psychological research and the undeniable usefulness of linking sex and power with a

It's not a stopper. It's a starter.

Uncork an Occasion.

Vintage methode champenoise, since 1872.
Imported by Codorniu U.S.A., Lake Success, New York.

ABSOLUT IMPOTENCE.

product, I contend that most of these visual and verbal puns and symbols are intended by the advertisers as yet another cynical ploy to influence us.

Ad after ad promises us that alcohol will give us great sex. The truth is exactly the opposite. Not only do high-risk quantities of alcohol often lead to sexual dysfunction, for women as well as for men, but they are also linked with other unwanted consequences, such as date rape, unwanted pregnancy, fetal alcohol syndrome, and sexually transmitted diseases, including AIDS. Alas, the parody "Absolut Impotence" comes closer to the real relationship between alcohol and sex. Perhaps Shakespeare put it best when he said that drink "provokes the desire, but it takes away the performance."

Again and again, advertising tells us that relationships with human beings are fragile and disappointing but that we can count on our products, especially our addictive products. A Winston ad features a greeting card that says, "I never really loved you," with the tagline, "Maybe there shouldn't be a card for every occasion." Another ad in the same campaign shows a cocktail napkin with a woman's name and phone number written on it. The copy says, "Please check the number and dial again." Oh well, at least we've got our cigarettes.

In truth, addiction increasingly corrupts and co-opts every desirable outcome of real connection. The initial sense of zest and vitality is replaced by depression and despair. Our ability to act productively is severely impaired and our lives stagnate. Blinded by denial, we are unable to see ourselves or others clearly. Corroded with self-hatred, we poison our relationships and end up alienated and alone. Our world narrows as our relationship with alcohol or another drug or substance becomes our central focus. We spiral downward.

Recovery reverses this downward spiral, widening our world and our possibilities. As we break through denial and learn to be honest with ourselves and others, our clarity and our sense of self-worth dramatically increase. All of this leads to a desire for more connection, both with other people and with some kind of life force. We find in recovery everything we had longed to find in addiction—but what addiction had in fact taken from us.

Denial blinds us to the many ironies of addiction, and advertising often supports this denial. In the case of alcohol, we drink to feel glamorous and sophisticated and often end up staggering, vomiting, screaming. We drink to feel courageous and are overwhelmed by fear and a sense of impending doom. We drink to have better sex, but alcohol eventually makes most of us sexually dysfunctional. We do this to ourselves because of our disease, but we also do it in a cultural climate in which people who understand the nature of our disease deliberately surround us with powerful images associating alcohol with glamour, courage, sexiness, and love, precisely what we need to believe in order to stay in denial.

Above all, we drink to feel connected and, in the process, we destroy all possiblity of real intimacy and end up profoundly isolated. Sadly, it is perhaps in recognition of this fact that advertisers so often romanticize and sexualize the bottle. Addicts often end up alone or in very dysfunctional relationships. We turn to alcohol or other drugs or activities for solace, for comfort, for the illusion of intimacy, and even for the illusion of sex appeal or sexual fulfillment. As addiction disrupts our human connections, the substance becomes ever more important, both to numb the pain and to continue the illusion that we are doing all right. What begins as a longing for a relationship, a romance, a grand passion, inexorably ends up as solitary confinement.

11

"YOU TALKIN' TO ME?"

Advertising and Disconnection

AT THE CORE OF EVERY ADDICTION IS LONELINESS, ISOLATION. ADDICTS FEEL isolated by definition. They feel that the substance they are dependent on is their only real friend and source of comfort—the very thing that keeps them going, rather than the very thing that is killing them. I used to say that without alcohol, I'd put a gun to my head. *But alcohol was the gun.* The smoker feels that the cigarette is her best friend, but the cigarette is really her assassin. In his classic novel *Under the Volcano,* Malcolm Lowry described the "cold shivering shell of palpitating loneliness" of his alcoholic protagonist and wrote, "God is it possible to suffer more than this, out of this suffering something must be born, and what would be born was his own death."

Jean Baker Miller refers to this terrible loneliness as "condemned isolation," an unbearable state in which a person feels both doomed to be alone and responsible for the isolation. One is alone because one deserves to be alone. One is unlovable. This state is the result of often violent *disconnection* in childhood, something that many addicts have experienced. Indeed, it is almost impossible to be in this state of condemned isolation without seeking respite from drugs or other addictions. Whereas women's yearning for connection has often been pathologized, Miller considers true pathology and psychological problems to be the result of disconnection or violation, especially in early relationships. These disconnections occur at the sociocultural level, as well as within families.

All addicts, male and female, become addicted to various substances for a variety of reasons. As I have discussed, scientists are increasingly discovering that most and perhaps all addictions, including eating disorders and behavioral addictions such as addictions to sex and gambling, have biochemical aspects, and that some people are genetically programmed to be more susceptible to addiction. However, it is also true that many addicts turn to alcohol, cigarettes, other drugs, sex, and food in an attempt to medicate ourselves against depression and despair and often to protect ourselves from the memories of very painful childhoods. At least two-thirds of patients in drug abuse treatment centers say they were physically or sexually abused as children. This is particularly true for women.

Female addicts weren't studied separately until the 1970s. Since then, research has found fundamental differences in the ways that women and men use drugs and other substances. Women are far more likely to use them to self-medicate, to cope with anger and depression, and as anesthesia to deal with traumatic events such as childhood sexual abuse or family alcoholism, whereas men are more likely to use them for recreation and pleasure. This has been known for several years about alcohol and cigarettes. More recently, it has been found to be true of binge eating as well. A survey of eleven hundred patients in weight-loss programs reports that women tend to binge when angry or sad or to use food for comfort when alone or depressed. Obese men were found to binge in positive social situations when celebrating or encouraged by others to eat.

One thing we have learned for sure is that *addictions for women are rooted in trauma*. Several studies have found that alcoholic women are more likely than alcoholic men to have experienced deprivation and rejection in childhood, including the absence, divorce, death, or alcoholism of a parent. They are also very likely to have been sexually abused. In fact, psychologist Sharon Wilsnack found in her 1997 study that childhood sexual abuse is the strongest predictor of alcohol dependency for women, even stronger than a family history of drinking. She estimates that half of the four million female alcoholics in the United States may have been sexually abused in childhood. In her study, those molested as children have more than double the depression rate of other women.

According to researcher Becky Thompson, at least half of women with eating problems were sexually abused as children. Various studies show that from 55 to 99 percent of women in treatment for drug addiction reported a history of physical or sexual trauma, most of which occurred before age eighteen and was related to repetitive childhood assaults. When the women were victims of both types of abuse, they were twice as likely to abuse drugs as those who experienced only one type of abuse. Other research has found that, whether the addiction is to alcohol, heroin, other drugs, or food, from 34 to 80 percent of female addicts are survivors of childhood sexual abuse. The huge gap in the statistics reflects how impossible it is to know the exact numbers, but even the lowest number, one-third, is astounding. And we do know that nothing else creates quite the same sense of "condemned isolation."

Sexual abuse is the most corrupt relationship, the most terrible disconnection. And, as we have learned in recent years, it is more common than many people are willing to believe. A review of 166 studies between 1985 and 1997 concluded that from 25 to 35 percent of girls and from 10 to 20 percent of boys are sexually abused, usually by men they know and trust. This abuse often leads to post-traumatic stress disorder, with its terrifying symptoms of panic attacks, nightmares, depression, flashbacks, and dissociative episodes. Various studies have found that from 30 to 60 percent of women in drug abuse treatment suffer from PTSD—two to three times higher than the rate among men in treatment. Men suffer terribly from abuse too, of course—multiple substance abuse among boys who were sexually abused was eighteen to twenty-one times greater than among boys who were not.

When the body itself is not safe, people often choose to "leave the body," to dissociate. Dissociation is a very common defense mechanism used by people who have been abused. According to feminist theologian Rita Nakashima Brock, "The estimates are that anywhere from 80 to 95 percent of prostitutes in the US are sexually abused as children. The psychological mechanisms of dissociation that they've learned, to survive sexual abuse, are what they also have to use to survive as a prostitute. The kinds of psychological devices people use to survive a business where they serve strangers in this oddly nonintimate sexual way are not healthy." When a person dissociates, he or she is essentially "not there"—not present in the relationship or capable of deep connection. In the immediacy of trauma, we dissociate at will. Years later some kind of drug or addiction is almost always necessary to maintain the dissociation. Seen in this light, some ads are chilling, such as the cigarette ad that says, "She's gone to Capri and she's not coming back," the alcohol ad that promises "Your own special island," and the chocolate ad that claims "Sometimes you're most in touch with the world when you're out of touch."

Alcohol is the perfect drug for someone both seeking and fearing connection, because it gives the illusion of intimacy, while making real intimacy impossible. This is reinforced by the alcohol ads that, with their amber light and cozy little scenes, continually promise an end to isolation—an isolation that alcohol abuse virtually guarantees. People with eating problems also escape their bodies in several ways. They can waste away until very little is left of them or they can hide under layers of fat. They can stuff themselves to feel full and then purge to feel empty and "clean" again. There are rarely clear boundaries between addictions these days: Many women, in particular, have suffered multiple traumas and most female addicts have multiple addictions.

There are many different ways to numb feelings. Some are far more acceptable in the culture than others. All of them, however, have similar roots in different forms of childhood abuse, shame, and rage. I don't think rage is the bedrock, however. I think the bedrock is grief. We turn to alcohol and cigarettes and other drugs and food because we fear we would not be able to bear the grief if we were truly conscious. We never want to go back there again. But we must, if we are to recover.

Of course, one doesn't have to be a woman to experience a sense of condemned isolation. Agonizing disconnections occur in men's lives too, but men are socialized to respond differently than women to these violations. Men who watch their mothers being battered in childhood are more likely to become batterers themselves, whereas women are more likely to become victims of batter-

ers. Men who are sexually abused as children are more likely to become preda-
tors, whereas women often end up more obviously damaging themselves, marrying child abusers or becoming prostitutes.

Even in childhood girls are made to feel more responsible than boys for the
failures of relationships. Many women, damaged as girls by their fathers, spend
their lives trying to heal damaged men, hoping each time to make the relationship right. The daughters of rejecting men reach out to men who will abuse them.
The sons of batterers and philanderers repeat the endless cycle.

Men are often taught to discount their need for connection, to strive to appear "independent" and "autonomous." And they pay a high price for this. Terence Real and others have written about the terrible unnamed depression that
afflicts many men. The cultural environment is only one part of what causes this,
of course, and advertising is only one part of this environment. But it is a powerful part. Advertising, especially advertising for addictive products, generally encourages men to stay disconnected, to be tough and alone—starting as children,
even as babies. "You talkin' to me?" asks a baby with a Harley-Davidson tattoo in
a Pepsi ad. The ad warns us not to mess with Joey or "he'll trench your front
yard." Sure, this is supposed to be cute and funny, but it's actually quite sad when
one thinks of how many real little boys are encouraged to be like this, with often
tragic consequences for themselves and their future partners and children.

"Have you ever seen a grown man cry?" asks a chilling ad for whiskey, as if the
only thing a grown man would cry over is spilled liquor. Miller beer uses the same
idea in a commercial featuring a bored guy trapped at a French movie with some
sobbing women who is brought to tears himself
only when his bottle of beer rolls beneath the
seats and smashes into pieces. A joke, to be sure,
but not too funny given that boys shamed for
crying often grow up into men afraid to feel very
much of anything, except rage.

Have you ever seen a grown man cry?

Women often use alcohol and other drugs
to cope with the pain and disappointment of
unhappy or abusive relationships with these
men. Millions of women have been given tranquilizers by doctors to help them cope with
marriages that should have been dissolved.
Countless battered women drink and smoke in a

misguided attempt to cope with their terror and despair. And many other women use food or alcohol or cigarettes to numb the soul-destroying loneliness they feel in relationships with men who have never learned how to be intimate, how to connect deeply with another human being (which is certainly not to say that all women know how to be intimate, but most of us have been socialized to value intimacy and to blame ourselves if it is absent in our relationships).

Canadian researcher Lorraine Greaves found in her study of women smokers that some women see their cigarettes as passive but comforting "partners." They like how their cigarettes are under their control, that they can have them whenever they want them. Greaves found that this is particularly true for abused women. There is so little security and predictability in their lives that the constancy of their cigarettes becomes very important. The irony, of course, is that the cigarette ends up controlling the smoker. And that most addictions make it almost impossible for women to leave abusive relationships and more difficult to resolve childhood trauma. Only in recovery can we come to terms with the abuse and make the connections that heal rather than harm.

"He loves me, he loves me not," says an ad featuring a daisy and a pack of cigarettes. "But one thing is sure. Carlton is lowest." You can't trust men, but you can trust your cigarettes. Meanwhile, an ad for Briones cigars features a man on a balcony, smoking a cigar while an angry woman far below looks up at him. The copy says, "It doesn't argue. It won't talk back. And it has no opinion." Looks like the woman needs a Carlton.

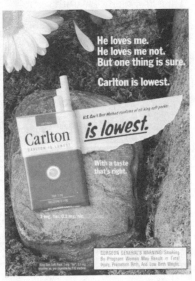

"Until I Find a Real Man, I'll Settle for a Real Smoke," declares a rather tough-looking woman in a cigarette ad. At first glance, this seems to be about sex, of course—the real man being the stud, the one in control. Another way to read it, however, is to think of the real man as one who is gentle, protective, caring. The woman who has never learned to think of men in this way, who has only been exploited by men, is likely indeed to settle for a cigarette or a drink instead. She is also likely to develop a veneer of toughness for self-protection. Not everything that advertisers do is intentional, but they do know what they are doing when they offer cigarettes—and alcohol and food—to women as a way to deal with anger and disappointment in relationships.

Addictions can also be viewed as an attempt to maintain connection in the face of often violent disconnection. We reach out to alcohol and cigarettes and food not simply to numb the pain, but also in an attempt to maintain some kind of relationship, even if it is a relationship with the very thing that will destroy us (a familiar pattern for those abused as children). As Jungian analyst Marian Woodman says, "An addiction reenacts a traumatized relationship to the body."

We don't become addicts because we are self-destructive. And we don't develop eating problems because we are vain or obsessed with our appearance. Most addictions start as survival strategies—logical, creative, even brilliant strategies. In the beginning, we are attempting to save ourselves, to make it possible to go on living in spite of all that we know (even if only unconsciously). In the beginning, alcohol and other drugs and substances make us feel *good*. Ultimately, addiction only deepens our despair and our shame. By the time that happens, however, we are too deep in denial to admit it.

Most addicts feel ashamed long before we become addicted. Childhood abuse makes all people, boys and girls, feel ashamed of themselves. The only way a child can make sense of abuse is by believing he or she deserves it. This leads to a terrible feeling of shame and worthlessness and rage against the self. It becomes necessary to create a false self to confront the world. R. D. Laing wrote brilliantly about this phenomenon in his classic book *The Divided Self*. Speaking of what he terms the "unembodied self," he says:

> In this position the individual experiences his self as being more or less divorced or detached from his body. *The body is felt more as one object among other objects in the world than as the core of the individual's own being.* Instead of being the core of his true self, the body is felt as the core of a *false self*, which a detached, disembodied, "inner," "true" self looks on at with tenderness, amusement, or hatred as the case may be.

The gap between the false self and the real self is unbearably painful. And one doesn't have to be an addict to experience it. Many social critics, such as Jeremy Iggers and Christopher Lasch, contend that we all, not just those of us who are addicts or who have experienced childhood abuse, suffer to a greater or lesser extent from a sense of emptiness. Our capitalistic culture encourages this because *people who feel empty make great consumers*. The emptier we feel, the more likely we are to turn to products, especially potentially addictive products, to fill us up, to make us feel whole.

We also live in a culture in which it is difficult not to feel trapped in a false self, not to feel that one's body is simply an "object among other objects in the world." This is especially true for women, since our bodies are routinely used as objects to sell every imaginable kind of product, from chainsaws to chewing gum. This affects all of us—but how could it not retraumatize people who were treated as objects in childhood?

Mary Gaitskill, in her collection *Because They Wanted To: Stories*, describes a billboard in which the model's:

> eyes were fixated, wounded, deprived. At the same time, her eyes were flat. Her body was slender, almost starved, giving her delicate beauty the strange, arrested sensuality of unsatisfied want. . . . The photograph loomed over the toiling shoppers like a totem of sexualized pathology, a vision of feeling and unfeeling chafing together. *It was a picture made for people who can't bear to feel and yet still need to feel* [italics mine]. It was a picture by people sophisticated enough to fetishize their disability publicly. It was a very good advertisement for a product called Obsession.

Many ads feature just a part of a woman's body—a derriere, a headless torso. An ad for an Internet terminal features a woman bending over. The copy says, "Your butt. It's practically a fixation. You look at it in the mirror. You exercise it. You dress it, so it looks good. You pinch it, for firmness, like a melon. How can we help improve it? Sit on it, and find out." Imagine—a part of one's body is being referred to as a separate object, "like a melon." How difficult it is to feel "embodied" in such a world. No wonder research studies keep finding that many women are depressed by exposure to advertisements and women's magazines.

Soft, smooth legs. No cuts.

We may not be conscious of this, but we are affected. I've been studying these issues for decades and I still feel awful almost every time I read a fashion magazine. My belly is too round

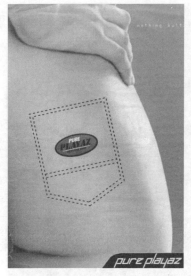

(ever since I gave birth to my daughter), my skin marred by sunspots and wrinkles, my teeth not white enough, my nails not perfect. It's easy to write this off as trivial vanity, but the impact can be deep and serious. It makes it difficult for a woman to feel safe, at home in her body and, therefore, in the world.

Marianne Apostolides, a young woman in recovery from anorexia and bulimia, wrote of her experience:

> I looked in the mirror and saw flabby arms, fatty hips, a rounded belly. I saw myself piece by piece. I didn't see the connections. I didn't see a form composed of curves and straight edges, of soft tissue and strong muscles. I didn't see *me*. My body image reflected my self-image: I hated my body because I hated myself, I doubted my body because I doubted myself, I was angry at my body because I was angry at myself.

It is almost impossible to imagine what our popular culture would look like if women's bodies weren't objectified and dismembered. We are so used to this that it is hard to believe that it has not always been so. In fact, the eroticized imagery of women has been part of the general cultural landscape, not relegated to the world of pornography and sex clubs, for only the past fifty years or so. It is true that there have been erotic images of women in art for centuries, but mass technology has made it possible for these images to constantly surround us. Unlike art, advertising always yokes these images to products. The point is not to arouse desire for the woman, but to arouse desire for the product. Robert Schultz describes these images as "scattered like parks or resorts, little retreats for the male imagination, strokes to the ego and hooks for commerce."

I've been talking about the exploitation of women in advertising since the late 1960s and it was the subject of my 1979 film *Killing Us Softly: Advertising's Image of Women*. It is certainly no longer news. However, it is more extreme and pervasive than ever before. Women's bodies are not only used to attract attention to the product in increasingly absurd ways, as when a nude woman is used to sell a watch or breasts are used to sell fishing line, but increasingly the woman's body

The most dependable fishing line in the world.

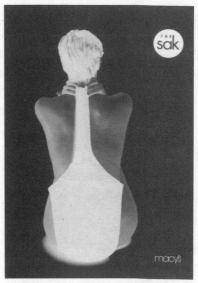

morphs into the product, as in the ad for "the Sak." And this objectification is related to addiction and substance abuse in ways that are complex and that have not been explored.

It is becoming clearer that this objectification has consequences, one of which is the effect that it has on sexuality and desire. Sex in advertising and the media is often criticized from a puritanical perspective—there's too much of it, it's too blatant, it will encourage kids to be promiscuous, and so forth. But sex in advertising has far more to do with trivializing sex than promoting it, with narcissism than with promiscuity, with consuming than with connecting. The problem is not that it is sinful, but that it is synthetic and cynical.

Sexual images in advertising and throughout the media define what is sexy and, more important, who is sexy. To begin with, sex in advertising in the mass media is almost entirely heterosexist—lesbian, gay, or bisexual sex is rarely even implied in the mainstream media (aside from the occasional male fantasy of lesbianism as two beautiful women waiting for Dick to arrive). We are surrounded by images of young, beautiful heterosexual couples with perfect hard bodies having sex. Women are portrayed as sexually desirable only if they are young, thin, carefully polished and groomed, made up, depilated, sprayed, and scented—rendered quite unerotic, in fact—and men are conditioned to seek such partners and to feel disappointed if they fail.

We never see eroticized images of older people, imperfect people, people with disabilities. The gods have sex, the rest of us watch—and judge our own im-

perfect sex lives against the fantasy of constant desire and sexual fulfillment portrayed in the media. To a great extent, the images define desirability—our own as well as others'. We can never measure up. Inevitably, this affects our self-images and radically distorts reality. "You have the right to remain sexy," says an ad featuring a beautiful young woman, her legs spread wide, but the subtext is "only if you look like this." And she is an object—available, exposed, essentially passive. She has the right to remain sexy, but not the right to be actively sexual.

Just as women and girls are offered a kind of ersatz defiance through drinking and smoking that interferes with true rebellion, so are we offered a pseudo-sexuality, a sexual mystique, that makes it far more difficult to discover our own unique and authentic sexuality. How sexy can a woman be who hates her body? She can act sexy, but can she feel sexy? How fully can she surrender to passion if she is worried that her thighs are too heavy or her stomach too round, if she can't bear to be seen in the light, or if she doesn't like the fragrance of her own genitals?

CONQUÊTE
DE LA FACE
NORD

BEST MOUNTAIN

In the world of advertising, only young people have sex. Not only are young women valued only for their sexuality, but the rest of us end up in a culture arrested in adolescence, surrounded by teenage fantasies of sex and romance, a culture that idealizes the very things that make real intimacy impossible—impulsive gratification, narcissism, distance and disconnection, romanticism, and eternal youth. Sex in advertising is about a constant state of desire and arousal—never about intimacy or fidelity or commitment. This not only makes intimacy impossible—it erodes real desire. The endless pursuit of passion is fueled by a sense of inner deadness, emptiness—and it is doomed to failure, like any addiction. Passion inevitably wanes and one is alone again, empty.

When we think about it, the people in ads aren't sexy because of anything unique to them. They have no personal histories. They mostly look alike and are interchangeable. They very rarely look at each other. "The only downside to fe-

The only downside to female guests that stay for breakfast is they leave with your nicest shirts.

male guests that stay over for breakfast is they leave with your nicest shirts," says an ad featuring a man getting dressed. His back is to the young woman in his bed, who is covering herself up as if embarrassed. People in ads like this aren't lovers—they are the users and the used. They are sexy because of the products they use. The jeans, the perfume, the car are sexy in and of themselves. The answer to the question posed by one ad, "What attracts?" is the perfume being advertised, which means these particular partners are irrelevant. They could easily be with any-

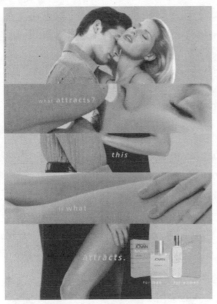

one else who happened to be wearing Jovan musk. Advertising even tells us that "Shi Cashmere is sexier than skin!" Often the people in the ads are grim—there is no humor, no quirkiness, none of the individuality that defines the truly erotic.

Although the sexual sell, overt and subliminal, is at a fever pitch in most advertising, depictions of sex as an important and profound human activity are notably absent. It is a cold and oddly passionless sex that surrounds us. A sense of joy is also absent; the models generally look either hostile or bored.

Passionate sex is one way that we can experience the oceanic, the transcendence of our own boundaries. But this can only occur between subjects, not objects. Sex certainly cannot and does not always have to be sacred and transcendent, but it is tragic for a culture when that possibility is diminished or lost. As psychologist Linda Pollock says, sexual pleasure is significantly more important and, at the same time, significantly less important than our culture holds it to be.

This notion that sexiness and sex appeal come from without rather than within is one of advertising's most damaging messages. Real sexiness has to do with a passion for life, individuality, uniqueness, vitality. It has nothing to do with products or with all the bored, perfect-looking models embracing that we see all around us. If Jeremy Iggers's definition of the erotic as "a heightened sense of aliveness" is true, then surely, in a world in which beautiful people so often look more dead than alive, it is the car ads that most promise an erotic experience. We live in a culture that is sex-crazed and sex-saturated, but strangely *unerotic.*

Advertising constantly confuses real sexuality with narcissism. Identical models parade alone through the commercials, caressing their own soft skin, stroking and hugging their bodies, shaking their long silky manes, sensually bathing and applying powders and lotions, and then admiring themselves at length in the mirror. We're subjected to a steady barrage of messages telling us that all that matters is the immediate fulfillment of our needs and desires. "We are hedonists and we want what feels good," declares a Nike ad. We are the he-

roes of every ad. "You deserve a break today." "Go for it." As an ad for a bath product says, "Entering Willow Lake. Population: One. You."

"A celebration of laughter . . . love . . . and intense happiness," says the ad for Amarige perfume. But all we see is a woman who seems to be in the throes of orgasm caressing her own throat. We don't need partners any more. This is perfect disconnection.

This has been taken even further in some recent ads where the models are literally kissing themselves. Supermodel Linda Evangelista appears in one such ad as a woman and a man. Transvestite RuPaul is featured in another, in which RuPaul the guy nuzzles RuPaul the babe. She is no doubt wearing "Narcisse" perfume and he "Egoiste."

This adolescent attitude toward sex is further reflected and reinforced by all the ads (and situation comedies and films) that turn sex into a dirty joke. Countless ads use sophomoric double entendres, such as "We keep it up longer" (for a radio station), "Your ability to score has just improved" (for a video game), and

"You never forget your first time" (for alcohol and for a discount store). An ad for shoes in a British magazine aimed at young people features a photo of a blonde in the throes of passion (or dead—it's hard to tell) and the copy, "Half way up Mount Caroline. Realised I'd forgotten my safety gear. Made a speedy descent." An American ad for cruises asks the question, "What's your idea of fun?" A beautiful woman slyly replies, "Licking the salt off my husband's margarita." When sexual jokes are used to sell everything from rice to roach-killer, from cars to carpets, it's hard to remember that sex can unite two

What's your idea of fun?

Carnival.

souls, can inspire awe. Individually these ads are harmless enough, sometimes even funny, but the cumulative effect is to degrade and devalue sex.

I do not mean to imply for a minute that sex has to be romantic, soft, nice, domesticated. We inevitably objectify ourselves and each other sexually, which is fine as long as there is reciprocity, as long as we all can be subjects as well, and never merely objects. As Ann Snitow says, "The danger of objectification and fragmentation depend on context. . . . The antipornography campaign introduces misleading goals into our struggle when it intimates that in a feminist world we will never objectify anyone, never take the part for the whole, never abandon ourselves to the mindlessness or the intensities of feeling that link sex with childhood, death, the terrors and pleasures of the oceanic." Far from abandoning the erotic, we need to take it back from the commercial culture that monopolizes it.

Perhaps most important, advertising and the popular culture define human connection almost entirely in terms of sex, thus overemphazing the relative importance of sex in our lives (and marriages) and underemphasizing other important things (friendship, loyalty, fun, the love of children, community). According to poet Robert Hass, the art of the pornographer "consists in the absence of scale." There is no sense of scale in advertising, no sense of what is of greater or lesser importance. Life is rich and varied, with so many aspects that are important and meaningful—political, occupational, educational, creative, artistic, religious, and spiritual aspects. Sex is certainly one of these important aspects but, as Sut Jhally says, "Never in history has the *iconography* of a culture been so obsessed or possessed by questions of sexuality and gender." Men's magazines are filled with erotic images of perfect women (which also litter our highways and fill our TV screens). And women's magazines are filled with desperate articles about how to keep our men sexually happy—explicit instructions for fellatio, recommendations to try new things like anal sex.

The magazines for single women, like *Cosmopolitan,* are breathless, risque ("Drive Him Wild in Bed: The Surprising Places He Wants You to Touch," "Be the Best Sex of His Life," and "Rated X: Sex Lessons of a Paris Madam" are typical cover stories). The ones for wives and mothers are more instructive (how to have romantic quickies, revive your sex life with a weekend in the Caribbean). When I read these magazines, I can almost feel the fatigue between the lines—oh, my God, in addition to working full-time and spending "quality time" with the children and remembering everyone's birthday and being responsible for all the planning of our lives and all the emotional work of the marriage, I also have to schedule passionate interludes and put on a garter belt and stockings and learn the latest sexual positions. No wonder I need a drink or a cigarette or a pint of ice cream.

Perhaps not surprisingly, at the same time that we are surrounded by these images and exhortations, many therapists and marriage counselors say that a chief complaint of many people, both single and married, these days is lack of desire. According to one sex therapist, "Sexual boredom is the most pandemic dysfunction in this country."

A 1999 study published in the *Journal of the American Medical Association* found that sexual dysfunction (such as lacking interest in or enjoyment of sex, performance anxiety, or inability to achieve or hold off orgasm) is an important public health concern, affecting 43 percent of women and 31 percent of men. The study, considered the most comprehensive look at American's sex lives since the Kinsey Report of the late 1940s, surprisingly found that the rate of sexual problems, aside from impotence, is not closely correlated with age. More than one in four women aged eighteen to twenty-nine said they do not find sex pleasurable and young women (aged eighteen to thirty-nine) were more likely than older women (in their forties and fifties) to report a lack of interest in sex, anxiety about performance, pain during intercourse, or an inability to achieve orgasm.

Not surprisingly, victims of childhood sexual abuse reported much higher rates of sexual dysfuntion, with male victims three times more likely to experience erectile dysfunction and female victims twice as likely to have arousal disorders. "Traumatic sexual acts continue to exert profound effects on sexual functioning, some effects lasting many years beyond the occurrence of the original event," the study authors wrote.

But even those who have not experienced trauma are often unhappy and dissatisfied with their sex lives. Another major survey found that a third of women respondents and a sixth of men were uninterested in sex. One-fifth of the women but only one-tenth of the men went so far as to say that sex gave them no pleasure. Although one advertiser joked about all this in an ad claiming that "37% of women prefer shoe shopping to sex," it is decidedly unfunny to those who are afflicted. Sexual dysfunction is associated with unhappiness and poor quality of life, especially for women. In a sea of sultry images, many people are dying of thirst, drying up. Now it may be that these people are perfectly "normal," but in an overheated culture have no idea of what normal desire is. We're not morons. We know that slipcovers won't lead to great sex and that a cruise won't bring a dying marriage back to life. However, it is hard not to believe that other people are having more fun and that there is something wrong with us.

Syndicated columnist Dan Savage thinks that the way we talk about sex contributes to this unhappiness and destroys a lot of perfectly decent relationships. "When we talk about trying to bring the divorce rate down," he says, "maybe we should do it by creating a society where we don't insist a relationship is over when the sexual passion is gone." Raymond C. Rosen, one of the authors of the JAMA study, said that too often people's perceptions of what their sex lives should be like are shaped by articles in magazines that suggest everyone else is having great sex all the time. "As a scientist, it makes my hair stand on end," he said. "It's terrible."

Perhaps these sexy images have the same effect as violent images: They lead more to desensitization than to imitation. As Norman Cousins said:

> The trouble with this wide-open pornography is not that it corrupts, but that it desensitizes; not that it unleashes the passions, but that it cripples the emotions; not that it encourages a mature attitude, but that it is a reversion to infantile obsessions; not that it removes the blinders, but that it distorts the view. Prowess is proclaimed but love is denied. What we have is not liberation, but dehumanization.

A recent issue of *Sky,* a magazine targeting young people, contained the following letter in the advice column: "My problem is that I don't enjoy sex any more. I am a virile 22-year-old. I regularly have sex with my girlfriend, but I have no pleasure any more. . . . Is there something that I'm doing wrong?" The advisor replied, "Shootin' air, eh, babe? You've caught the sex problem of the 90s: pelvic apathy. . . . Actually all that's happening to you and your bald best mate of 22 years is that you've both managed to forget there's another human being slaving away at the far end of your plank. Remember that person with the high voice and the lipstick?" This exchange was an unwittingly ironic counterpart to all the "sexy" ads throughout the issue. And how dehumanizing to refer to a woman, someone's lover, as "that person with the high voice and the lipstick."

Meanwhile, *Mademoiselle* offered this advice to young women whose arms start to ache while pleasuring their partners: "Your best bet—short of looking meaningfully at the bedside clock or developing the forearms of Martina Navratilova—is to get him to give you a hand."

In 1997 NBC featured a story about some college students—men and women—who regularly make a practice of getting drunk together and then having sex with whomever happens to be nearest at hand. According to one student, it is a great way to get his sexual needs met quickly without the "time-consuming" hassle of actually dating and getting to know somebody.

In a world filled with fast-food chains and junk-food advertising, many people are deliberately starving themselves or gorging themselves into oblivion. Consuming food for which we have no real appetite, we are never satisfied and lose our ability to gauge our own hunger. In a similar way, the barrage of constant sexual images and perfect bodies being offered up to us like delectable pastries (or perhaps popsicles) leave us sexually numb and out of touch with our own desire. We can get almost any kind of ethnic food in our own hometowns these days, and we also have more sexual choices than ever before in terms of partners and techniques. But when eating is divorced from hunger and appetite and sex is divorced from desire and relationships, both experiences become onanistic, solitary, unfulfilling.

Of course, all these sexual images aren't intended to sell us on sex—they are intended to sell us on shopping. The desire they want to inculcate is not for orgasm but for more gismos. This is the intent of the advertisers—but an unintended consequence is the effect these images have on real sexual desire and real lives. When sex is a commodity, there is always a better deal. The wreckage that ensues when people try to emulate the kind of sexuality glorified in the ads and the popular culture is everywhere, from my house to the White House. And many who choose not to act on these impulsive sexual mandates nonetheless end up worrying that something is wrong with them, with their flawed and ordinary and all-too-human relationships.

So, all these blatant sexual images that surround us actually are more likely to lead to disconnection rather than to connection. And substance abuse and addiction, especially for women, is often a response to disconnection. Advertising doesn't cause this disconnection, of course, just as it doesn't cause addiction. But it does objectify women's bodies, making it more difficult for women to feel safely "embodied" and thus furthering a sense of dissociation. And it creates a climate in which disconnection and dissociation are normalized, even glorified and eroticized. And finally it deliberately offers addictive products—alcohol, cigarettes, food—as a way to cope with the pain this causes.

Far from improving, the situation continues to get worse. We are so used to blatant sexual images these days that advertisers have to constantly push the envelope in order to attract our attention, to break through the clutter. Increasingly, in order to shock us into paying attention, they borrow images from the world of pornography—which is a world of violence, a world of utter disconnection.

12

"TWO WAYS A WOMAN CAN GET HURT"

Advertising and Violence

Two Ways A Woman Can Get Hurt.

(Heartbreaker)

(Soap and water shave)

Skintimate® Shave Gel Ultra Protection formula contains
75% moisturizers, including vitamin E, to protect your
legs from nicks, cuts and razor burn. So while guys may
continue to be a pain, shaving most definitely won't.

SKINTIMATE® SHAVE GEL
LOVE YOUR LEGS

© 1997 S.C. Johnson & Son, Inc. All rights reserved. www.skintimate.com

SEX IN ADVERTISING IS MORE ABOUT DISCONNECTION AND DISTANCE THAN connection and closeness. It is also more often about power than passion, about violence than violins. The main goal, as in pornography, is usually power over another, either by the physical dominance or preferred status of men or what is seen as the exploitative power of female beauty and female sexuality. Men conquer

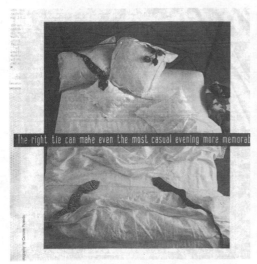

The right tie can make even the most casual evening more memorab

and women ensnare, always with the essential aid of a product. The woman is re-warded for her sexuality by the man's wealth, as in an ad for Cigarette boats in which the woman says, while lying in a man's embrace clearly after sex, "Does this mean I get a ride in your Cigarette?"

Sex in advertising is pornographic because it dehumanizes and objectifies people, especially women, and because it fetishizes products, imbues them with an erotic charge—which dooms us to disappointment since products never can fulfill our sexual desires or meet our emotional needs. The poses and postures of advertising are often borrowed from pornography, as are many of the themes, such as bondage, sadomasochism, and the sexual exploitation of children. When a beer ad uses the image of a man licking the high-heeled boot of a woman clad in leather, when bondage is used to sell neckties in *The New York Times*, per-fume in *The New Yorker*, and watches on city buses, and when a college maga-zine promotes an S&M Ball, pornography can be considered mainstream.

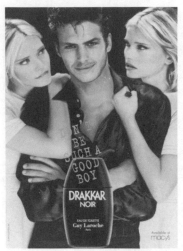

Most of us know all this by now and I suppose some consider it kinky good fun. Pornography is more dangerously mainstream when its glorification of rape and violence shows up in mass media, in films and television shows, in comedy and music videos, and in advertising. Male violence is subtly encouraged by ads that encourage men to be forceful and dominant, and to value sexual intimacy more than emotional intimacy. "Do you want to be the one she tells her deep, dark secrets to?" asks a three-page ad for men's cologne. "Or do you want to be her deep, dark secret?" The last page advises men, "Don't be such a good boy." There are two identical women looking adoringly at the man in the ad, but he isn't looking at either one of them. Just what is the deep, dark secret? That he's sleeping with both of them? Clearly the way to get beautiful women is to ignore them, perhaps mistreat them.

"Two ways a woman can get hurt," says an ad for shaving gel, featuring a razor and a photo of a handsome man. My first thought is that the man is a batterer or date rapist, but the ad informs us that he is merely a "heartbreaker." The gel will protect the woman so that "while guys may continue to be a pain, shaving most definitely won't." Desirable men are painful—heartbreakers at best.

Wouldn't it be wonderful if, realizing the importance of relationships in all of our lives, we could seek to learn relational skills from women and to help men develop these strengths in themselves? In fact, we so often do the opposite. The popular culture usually trivializes these abilities in women, mocks men who have real intimacy with women (it is almost always married men in ads and cartoons who are jerks), and idealizes a template for relationships between men and women that is a recipe for disaster: a template that views sex as more important than anything else, that ridicules men who are not in control of their women (who are "pussy-

POSSESSION
SHIRTS AND SHORTS
1-800-229-CRVPO

whipped"), and that disparages fidelity and commitment (except, of course, to brand names).

Indeed the very worst kind of man for a woman to be in an intimate relationship with, often a truly dangerous man, is the one considered most sexy and desirable in the popular culture. And the men capable of real intimacy (the ones we tell our deep, dark secrets to) constantly have their very masculinity impugned. Advertising often encourages women to be attracted to hostile and indifferent men while encouraging boys to become these men. This is especially dangerous for those of us who have suffered from "condemned isolation" in childhood: like heat-seeking missiles, we rush inevitably to mutual destruction.

Men are also encouraged to never take no for an answer. Ad after ad implies that girls and women don't really mean "no" when they say it, that women are only teasing when they resist men's advances. "NO" says an ad showing a man leaning over a woman against a wall. Is she screaming or laughing? Oh, it's an ad for deodorant and the second word, in very small print, is "sweat." Sometimes it's "all in good fun," as in the ad for Possession shirts and shorts featuring a man ripping the clothes off a woman who seems to be having a good time.

And sometimes it is more sinister. A perfume ad running in several teen magazines features a very young woman, with eyes blackened by makeup or perhaps something else, and the copy, "Apply generously to your neck so he can smell the scent as you shake your head 'no.'" In other words, he'll understand that you don't really mean it and he can respond to the scent like any other animal.

Sometimes there seems to be no question but that a man should force a

woman to have sex. A chilling newspaper ad for a bar in Georgetown features a closeup of a cocktail and the headline, "If your date won't listen to reason, try a Velvet Hammer." A vodka ad pictures a wolf hiding in a flock of sheep, a hideous grin on its face. We all know what wolves do to sheep. A campaign for Bacardi Black rum features shadowy figures almost obliterated by darkness and captions such as "Some people embrace the night because the rules of the day do not apply." What it doesn't say is that people who are above the rules do enormous harm to other people, as well as to themselves.

These ads are particularly troublesome, given that between one-third and three-quarters of all cases of sexual assault involve alcohol consumption by the perpetrator, the victim, or both. "Make strangers your friends, and your friends a

lot stranger," says one of the ads in a Cuervo campaign that uses colorful cartoon beasts and emphasizes heavy drinking. This ad is especially disturbing when we consider the role of alcohol in date rape, as is another ad in the series that says, "The night began with a bottle of Cuervo and ended with a vow of silence." Over half of all reported rapes on college campuses occur when either the victim or the assailant has been drinking. Alcohol's role has different meaning for men and women, however. If a man is drunk when he commits a rape, he is considered less responsible. If a woman is drunk (or has had a drink or two or simply met the man in a bar), she is considered more responsible.

In general, females are still held responsible and hold each other responsible when sex goes wrong—when they become pregnant or are the victims of rape and sexual assault or cause a scandal. Constantly exhorted to be sexy and attractive, they discover when assaulted that that very sexiness is evidence of their guilt, their lack of "innocence." Sometimes the ads play on this by "warning" women of what might happen if they use the product. "Wear it but beware it," says a perfume ad. Beware what exactly? Victoria's Secret tempts young women with blatantly sexual ads promising that their lingerie will make them irresistible. Yet when a young woman accused William Kennedy Smith of raping her, the fact that she wore Victoria's Secret panties was used against her as an indication of her immorality. A jury acquitted Smith, whose alleged history of violence against women was not permitted to be introduced at trial.

It is sadly not surprising that the jury was composed mostly of women. Women are especially cruel judges of other women's sexual behavior, mostly because we are so desperate to believe we are in control of what happens to us. It is too frightening to face the fact that male violence against women is irrational and commonplace. It is reassuring to believe that we can avoid it by being good girls, avoiding dark places, staying out of bars, dressing "innocently." An ad featuring two young women talking intimately at a coffee shop says, "Carla and Rachel considered themselves open-minded and non-judgmental people. Although they did agree Brenda was a tramp." These terrible judgments from other women are an important part of what keeps all women in line.

If indifference in a man is sexy, then violence is sometimes downright erotic. Not surprisingly, this attitude too shows up in advertising. "Push my buttons," says a young woman, "I'm looking for a man who can totally floor me." Her vulnerability is underscored by the fact that she is in an elevator,

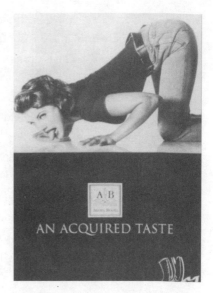

AN ACQUIRED TASTE

often a dangerous place for women. She is young, she is submissive (her eyes are downcast), she is in a dangerous place, and she is dressed provocatively. And she is literally asking for it.

"Wear it out and make it scream," says a jeans ad portraying a man sliding his hands under a woman's transparent blouse. This could be a seduction, but it could as easily be an attack. Although the ad that ran in the Czech version of *Elle* portraying three men attacking a woman seems unambiguous, the terrifying image is being used to sell jeans *to women.* So someone must think that women would find this image compelling or attractive. Why would we? Perhaps it is simply designed to get our attention, by shocking us and by arousing unconscious anxiety. Or per-

haps the intent is more subtle and it is designed to play into the fantasies of domination and even rape that some women use in order to maintain an illusion of being in control (we are the ones having the fantasies, after all, we are the directors).

A camera ad features a woman's torso wrapped in plastic, her hands tied behind her back. A smiling woman in a lipstick ad has a padlocked chain around her neck. An ad for MTV shows a vulnerable young woman, her breasts exposed, and the simple copy "Bitch." A perfume ad features a man shadowboxing with what seems to be a woman.

ÉGOÏSTE
"PLATINUM"
CHANEL

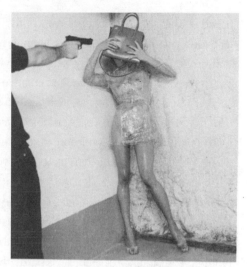

La Borsa è la Vita

Sometimes women are shown dead or in the process of being killed. "Great hair never dies," says an ad featuring a female corpse lying on a bed, her breasts exposed. An ad in the Italian version of *Vogue* shows a man aiming a gun at a nude woman wrapped in plastic, a leather briefcase covering her face. And an ad for Bitch skateboards, for God's sake, shows a cartoon version of a similar scene, this time clearly targeting young people. We believe we are not affected by these

bitch skateboards

images, but most of us experience visceral shock when we pay conscious attention to them. Could they be any less shocking to us on an unconscious level?

Most of us become numb to these images, just as we become numb to the daily litany in the news of women being raped, battered, and killed. According to former surgeon general Antonia Novello, battery is the single greatest cause of injury to women in America, more common than automobile accidents, muggings, and stranger rapes combined, and more than one-third of women slain in this country die at the hands of husbands or boyfriends. Throughout the world, the biggest problem for most women is simply surviving at home. The Global Report on Women's Human Rights concluded that "Domestic violence is a leading cause of female injury in almost every country in the world and is typically ignored by the state or only erratically punished." Although usually numb to these facts on a conscious level, most women live in a state of subliminal terror, a state that, according to Mary Daly, keeps us divided both from each other and from our most passionate, powerful, and creative selves.

Ads don't directly cause violence, of course. But the violent images contribute to the state of terror. And objectification and disconnection create a climate in which there is widespread and increasing violence. Turning a human being into a thing, an object, is almost always the first step toward justifying violence against that person. It is very difficult, perhaps impossible, to be violent to someone we think of as an equal, someone we have empathy with, but it is very easy to abuse a thing. We see this with racism, with homophobia. The person becomes an object and violence is inevitable. This step is already taken with women. The violence, the abuse, is partly the chilling but logical result of the objectification.

An editorial in *Advertising Age* suggests that even some advertisers are concerned about this: "Clearly it's time to wipe out sexism in beer ads; for the brewers and their agencies to wake up and join the rest of America in realizing that sexism, sexual harassment, and the cultural portrayal of women in advertising are inextricably linked." Alas, this editorial was written in 1991 and nothing has changed.

It is this link with violence that makes the objectification of women a more serious issue than the objectification of men. Our economic system constantly re-

quires the development of new markets. Not surprisingly, men's bodies are the latest territory to be exploited. Although we are growing more used to it, in the beginning the male sex object came as a surprise. In 1994 a "gender bender" television commercial in which a bevy of women office workers gather to watch a construction worker doff his shirt to quaff a Diet Coke led to so much hoopla that you'd have thought women were mugging men on Madison Avenue.

There is no question that men are used as sex objects in ads now as never before. We often see nude women with fully clothed men in ads (as in art), but the reverse was unheard of, until recently. These days some ads do feature clothed and often aggressive women with nude men. And women sometimes blatantly objectify men, as in the Metroliner ad that says, "'She's reading Nietzsche,' Harris noted to himself as he walked towards the cafe car for a glass of cabernet. And as he passed her seat, Maureen looked up from her book and thought, 'Nice buns.'"

Although these ads are often funny, it is never a good thing for human beings to be objectified. However, there is a world of difference between the objectification of men and that of women. The most important difference is that there is no danger for most men, whereas objectified women are always at risk. In the Diet Coke ad, for instance, the women are physically separated from the shirtless man. He is the one in control. His body is powerful, not passive. Imagine a true role reversal of this ad: A group of businessmen gather to leer at a beautiful woman worker on her break, who removes her shirt before drinking her Diet Coke. This scene would be frightening, not funny, as the Diet Coke ad is. And why is the Diet Coke ad funny? Because we know it doesn't describe any truth. However, the ads featuring images of male violence against women do describe a truth, a truth we are all aware of, on one level or another.

When power is unequal, when one group is oppressed and discriminated against *as a group*, when there is a context of systemic and historical oppression, stereotypes and prejudice have different weight and meaning. As Anna Quindlen said, writing about "reverse racism": "Hatred by the powerful, the majority, has a different weight—and often very different effects—than hatred by the powerless, the minority." When men objectify women, they do so in a cultural context in which women are constantly objectified and in which there are consequences— from economic discrimination to violence—to that objectification.

For men, though, there are no such consequences. Men's bodies are not routinely judged and invaded. Men are not likely to be raped, harassed, or beaten (that is to say, men presumed to be heterosexual are not, and very few men are abused in these ways by women). How many men are frightened to be alone with a woman in an elevator? How many men cross the street when a group of women approach? Jackson Katz, who writes and lectures on male violence, often begins his workshops by asking men to describe the things they do every day to protect themselves from sexual assault. The men are surprised, puzzled, sometimes amused by the question. The women understand the question easily and have no trouble at all coming up with a list of responses. We don't list our full names in the phone directory or on our mailboxes, we try not to be alone after dark, we carry our keys in our hands when we approach our cars, we always look in the back seat before we get in, we are wary of elevators and doorways and bushes, we carry pepper sprays, whistles, Mace.

Nonetheless, the rate of sexual assault in the United States is the highest of any industrialized nation in the world. According to a 1998 study by the federal government, one in five of us has been the victim of rape or attempted rape, most often before our seventeenth birthday. And more than half of us have been physically assaulted, most often by the men we live with. In fact, three of four women in the study who responded that they had been raped or assaulted as adults said the perpetrator was a current or former husband, a cohabiting partner or a date. The article reporting the results of this study was buried on page twenty-three of my local newspaper, while the front page dealt with a long story about the New England Patriots football team.

A few summers ago, a Diet Pepsi commercial featured Cindy Crawford being ogled by two boys (they seemed to be about twelve years old) as she got out of her car and bought a Pepsi from a machine. The boys made very suggestive comments, which in the end turned out to be about the Pepsi's can rather than Ms. Crawford's. There was no outcry: The boys' behavior was acceptable and ordinary enough for a soft-drink commercial.

Again, let us imagine the reverse: a sexy man gets out of a car in the countryside and two preteen girls make suggestive comments, seemingly about his body, especially his buns. We would fear for them and rightly so. But the boys already have the right to ogle, to view women's bodies as property to be looked at, commented on, touched, perhaps eventually hit and raped. The boys have also learned that men ogle primarily to impress other men (and to affirm their heterosexuality). If anyone is in potential danger in this ad, it is the woman (regardless of the age of the boys). Men are not seen as *property* in this way by women. Indeed if a woman does whistle at a man or touches his body or even makes direct eye contact, it is still *she* who is at risk and the man who has the power.

"I always lower my eyes to see if a man is worth following," says the woman in an ad for men's pants. Although the ad is offensive to everyone, the woman is endangering only herself.

"Where women are women and men are roadkill," says an ad for motorcycle clothing featuring an angry-looking African-American woman. Women are sometimes hostile and angry in ads these days, especially women of color who

where women are women
and men are
roadkill.

are often seen as angrier and more threatening than white women. But, regardless of color, we all know that women are far more likely than men to end up as roadkill—and, when it happens, they are blamed for being on the road in the first place.

Even little girls are sometimes held responsible for the violence against them. In 1990 a male Canadian judge accused a three-year-old girl of being "sexually aggressive" and suspended the sentence of her molester, who was then free to return to his job of babysitter. The deeply held belief that all women, regardless of age, are really temptresses in disguise, nymphets, sexually insatiable and seductive, conveniently transfers all blame and responsibility onto women.

All women are vulnerable in a culture in which there is such widespread objectification of women's bodies, such glorification of disconnection, so much violence against women, and such blaming of the victim. When everything and everyone is sexualized, it is the powerless who are most at risk. Young girls, of course, are especially vulnerable. In the past twenty years or so, there have been several trends in fashion and advertising that could be seen as cultural reactions to the women's movement, as perhaps unconscious fear of female power. One has been the obsession with thinness. Another has been an increase in images of violence against women. Most disturbing has been the increasing sexualization of children, especially girls. Sometimes the little girl is made up and seductively posed. Sometimes the language is suggestive. "Very cherry," says the ad featuring a sexy little African-American girl who is wearing a dress with cherries all over it. A shocking ad in a gun magazine features a smiling little girl, a toddler, in a bathing suit that is tugged up suggestively in the rear. The copy beneath the photo says, "short BUTTS from FLEMING FIREARMS."

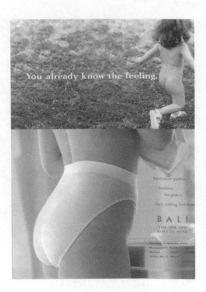

Other times girls are juxtaposed with grown women, as in the ad for underpants that says "You already know the feeling."

This is not only an American phenomenon. A growing national obsession in Japan with schoolgirls dressed in uniforms is called "Loli-con," after Lolita. In Tokyo hundreds of "image clubs" allow Japanese men to act out their fantasies with make-believe schoolgirls. A magazine called *V-Club* featuring pictures of naked elementary-school girls competes with another called *Anatomical Illustrations of Junior High School Girls.* Masao Miyamoto, a male psychiatrist, suggests that Japanese men are turning to girls because they feel threatened by the growing sophistication of older women.

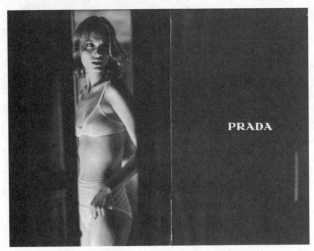

In recent years, this sexualization of little girls has become even more disturbing as hints of violence enter the picture. A three-page ad for Prada clothing features a girl or very young woman with a barely pubescent body, clothed in what seem to be cotton panties and perhaps a training bra, viewed through a partially opened door. She seems surprised, startled, worried, as if she's heard a strange sound or glimpsed someone watching her. I suppose this could be a woman awaiting her lover, but it could as easily be a girl being preyed upon.

The 1996 murder of six-year-old JonBenet Ramsey was a gold mine for the media, combining as it did child pornography and violence. In November of 1997 *Advertising Age* reported in an article entitled "JonBenet keeps hold on magazines" that the child had been on five magazine covers in October, "Enough to capture the Cover Story lead for the month. The pre-adolescent beauty queen, found slain in her home last Christmas, garnered 6.5 points. The case earned a *triple play* [italics mine] on the *National Enquirer,* and one-time appearances on *People* and *Star.*" Imagine describing a six-year-old child as "pre-adolescent."

Sometimes the models in ads are children, other times they just look like children. Kate Moss was twenty when she said of herself, "I look twelve." She epitomized the vacant, hollow-cheeked look known as "heroin chic" that was popular in the mid-nineties. She also often looked vulnerable, abused, and exploited. In one ad she is nude in the corner of a huge sofa, cringing as if braced for an impending sexual assault. In another, she is lying nude on her stomach, pliant, available, androgynous enough to appeal to all kinds of pedophiles. In a music video she is dead and bound to a chair while Johnny Cash sings "Delia's Gone."

It is not surprising that Kate Moss models for Calvin Klein, the fashion designer who specializes in breaking taboos and thereby getting himself public out-

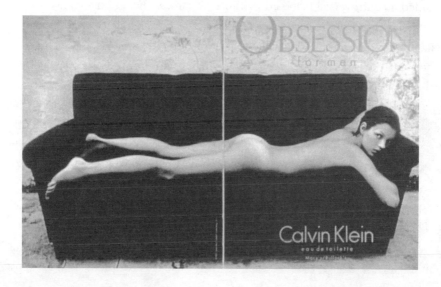

rage, media coverage, and more bang for his buck. In 1995 he brought the federal government down on himself by running a campaign that may have crossed the line into child pornography. Very young models (and others who just seemed young) were featured in lascivious print ads and in television commercials designed to mimic child porn. The models were awkward, self-conscious. In one commercial, a boy stands in what seems to be a finished basement. A male voiceover tells him he has a great body and asks him to take off his shirt. The boy seems embarrassed but he complies. There was a great deal of

protest, which brought the issue into national consciousness but which also gave Klein the publicity and free media coverage he was looking for. He pulled the ads but, at the same time, projected that his jeans sales would almost double from $115 million to $220 million that year, partly because of the free publicity but also because the controversy made his critics seem like prudes and thus positioned Klein as the daring rebel, a very appealing image to the majority of his customers.

Having learned from this, in 1999 Klein launched a very brief advertising campaign featuring very little children frolicking in their underpants, which included a controversial billboard in Times Square. Although in some ways this campaign was less offensive than the earlier one and might have gone unnoticed had the ads come from a department store catalog rather than from Calvin Klein, there was the expected protest and Klein quickly withdrew the ads, again getting a windfall of media coverage. In my opinion, the real obscenity of this campaign

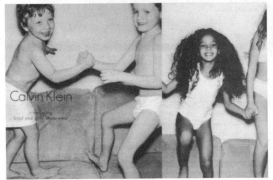

is the whole idea of people buying designer underwear for their little ones, especially in a country in which at least one in five children doesn't have enough to eat.

Although boys are sometimes sexualized in an overt way, they are more often portrayed as sexually precocious, as in the Pepsi commercial featuring the young boys ogling Cindy Crawford or the jeans ad portraying a very little boy looking up a woman's skirt. It may seem that I am reading too much into this ad, but imagine if the genders were reversed. We would fear for a little girl who was unzipping a man's fly in an ad (and we would be shocked, I would hope). Boys are vulnerable to sexual abuse too, but cultural attitudes make it difficult to take this seriously. As a result, boys are less likely to report abuse and to get treatment.

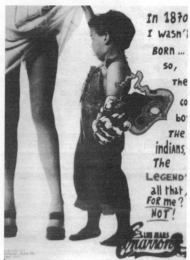

Many boys grow up feeling that they are unmanly if they are not always "ready for action," capable of and interested in sex with any woman who is available. Advertising doesn't cause this attitude, of course, but it contributes to it. A Levi Strauss commercial that ran in Asia features the shock of a schoolboy who discovers that the seductive young woman who has slipped a note into the jeans of an older student is his teacher. And an ad for BIC pens pictures a young boy wearing X-ray glasses while ogling the derriere of an older woman. Again, these ads would be unthinkable if the genders were reversed. It is increasingly difficult in such a toxic environment to see children, boys or girls, as *children*.

In the past few years there has been a proliferation of sexually grotesque toys for boys, such as a Spider Man female action figure whose exaggerated breasts have antennae coming out of them and a female Spawn figure with carved skulls for breasts. Meantime even children have easy access to pornography in video games and on the World Wide Web, which includes explicit photographs of women having intercourse with groups of men, with dogs, donkeys, horses, and snakes; photographs of women being raped and tortured; some of these women made up to look like little girls.

It is hard for girls not to learn self-hatred in an environment in which there is such widespread and open contempt for women and girls. In 1997 a company called Senate distributed clothing with inside labels that included, in addition to the usual cleaning instructions, the line "Destroy all girls." A Senate staffer explained that he thought it was "kind of cool." Given all this, it's not surprising that when boys and girls were asked in a recent study to write an essay on what it

would be like to be the other gender, many boys wrote they would rather be dead. Girls had no trouble writing essays about activities, power, freedom, but boys were often stuck, could think of nothing.

It is also not surprising that, in such an environment, sexual harassment is considered normal and ordinary. According to an article in the journal *Eating Disorders:*

> In our work with young women, we have heard countless accounts of this contempt being expressed by their male peers: the girls who do not want to walk down a certain hallway in their high school because they are afraid of being publicly rated on a scale of one to ten; the girls who are subjected to barking, grunting and mooing calls and labels of "dogs, cows or pigs" when they pass by groups of male students; those who are teased about not measuring up to buxom, bikini-clad [models]; and the girls who are grabbed, pinched, groped and fondled as they try to make their way through the school corridors.
>
> Harassing words do not slide harmlessly away as the taunting sounds dissipate. . . . They are slowly absorbed into the child's identity and developing sense of self, becoming an essential part of whom she sees herself to be. Harassment involves the use of words as weapons to inflict pain and assert power. Harassing words are meant to instill fear, heighten bodily discomfort, and diminish the sense of self.

It is probably difficult for those of us who are older to understand how devastating and cruel and pervasive this harassment is, how different from the "teasing" some of us might remember from our own childhoods (not that that didn't hurt and do damage as well). A 1993 report by the American Association of University Women found that 76 percent of female students in grades eight to eleven and 56 percent of male students said they had been sexually harassed school. One high-school junior described a year of torment at her vocational school: "The boys call me slut, bitch. They call me a 10-timer, because they say I go with 10 guys at the same time. I put up with it because I have no choice. The teachers say it's because the boys think I'm pretty."

High school and junior high school have always been hell for those who were different in any way (gay teens have no doubt suffered the most, although "overweight" girls are a close second), but the harassment is more extreme and more physical these days. Many young men feel they have the right to judge and touch young women and the women often feel they have no choice but to submit. One young woman recalled that "the guys at school routinely swiped their hands across girls' legs to patrol their shaving prowess and then taunt them if they were slacking off. If I were running late, I'd protect myself by faux shaving—just doing the strip between the bottom of my jeans and the top of my cotton socks."

Sexual battery, as well as inappropriate sexual gesturing, touching, and fondling, is increasing not only in high schools but in elementary and middle schools as well. There are reports of sexual assaults by students on other students as young as eight. A fifth-grade boy in Georgia repeatedly touched the breasts and genitals of one of his fellow students while saying, "I want to get in bed with you" and "I want to feel your boobs." Authorities did nothing, although the girl complained and her grades fell. When her parents found a suicide note she had written, they took the board of education to court.

A high-school senior in an affluent suburban school in the Boston area said she has been dragged by her arms so boys could look up her skirt and that boys have rested their heads on her chest while making lewd comments. Another student in the same school was pinned down on a lunch table while a boy simulated sex on top of her. Neither student reported any of the incidents, for fear of being ostracized by their peers. In another school in the Boston area, a sixteen-year-old girl, who had been digitally raped by a classmate, committed suicide.

According to Nan Stein, a researcher at Wellesley College:

Schools may in fact be training grounds for the insidious cycle of domestic violence. . . . The school's hidden curriculum teaches young women to suffer abuse privately, that resistance is futile. When they witness harassment of others and fail to respond, they absorb a different kind of powerlessness—that they are incapable

injustice or acting in solidarity with their peers. Similarly, in
? permission, even training, to become batterers through the
.assment.

This pervasive harassment of and contempt for girls and women constitute a
kind of abuse. We know that addictions for women are rooted in trauma, that
girls who are sexually abused are far more likely to become addicted to one substance or another. I contend that all girls growing up in this culture are sexually
abused—abused by the pornographic images of female sexuality that surround
them from birth, abused by all the violence against women and girls, and abused
by the constant harassment and threat of violence. Abuse is a continuum, of
course, and I am by no means implying that cultural abuse is as terrible as literally
being raped and assaulted. However, it hurts, it does damage, and it sets girls up
for addictions and self-destructive behavior. Many girls turn to food, alcohol, cigarettes, and other drugs in a misguided attempt to cope.

As Marian Sandmaier said in *The Invisible Alcoholics: Women and Alcohol
Abuse in America,* "In a culture that cuts off women from many of their own possibilities before they barely have had a chance to sense them, that pain belongs
to all women. Outlets for coping may vary widely, and may be more or less addictive, more or less self-destructive. But at some level, all women
know what it is to lack access to their own power, to live with a piece
of themselves unclaimed."

Today, every girl is endangered, not just those who have been physically and
sexually abused. If girls from supportive homes with positive role models are at
risk, imagine then how vulnerable are the girls who have been violated. No wonder they so often go under for good—ending up in abusive marriages, in prison,
on the streets. And those who do are almost always in the grip of one addiction
or another. More than half of women in prison are addicts and most are there
for crimes directly related to their addiction. Many who are there for murder
killed men who had been battering them for years. Almost all of the women who
are homeless or in prisons and mental institutions are the victims of male violence.

Male violence exists within the same cultural and sociopolitical context that
contributes to addiction. Both can be fully understood only within this context,
way beyond individual psychology and family dynamics. It is a context of systemic violence and oppression, including racism, classism, heterosexism, weight-

ism, and ageism, as well as sexism, all of which are traumatizing in and of themselves. Advertising is only one part of this cultural context, but it is an important part and thus is a part of what traumatizes.

All right, you might think, these ads are shocking. They are probably not good for us. But just what is the relationship of all these sexist and violent ads to addiction? Am I blaming advertisers for everything now? No. But I do contend that ads that contribute to a climate of disconnection also contribute to addiction. Ads that objectify women and sexualize children also play a role in the victimization of women and girls that often leads to addiction. When women are shown in positions of powerlessness, submission, and subjugation, the message to men is clear: Women are always available as the targets of aggression and violence, women are inferior to men and thus deserve to be dominated, and women exist to fulfill the needs of men.

There is a further connection between images that legitimize male domination of females and addiction. In his classic essay "The Cybernetics of Self" Gregory Bateson describes the fundamental belief of Western culture that we can dominate, control, and have power over almost every aspect of our experience. We can get rid of pain, we can dominate people who threaten us, we can win in any interaction, we can be invulnerable. Bateson theorizes that this belief is fundamentally erroneous and leads to addiction, which he sees as a disordered attempt to get to a more "correct" state of mind, one in which we permit dependency, vulnerability, and mutuality. Bateson argues that we have no culturally sanctioned, nonaddictive way to achieve this state.

Claudia Bepko takes Bateson's theory further by arguing that the stage is set for addiction by the overriding belief system maintaining that men have power and women are the objects of that power. This assumption is as erroneous as is the assumption that we can control our emotions. But our entire culture is predicated on this illusion of male dominance, and our institutions are set up in ways that perpetuate it. According to Bepko, being socialized in an erroneous belief system leads to addiction because incongruity may arise between what one believes and how one actually feels. A man who feels he must be dominant but who actually feels vulnerable might use an addictive substance to lessen his feeling of vulnerability or to enhance his sense of dominance. A woman forced to show dependence who really feels powerful might use a drug or other substance either to enhance or disqualify the impulse to be powerful (as the old Jefferson Airplane song says, "One pill makes you larger and one pill makes you small"). Thus gen-

der-role socialization both shapes and is continually challenged by addictive behavior.

Bepko describes what she calls "the yin and yang of addiction." Both men
and women become addicted and suffer, but their individual addictions arise
from their different positions in the world and have different effects. Men oper-
ate within a context in which both autonomy and entitlement to be taken care of
are assumed; women within a context in which both dependency on a man and
emotional and physical nurturing and caretaking are assumed. The contradictions in these prescriptions obviously create a bind: The male is independent but
taken care of and the woman is dependent but the caretaker. Addiction is one response to the pain created by these contradictions.

Although the critical issues are dependency and control, these have radically
different meanings and outcomes for women and men. Since money, sexuality,
size, strength, and competitive work convey power and status for men, gambling,
sexual addictions, and work addiction tend to be predominantly male forms of
compulsive behavior (although women are catching up as gender roles change).
Women are still socialized to be physically and emotionally nurturing, so eating
disorders, obsessive shopping or cleaning, self-mutilation, and compulsive behavior in relationships are common female forms of addictive behavior, as is prescription drug abuse, which reflects the cultural belief that women's emotions
need to be subdued and controlled. A man is more likely to engage in addictive
behavior that involves having power over others, whereas a woman's attempt at
control is often focused on her own body.

It would be foolish to suggest that advertising is *the cause* of violence against
women—or of alcoholism or eating disorders or any other major problem. These
problems are complex and have many contributing factors. There is no doubt
that flagrant sexism and sex role stereotyping abound in all forms of the media.
There is abundant information about this. It is far more difficult to document the
effects of these stereotypes and images on the individuals and institutions exposed to them because, as I've said, it is difficult to separate media effects from
other aspects of the socialization process and almost impossible to find a comparison group (just about everyone in America has been exposed to massive
doses of advertising).

But, at the very least, advertising helps to create a climate in which certain
attitudes and values flourish, such as the attitude that women are valuable only as
objects of men's desire, that real men are always sexually aggressive, that vio-

lence is erotic, and that women who are the victims of sexual assault "asked for it." These attitudes have especially terrible consequences for women abused as children, most of whom grow up feeling like objects and believing they are responsible for their own abuse. These are the very women who are likely to mutilate and starve themselves, to smoke, to become addicted to alcohol and other drugs. As Judith Herman wrote in her classic book *Father-Daughter Incest:*

> These women alone suffered the consequences of their psychological impairment. Almost always, their anger and disappointment were expressed in self-destructive action: in unwanted pregnancies, in submission to rape and beatings, in addiction to alcohol and drugs, in attempted suicide.
>
> . . . Consumed with rage, they nevertheless rarely caused trouble to anyone but themselves. In their own flesh, they bore repeated punishment for the crimes committed against them in their childhood.

Addictions are not incidental in the lives of women. Most often they are caused by (or at least related to) disturbances in relationships in childhood, often violent disturbances. They are fueled by a culture that sexualizes children, objectifies, trivializes, and silences women, disparages our interest in and skill at relating, and constantly threatens us with violence. Feeling isolated and disconnected, a girl or a woman reaches out to a substance to numb her pain, to be sure, but also to end her isolation, to relate, to connect. She reaches for alcohol or other drugs, she reaches for cigarettes, she reaches for men who don't love her, or she reaches for food. The advertisers are ready for her.

"RELAX. AND ENJOY THE REVOLUTION"

Redefining Rebellion

WE LIVE IN A TOXIC CULTURAL ENVIRONMENT. OUR CHILDREN ARE BEING grossly exploited for commercial gain, buried alive in what David Denby so accurately calls "an avalanche of crud." Millions of people are suffering in the prison of addiction, while others profit from their misery. What can we do about this? How can we break through the climate of denial? The first thing we must do is to get past the cultural belief, promoted so heavily by advertising, that there is a quick fix, an instant solution to every problem—and that one shouldn't even discuss a problem unless one has this solution firmly in mind. There is no quick fix for the problems discussed in this book, no panacea, but there are many things we can and must do.

We must recognize that all of these problems—addictions, eating disorders, male violence (including battering and rape), child abuse, the increasing commercialization of the culture, the exploitation of children by advertisers, gun violence, and the objectification of women and girls—are related. We cannot solve these problems by treating them as separate issues. They are all public health problems and must be treated as such. The public health perspective teaches us that no illness is ever brought under control by treating only the casualties—by having ambulances at the base of the cliff. Just as we can't solve the problems of the physical environment by treating the cancer with chemotherapy, by removing the oil bird by bird, by developing better artificial limbs for the children born with arms and legs missing, we can't solve the problems of the cultural environment by getting alcoholics into support groups, putting metal detectors in our schools, sentencing drunk drivers to stiff prison terms, creating patches and other devices to cut the craving for nicotine, or putting counselors specializing in eating disorders and dating violence in our schools and colleges.

Of course, we need to do some of these things and more to help the casualties. We must build more shelters and safe houses for battered women and children (as things stand now, we have more shelters for animals). We must get addicts into treatment, with separate kinds of treatment programs for adolescents, for girls and women, for prison inmates. We must change the focus of the war on drugs (which has been a dismal failure) from punishment to treatment and prevention. Two-thirds of the almost $18 billion federal drug control budget is spent on law enforcement and only one-third on prevention and treatment—although every person knowledgeable about addiction knows that the percentages should be reversed (and then some). Among industrialized nations, the United States is second only to Russia in the number of its citizens it imprisons, most for drug offenses.

Of course, we have to punish violent criminals, drunk drivers, and so forth. Addiction is not an excuse for criminal acts. But if we imprison people without treating them, we are just putting ourselves at greater risk. Treatment is not a reward for a criminal—it is a proven way to reduce recidivism and thus risk for the rest of us. We should insist that prison inmates be treated for addiction (and probably for post-traumatic stress syndrome, stemming from childhood, as well). This isn't "coddling criminals": This is acting in our own best interest.

Traditionally the approach to addiction in the United States has been consonant with our national ideology of rugged individualism and self-determination. The belief has been that a few unlucky people, through character flaws and general weakness, become addicted. As a culture, we tend to despise these people, just as we despise anyone (the poor, children, the disabled) who reminds us that we are all vulnerable and that no one is really independent. The solution has been to get addicts into treatment as individuals (or, in the case of the less popular drugs or the drugs used by African-Americans, to imprison them).

"Prevention" traditionally has also had an individual focus—"just say no," resist peer pressure, and so forth. But how can we expect kids to say "no" to drugs, when their environment tells them "yes!" People make choices, for better or worse, in a physical, social, economic, and legal environment. The credo of individualism and self-determination ignores the fact that people's behavior is profoundly shaped by their environment, which in turn is shaped by public policy. Certainly individual behavior and responsibility matter, but they don't occur within a vacuum. The American tradition of individual responsibility and promise has been perverted to an extreme form of isolated individualism, an individualism no longer connected with active citizenship and community participation. The result is isolation, alienation, a failure to nurture the next generation or to care for the earth. As social critic Stanley Crouch said, "We get confused about the difference between heroic individuality, which makes possible a greater social freedom, and anarchic individuality, which is ruthless, narcissistic, amoral and dangerous. A long time ago, Alexis de Tocqueville suggested that America's strength was also its vulnerability, that the nation's vibrant individualism might in the long run "attack and destroy" society itself, for it can create individuals so atomized or self-involved that they "no longer feel bound by a common interest."

Advertising's point of view is always and necessarily extremely individualistic. The basic message of advertising, after all, is that an individual has a need or a problem that a product can meet or fix. We are constantly told by advertising that all we need to do is use the right products and get our own individual acts together and all will be fine. If we are unhappy, there is something wrong with us that can be solved by buying something. We can smoke a cigarette or have a drink or eat some ice cream. Or we can lose some weight (instantly, of course). If the problem is a headache, the solution is a stronger aspirin, rather than to question why we have so many headaches, what is going on in our buildings, our food, our environment, why we are so stressed. If the problem is lack of communication in our family, the solution is a different telephone service or a new kind of frozen dinner.

We are especially encouraged to stay focused on the individual and on small changes in personal behavior when the problems involve addiction. If you drink so much you wake up with a hangover . . . take an Alka-Seltzer, don't worry about your drinking. If you're afraid you might kill someone while you're drinking and driving . . . get a designated driver. If you're getting fat, the answer is to use a diet product, not to cut out the junk food and get off the couch. If your dieting is destroying your bones . . . take some calcium. If your teeth are rotting because you are bulimic . . . use a whitening gel. Don't ever look at what this all might mean or try to put it in a larger context. That would disrupt the climate of denial that is so vitally important to the sellers of addictive products.

We must constantly perfect and change ourselves, working for self-improvement rather than social change. "Change is a beautiful thing," says an ad featuring a smiling woman. But the fine print tells us that what we can change is our image, our eye color. "So you're out to change the world—we can do it together," said an ad in the 1970s . . . for shoe coloring. Twenty-five years later another ad features two young women, one white, one African-American, both in very trivializing poses. "Gotta problem? Solve it!" says the ad. What's the ad for? An anti-racism seminar? A consciousness-raising group? No . . . "beauty organizers," kits for holding cosmetics. The more things change, the more they stay the same. These ads exemplify the way that advertising co-opts any movement for social change and reduces it to the narcissistic pursuit of pleasure and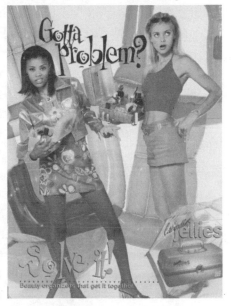

perfection. It has done this most glaringly in the case of the women's movement. "Relax. And enjoy the revolution," declared a woman in an ad in the late sixties, inspiring thoughts of women's liberation. Turns out she was hawking flavored douches. "New Freedom" is a maxipad. "ERA" is a laundry detergent. "Day Care" is a cold medicine. The solution to women being overworked, having a "second shift," is a new kind of potato . . . or a bath oil . . . or a candy bar. An ad for frozen food says, "For me, freedom comes in a bright red package." Another ad, which proclaims, "We believe women should be running the country," turns out to be for expensive sneakers, not political change.

"A woman's life isn't always easy on her," says an ad featuring a woman walking into the kitchen, wearing business clothes, with groceries in her arms and a little child on the floor. What is the ad offering her—child care, more pay, a vacation, a helpful husband? No. The punchline is, "Her laxative should be." The copy continues, "With all the demands on a woman's life, it's no wonder women suffer constipation three times more often than men."

"Win a year at home with your baby," declares an ad for a sweepstakes sponsored by an apple juice company, which continues, "Wouldn't it be wonderful if you could stay at home with your baby for a whole year instead of going off to work?" Women in most other developed nations can count on a year at home with their babies, without having to rely on a lottery. We could too, if we collectively fought for it.

"With Tide, my kid's clothes have a very bright future," says a smiling African-American woman hugging her little girl. Of course, unless we deal with racism in our society, the child herself may not have so bright a future.

The wider world of discrimination, poverty, child abuse, and oppression simply doesn't exist in advertising. There is never the slightest hint that people suffer because of socioeconomic and political situations that could be changed. If we are having difficulty with child care, the solution is to give our children sweets so they will love us, not to lobby for a national child care policy. In the early 1980s an ad campaign for Excedrin used the slogan "Life Got Tougher. We Got Stronger." In one of these ads, a woman is in distress at her office. The copy says, "Life seems tougher when you're raising a family and working too." Indeed it does, but the solution according to this ad is not more equal partnerships in marriage or a national child care policy but simply a stronger aspirin.

Ads such as these have contributed to the myth of superwoman, one of the most damaging stereotypes of all. Young women are encouraged to feel that they effortlessly can combine marriage and a career. Advertising images obscure the fact that the overwhelming majority of women are in low-status, low-paying jobs and are as far removed from superwoman's elite executive status as the majority

of men have always been removed from her male counterpart. In addition, the myth of superwoman places total responsibility for change on the individual woman and exempts men from the responsibilities and rewards of domestic life and child care. It also diverts attention from the political policies that would truly change our lives.

When social problems are mentioned in advertising, it is only to be trivialized and reduced once again to the personal. "Urban decay" is simply the brand name of a cosmetics line. Several ads illustrate advertising's approach to the threat of environmental destruction. "Scientists predict global warming," says one ad, which continues, "Miller says no problem." The icy cold six-pack of beer in the ad is the obvious solution. "How best to combat global warming?" asks another ad, featuring a young woman in a sleeveless dress. "Something in lightweight wool perhaps." "You know what's happening to the ozone," says an ad for makeup. "Imagine what it's doing to your skin." "Help keep America beautiful" is the headline for an ad . . . not about litter but about lingerie, an ad featuring dismembered parts of a woman's body against scenic backdrops.

One of the most unintentionally hilarious ads I've ever seen features an earnest-looking young woman, fashionably dressed in denim, with the copy, "I get really angry when I hear about all the selfish people who are destroying our environment. Polluting the beaches. Burying toxic wastes. Causing acid rain. Someday I want to travel and see the world. I only hope it isn't all screwed up by then." What is she selling—the Peace Corps, community volunteerism? No—gold bracelets! This is reminiscent of the notorious Benetton campaign that yokes shocking im-

"I like to give each piece a chance."
(Carrie Bell, Student)

THERE'S
NO WRONG WAY
TO EAT A

Reese's
PEANUT BUTTER CUPS

INTERNATIONAL SYMBOL FOR PEACE.   INTERNATIONAL SYMBOL FOR FREEDOM.

Jeep

ages of tragedy and misery, such as a dying AIDS patient, drowning Romanian refugees, and the bloody uniform of a dead Croat soldier, with overpriced sweaters.

Movements for political change are also trivialized. The peace symbol from the 1960s has shown up in ads for everything from candy to Jeeps. "Give peace a chance" is used again and again to sell spas and vacation getaways, while images of Woodstock are used to sell tampons. "Tampax was there," says the commercial, undoubtedly true but so what? As Bob Garfield said, so were a lot of things, like shoelaces, rubber bands, and the cold virus. Cynicism about politics shows up in many ads targeting young people, such as one for Wonderbra that offers readers a chance to vote for their favorite model, with the headline "Sure beats voting for president." A television commercial for Miller beer in election year 1996 shows a young man strolling on a giant political game board, celebrating his right to choose, whether it be candidates or beer. Unctuous politicians spring up in his path, but he chooses a smiling blonde waitress with Lite beer. The commercial ends with bumper stickers bearing slogans such as "Join the party" and "Choose Miller Lite" and the notice that the ad was "Paid for by the Miller Lite Party." Don't bother voting or trying to change the world—just have another beer. Again and again, everything comes down to the individual and his or her choice of a product.Of course, we can't expect anything else from advertising. The advertiser's job is to sell products, not to solve the world's problems. But the powerful impact of advertising on our culture affects how we conceptualize and approach these problems.

A sea change in the public health approach to alcohol and tobacco problems in recent years has shifted the focus from the indivbidual to the environment. We are learning that many, if not all, of these problems can be reduced by changing the environment. As we see the effectiveness of this approach in dealing with alcohol and tobacco problems, we must widen it to include other addictions and societal problems as well.

Public health experts generally refer to this approach as a "systems" approach, which recognizes that dynamic interactions occur, not only between the individual and the environment, but among various levels of the environment. The individual is viewed as part of a complex social, physical, and political web— family, school, community, workplace, state, and so forth. Changes at one level of the system affect all other parts, so prevention programs must be comprehensive. Single approaches to prevention are bound to be ineffective.

Some absurd examples of the single-minded approach emerged in the wake of the school shootings in Colorado. At least one high school principal banned the wearing of black trenchcoats in his school (because that's what the killers were wearing), others proposed metal detectors and more armed guards (although there was an armed guard in the Colorado school), and a religious leader recommended posting the Ten Commandments in every classroom (an idea that made its way to Congress). Several people suggested that the problem was *not enough guns in schools*—if teachers had been armed, they could have taken out the killers. The environmental approach to this tragedy calls for many things—an examination of the socialization of boys in America, the impact of violent video games and other violent media, outreach programs early on to troubled and alienated boys and, of course, gun control. High school has always been hell for misfits but until recently they didn't have access to guns. Sometimes the people recommending gun control fight with those pointing their fingers at the media, as if there were one reason for this reoccurring catastrophe and everyone must protect his or her turf. The roots are many and the solutions must also be deep and multifaceted.

Antismoking organizations used to focus on the individual smoker as the problem and offered health information, pictures of diseased lungs, and advice for quitting. As data showed that this was not the most effective way of improving public health, these organizations switched their strategies to emphasize the role of the environment and the institutional responsibility of the tobacco industry. They fought for a ban on cigarette advertising and promotion, aggressive counteradvertising, much higher taxes and better warning labels, the removal of vending machines, product liability suits, and a crackdown on those who sell cigarettes to minors. With this approach, the focus shifted from individual responsibility to changing public policy.

Does this work? Indeed it does. Since Massachusetts increased taxes on cigarettes and launched an aggressive antitobacco campaign in 1993, consumption of cigarettes has dropped 31 percent, the steepest decline in smoking rates in the nation. In Florida, smoking by middle-school students dropped 19 percent since the state launched an aggressive antitobacco campaign. And several studies have documented that in the 1990s smoking has declined more than twice as fast in California, which has the oldest such program, as nationwide. There have been similar success stories in countries around the world, from Canada to New Zealand. And the norms for cigarette smoking have changed dramatically in the past twenty years.

We can change the norms about alcohol use, dieting, and violence with many of the same measures. To help resolve the problem of high-risk drinking, the individual approach calls for such measures as designated drivers, meaningless slogans such as "Know when to say when" and the oxymoronic "Think when you drink," and brawnier bouncers at bars. The systems approach calls for higher taxes on alcohol, better warning labels on the bottles and the ads, server training for waitstaff in bars and restaurants, and equal-time provisions for aggressive counteradvertising, among other things. This approach has been adopted by many colleges seeking to reduce the high levels of binge drinking by their students. Some of the strategies include working with local bars and restaurants to curb happy hours and promotions involving cheap booze and publicizing information letting students know that the majority are *not* binge drinkers, thus diminishing the impact of "imaginary peers." As a report from the Higher Education Center for Alcohol and Other Drug Prevention says, "Students do not make decisions about the use of alcohol and other drugs entirely on their own, but rather are influenced by campus social norms and expectancies and by policy decisions affecting the availability of alcohol and other drugs on and off campus, the level of enforcement of regulations and laws, and the availability and attractiveness of alcohol-free social and recreational opportunities."

The alcohol and tobacco industries do not like the systems approach not only because it works to reduce consumption (and therefore their profits) but also because it undermines their marketing messages and reduces the attractiveness of their products, especially to young people, whereas their little slogans emphasizing individual responsibility are designed to have no effect. In general, if we want to know what will really work to solve these problems, we should look at what the industries are fighting hardest against. The alcohol industry loves the designated driver campaign, which has no effect on consumption, but lobbies hard against increased taxes or any restrictions on advertising. Most industries wants the focus to stay on the individual, because a focus on the environment inevitably leads to corporate accountability and restrictions. As the gun industry loves to say, "Guns don't kill people. People do." When Ralph Nader first spoke up about the role of unsafe cars in automobile crashes, the automobile industry immediately attacked him and responded with a campaign stating that only the individual driver is responsible: Their slogan was "It's the nut behind the wheel." We've known for a long time, of course, that Nader was right.

The systems approach is easily misunderstood because some of the interventions can seem trivial, especially in light of the extent of the problems. When some parents in a Boston suburb complained about an advertisement for beer in a Little League field, a well-known Boston columnist ridiculed them as "touchy-feely, politically correct busybodies" who thought the ad would immediately "turn their kids into drunks." He concluded, "It's a bad sign when adults figure their own kids are such weak little simpletons that they might commit an error based on a billboard when any sane liberal knows: Ads don't drink. People do." Like a lot of people, he completely missed the point, which is that we give a message to our children about the normalcy of beer-drinking and about societal expectations when we allow such an ad on a Little League field. A single ad—or scores of ads—won't turn kids into drunks, but they are part of a climate that normalizes and glamorizes drinking, and research proves that this especially affects young people.

There has been a great deal of publicity in recent years about alcohol and cigarette campaigns that have targeted African-Americans (for example, Uptown cigarettes and Powermaster malt liquor) and children (for example, the Joe Camel campaign). There should be similar widespread publicity about the diet ads and the ads featuring risky attitudes about eating. Eating disorders must also be treated as a dysfunction of the culture, not just of the individual.

If we were to combat the obsession with thinness from a public health perspective, what would we do? We would demand that Congress, the Federal Trade Commission, and the Food and Drug Administration take an active role in investigating and regulating diet programs and products. We would put warning labels on the ads and demand that the ads include the success rate (it is important for consumers to know that 95 percent of all diets fail). I sometimes fantasize putting warning labels on ads featuring very thin models as well—"Warning: Attempting to achieve this look can ruin your life." We would have prevention programs starting in elementary school, as we do for alcohol and other drugs. But we must also be sure, via scientific evaluation, that these programs are effective. A lot of money has been wasted on prevention programs that are useless at best and sometimes harmful (such as programs that are more likely to teach kids how to use drugs or practice bulimia than to prevent anything).

Therapists, many of whom have moved to a great extent in recent years from an individual to a familial approach, must take the cultural context into consideration too. Just as they can't successfully treat lesbians or gay men or people of color without taking homophobia and racism into account, they can't treat anyone without taking sexism into account. They certainly can't treat young women with eating disorders without considering an environment that demonizes large women and rewards those who starve themselves. They can't treat depression without considering addiction, and they can't treat female addicts without understanding male violence and sexual abuse. Family therapists must recognize that marriages fall apart because of individual failures, to be sure, but also because they exist in a culture that is hostile to marriage, commitment, delayed gratification, and families. We are always responsible as adult individuals for our choices and actions, but our cultural environment makes it exceedingly difficult to raise healthy children, to have successful marriages, to avoid addiction, and to have nonmaterialistic values.

We can learn a great deal from the public policy advocates who have been battling the alcohol and tobacco industries for the past several years, with some striking success. Knowing that statistics can often be numbing and meaningless, they have developed strategies to bring them to life and to capture the attention of the media and the public. For example, when Perrier withdrew its product from the shelves because some of it was tainted with benzene, the antismoking activists pointed out that it would take thirty-three bottles of tainted Perrier to equal the benzene in just one pack of cigarettes. They held a press conference with the thirty-three bottles of Perrier lined up behind them. We need to be equally creative in dramatizing the damage that the obsession with thinness, for example, is doing to women and girls.

We must adopt a similar public health approach to other social problems, such as rape and violence against women and the sexual abuse of children. Former U.S. surgeon generals Antonia Novello and C. Everett Koop, who spoke out bravely about alcohol and tobacco, have also spoken out about violence against women as a public health issue. We should encourage other public health leaders to become involved with these issues. These are all major public health problems that endanger the lives of women and girls, indeed that cut to the very heart of women's energy, power, and self-esteem.

Child abuse is perhaps the most important public health issue. It is terrible in and of itself and it is also at the root of many other societal problems, from addiction to violent crime to domestic violence. Our current approach to child abuse is haphazard, chaotic, and underfunded. As with all public health problems, we need an emphasis on prevention. We should teach parenting skills and basic child psychology in our schools (and have the courses be at least as important as driver's ed!). Studies in Tennessee and New York find that home visits by nurses following the birth of a child reduce subsequent health problems in both the mother and the child and also reduce child abuse and neglect, criminal behavior, and the use of welfare. It costs a great deal less to have a team of people help stressed young parents learn about parenting than it does to intervene when the child has already been damaged. Many states are moving toward a team approach to child abuse, each team consisting of a pediatrician, a nurse, a psychologist, a social worker, and a law enforcement expert. I would like to see these teams on the scene *before* children are abused—they could get involved immediately with high-risk families. Everyone on the team should be knowledgeable about addiction, since it is a factor in the majority of cases of child abuse. Indeed all gatekeepers—teachers, doctors, law enforcement people, clergy, psychologists—should be truly educated about addiction and look for it automatically wherever there is trouble. *Assume addiction* until one discovers otherwise.

A systems approach to child abuse would also recognize the link between poverty, unemployment, neighborhood deterioration, and lack of economic opportunity and all kinds of domestic violence. Community-level interventions that reduce parental stress, such as flexible work schedules, adequate child care services, and parent support groups, are important prevention strategies that work on an environmental level rather than focusing exclusively on high-risk families.

Among many powerful tools that can change the environment is counteradvertising—advertising that gives us honest information and advertising that

WARNING: SMOKING CAUSES IMPOTENCE

deglamorizes products such as alcohol and tobacco. Contrary to what Audre Lorde said, sometimes the master's tools can dismantle the master's house. I had a wonderful experience working with young advertisers in Boston preparing the Tobacco Control Program counteradvertising campaign. Many people in advertising are creative and smart and thrilled to be able to use their skills in a positive way. Counteradvertising should be mandated through the fairness doctrine for electronic media and paid for by alcohol and tobacco taxes.

Counteradvertising is very different from campaigns that target individuals (such as ads that recommend quitting smoking or not driving while drunk). True counteradvertising takes on the industries. As one California ad said, "Warning: The tobacco industry is not your friend." Another in this campaign features two cowboys riding into the sunset with the headline, "I miss my lung, Bob." Parodies of popular ads, such as the Absolut ads that run in *Adbusters,* are very effective. Kalle Lasn, editor of *Adbusters,* calls this use of parody and satire against ads "culture-jamming." Young people generally love designing ads like this, so it is not difficult to get them involved in campaigns and contests.

Another extremely important aspect of breaking through the climate of denial is to teach media literacy in our schools, starting in kindergarten. The United States is one of the few developed nations in the world that does not teach media literacy, but a growing national movement is trying to change that. We all need to be educated to become critical viewers of the media. Without this education, we are indeed sitting ducks. We also need to insist that our schools be Ad-Free Zones.

In recent years, there has been increasing understanding of the relationship of media literacy to substance abuse, violence, and other societal problems. A program called Flashpoint teaches media literacy to adolescents in the juvenile justice system. The American Academy of Pediatrics offers a course called Media Matters to all its members and urges them to do a media history along with a health history with every patient. Scores of other organizations and groups are

incorporating media education into their agendas. Huge and powerful industries—alcohol, tobacco, junk food, diet, guns—depend upon a media-illiterate
population. Indeed, they depend upon a population that is disempowered and
addicted. They fight our efforts with all their mighty resources. And we fight
back, using the tools of media education that enable us to understand, analyze,
interpret, to expose hidden agendas and manipulation, to bring about constructive change, and to further positive aspects of the media.

As parents, we can help our children to become media-literate, both by
fighting for media literacy programs in our schools and by talking with them
about the media. We should watch television with our children, choosing programs with care. My daughter and I look at the television schedule every week
and select a few programs to tape. We then watch them together, usually skip-
ping through the commercials. We should listen to our children's music, being
careful never to condemn the media they love or blame them for loving it. We
should pay attention to it and help our children and ourselves to be more critical
viewers and listeners. About the only autocratic thing I do with my daughter is to
forbid her to wear clothing that advertises a store or a product (and, of course, I
don't wear such things myself). I also try not to buy anything for either of us that
is advertised on television. When she was young, this eliminated many problems,
since almost everything that is advertised on television for children is unhealthy
and unimaginative. The food is terrible for them, the toys stupid, sexist, and disappointing.

We can limit our own consumption and television watching and both encourage and engage in other activities, such as reading, sports, drama, volunteerism, environmentalism. We can also start small discussion groups with our
children (beginning when they are young enough to be thrilled by the idea!).
When my daughter was ten, I started a mother-daughter group with several of
her best friends and their mothers. We meet monthly and talk about a variety of
issues, such as homework, dating, clothes, money, food, and the media. I think we
all enjoy the mutual support, the openness, and the close connection. And, of
course, we can model citizen activism for our children as we work to improve the
cultural environment in our communities and throughout the nation and world.

In addition to the media literacy movement, another movement that is gathering steam is what is sometimes called the "voluntary simplicity" movement.
This consists of many diverse groups and organizations trying to reduce consumption in general, not only to save the earth but also to save our souls. Many of

these organizations, as well as public health and media literacy organizations, are listed on the resource list on my Website (www.jeankilbourne.com). They all have abundant ideas for action, far more than I could possibly include in this chapter.

The systems approach to public health problems is inherently political. The individual approach doesn't rock the boat—it basically says that the world is fine, the environment is fine, but you, the individual, must shape up, resist temptation, stop being so weak-willed. An environmental approach questions the nature of the world—and inevitably confronts the corporations that depend on addiction for profit. For this reason, it has been very difficult to get the government, increasingly dependent on donations from big business, to use this approach. It is also almost impossible to shift the focus from the individual to the environment without "offending the sponsor," which explains the general reluctance of the media to adopt this perspective. By now, many people no longer have the attention span necessary to track an issue for a long time. They can follow O. J. Simpson's trial, but would never stay tuned for a year-long discussion of the roots of domestic violence and the public policy measures necessary to curb it.

As large, diversified corporations merge to create media dynasties, it becomes more and more difficult to get accurate information about anything. Perhaps most insidiously, it becomes difficult to get information about the media conglomerates themselves. There was a virtual news blockade on information concerning the Telecommunications Act of 1996, a bill that effectively threw open the doors to media monopolies. Neither the passage nor the signing of the most sweeping telecommunications legislation in sixty years made the top-ten stories in their respective weeks. The media are now almost completely under corporate control and corporate interests structure almost every message we get. Truly alternative perspectives have vanished. Of course, we must support alternative media, but we must also fight to take back the public airways (that belong to us, after all) and to insist on access and diversity.

It is not surprising that criticism of this situation rarely makes it into the mass media. Indeed corporate criticism in general is seldom allowed. Challenging the culture of commercialism is especially taboo. The Vancouver-based Media Foundation has been trying for years, without success, to get some of its anticonsumerism advertisements into the mass media. According to the foundation, a television spokesman said, "We don't want the business. We don't want any advertising that's inimical to our legitimate business interests." As prize-winning reporter Bill Lazarus says, "When you write about government, the attitude of [editors] tends to be 'no holds barred.' When you write about business, the attitude tends to be one of caution. And for businesses who happen to be advertisers, the caution turns frequently to timidity."

No wonder there is very little mainstream media coverage of serious, chronic, and pervasive abuses of corporate power. Health coverage almost always focuses on personal health habits, on exercise and weight control, for example, rather than on problems such as toxins in the environment, put there by corporations that underwrite public broadcasting and advertise in the media. Endless blame is heaped on welfare mothers but corporate welfare, such as the savings and loan bailout, which costs the taxpayers far more, is barely mentioned. The news brings us a daily litany of crimes committed by individuals but rarely anything about corporate crime, although far more people will die because of inadequate health insurance, faulty products, or toxic waste than from serial killers. Mass murderers have nothing on tobacco industry executives, yet the executives get away with committing perjury before Congress. Each year sixty thousand workers die from workplace injuries and diseases, almost three times the number of people "murdered," yet we hear litle about that. Thus, the role of corporations in major problems of our times is erased and, in this Information Age, people are literally dying from lack of information.

Democracy itself is endangered when information is given to foster private economic gain rather than to educate and enlighten the public so it can make intelligent decisions. As Studs Terkel said, "If journalists cannot freely report the news which disturbs the wealthy and the powerful, then we'll learn only what the big boys want us to learn." These days the big boys don't want us to learn much more than what brands to buy (of politicians as well as of beer and cars).

Politicians are examined with a microscope by the media and are assumed to be corrupt (as indeed they sometimes are), but the men who control the conglomerates are usually invisible. Thus, it is fashionable to hate the government, to be cynical and apathetic about politics, and yet to remain completely ignorant about the people who have even more influence on our lives. In recent years there has been almost complete alienation of the citizenry from its government. In 1966, 58 percent of incoming college freshmen said keeping up with political affairs is "very important." In 1998, only 27 percent agreed. A profound distrust of government is encouraged by the big corporations because it is in their interest. After all, it is only the government that can regulate them. We need enlightened government now more than ever, both to protect us from corporate control and to pursue progressive public policies. Public policy won't change until ordinary citizens hold elected officials accountable for their votes.

Although advertising tries to convince us that freedom is our right to buy things and democracy our ability to choose from a variety of consumer goods, most of us know better. We know that democracy requires active participation from an informed citizenry. Journalistic integrity is crucial to democracy, as is an aware and skeptical public audience. We have a cynical audience, an audience so apathetic that most people don't even bother to vote (more people watched the Superbowl than voted in the 1996 presidential election), but we certainly don't have an educated and informed audience. According to the funder of a 1998 national report on the state of U.S. civil life, "Corrosive cynicism has crippled our civic spirit, and a sense of helplessness has sapped our civic strength." When people are working hard to earn money to buy a lot of stuff and then spending their free time shopping, it's hard to get involved in community issues or civic affairs—especially if they believe that nothing they do will make any difference anyway.

Ever since Ronald Reagan's reign, big business's political allies have been pushing a sweeping deregulatory agenda, unraveling some of the few public controls we have left as "watchdogs" over corporate abuses. This burgeoning corporate power threatens the very core of our democracy, and it poses a growing threat to human health and the environment. We have much more to fear these days from corporate giantism than from big government, but it is very difficult to get people to understand this. Most Americans define freedom very narrowly as freedom from government, as if nothing else could pose a threat. And George Soros, one of the most successful capitalists in history, says, "Although I have made a fortune in the financial markets, I now fear that the untrammeled intensification of laissez-faire capitalism and the spread of market values into all areas of life is endangering our open and democratic society. The main enemy of the open society, I believe, is no longer the communist but the capitalist threat."

It is the increasingly important role of advertising in political elections that necessitates huge campaign coffers, which in turn makes politicians dependent on corporations. Most of the half-billion dollars spent during the 1996 presidential election came from American corporations and Wall Street. As these giants become global, the campaign money increasingly comes from everywhere around the globe—and, of course, with strings attached. Campaign finance re-

THE WORLD HAS A THIRST FOR FREEDOM

PILSNER URQUELL
CZECHOSLOVAKIA

The Original Pilsner, Since 1292

form might well be the most important issue of our time, but it is hard to put a sexy spin on it—it won't sell a lot of newspapers or draw huge television audiences. It also isn't in the interest of newspaper and television owners who reap huge sums from political advertising and contribute mightily to politicians themselves. As Richard Goodwin says, the issue is "not about how politicians should be financed, but how America should be governed, not about how we elect officials, but how they rule the nation. . . . Under the deceptive cloak of campaign contributions, access, and influence, votes and amendments are bought and sold." One obvious solution to this problem is to ban political advertising or at least to limit it to head shots of the candidates talking about their beliefs and policies. No music, no fancy images, no attack ads, no gimmicks. We could also put a cap on what politicians can spend on elections and resurrect the fairness doctrine, so that every commercial would trigger a free response.

We must also reclaim and redefine the concepts of freedom and rebellion that have been so distorted and co-opted by advertisers. They spend billions of dollars a year trying to convince us that we can buy freedom—most ironically, that we can buy freedom via the purchase of addictive products. "The world has a thirst for freedom," says an ad for an imported beer, while in another ad, the end of the Cold War is reduced to "Freedom of vodka." To paraphrase Kris Kristofferson, freedom's just another word for something else to buy. "It's not just fashion, it's freedom," says an ad for wool. "A declaration of independence" is a statement about perfume, and nail polish "sets you free in 90 seconds!" A bus shelter poster in Montreal features a young woman representing the Statue of Liberty, but with a crown com-

ÇA GOÛTE VRAI

VRAI COMME J'AI SOIF DE LIBERTÉ

posed of Coca-Cola bottles—"It tastes real," says the ad, "as real as I thirst for freedom." "Not since the fork-in-the-road sign, has the world been witness to such a pure example of choice," proclaims an ad for Diet Snapple drinks. Consumption becomes a substitute for democracy, with the choice of what to eat or wear or drink taking the place of meaningful political choice. People all around the world are being told that the way to experience American individualism and success is to smoke Marlboros and drink Budweiser. We must never forget that this is a global issue.

Young people are especially targeted because advertisers know that freedom and rebellion are of great importance to them. So they put smokers on the Statue of Liberty to sell cigarettes, Phillip Morris buys the rights to our Bill of Rights, the diet industry offers "the taste of freedom," and Calvin Klein and his ilk surround us with messages lauding casual, uncommitted sex and pornography as freedom of expression. Be free, be a rebel . . . be addicted, be a consumer! A lot of children and young people fall for this propaganda. Desperate to be unique in a conformist culture, they follow the crowd right over the cliff—drinking, smoking, engaging in dangerous sex, compulsively shopping for recreation, stuffing and starving themselves. O brave new world, where Addiction is Freedom and Conformity is Rebellion.

Those who resist this message are labeled "antifreedom." If we protest the targeting of children by the tobacco industry, we are called "lifestyle police" and "public health Nazis." If we suggest that popsicles containing alcohol and beer commercials using talking frogs are inappropriate, we are called "neo-Prohibitionists" and "Carrie Nations." If we complain about Calvin Klein's appropriation of child pornography in his ads, we are "the nation's nannies," antisexual prudes, in bed (so to speak) with the Christian right. If we protest the casual sex, the violence, the consumerism, we are part of a Big Brother government trying to tell everyone what to do. The alcohol industry, the tobacco industry, the junk food industry all have billions of dollars with which to frame the debate in this way and they are very successful. In 1999 a bill before Congress designed to prevent children from starting to smoke was defeated after the tobacco industry spent $40 million on advertising framing the issue as big government versus freedom-loving individuals.

One of the most disturbing displays of corporate power in recent years has been the hijacking of the First Amendment. Philip Morris did this quite literally by buying the right to use the Bill of Rights in an advertising campaign. But, on a more subtle level, as giant corporations spend billions of dollars on public relations and systematically construct their images, they have increasingly become the citizens whose rights need protecting, while the rest of us are merely consumers. Since many Americans are ardently and correctly concerned with protecting the First Amendment, it has been easy for corporations to get us to confuse our rights with their rights. Eminent legal scholars not tied to the alcohol and tobacco industries conclude that reasonable regulations on alcohol and tobacco advertising that do not unduly restrict adults from obtaining accurate information about the availability of these products (for example, price advertising and accurate advertising in adult-oriented media) do not violate the First Amendment.

The truth is that the First Amendment was not meant to protect commercial free speech and that commercial free speech today is often the enemy of private speech. What chance do grass-roots public health groups have against the huge assets and political power of the tobacco, alcohol, junk food, diet, and other such industries? How can someone be elected to office who can't afford advertising to counter the mudslinging of special interest groups? How can speech be considered free when television routinely excludes unusual or extreme or even merely progressive points of view from the news and political programs? How can individuals speak out about food safety if they risk being sued by the food industry, as Oprah Winfrey was by the Texas cattlemen? She won, but had to spend almost a million dollars on her defense. As Max Frankel says, this "relatively recent reading of the Constitution produces a false equality between a corporate shout and every ordinary citizen's whisper." Corporate wealth monopolizes debate, corrupts politicians, and dictates policy. Increasingly, the First Amendment is being used as a shield to protect the wealthy and the powerful, such as tobacco advertisers and pornographers.

It is time for us to fight back, to resist this name-calling and to redefine freedom, liberation, and rebellion in our own terms. We can turn these advertising messages inside out. We are free when we are not addicted, when we can be our real selves, when we are as healthy as possible in body and soul, when we are authentically sexual (which means loving and treasuring our imperfect bodies, as well as each other). We are rebels with a cause when we take on these industries and their destructive advertising messages. We can and must unhook ourselves from the lure, the bait of advertising.

We need connection—not the illusion of connection provided by advertising, but real connection—in our private lives and in our public policy. These days our public policies often reflect our evasion of connection and of committed relationships—our short-term solutions, our abandonment of the poor, disabled, and mentally ill, our refusal to provide basic health care for everyone, even children, our dismissal of workers' rights, and our eagerness to imprison and execute people when they are adolescents or adults as opposed to investing in programs that would help them while they are children and babies. At a time when we desperately need to encourage people to care for each other, to restore a sense of communal life, we often seem to be doing exactly the opposite.

As parents, the most important thing we can do for our children is to connect deeply and honestly with them. A two-year study of over twelve thousand adolescents reported on in the *Journal of the American Medical Association* found that the best predictor of health and the strongest deterrent to high-risk behavior in teens was a strong connection with at least one adult, at home or at school. This finding held up regardless of family structure, income, race, education, amount of time spent together, where or with whom the child lives, or whether one or both parents work. The message is clear: Good relationships create the resilience that prevents dangerous, acting-out behaviors in our children.

Of course, we also need to work politically to create the kind of culture that makes it easier to have successful relationships with our children. Sylvia Ann Hewlett and Cornel West, who have formed a parenting movement called the National Parenting Association, argue that "at the root of the assault on families is the triumph of a marketing culture which promotes hedonistic, narcissistic, and individualistic ways of being in the world. These ways of being make it harder for anyone to support or to honor non-market activity, of which parenting is a primary example. . . . Compassion and conscience are constructed through the child-parent relationship." We must recognize that many children don't have the possibility of a strong connection with a parent, so we must make sure they get these connections elsewhere. We must support youth centers and organizations, good schools, mentoring programs, and programs to identify children of addicts and other children at risk.

We must cherish all children, not just our own. The emphasis on "parental responsiblity" overlooks the fact that millions of children have absent, addicted, crazy, and irresponsible parents—parents driven so mad by their own childhoods that they blindly perpetuate the legacy of abuse, addiction, violence, and destruction. Maybe it's too late to save most of these parents, but it's not too late to save their children and thus in turn their children's children.

We can't have good relationships with our children or anyone else if we are addicted. So we must have the courage to kick our addictions, no matter what form they take. Isolation is at the core of addiction and connection is what heals us. Both advertising and addiction lead us into narcissism, and recovery is possible only if we move away from this self-obsessed focus. The brilliance of Alcoholics Anonymous (and other programs modeled on it) is the recognition of this fact. Addicts recover by helping other addicts. Self-help is completely the wrong term for what goes on in these groups. As Margaret Bullitt-Jonas says about recovering from an eating disorder, "It is fear that drove me into recovery, but it is love that keeps me there."

We need to come together and speak out about our addictions, our abuse, our recovery. We will discover, as women did in consciousness-raising groups years ago, that we are not alone. There is and will continue to be a backlash that will label us "whiners" or "victims" if we speak out in this way (and indeed there have been some whiners on the scene). We do not consider ourselves victims, but most of us were indeed victimized as children and we want to prevent today's children from being similarly victimized. We are survivors, we are legion, and we will share our experience, strength, and hope with each other.

As Jill Nelson says, "I have learned to control and use my rage because if I don't, it will control and use me. This is why I gave up those things I once used to stifle my rage, the liquor and drugs and late-night fats and disembodied sex—universal vices, escape routes women often take to deaden the pain, repress our frustration, suppress those niggerbitchfits. Turning my rage outward, I have not committed homicide or suicide because the flip side of my rage is my conviction that change is possible, that communication is key. I have learned that the only thing to do with my rage is recognize it, temper it with love, and blend the two together into hopeful action."

Of course, it is not just addicts who need healing. Heart specialist Dean Ornish instructs his patients to do acts of kindness for one another. He has written, "Anything that leads to real intimacy and feelings of connection can be healing in the real sense of the word: to bring together, to make whole."

We need coalitions, networks, conferences, public outcries. We need all kinds of people coming together—in our communities, in our schools, in our places of work and our places of worship. We need what George Gerbner calls, and has founded: a Cultural Environment Movement. We need parents, educators, pediatricians, business people, psychologists, the clergy—everyone speaking out and saying, as anchor man Howard Beale so memorably did in Paddy Chayevsky's *Network*, "I'm as mad as hell and I'm not going to take it any more!" Our survival is at stake. We literally cannot go on like this—we will destroy the planet. We must rise up, break through the denial, and act to save ourselves, our children, and future generations.

I once heard a parable about a wise old woman who lived in a village. A boy in the village decided to trick her. He trapped a small bird and told his friends that he would take it to the woman and ask her if it were dead or alive. "If she says it is dead, I will release it," he said, "and if she says it is alive, I will crush it to death." The children went to the old woman and the boy said, "I have a bird in my hands. Is it dead or alive?" The old woman looked at him and replied, "It is in your hands."

NOTES

CHAPTER 1. "BUY THIS 24-YEAR-OLD…"

page

33   *"over $200 billion a year on advertising"*: Coen, 1999, 136.
33   *"over $250,000 to produce an average television commercial"*: Garfield, 1998, 53.
34   *"they will gladly spend over a million dollars"*: Reidy, 1999, D1.
34   *"Victoria's Secret"*: Ryan, 1999, D1.
34   *"Ad agency Arnold Communications"*: Reidy, 1999, E1, E2.
34   *"the Super Bowl is one of the few sure sources"*: Carter, 1999, BU1.
34   *"the Super Bowl is more about advertising"*: Twitchell, 1996, 71.
34   *"The Oscar ceremony"*: Johnson, 1999, C5.
34   *"Advertising supports more than 60 percent"*: Twitchell, 1996, 46.
35   *"Over $40 billion a year in ad revenue is generated"*: Endicott, 1998, S-50.
35   *"As one ABC executive said"*: Collins, 1992. 13.
35   *"the CEO of Westinghouse Electric"*: Ross, 1997, 14.
35   *"Dr. Quinn, Medicine Woman"*: Bierbaum, 1998, 18.
35   *"The Daily Herald"*: Masterman, 1990, 3.
35   *"According to Dean Valentine"*: Hirschberg, 1998, 59.
38   *"Early in 1999 William Eisner"*: Berke, 1999, 17.
38   *"Ethnic minorities will soon account"*: Woods, 1995.
38   *"Nearly half of all Fortune 1000"*: Cortese, 1999.
38   *"African-Americans"*: Winski, 1992, 18.
38   *"about 87 percent"*: Bowen and Schmid, 1997, 138. The totals do not add up to 100 percent because only individuals were counted, not mixed ethnic groups.
38   *"advertisers, such as IBM, Benetton"*: Wilke, 1997, 1.
38   *"Hartford Financial Services Group"*: Petrecca and Arndorfer, 1998, 12.
39   *"Molson beer launched"*: Wilke, 1997, 10.
39   *"A Subaru print ad"*: Wilke, 1996, 8.
39   *"American Express ran an ad"*: Wilke, 1998, 3.
39   *"American Express spent $250,000"*: Wilke, 1998, 3.
39   *"a major gay-market study in 1997"*: Wilke, 1998, 30.
39   *"More than two-thirds of gay-market advertisers"*: Be out front on gay ads, 1997, 14.
39   *"gay consumers drink about twice as much"*: Pruzan, 1996, 13. Also Wilsnack, Plaud, Wilsnack, and Klassen, 1997, 259–60.
39   *"Australian brewers Lion Nathan"*: "Gay beer" in Australia, 1997, January, 23.

40   *"spend a fortune"*: Market research was a $2.5-billion business in 1994, growing at about 4.2 percent a year (after adjustment for inflation). Savan, 1994, 2.

40   *"Many companies these days are hiring anthropologists"*: Wells, 1999, B1.

40   *"One new market research technique involves monitoring brain-wave signals"*: Skull tapping, 1998, 33.

41   *"'Mass marketing is like defoliating Vietnam'"*: Reidy, 1996, 47.

41   *"'We're in an era of global marketing warfare'"*: Trout, 1996, 7.

42   *"Bronner Slosberg Humphrey Inc."*: Reidy, 1996, 47.

42   *"Another company recently launched"*: Williamson, 1997, 60.

43   *"As a writer for* Advertising Age *said"*: Webster, 1998, 26.

43   *"Some sites offer prizes"*: Rich, 1997, E15.

43   *"Companies unrelated to children's products"*: Austen, 1999, E8.

43   *"Belgium, Denmark, Norway"*: Jacobson and Mazur, 1995, 28. Also Weber, 1997, F4.

43   *"Sweden and Greece"*: Koranteng, 1999, 2.

44   *"The Turner Cartoon Network tells advertisers"*: Ad in *The New York Times,* 1993, February 8, C7 (California edition).

44   *"Mike Searles, president of Kids 'R' Us"*: Harris, 1989, A1.

44   *"Levi Strauss & Co. finds it worthwhile"*: Krol, 1998, 29.

44   *"Nintendo U.S. has a research center"*: Interview with Stephen Kline, author of *Out of the Garden: toys and children's culture in the age of TV marketing,* in McLaren, 1997, 10.

44   *"Kid Connection, a unit of the advertising agency Saatchi & Saatchi"*: Austen, 1999, E8.

44   *"Center for Media Education"*: Center for Media Education, 1511 K Street N.W., Suite 518, Washington, DC 20005, 202-628-2620.

45   *"One company has initiated"*: Carroll, 1995, D5.

45   *"The editor-in-chief of* KidStyle"*: Kerwin, 1997, 46.

45   *"Channel One is hardly free"*: Reading, writing, 1999, 10.

45   *"'Our relationship with 8.1 million teenagers'"*: Advertising Age, 1998, June 29, S27.

45   *"Imagine the public outcry"*: Rank, 1992, April.

46   *"Advertisers are reaching nearly 8 million"*: Some corporations sponsor contests and incentive programs, such as an essay-writing contest sponsored by Reebok shoes, which then uses the information to fine-tune the appeal of its advertisements to youth (*Not for Sale,* 1997, 1), and a Kellogg's contest which had kids make sculptures out of Rice Krispies and melted marshmallows (Labi, 1999, 44). Schools can earn points for every Campbell's soup label or AT&T long-distance phone call, which can then be redeemed for athletic and educational equipment. And a math textbook introduces a decimal division problem as follows: "Will is saving his allowance to buy a pair of Nike shoes that cost $68.25. If Will earns $3.25 per week, how many weeks will Will need to save?" Beside the text is a full-color picture of a pair of Nikes (Hays, 1999, 1).

45   *"'Perhaps fewer libraries'"*: Wilkins, 1997, 32.

46   *"According to the Council for Aid to Education"*: Zernike, 1997, B6.

46   *"The Seattle School Board"*: Not for Sale!, 1997, 1.

46   *"market-driven educational materials"*: Carroll, 1996, D5.

46   *"and a kindergarten curriculum"*: Not for Sale!, 1999, 1.

46   *"Mike Cameron, a senior at Greenbrier High School"*: Associated Press, 1998, A3.

46   *"Coke has several 'partnerships'"*: Foreman, 1999, C1.

48   *"The truth is that African-American and Latinos"*: In 1990, 68.3 percent of whites, 64.5 percent of Hispanics, and 55.6 percent of African-Americans used alcohol. National Institute on Drug Abuse, 1991.

48   *"A few years later* Ebony"*: Ebony, 1991, November, 120–24.

49   *"Up to 85 percent of the news"*: Lyon, 1997, 15.

49   *"Nike's sponsorship of CBS's Olympic coverage"*: Herbert, 1998, 13.
49   *"In 1996 Chrysler Corporation"*: Baker, 1997, 30.
50   *"in 1997 a major advertiser"*: Baker, 1997, 30.
50   *"According to Kurt Andersen"*: Baker, 1997, 31.
50   *"the CBS executives who canceled Ed Asner's series"*: Cooper, 1999, 26.
50   *"several radio stations in the Midwest"*: Soley, 1999, 21.
51   *"Gloria Steinem provides a striking example"*: Steinem, 1990, 18–28.
51   *"New Woman magazine"*: Martin, 1998, 4.
52   *"An informal survey"*: Jackson, 1996, 21.
53   *"the silence in women's magazines"*: Amos, 1999, 6–7.
53   *"Dr. Holly Atkinson"*: Collins, 1992, 41.
53   *"As Helen Gurley Brown"*: Ibid.
54   *"The government is spending $195 million"*: Wren, 1999, 1.
54   *"Thirty percent of Americans"*: Jacobson and Mazur, 1995, 160.
54   *"In 1996 the Seagram Company"*: Pruzan and Ross, 1996, 26.
54   *"Today, Time Warner, Sony, Viacom"*: Schamus, 1999, 34–35. Also McChesney and Herman, 1997.
54   *"these companies will own 90 percent"*: Duncan, 1997, 4.
54   *"We may be able to change the channel"*: I believe that Kalle Lasn, editor of *Adbusters,* first said this.
55   *"Not the American culture of the past"*: Kakutani, 1997.
55   *"As Simon Anholt"*: Anholt, 1998, 12.
56   *"As George Gerbner"*: Gerbner, 1994. 385.

CHAPTER 2. "IN YOUR FACE…ALL OVER THE PLACE"

page

58   *"advertising's messages are inside"*: Jhally, 1998.
58   *"almost half of all automobile crashes"*: According to the U.S. Department of Transportation, over 40 percent of all fatal traffic accidents in 1996 were alcohol-related. National Highway Traffic Safety Administration, 1999.
58   *"'This is my best idea ever'"*: Sharkey, 1998, 2.
58   *"Their next big idea"*: Rosenberg, 1999, A3.
58   *"In England the legendary white cliffs of Dover"*: Liu, 1999, 15A.
58   *"American consumers have recently joined Europeans"*: Mohl, 1999, A1. Also Tagliabue, 1997, 1.
58   *"Conversations are interrupted"*: Bidlake, 1997, 149.
58   *"beer companies have experimented"*: Twitchell, 1996, 62.
58   *"The average American is exposed"*: Jacobson and Mazur, 1995, 13.
58   *"Advertising makes up about 70 percent of our newspapers"*: Twitchell, 1996, 71.
59   *"40 percent of our mail"*: McCarthy, 1990, F3.
59   *"According to Rance Crain"*: Crain, 1997, 25.
59   *"advertising is subliminal"*: Twitchell, 1996, 116.
59   *"Grapevine Mills in Texas"*: Grunwald, 1997, A1.
59   *"the world David Foster Wallace imagined"*: Wallace, 1996.
59   *"In 1998 the museum's Monet show"*: Monet show sets world record, 1999, E2.
59   *"Bob Dole plays on his defeat"*: Angier, 1996, 4E.
59   *"Sarah Ferguson"*: Lewis, 1997, 22.
60   *"And the Rolling Stones, those aging rebels"*: Pareles, 1998, D1.

60 *"when Neil Young recorded a video":* Twitchell, 1996, 21–22.
60 *"Stars such as Harrison Ford":* Angier, 1996, 4E.
60 *"Antonio Banderas and Kevin Costner have pushed cars":* Ads not infinitum, 1998, 10.
60 *"Leonardo DiCaprio was paid $4 million":* Wentz, 1998, 12.
61 *"In 1983 Sylvester Stallone wrote":* What do they have in common? 1994, 4. Also Levin, 1994, 1.
61 *"New technology allows":* Bauder, 1999, E6.
61 *"Writer and cartoonist Mark O'Donnell":* O'Donnell, 1995, 64.
61 *"Diet Coke obtained the rights":* Gleason, 1997, S1.
61 *"In 1997 ABC and American Airlines":* Cheers & Jeers, 1997, 10.
61 *"a character in the hit show* Baywatch*":* Logan, 1998, 8.
62 *"'People have become less capable'":* Kakutani, 1997, 32.
62 *"Steven Stark, another media critic":* Stark, 1990, 15.
62 *"As Jerry Seinfeld, star of the show, said":* Mandese, 1995, 1.
62 *"The 1997 James Bond film":* Arndofer, 1997, 24.
63 *"the 1998 hit movie* You've Got Mail*":* Maddox and Jensen, 1998, 48.
63 *"And independent films are becoming as tight":* Hudes, 1998, 43.
63 *"Hilfiger provided the wardrobe":* Lee, 1998, 2 ST.
63 *"Maurice Malone":* Ryan, 1999, F1.
63 *"Chris Gore, publisher of the Webzine* Film Threat*":* Lee, 1998, 2 ST.
64 *"This argument was made by Jacob Sullum":* Sullum, 1997, A31.
64 *"As Sut Jhally says":* Jhally, 1998.
64 *"As Joseph Goebbels":* Goebbels, 1933, March 28. Quoted in Jacobson and Mazur, 1995, 15.
65 *"no wonder that Evian backwards":* My thanks to Bob McCannon for this observation.
65 *"When Nike wanted to reach skateboarders":* Nike, 1997, 54.
66 *"Some advertisers use what they chillingly call":* Espen, 1999, 54–59.
66 *"One marketing consultant suggests":* Crain, 1997, 25.
66 *"A study of children done by researchers at Columbia University":* Bever, Smith, Bengen, and Johnson, 1975, 119.
66 *"'7- to 10-year-olds are strained'":* Bever, Smith, Bengen, and Johnson, 1975, 120.
67 *"Rance Crain of* Advertising Age*":* Crain, 1999, 23.
67 *"When Pope John Paul II":* Chacon and Ribadeneira, 1999, A8.
68 *"Neil Postman refers":* Curtis, 1998, 49.
68 *"'The Jolly Green Giant'":* Twitchell, 1996, 30.
70 *"'It's no fun to spend $100 on athletic shoes'":* Peppers and Rogers, 1997, 32.
70 *"the city health commissioner in Philadelphia":* Worthington, 1992, 15.
70 *"A* USA Today*-CNN-Gallup Poll":* Jacobson and Mazur, 1995, 26.
70 *"Leydiana Reyes":* Leonhardt, 1997, 65.
70 *"Danny Shirley":* Espen, 1999, 59.
70 *"sweatshirts with fifteen-inch 'Polo' logos":* Ryan, 1996, D1.
71 *"Consumer behavior":* Woods, 1995.
71 *"Most shampoos":* Twitchell, 1996, 252.
71 *"Blindfolded smokers":* Twitchell, 1996, 125.
72 *"This campaign has been so successful":* Enrico, 1997, 4B.
72 *"Collecting Absolut ads":* Tye, 1997, 1, 13.
72 *"Carol Nathanson-Moog, an advertising psychologist":* Nathanson-Moog, 1984, 18.
72 *"'product image is probably the most important element'":* Nathanson-Moog, 1984, 18.
73 *"'A strange world it is'":* Bernstein, 1978, August 7.
73 *"According to Bob Wehling":* Crain, 1998, 24.

73   *"A commercial for I Can't Believe It's Not Butter"*: Haran, 1996, 12.

74   *"Tamagotchis"*: Goldner, 1998, S43.

74   *"And Gardenburger"*: Gardenburger hits the spot, 1998, 17.

74   *"In 1998 a Miller beer campaign"*: Crain, 1998, 24.

74   *"The 1989 Nissan Infiniti"*: Horton, 1996, S28.

74   *"the Edsel"*: Horton, 1996, S30.

74   *"An ad for Gap khakis"*: Cortisoz, 1998, A10.

74   *"James Twitchell argues"*: University of Florida news release, quoted by Orlando, 1999, http://www.sciencedaily.com/releases/1999/05/990518114815.htm.

74   *"Critic and novelist George Steiner"*: Dee, 1999, 65–66.

75   *"As Richard Pollay"*: Pollay, 1986.

75   *"there has never been a propaganda effort"*: Jhally, 1998.

CHAPTER 3. "BATH TISSUE IS LIKE MARRIAGE"

page

78   *"A commercial for a minivan"*: Cheers & Jeers, 1999, 10.

78   *"people say they spend about forty minutes"*: Armour, 1999, 3B.

82   *"We can dine on Christian Dior dinnerware"*: Horovitz, 1997, B1.

82   *"Bill Blass put his signature"*: Hyde, 1980, C3.

82   *"According to the Center for Media Education"*: Rich, 1997, E15.

82   *"According to Klein"*: Ryan, 1998, D8.

83   *"One researcher, interviewing ninth-grade"*: Fox, 1997, 38.

83   *"'Attention: Big Mac lovers'"*: Commercial for McDonald's, broadcast February 25, 1997, on ABC.

83   *"According to Steve Chinn"*: Grimes, 1996, 65.

83   *"'Know the heart of the consumer'"*: Houlahan, 1998, S4.

83   *"Many chains, from pizza stores to moviehouses"*: Canellos, 1999, C1.

83   *"According to market analyst Faith Popcorn"*: Popcorn and Hanft, 1997, 26.

83   *"market researcher Bernadette Tracy"*: Tracy, 1997, 32.

84   *"Kraft recently announced"*: Pollack, 1998, s2.

87   *"The average wedding in America"*: White, 1998, C7.

88   *"a man is snoring in bed"*: Commercial for Wamsutta sheets, broadcast April 5, 1997.

88   *"a heavy woman dances with a man"*: Commercial for lingerie, broadcast during *Feds* on April 3, 1997.

89   *"Jean Baker Miller"*: Miller, 1976.

93   *"a clever commercial that features a woman at a restaurant table"*: Commercial for credit card, broadcast during *Mad About You* on NBC, February 22, 1999.

93   *"Half of all marriages"*: Sandmaier, 1997, 24.

93   *"life after infatuation"*: Ibid.

93   *"Actor Charlie Sheen"*: Kuczynski, 1998, 8.

CHAPTER 4. "CAN AN ENGINE PUMP THE VALVES...?"

page

96   *"One-third of the land in our cities"*: Dittmar, 1999.

96   *"Although we are only 5 percent of the world's population"*: Kiefer, 1997, A13.

96   *"40 percent of the oil"*: Goodman, 1990, 23.

96   *"The top three automakers spend about six billion dollars a year"*: *Advertising Age*, 1997, data-base (www.adage.com). General Motors spent $3,087,400, Chrysler $1,532,400, and Ford $1,281,800 in 1997.

96   *"Jeep runs an annual"*: Halliday, 1996, 24.

96   *"commercial for Toyota's Tacoma"*: Breaking: Toyota Tacoma, 1998, 4.

97   *"a 1999 Toyota commercial"*: Broadcast on ABC during *The Practice*, January 18, 1999.

99   *"a newspaper ad for Autique stores"*: *Advertising Age International*, 1998, 42.

99   *"Robyn Meredith suggests"*: Meredith, 1999, WK3.

101   *"'How to build a lasting relationship'"*: Broadcast on NBC during *Law and Order*, May 12, 1999.

101   *"'Autoeroticism'"*: Snook, 1997, 230.

102   *"a 1999 television commercial for BMW"*: Broadcast on ABC during *The Practice*, January 24, 1999.

102   *"'I'm Autobahn'"*: Broadcast on NBC during *Homicide*, January 1997.

103   *"Nissan's president of North American design"*: Bradsher, 1997, 2.

103   *"sociology professor Pepper Schwartz"*: Quoted in Bradsher, 1997, 2.

103   *"Sales for these light trucks"*: Halliday, 1998, S12.

103   *"Nature, often personified"*: Andersen, 1998, 22.

103   *"One marketing consultant"*: Cedergren, quoted in Halliday, 1998, S12.

103   *"The 13 percent of SUVs"*: Andersen, 1998, 22.

104   *"Sport utility vehicles are especially dangerous"*: Bradsher, 1998, 4.

104   *"Somebody's Under the Vehicle"*: Levingston, 1999, C4.

104   *"When cars and SUVs collide"*: Andersen, 1998, 23.

104   *"SUV drivers"*: Andersen, 1998, 23.

104   *"In 1998, Americans bought more vans"*: Ford, 1999, A1.

104   *"The 2000 Ford Excursion"*: Ford, 1999, D1.

104   *"A 1997 study"*: *Boston Globe*, 1997, A18.

105   *"a study by the American Automobile Association"*: Sharkey, 1997, 1.

105   *"'a cultural illness'"*: Keller, 1998, A19.

105   *"According to the National Highway Traffic Safety Administration"*: Chronicle News Services, 1997, A3.

106   *"Ad critic Bob Garfield"*: Garfield, 1997, 61.

106   *"The man's hand"*: Broadcast on NBC during *Law and Order*, September 1997.

CHAPTER 5. "PLEASE, PLEASE, YOU'RE DRIVING ME WILD"

page

109   *"Beautiful women"*: Tierney, 1996, 50.

110   *"'From you to you'"*: Commercial for Nestle's Treasures, broadcast March 7, 1999.

111   *"Family therapist Jill Harkaway"*: Wylie, 1997, 29.

112   *"sales of Häagen-Dazs in Great Britain"*: Inside advertising, 1992, 38.

112   *"In a commercial broadcast on Valentine's Day"*: Broadcast on ABC during *The Practice*, February 14, 1999.

113   *"A television commercial broadcast during* Sabrina, the Teenage Witch*"*: SnackWell commercial broadcast on ABC, February 1998.

113   *"an extreme closeup of the peaks and swirls of frosting on a cake"*: Broadcast during *Law and Order*, October 15, 1997.

115   *"thinness becomes the equivalent of virginity"*: Steiner-Adair, 1994, 386.

116   *"About eighty million Americans"*: Iggers, 1996, xi.

116   *"Eight million Americans"*: Davis, 1994, 8.

116   *"the third most common"*: Steiner-Adair, 1996.
117   *"American children see"*: PBS *Frontline: Obesity,* November 11, 1998.
117   *"Americans spend an estimated $14 billion"*: Wylie, 1997, 25.
119   *"Oprah Winfrey"*: Winfrey, 1996, 8–9.
119   *"A 1999 study, published in the American Medical Association's"*: Associated Press, 1999, A5.
119   *"The frequency of eating disorders"*: Jonas, 1989, 267–71. Also Krahn, 1991, 239–53. Also Lilenfeld and Kaye, 1996, 94–106.
120   *"A 1998 SnackWell's campaign"*: Pollack, 1998, 6.
120   *"Even Bob Garfield"*: Garfield, 1998, 33.
123   *"A photograph of Julia Roberts"*: Schneider, 1996, 73.
123   *"at least 85 percent of body doubles"*: Ibid.
123   *"The diet industry"*: Black, 1990, 1. Also Rothblum, 1994, 55.
124   *"Ninety-five percent of all women"*: Seid, 1994, 8.
124   *"more than half the adult women"*: Surrey, 1984, 2.
125   *"the drug combination of fenfluramine"*: Kolata, 1997, E3.
125   *"dieters often experience a temporary drop"*: Study done at the Institute of Food Research in Reading, England, reported in *Cooking Light,* 1997, January, 16.
126   *"Ninety-five percent of dieters"*: Fraser, 1997, 47.

CHAPTER 6. "THE MORE YOU SUBTRACT, THE MORE YOU ADD"

page

129   *"As Margaret Mead"*: In a speech at Richland College in Dallas, Texas, on February 24, 1977.
129   *"According to the Carnegie Corporation"*: Carnegie Corporation, 1995.
129   *"As Carol Gilligan, Mary Pipher"*: Gilligan, 1982; Pipher, 1994; Sadker and Sadker, 1994.
129   *"Teenage women today"*: Roan, 1993, 28.
129   *"a 1998 status report"*: Vobejda and Perlstein, 1998, A3.
130   *"The socialization that emphasizes passivity"*: Thompson, 1994.
130   *"Eating problems affect girls from African-American"*: Steiner-Adair and Purcell, 1996, 294.
130   *"Handbook on Adolescent Psychology"*: English, 1998, C7.
131   *"In Raising Cain"*: Kindlon and Thompson, 1999.
131   *"In Real Boys"*: W. Pollack, 1998.
131   *"Teenage girls spend over $4 billion"*: Brown, Greenberg, and Buerkel-Rothfuss, 1993.
132   *"A researcher at Brigham and Women's Hospital"*: Field, Cheung, Wolf, Herzog, Gortmaker, and Colditz, 1999, 36.
133   *"Studies at Stanford University"*: Then, 1992. Also Richins, 1991, 71.
133   *"this one of 350 young men and women"*: Fredrickson, 1998, 5.
133   *"Male college students who viewed just one episode"*: Strasburger, 1989, 757.
134   *"Taco Bell"*: Garfield, 1997, 43.
134   *"A ten-year-old girl wrote to New Moon"*: E-mail correspondence with Heather S. Henderson, editor-in-chief of HUES Magazine, New Moon Publishing, March 22, 1999.
134   *"from 40 to 80 percent of fourth-grade girls"*: Stein, 1986, 1.
134   *"one-third of twelve- to thirteen-year-old girls"*: Rodriguez, 1998, B9.
134   *"63 percent of high-school girls"*: Rothblum, 1994, 55.
134   *"a survey in Massachusetts"*: Overlan, 1996, 15.
134   *"our last 'socially acceptable' prejudice—weightism"*: Steiner-Adair and Purcell, 1996, 294.
135   *"Although eating problems are often thought to result"*: Smith, Fairburn, and Cowen, 1999, 171–76. Also Thompson, 1994. Also Krahn, 1991. Also Hsu, 1990. Also Jonas, 1989, 267–71.
135   *"a recent study that found a sharp rise in eating disorders"*: Becker and Burwell, 1999.

135   *"As Ellen Goodman says"*: Goodman, 1999, A23.

137   *"Some argue that it is men's awareness"*: Faludi, 1991. Also Kilbourne, 1986.

138   *"Catherine Steiner-Adair suggests"*: Steiner-Adair, 1986, 107, 110.

139   *"A 1999 study done at the University of Michigan"*: Martin, 1998, 494–511.

139   *"a very young woman lying on a bed"*: A commercial for Tresor perfume, broadcast on NBC on December 5, 1997.

140   *"colored contact lenses"*: Commercial for Focus Softcolors, broadcast on Fox during *Ally McBeal*, June 15, 1998.

141   *"Erving Goffman"*: Goffman, 1978.

142   *"The exception to the rule involves African-American children"*: Seiter, 1993.

144   *"it also boosted sales of Candies shoes"*: Grierson, 1998, 21.

145   *"Teachers report a steady escalation of sex talk"*: Moltz, 1997, F1, F4.

146   *"consequences of all this sexual pressure"*: Brown, Greenberg, and Buerkel-Rothfuss, 1933, 511.

146   *"seven in ten girls who had sex"*: Kaiser Family Foundation, 1996, 1.

146   *"One of every ten girls"*: Brown, Greenberg, and Buerkel-Rothfuss, 1993, 511.

146   *"twice as high as in England"*: Kaiser Family Foundation, 1996, 2.

147   *"typical teenage viewer"*: Brown, Greenberg, and Buerkel-Rothfuss, 1993, 513.

147   *"abundant sexual activity"*: Brown, Greenberg, and Buerkel-Rothfuss, 1993, 512–14.

147   *"sex can hurt or kill them"*: Bernstein, 1995, 49.

147   *"the few existing studies"*: Brown and Steele, 1995, 22.

147   *"Two studies"*: Ibid.

148   *"Jane Brown and her colleagues"*: Brown, Greenberg, and Buerkel-Rothfuss, 1993, 523.

149   *"No wonder most teenage pregnancies occur"*: Reed, 1991, 130–49.

149   *"Carol Gilligan terms the 'tyranny of nice and kind'"*: Brown and Gilligan, 1992, 53.

150   *"And Barbie continues to rake in"*: Goldsmith, 1999, D3.

150   *"according to Anthony Cortese"*: Cortese, 1999, 57.

153   *"Joan Jacobs Brumberg describes this difference vividly"*: Brumberg, 1997, xxi.

CHAPTER 7. "FORGET THE RULES! ENJOY THE WINE"

page

155   *"Although we hear a lot about marijuana"*: National Institute on Drug Abuse, 1991.

155   *"A 1999 study found"*: National Parents' Resource Institute for Drug Education, 1999, April 7. Reported on Join Together Online (www.jointogether.org).

155   *"Fifteen percent of eighth-graders"*: Johnston, O'Malley, and Bachman, 1998, 18.

156   *"the percentage of binge drinkers"*: Presley, Leichliter, and Meilman, 1998, 6.

156   *"Alcohol is the leading killer of young people"*: Ninth special report to the U.S. Congress on alcohol and health from the Secretary of Health and Human Services, 1997.

156   *"The younger people are when they start to drink"*: Early drinking said to increase alcoholism risk, 1998, 46.

156   *"According to Dr. Bernadine Healey"*: Masse and Tremblay, 1997, 62.

156   *"Ten percent of drinkers"*: Greenfield and Rogers, 1999, 81.

156   *"As August Busch III"*: Anheuser-Busch Annual Report, 1996, 3.

156   *"if every adult American drank"*: ARIS (Alcohol Research Information Service), 1997, 3.

156   *"As one researcher said, 'Though problem-free drinking'"*: Ragels, 1996, 51.

156   *"Thomas Greenfield of the Alcohol Research Group"*: Greenfield and Rogers, 1999, 78.

157   *"heavy drinkers who are not alcoholic"*: Mangione, Howland, and Lee, 1998.

157   *"The top 2.5 percent"*: Greenfield and Rogers, 1999, 81.

157   *"According to the U.S. Department of Health"*: Kusserow, 1991.

158 *"Anheuser-Busch, the largest brewer in the world":* Emert, 1998, B1. This figure is for measured media only (television, radio, billboards, newspapers, magazines) and does not include unmeasured media, such as promotions, sponsorships, and giveaways.

158 *"As one Anheuser-Busch marketing executive":* Castellano, quoted in Hume, 1986, S6.

158 *"Introduced during the 1995 Super Bowl":* Beer advertising: the "unintended market," 1996, 6.

158 *"The frogs have been criticized":* Balu, 1998, B6.

158 *"Frank and Louie, the sardonic lizards":* Kauffman, 1998, D1.

158 *"According to* Supermarket News*":* Supermarket News, 1997, January 13, 14.

159 *"As one liquor store owner said":* Jobson's Beverage Dynamics, 1994, May, 53.

159 *"'a beer-guzzling holiday'":* Lipman, 1989, B6.

159 *"According to a Coor's marketing executive":* Ibid.

159 *"the Budweiser frog campaign":* Campbell Mithun Esty (Minneapolis). Reported in Harper's Index, 1999, 15. Also national study reveals kids' favorite TV ads, 1998, March 24, Yahoo PR Newswire. Online.

159 *"According to a 1996 survey":* Leiber, 1996.

160 *"A survey of eight- to twelve-year-olds":* Center for Science in the Public Interest, 1988, September 4. Kids are as aware of booze as presidents, survey finds. Washington, D.C.: CSPI press release.

160 *"And a 1998 study":* Emert, 1998, B1.

160 *"As Bob Garfield, ad reviewer":* Garfield, 1997, 59.

160 *"Garfield also acknowledges":* Garfield, 1999, 77.

160 *"A 1919 article ran in* Printer's Ink*":* Varley, 1919.

160 *"an editorial in* Advertising Age*":* Bernstein, 1986, 17.

161 *"As one marketing executive said":* Defoe and Breed, 1979, 195.

161 *"various research studies":* Austin, 1998. Also Saffer, 1996; Slater, 1996; Grube, 1995; Grube and Wallack, 1999; Aiken, Eadie, Leather, McNeill, Scott, and Scott, 1988; Aiken and Block, 1981.

161 *"creates an unconscious presumption":* Sherman, 1985, 1122.

161 "Seventh Special Report to the U.S. Congress": Seventh special report to the U.S. Congress on alcohol and health, 1990, 53.

161 *"So the brewers broadcast their ads":* Kane's Beverage Week, 1998, September 21, 5.

161 "Beavis and Butthead": Wall Street Journal, 1997, B1.

161 *"leading brewers have run commercials":* Ross and Teinowitz, 1997, 4.

161 *"Both Budweiser and Miller":* Brandweek, 1997, 25.

161 *"According to a Jose Cuervo tequila spokesperson":* Fitzgerald, 1997, 28.

161 *"In 1998 the Center for Media Education":* Beatty, 1998, 14.

161 *"At Absolutvodka.com":* Ibid.

162 *"'One might say that this product'":* Maxwell, 1985, 45.

162 *"Wine coolers quickly":* Winters, 1987, 110.

162 *"Junior and senior high-school students drink over 35 percent":* Kusserow, 1991, 1.

162 *"This marketing strategy began in Britain":* Neighborhood convenience stores push lemon drops, butter balls and 30-proof oatmeal cookies, 1996, Spring, 8–9. A complete copy of the report is available from the Royal College of Physicians, 11 St. Andrew's Place, Regent's Park, London NW1 4LE.

162 *"In 1995 the Royal College of Physicians":* Ibid.

162 *"Tumblers is a twenty-four-proof":* Halbfinger, 1997, E5.

162 *"T.G.I. Friday's, the restaurant chain":* Ibid.

163 *"Blenders, an ice cream product":* Frazeur, 1997, 1–4.

163 *"A full-page ad for Tattoo":* Beverage & Food Dynamics, 1997, May, 7.

163 *"Promotional merchandise":* Advertising Age, 1997, May 12, 88.

163   *"Moo and Super Milch"*: Herald Sun, 1997, May 11, 45. Also *Impact International*, 1997, June 15, 29.

163   *"And Australian company Candyco"*: Herald Sun, 1997, May 14, 31.

163   *"'entry-level' drinks"*: Impact, 1998, May 15, 12.

164   *"Rapper King Tee sings"*: Carroll, 1992, March 29, 70.

164   *"In 1997 protests by public health advocates"*: Modern Brewery Age, 1997, August 4, 3.

165   *"alcohol abuse is the leading health"*: Jacobson and Mazur, 1995, 170.

166   *"College students spend $4 billion"*: Prevention File, 1992, Spring, 2. Also Commission on Substance Abuse at Colleges and Universities, 1994, 2.

166   *"Over half of all cases of violent crime"*: Abbey, Ross, and McDuffie, 1991. Also Martin, 1992, 230–37.

166   *"Almost all of these crimes"*: Perkins, 1992, 458.

166   *"Of students in college in America"*: Commission on Substance Abuse at Colleges and Universities, 1994, 4.

166   *"According to Henry Wechsler"*: Nicklin, 1999, 39.

166   *"Five students died"*: Update: binge drinking, 1998, 10.

166   *"Virginia Tech's Mindy Somers fell"*: Business Wire Features, 1998, 2.

166   *"Bradley McCue"*: Bunkley, 1999.

166   *"Nicholas Armstrong"*: Hanna, 1999.

166   *"at least thirty-four alcohol-related deaths"*: McNamara, 1999, B1.

167   *"Eric Clapton"*: Gunderson, 1989, 2D.

167   *"Adolescent females are significantly more at risk"*: National Household Survey on Drug Abuse, 1997.

167   *"In the early 1960s about 7 percent of the new female users of alcohol"*: Trends in prevalence, 1997.

168   *"Females have less gastric alcohol dehydrogenase"*: Frezza, DiPadova, Pozzato, Terpin, Baraona, and Lieber, 1990.

168   *"the personality traits that influence high-risk drinking choices"*: Jessor and Jessor, 1977. Also Donovan, 1993. Also Donovan and Jessor, 1985.

169   *"According to the Justice Department"*: Associated Press, 1998, A8.

169   *"the majority of our nation's prisoners"*: National Center on Addiction and Substance Abuse, 1998, iii.

170   *"Given that alcohol and other drugs"*: Ibid.

171   *"As Marian Sandmaier says"*: Sandmaier, 1980.

172   *"A 1999 television commercial for Finlandia vodka"*: Monday Morning Report, 1999, 4.

175   *"Heavy drinking is seen by the culture"*: Sandmaier, 1980.

176   *"The waterskier in a Smirnoff ad"*: Williamson, 1986, 50.

177   *"Several researchers have identified shame"*: Sandmaier, 1980. Also Bepko, 1991.

178   *"Many theorists believe that gender socialization"*: Ibid.

178   *"According to researcher F. B. Parker"*: Parker, 1972, 656.

CHAPTER 8. "WHAT YOU'RE LOOKING FOR"

page

180   *"three thousand children to start smoking every day"*: Altman, Foster, and Rasenick-Douss, 1989, 80–83.

181   *"90 percent of all smokers"*: DiFranza, Richards, Paulman, Wolf-Gillespie, Fletcher, Jaffe, and Murray, 1991, 3149. Also Barbeau, DeJong, Brugge, and Rand, 1998, 473.

181   *"the age of initiation"*: U.S. Department of Health and Human Services, 1995.

181   *"about one-third of high-school-aged adolescents"*: U.S. Department of Health and Human Services, 1994, 5.

181   *"nicotine is the most addictive drug"*: Anthony, Warner, and Kessler, 1994, 244–68. Also U.S. Department of Health and Human Services, 1994, 31.

181   *"a 'pediatric disease'"*: FDA Commissioner David Kessler, in a speech at Columbia University School of Law, March 8, 1995.

181   *"Seventy percent will regret"*: Gallup Institute, 1992, 54.

181   *"Joseph Califano, Jr., former secretary of health"*: Califano, 1995, 1215.

181   *"smoking in the teenage years causes permanent genetic changes"*: Wiencke,Thurston, Kelsey, Varkonyi, Wain, Mark, and Christiani, 1999.

181   *"Cigarettes kill more Americans each year"*: Lynch and Bonnie, 1994.

181   *"according to former surgeon general C. Everett Koop"*: Bartecchi, MacKenzie, and Schrier, 1994, 907.

182   *"by the year 2030"*: World Health Organization, 1999.

182   *"cigarette smoke is also harmful to nonsmokers"*: Environmental tobacco smoke (ETS) can cause a number of adverse health consequences, including acute respiratory disease in children. ETS kills about fifty thousand people a year in the United States, more than are killed by all illicit drugs combined, and sends at least four million children to their doctors. Environmental Protection Agency, 1992.

      Yet in 1996 R.J. Reynolds Tobacco Company chairman Charles Harper said, defending his belief that smokers should never be restricted, "If children don't like to be in a smoky room, they'll leave." Asked by a shareholder about infants who would be unable to leave, Harper replied, "At some point they begin to crawl." Harper, quoted in *USA Today,* 1996, April 18, B1.

182   *"The World Bank has estimated"*: World Health Organization, 1997. Also Advocacy Institute, 1997.

182   *"over five billion dollars a year"*: Federal Trade Commission, 1998.

182   *"10 percent of the nation's fifty-five million smokers"*: Tye, Warner, and Glantz, 1987, 492–508.

182   *"Marlboros began as a cigarette designed for women"*: Jacobson, 1982, 60.

183   *"in 1956 Marlboro was repositioned"*: Kluger, 1996. In Massing, 1996, 34.

183   *"Almost one-third of American smokers smoke Marlboros"*: Top 10 cigarette brands, 1997, S20.

183   *"one writer for the magazine"*: Garfield, 1999, 18.

183   *"more than two-thirds of the fifty G-rated animated films"*: Goldstein, Sobel, and Newman, 1999, 1131–36.

183   *"tobacco advertising has two major effects"*: U.S. Department of Health and Human Services, 1994, vii.

183   *"This camel, known as Old Joe"*: Fischer, Schwartz, Richards, Goldstein, and Rojas, 1991, 3145–48.

184   *"After the introduction of Joe Camel"*: DiFranza, Richards, Paulman, Wolf-Gillespie, Fletcher, Jaffe, and Murray, 1991, 3149–53. According to Arnett and Terhanian, 13 percent of teen smokers now smoke Camels. Arnett and Terhanian, 1998, 129–33.

184   *"Eighty-six percent of all teenage smokers"*: Centers for Disease Control, 1994, 578–79.

184   *"70 percent of young African-American smokers"*: Todt, 1998, A16. According to this article, a class-action suit has been filed against the tobacco industry accusing it of violating the civil rights of African-Americans by trying to sell them menthol cigarettes, which are especially dangerous.

184   *"Recent research also supports this"*: King, Siegel, Celebucki, and Connolly, 1998, 516–20. Also Feighery, Borzekowski, Schooler, and Flora, 1998, 123–28. Also Arnett and Terhanian, 1998, 129–33. Also Evans, Farkas, Gilpin, Berry, and Pierce, 1995, 1538–45. Also O'Connell, Alexander, Dobson, Lloyd, Hardes, and Springthorpe, 1990, 223–31. Also Armstrong, DeKlerk, Shean,

Dunn, and Dolin, 1990, 117–24. According to Kluger, "The tobacco companies insult common sense with their claims that they do not advertise or promote cigarettes with the intention of enlisting the young. Cigarette makers lose two millions customers a year—80 percent quit and the rest die. If these smokers weren't replaced, the manufacturers would soon have to close down. And since 90 percent of all smokers take up the practice in their teen-age years, where else would the industry logically look for fresh recruits? The result is advertising that struts heroically taciturn cowboys, sportive cartoon camels and death-defying adventurers, brand-name promotional events like rock concerts, stock car races and tennis tournaments, and merchandising offers of T-shirts and camping gear embossed with brand logos." Kluger, 1996, 28.

184 *"According to one of these studies, tobacco advertising and promotion":* Evan, Farkas, Gilpin, Berry, and Pierce, 1995, 1538–45.

184 *"In 1998 Pierce conducted a longitudinal study":* Pierce, Choi, Gilpin, Farkas, and Berry, 1998, 511–15.

184 *"In one poll, 71 percent of advertising executives":* Novelli, National Center for Tobacco-Free Kids, Washington, D.C.

184 *"According to Rance Crain":* Crain, 1995, 20.

185 *"The late Emerson Foote":* Foote, 1981, 1667.

185 *"Bob Garfield, advertising reviewer":* Garfield, 1997, 59.

185 *"people in their early and mid-teens":* Hilts, 1996. In Massing, 1996, 34.

185 *"about thirty countries":* Pollack, 1997, E5.

185 *"including those of the European Union":* Bidlake, 1998, 56.

185 *"A survey conducted by the American Cancer Society":* American Cancer Society, 1990.

185 *"In 1997 the Liggett Group":* Flint, 1997, 1.

185 *"Tobacco industry documents":* Glantz, 1996.

186 *"As one R.J. Reynolds document":* R.J. Reynolds Tobacco Company internal memorandum, 1986, in Advocacy Institute, 1998.

186 *"Brown & Williamson Company's efforts":* Brown & Williamson Company memo, 1972.

186 *"The company also considered tobacco-based lollipops":* Associated Press, 1999, May 23.

186 *"a study in which Philip Morris researchers":* Ryan, 1974.

186 *"As an R. J. Reynolds memo says":* Hind, 1975.

186 *"'The base of our business'":* Advocacy Institute, 1998.

186 *"a Philip Morris report says":* Ibid.

186 *"In 1968 Virginia Slims was introduced by Philip Morris":* Pierce, Lee, and Gilpin, 1994, 608–11.

187 *"The co-optation of women's liberation":* Brandt, 1996, 63–66.

187 *"Hill reportedly said":* Ibid.

187 *"Today 25 million American women":* Blumenthal, 1996, 8.

187 *"The highest rates are among whites and Native Americans":* French and Perry, 1996, 25–28.

187 *"Lesbian and bisexual rates":* Gay and lesbian smoking and health survey, Santa Barbara Gay and Lesbian Resource Center, Santa Barbara, California. Quoted in Redefining liberation: Fact sheet for the women's health project, 1997. Washington, D.C.: National Organization for Women.

188 *"most smokers wish they could quit":* Berman and Gritz, 1991, 221–28.

188 *"tobacco companies used coercion":* Levin, 1999.

188 *"lung cancer in women has increased nationwide":* Califano, 1995, 1215. Smoking is also associated with increased menstrual abnormalities and reduced fertility. When women do conceive, their babies run extra risks of low birth weight, fetal death, prematurity, fetal distress, and other complications. In spite of this, one out of every five pregnant women smokes. Smoking also impairs lactation. Children exposed to tobacco smoke are at much greater risk for ear infections, asthma, respiratory infections such as bronchitis and pneumonia, and lung damage. As if all this

weren't enough, smoking also accelerates bone loss in older women and increases the risk of osteoporosis.

188 *"Smoking only a few cigarettes a day"*: Budris, 1997, 6.

189 *"genetically at risk"*: Associated Press, 1999, January 25. Also Knox, 1998, A3.

189 *"A heavy smoker is as much as four times more likely"*: Borelli, Bock, King, Pinto, and Marcus, 1996, 378–87. Also Glassman, Helzer, Covey, Cottler, Stetner, Jayson, and Johnson, 1990, 1546–49. Also Anva, Williamson, Escobedo, Mast, Giovino, and Remington, 1990, 1541–45.

189 *"teenage smokers were twice as likely as nonsmokers"*: Brown, Lewinsohn, Seeley, and Wagner, 1996, 1602–10.

189 *"to report a suicide attempt"*: Associated Press, 1997, June 3, A3.

189 *"One middle-school girl"*: Women and Tobacco Task Force, 1995. This girl was a participant in a series of roundtable discussions run by the Commission for a Healthy New York in 1995. The surveyors asked many questions of girls and women throughout the state. They asked girls under eighteen their reasons for smoking and found that weight control and coping with stress were cited more frequently by older girls and curiosity and peer pressure were referred to more often by younger girls.

189 *"a woman in an unhappy marriage said"*: Jacobson, 1982, 4.

190 *"Worldwide cross-cultural studies"*: Gitlin and Pasnau, 1989, 7–15.

190 *"A 1997 nationwide survey of college freshmen"*: Survey finds serious stress on campus, 1997, A5.

190 *"Women are also more likely than men"*: Gritz, Nielsen, and Brooks, 1996, 35–42. Also Borelli, Bock, King, Pinto, and Marcus, 1996, 378–87. Also Berman and Gritz, 1991, 221–38. Also Warburton, 1988, 27–49. Also Kleinke, Staneski, and Mason, 1982, 877–89.

190 *"women experience greater anxiety"*: Gritz, Nielsen, and Brooks, 1996, 35–42. Also Husten, Chrismon, and Reddy, 1996, 11–18. Also Fant, Everson, Dayton, Pickworth, and Henningfield, 1996, 19–24.

190 *"According to Dr. Teresa Bernardez"*: Bernardez, 1978, 22.

191 *"Women who are doubly or triply oppressed"*: Borelli, Bock, King, Pinto, and Marcus, 1996, 378–87.

191 *"In Straight, No Chaser"*: Nelson, 1997, 94.

191 *"suppressed anger also plays an important role"*: Wilsnack, Wilsnack, and Kristjanson, 1998, 199–230. Also Thompson, 1994.

191 *"Jennifer, a fourteen-year-old anorexic"*: McFarland, 1997, 41.

191 *"And Bone, the abused girl"*: Allison, 1992, 98.

191 *"A study reported by British researcher Bobbie Jacobson"*: Jacobson, 1982, 28.

191 *"Canadian researcher Lorraine Greaves found"*: Greaves, 1990.

191 *"the story of a girl named Lauren"*: Martin-Morris, 1998, 62.

193 *"As Barbara Ehrenreich said"*: Ehrenreich, 1999, 46.

195 *"women still don't get equal pay"*: Goodman, 1999, C7. According to this article, women earn 74 cents for every dollar men earn.

197 *"When psychologist Judith Jordan"*: in private conversation, March 1999.

199 *"The Commission for a Healthy New York study"*: Commision for a Healthy New York, 1995.

200 *"Adolescent girls in particular"*: Nichter, Nichter, Vuckovic, Quintero, and Ritenbaugh, 1997, 285–95.

203 *"We have the little surveyor in our head"*: Berger, 1972.

203 *"terror of gaining weight"*: French and Perry, 1996, 25–28.

205 "Advertising Age *published a letter from a copywriter"*: Rotterdam, 1986, 21. Mr. Rotterdam was a promotion copywriter for *USA Weekend*.

205 *"As psychologist Karen Horney"*: Paris, 1994, 68–70.

206 *"Richard Pollay, curator of the Advertising Archives"*: Pollay, 1995, 189.

207   *"Elizabeth Hirschman, a marketing professor":* Hirschman, 1995, 193.

208   *"According to a Philip Morris document":* Advocacy Institute, 1998.

209   *"cigarettes, like alcohol, are linked with impotence":* Mannino, Klevens, and Flanders, 1994, 1003–8.

209   *"A 1959 tobacco industry study":* Rosenbaum, 1995, 55.

210   *"Teenage girls, who identify smoking with independence":* Nichter, Nichter, Vuckovic, Quintero, and Ritenbaugh, 1997, 285–95.

212   *"According to media critic Mark Crispin Miller":* Miller, 1994, 23.

214   *"Bill Clinton is the first president":* Ferguson, 1999, 11–15.

215   *"Its international sales have quadrupled":* Philip Morris steps up international influence, 1997, 5.

215   *"Worldwide today, 47 percent of men":* Women, girls and tobacco: An appeal for global action, 1998, 7.

215   *"In developing countries":* Haglund, 1998, 1.

215   *"Two out of the top three global tobacco":* World Tobacco File, 1994.

215   *"'Camel Planet,' says an ad":* INFACT Update, 1997, 5.

215   *"Mark Palmer, the U.S. ambassador":* Palmer, 1998, A25.

215   *"or the Chinese opium":* Mintz, 1991.

215   *"As Barbara Gordon said":* Gordon, 1979, 176.

216   *"As one former smoker":* Commission for a Healthy New York, 1995, 27.

216   *"As Sue Delaney said":* Delaney, 1989, 8.

216   *"As Jill Nelson, writing about the rage of African-American women":*: Nelson, 1997, 95.

CHAPTER 9. "THE DREAM BEGINS AS SOON AS YOU OPEN THE DOOR"

page

218   *"A 1997 commercial for Levi jeans":* Cuneo, 1997, 1, 31.

218   *"The director of the commercial":* Garfield, 1997, 29.

220   *"Heavy drinkers tend to believe that alcohol is a 'magic elixir'":* Seventh special report to the U.S. Congress on alcohol and health, 1990, 53.

220   *"Teenage alcohol abusers expect more positive effects":* Op. cit., 60.

222   *"Coca-Cola and Pepsi alone":* Jacobson, 1998, 8.

223   *"A 1999 Mountain Dew commercial":* Breaking: Mountain Dew, 1999, 54.

223   *"According to Michael Bainbridge, a brand identity consultant":* Barboza, 1997, D5.

224   *"'Postpone adulthood,' says yet another car commercial":* Mitsubishi commercial broadcast on Fox during *Ally McBeal,* May 10, 1999.

225   *"According to child psychiatrist and author Robert Coles":* Kakutani, 1997, 22.

225   *"Media critic Steven Stark adds":* Ibid.

226   *"As William James said":* Goodman, 1988, 168. I am grateful to Nancy Holloway for bringing this to my attention.

226   *"Carl Jung described a craving for alcohol":* Jung, 1961, January 30. In a letter to Bill Wilson, the founder of Alcoholics Anonymous. Reprinted in the *Grapevine,* January 1968.

227   *"Some research indicates that we may have lower levels":* Royce, 1981, 105.

228   *"In the strictest scientific sense, addiction is a state":* Jonas, 1989, 269.

228   *"As James Royce said":* Royce, 1981, 67.

229   *"The pharmaceutical industry":* Carroll, 1999, F1.

229   *"the majority of students, if surveyed":* Perkins and Berkowitz, 1986, 961–76.

232   *"According to ad reviewer Bob Garfield":* Garfield, 1998, 57.

233   *"The alcohol industry spends over one billion dollars a year"*: Fleming, 1998.
233   *"According to a recent Gallup survey, one out of three"*: McAnemy, 1997.

CHAPTER 10. "IN LIFE THERE ARE MANY LOVES…"

page

235   *"A very powerful 1997 commercial"*: Broadcast on CBS during *Michael Hayes*, October 1997.
235   *"As the chairman of one advertising agency"*: Reidy, 1997, D7.
236   *"whole lexicon of smoking"*: Klein, 1993.
237   *"And smokers are 53 percent more likely to have been divorced"*: Doherty and Doherty, 1998, 393–400.
237   *"Caroline Knapp used this idea"*: Knapp, 1996, xv.
237   *"Margaret Bullitt-Jonas titled her book"*: Bullitt-Jonas, 1999.
238   *"so much of our drinking is connected with our relationships"*: Wilsnack, Wilsnack, and Kristjanson, 1998, 199–230. Also Covington and Surrey, 1994. Also Finkelstein, 1996. Also Gleason, 1994.
246   *"Alcohol is involved in over half of all cases"*: Greenfield, 1998.
246   *"One of the most chilling commercials"*: Michelob commercial broadcast on Fox during *Ally McBeal*, May 10, 1999.
249   *"Perhaps Shakespeare put it best"*: Shakespeare, W. *Macbeth*. Act 2, Scene 3.
250   *"Recovery reverses this downward spiral"*: Stephanie Covington, who lectures and writes on addiction, introduced me to the idea of addiction and recovery as spirals.

CHAPTER 11. "YOU TALKIN' TO ME?"

page

252   *"In his classic novel* Under the Volcano": Lowry, 1947, 349–50.
252   *"Jean Baker Miller refers to this terrible sadness"*: Miller and Stiver, 1997, 75–81.
252   *"scientists are increasingly discovering"*: Associated Press, 1999, February 15, A5. Also Thompson, 1994. Also Krahn, 1991, 239–53. Also Hso, 1990. Also Jonas, 1989, 267–71. Also Royce, 1981.
252   *"At least two-thirds of patients"*: Leshner, 1998, 3.
252   *"research has found fundamental differences"*: Wilsnack and Wilsnack, 1997. Also National Center on Addiction and Substance Abuse, 1996.
253   *"alcoholic women are more likely than alcoholic men"*: Bepko, 1989, 406–26.
253   *"psychologist Sharon Wilsnack"*: Wilsnack, Vogeltanz, Klassen, and Harris, 1997, 264–72.
253   *"According to researcher Becky Thompson"*: Thompson, 1994, 8.
253   *"Various studies show"*: Thompson, 1994. Also Wilsnack, Vogeltanz, Klassen, and Harris, 1997; Wooley, 1994; Russell and Wilsnack, 1991; Wilsnack and Beckman, 1984; and Sandmaier, 1980.
253   *"A review of 166 studies"*: Holmes and Slap, 1998, 1855–62. According to Ellen Bass and Laura David, at least one out of four girls and one out of seven boys are sexually abused, usually by a man they know and trust. Bass and Davis, 1988.
253   *"from 30 to 60 percent of women in drug abuse treatment suffer from PTSD"*: Swan, 1998, 5.
253   *"Men suffer terribly"*: Clark, Lesnick, and Hegedus, 1997.
254   *"According to feminist theologian Rita Nakashima Brock"*: Koch, 1999, 8.
254   *"When a person dissociates"*: Covington and Surrey, 1994.
255   *"Terence Real and others have written"*: Real, 1997.
256   *"Canadian researcher Lorraine Greaves"*: Greaves, 1996.
257   *"'addiction reenacts a traumatized relationship'"*: Woodman, 1990, 38.

257 *"R. D. Laing wrote brilliantly"*: Laing, 1960, 69.
257 *"such as Jeremy Iggers and Christopher Lasch"*: Iggers, 1996; Lasch, 1979.
258 *"Mary Gaitskill, in her collection"*: Gaitskill, 1997, 137.
258 *"research studies keep finding that many women"*: Then, 1992. Also Richins, 1991.
259 *"Marianne Apostolides"*: Apostolides, 1998, 50.
259 *"Robert Schultz describes these images"*: Schultz, 1995, 369.
262 *"The endless pursuit of passion"*: Moog, 1991, 20–22.
263 *"As psychologist Linda Pollock"*: Pollock, 1998, 20.
263 *"'a heightened sense of aliveness'"*: Iggers, 1996, 110.
263 *"Identical models parade alone"*: Kilbourne, 1977, 293–94.
265 *"As Ann Snitow says"*: Snitow, 1985, 116.
265 *"According to poet Robert Hass"*: Schultz, 1995, 378–79.
266 *"as Sut Jhally says"*: Jhally, 1989.
266 *"According to one sex therapist"*: Johnson, 1998, 59.
266 *"A 1999 study"*: Laumann, Paik, and Rosen, 1999, 537–44.
266 *"victims of childhood sexual abuse"*: Laumann, Paik, and Rosen, 1999, 542.
267 *"a third of women respondents and a sixth of men"*: Kolata, 1998, 3.
267 *"Sexual dysfunction is associated"*: Laumann, Paik, and Rosen, 1999, 543.
267 *"Syndicated columnist Dan Savage"*: Johnson, 1998, 60.
267 *"Raymond C. Rosen"*: Howe, 1999, A18.
267 *"As Norman Cousins said"*: Cousins, 1975.
267 *"A recent issue of Sky"*: Dear Karen, 1996, 226.
268 *"Mademoiselle offered this advice"*: Geggis, 1997, C1.
268 *"In 1997 NBC featured a story"*: Wylie, 1997, 29.

CHAPTER 12. "TWO WAYS A WOMAN CAN GET HURT"

page

274 *"between one-third and three-quarters of all cases"*: Wilsnack, Plaud, Wilsnack, and Klassen, 1997, 262.
274 *"over half of all reported rapes"*: Abbey, Ross, and McDuffie, 1991. Also Martin, 1992, 230–37.
277 *"According to former surgeon general Antonia Novello"*: Novello, 1991. Also Blumenthal, 1995.
277 *"The Global Report on Women's Human Rights"*: Wright, 1995, A2.
278 *"according to Mary Daly"*: Weil, 1999, 21.
278 *"An editorial in Advertising Age"*: Brewers can help fight sexism, 1991, 28.
278 *"In 1994 a 'gender bender' television commercial"*: Kilbourne, 1994, F13.
279 *"As Anna Quindlen said"*: Quindlen, 1992, E17.
280 *"the rate of sexual assault in the United States"*: Blumenthal, 1995, 2.
280 *"According to a 1998 study"*: Tjaden and Thoennes, 1998.
281 *"In 1990 a male Canadian judge"*: Two men and a baby, 1990, 10.
281 *"A shocking ad in a gun magazine"*: Herbert, 1999, WK 17.
282 *"A growing national obsession in Japan"*: Schoolgirls as sex toys, 1997, 2E.
282 *"Masao Miyamoto, a male psychiatrist"*: Ibid.
283 *"In November of 1997 Advertising Age"*: Johnson, 1997, 42.
283 *"Kate Moss was twenty"*: Leo, 1994, 27.
284 *"In 1995 he brought the federal government down on himself"*: Sloan, 1996, 27.
284 *"in 1999 Klein launched a very brief advertising campaign"*: Associated Press, 1999, February 18, A7.

285 *"In 1997 a company called Senate":* Wire and *Times* staff reports, 1997, D1.
286 *"According to an article in the journal* Eating Disorders": Larkin, Rice, and Russell, 1996, 5–26.
286 *"A 1993 report by the American Association of University Women":* Daley and Vigue, 1999, A12.
287 *"One high-school junior":* Hart, 1998, A12.
287 *"One young woman recalled":* Mackler, 1998, 56.
287 *"Sexual battery":* Daley and Vigue, 1999, A1, A12.
287 *"A fifth-grade boy in Georgia":* Shin, 1999, 32.
287 *"A high-school senior":* Daley and Vigue, 1999, A12.
287 *"In another school in the Boston area":* Vigue and Abraham, 1999, B6.
287 *"According to Nan Stein":* Stein, 1993, 316–17.
288 *"As Marian Sandmaier said":* Sandmaier, 1980, xviii.
288 *"More than half of women in prison":* Snell, 1991.
289 *"In his classic essay 'The Cybernetics of Self' Gregory Bateson":* Bateson, 1972.
289 *"Claudia Bepko takes Bateson's theory further":* Bepko, 1989.
291 *"As Judith Herman wrote":* Herman and Hirschman, 1981, 107–8.

CHAPTER 13. "RELAX.W AND ENJOY THE REVOLUTION"

page

292 *"David Denby so accurately calls 'an avalanche of crud'":* Denby, 1996, 48.
293 *"Two-thirds of the almost":* Palmer, 1999, A9.
293 *"Among industrialized nations":* Califano, 1995, 40. Also Reich, 1997, 11.
294 *"acting in our own best interest":* Getting smarter in the war on drugs, 1999. Also Treatment of drug offenders, 1999.
294 *"The result is isolation, alienation":* Greenfield, 1996, F2.
294 *"As social critic Stanley Crouch said":* DeWitt, 1996, 10.
294 *"Alexis de Tocqueville suggested":* Derber, 1996, 15.
298 *"As Bob Garfield said, so were a lot of things":* Garfield, 1999, March 15, 57.
299 *"Public health experts":* Mosher, 1997, 74–91.
300 *"Since Massachusetts increased":* Phillips, 1998, A32.
300 *"In Florida":* Mays, 1999, A8.
300 *"And several studies have documented that in the 1990s smoking":* Pérez-Peña, 1999, 23.
300 *"As a report from the Higher Education Center for Alcohol":* Zimmerman, 1997, vii.
301 *"a well-known Boston columnist":* Barnicle, 1998, B1.
303 *"Studies in Tennessee and New York":* Welch, 1999, A17.
304 *"Kalle Lasn, editor of* Adbusters": Lasn, 1999.
306 *"There was a virtual news blockade":* Frankel, 1999, 29. Also McChesney, 1996, 98–124.
306 *"The Vancouver-based Media Foundation":* Adbusters Media Foundation, 1243 W. Seventh Avenue, Vancouver, British Columbia, V6H 1B7.
306 *"As prize-winning reporter Bill Lazarus":* Collins, 1992, 61.
307 *"Each year sixty thousand workers die":* Leigh, Markowitz, Fahs, Shin, and Landrigan, 1997.
307 *"In 1966, 58 percent of incoming college freshmen":* Nyhan, 1999, A23.
308 *"And George Soros":* Nyhan, 1997, A15.
309 *"As Richard Goodwin says":* Goodwin, 1997, A13.
310 *"In 1999 a bill before Congress":* Frankel, 1999, 29.
311 *"as Oprah Winfrey was by the Texas cattlemen":* Hatherill, 1999.
311 *"As Max Frankel says":* Frankel, 1999, 29.

312   *"A two-year study of over twelve thousand adolescents"*: Dooley and Fedele, 1999.
312   *"Sylvia Ann Hewlett and Cornel West"*: Hewlett and West, 1999.
313   *"As Margaret Bullitt-Jonas says"*: Bullitt-Jonas, 1999, 250.
313   *"As Jill Nelson says"*: Nelson, 1997, 95.
313   *"Heart specialist Dean Ornish"*: Rowe, 1996, 28.
313   *"We need what George Gerbner calls"*: Cultural Environment Movement, P.O. Box 31847, Philadelphia, PA 19104, 215-387-5202.

BIBLIOGRAPHY

Abbey, A., Ross, L., and McDuffie, D. (1991). Alcohol's role in sexual assault. In Watson, R., ed. *Addictive behaviors in women.* Towota, NJ: Humana Press.

Ads not infinitum (1998, December 14). *People,* 10–11.

Advocacy Institute (1997, April 30). Issue: Tenth annual world no-tobacco day, May 31,1997. *Action Alert,* 3.

Advocacy Institute (1998, April 15). *Action Alert.*

Advocacy Institute (1998, April 15). Draft report to the Philip Morris Board of Directors. *Action Alert.*

Advocacy Institute (1998, April 15). R. J. Reynolds Tobacco Company internal memorandum (1986). *Action Alert.*

Aiken, P., Eadie, D., Leathar, D., McNeill, R., Scott, R., and Scott, A. (1988). Television advertisements for alcoholic drinks do reinforce under-age drinking. *British Journal of Addiction,* 83, 1399–1419.

Allison, D. (1992). *Bastard Out of Carolina.* New York: Dutton.

Altman, D., Foster, V., and Rasenick-Douss, L. (1989). Reducing the illegal sale of cigarettes to minors. *Journal of the American Medical Association,* vol. 261, 80–83.

American Cancer Society (1990, Spring). Government tobacco promotion policies and consumption trends in thirty-three countries from 1970 to 1986. *World Smoking and Health,* vol. 15, no. 1.

Amos, A. (1999, Winter). *The Net (International Network of Women Against Tobacco),* 6–7.

Anda, R. F., Williamson, D. F., Escobedo, L. G., Mast, E. E., Giovino, G. A., and Remington, P. L. (1990, September 26). Depression and the dynamics of smoking. *Journal of the American Medical Association,* vol. 264, no. 12, 1541–45.

Andersen, R. (1998, September/October). Road to ruin. *Extra!,* 22, 23.

Angier, N. (1996, November 24). Who needs this ad most? *New York Times,* 4E.

Anholt, S. (1998, March 30). Brazil should follow lead of brand U.S.A. *Advertising Age International,* 12.

Anthony, J. C., Warner, L. A., and Kessler, R. C. (1994). *Comparative epidemiology of dependence on tobacco, alcohol, controlled substances and inhalants: Basic findings from the National Comorbidity Survey,* 244–68.

Apostolides, M. (1998). *Inner hunger: a young woman's struggle through anorexia and bulimia.* New York: W.W. Norton.

ARIS (1997, November 3). Alcohol issues. *Monday morning report,* vol. 21, no. 21, ISSN 0891–8651.

Armour, S. (1999, March 2). You have (too much) e-mail. *USA Today,* 3B.

Armstrong, B. K., DeKlerk, N. H., Shean, R. E., Dunn, D. A., and Dolin, P.H. (1990). Influence of education and advertising on the uptake of smoking by children. *Medical Journal of Australia,* vol. 152, 117–24.

Arndofer, J.B. (1997, July 28). 007's sponsor blitz. *Advertising Age,* 24.

Arnett, J. J. and Terhanian, G. (1998, Summer). Adolescents' response to cigarette advertisements: Links between exposure, liking, and the appeal of smoking. *Tobacco Control*, vol. 7, no. 2, 129–33.

Associated Press (1997, June 3). Study lists factors common in teenage suicide. *Boston Globe*, A15.

Associated Press (1998, March 26). Pepsi prank goes flat. *Boston Globe*, A3.

Associated Press (1998, April 6). Study links alcohol to many violent crimes. *Boston Globe*, A8.

Associated Press (1998, February 6). Tobacco firms lured youth at age 13, data show. *Boston Globe*, 6.

Associated Press (1999, January 25). Another gene linked to smoking, scientists say. *Boston Globe*, A4.

Associated Press (1999, February 15). Chemical malfunction suspected in cause of bulimia. *Boston Globe*, A5.

Associated Press (1999, February 18). Calvin Klein retreats on ad. *Boston Globe*, A7.

Associated Press (1999, May 23). Document: Tobacco candy considered. From Join Together Online (1999, May 25), www.jointogether.org.

Atkin, C. and Block, M. (1981). *Content and effects of alcohol advertising.* Washington, DC: Bureau of Tobacco, Alcohol and Firearms, Report PB-82-12314.

Austen, I. (1999, February 18). But first, another word from our sponsors. *New York Times*, E1, E8.

Austin, E. W. (1998, July). What makes media illiteracy a public health issue? Presentation at 1998 National Media Education Conference, Colorado Springs, CO.

Baker, R. (1997, September/October). The squeeze. *Columbia Journalism Review*, 30–36.

Balu, R. (1998, April 10). Anheuser lizard ads called cold-blooded. *Wall Street Journal*, B6.

Barbeau, E. M., DeJong, W., Brugge, D. M., and Rand, W. M. (1998, Winter). Does cigarette print advertising adhere to the Tobacco Institute's voluntary advertising and promotion code? An assessment. *Journal of Public Health Policy*, vol. 19, no. 4, 473–88.

Barboza, D. (1997, August 22). More hip, higher hop. *New York Times*, D1, D5.

Barnicle, M. (1998, May 10). Overreaction is a bad sign. *Boston Globe*, B1.

Bartecchi, C. E., MacKenzie, T. D., and Schrier, R. W. (1994, March 31). The human costs of tobacco use, I. *New England Journal of Medicine*, vol. 330, no. 13, 907–12.

Bass, E. and Davis, L. (1988). *The courage to heal: a guide for women survivors of child sexual abuse.* New York: Harper & Row.

Bateson, G. (1972). The cybernetics of self. In *Steps to an ecology of mind.* New York: Chandler Publishing.

Bauder, D. (1999, March 31). Ads creep into TV content. *Boston Globe*, E6.

Be out front on gay ads (1997, August 11). *Advertising Age*, 14.

Beatty, S. (1998, December 17). Alcohol firms boost online ads to youth. *Wall Street Journal*, 14.

Beavis and Butthead (1997, January 6). *Wall Street Journal*, B1.

Becker, A. E. and Burwell, R. A. (1999). Acculturation and disordered eating in Fiji. Poster presented at the American Psychiatric Association Annual Meeting, Washington, DC, May 19, 1999.

Beer advertising: the "unintended market" (1996, Summer). *The bottom line on alcohol in society*, vol. 7, no. 2, 5–10.

Beer companies tone down campus promotions (1992, Spring). *Prevention File*, 2.

Bepko, C. (1989). Disorders of power: women and addiction in the family. In McGoldrick, M., Anderson, C. M., and Walsh, F., eds. (1989). *Women in families: a framework for family therapy.* New York: W. W. Norton, 406–26.

Bepko, C., ed. (1991). *Feminism and addiction.* New York: Haworth Press.

Berg, F. M. (1997). Afraid to eat: children and teens in weight crisis. Hettinger, ND: *Healthy Weight Journal.*

Berger, J. (1972). *Ways of seeing.* London: British Broadcasting Corporation.

Berke, R. L. (1999, May 30). Fitting Forbes for Oval Office is advertising man's assignment. *New York Times*, 1, 17.

Berman, B. A. and Gritz, E. R. (1991). Women and smoking: Current trends and issues for the 1990s. *Journal of Substance Abuse,* vol. 3, 221–38.

Bernardez, T. (1978, November). Women and anger. *The Sciences,* 21–22, 32–33.

Bernstein, N. (1995, January/February). Learning to love. *Mother Jones,* 45–49, 54.

Bernstein, S. (1978, August 7). Do ads promote spirited imbibing? *Advertising Age,* 14.

Bernstein, S. (1986, January 27). Advertising still presells. *Advertising Age,* 17.

Bever, T. G., Smith, M. L., Bengen, B., and Johnson, T. G. (1975). Young viewers' troubling response to TV ads. *Harvard Business Review,* 53, 109–20.

Bidlake, S. (1997, September). Commercials support free phone calls. *Advertising Age International,* 147, 149.

Bidlake, S. (1998, May 18). Europe to halt tobacco ads, sponsorships. *Advertising Age,* 56.

Bierbaum, T. (1998, June 8–June 14). Ailing demos bag 'Dr. Quinn.' *Variety,* 18.

Black, C. (1990, April 21). Diet fad fattens firms. *Boston Globe,* 1.

Blumenthal, S. J. (1995, July). *Violence against women.* Washington, DC: Department of Health and Human Services.

Blumenthal, S. J. (1996, January/April). Smoking v. women's health: The challenge ahead. *Journal of the American Medical Women's Association,* vol. 51, nos. 1 and 2, 8.

Borelli, B., Bock, B., King, T., Pinto, B., and Marcus, B. H. (1996). The impact of depression on smoking cessation in women. *American Journal of Preventive Medicine,* vol. 12, no. 5, 378–87.

Bowen, L. and Schmid, J. (1997, Spring). Minority presence and portrayal in mainstream magazine advertising: an update. *Journalism & Mass Communication Quarterly,* vol. 74, no. 1, 134–45.

Bradsher, K. (1997, March 23). Domination, submission and the Chevy Suburban. *New York Times,* 2.

Bradsher, K. (1998, January 18). Drivers on a collision course. *New York Times,* 4.

Brandt, A. M. (1996, January/April). Recruiting women smokers: The engineering of consent. *Journal of the American Medical Association,* vol. 51, nos. 1 and 2, 63–66.

Brandweek (1997, January 27), vol. 38, no. 4, 25.

Breaking: Mountain Dew (1999, March 15). *Advertising Age,* 54.

Breaking: Toyota Tacoma (1998, September 21). *Advertising Age,* 4.

Brewers can help fight sexism (1991, October 28). *Advertising Age,* 28.

Brown, J. D., Greenberg, B. S., and Buerkel-Rothfuss, N. L. (1993). Mass media, sex and sexuality. In Strasburger, V. C. and Comstock, G. A., eds. *Adolescent medicine: adolescents and the media.* Philadelphia, PA: Hanley & Belfus.

Brown, J. D. and Steele, J. R. (1995, June 21). *Sex and the mass media. A report prepared for the Henry J. Kaiser Family Foundation.*

Brown, L. M. and Gilligan, C. (1992). Meeting at the crossroads: women's psychology and girls' development. New York: Ballantine Books.

Brown, R. A., Lewinsohn, P. M., Seeley, J. R., and Wagner, E. F. (1996). Cigarette smoking, major depression, and other psychiatric disorders among adolescents. *Journal of the American Academy of Child and Adolescent Psychiatry,* vol. 35, no. 12, 1602–10.

Brumberg, J. J. (1997). *The Body Project: An Intimate History of American Girls.* New York: Random House.

Buchwald, E., Fletcher, P., and Roth, M. (1993). *Transforming a rape culture.* Minneapolis: Milkweed Editions.

Budris, J. (1997, October 19). Where there's smoke. *Boston Globe Magazine,* 6, 7, 16.

Bullitt-Jonas, M. (1999). *Holy hunger: a memoir of desire.* New York: Alfred A. Knopf.

Bunkley, N. (1999, February 22). MSU alcohol incidents prompt community action. *Michigan Daily Online.* Obtained from the online news service of the Higher Education Center for Alcohol and Other Drug Prevention.

Business Wire Features (1998, November 11). Binge drinking: big killer on campus, 1–4.

Califano, J. A. (1995, November 2). The wrong way to stay slim. *New England Journal of Medicine*, vol. 333, no. 18, 1215.

Califano, J. A. (1995, January 29). It's drugs, stupid. *New York Times Magazine*, 40–41.

Campbell Mithun Esty (Minneapolis). Reported in Harper's Index (1999, January). *Harper's*, 15.

Canellos, P. S. (1999, February 28). Smile . . . or else. *Boston Globe*, C1, C2.

Carnegie Corporation (1995). *Great transitions: preparing adolescents for a new century.* New York: Carnegie Corporation.

Carroll, J. (1992, March 29). When puffery turns to perfidy. *Boston Globe*, 70.

Carroll, J. (1996, November 24). Adventures into new territory. *Boston Globe*, D1, D5.

Carroll, J. (1999, January 24). Drugs on TV: It all ads up. *Boston Globe*, F1, F3.

Carter, B. (1999, January 30). Where the boys are. *New York Times*, BU1, BU2.

Center for Science in the Public Interest (1998, September 4). Kids are as aware of booze as presidents, survey finds. Washington, DC: CSPI press release.

Centers for Disease Control (1994, August 19). Changes in the cigarette brand preferences of adolescent smokers—United States, 1989–1993. *Morbidity and Mortality Weekly Report*, vol. 43, no. 32, 577–81.

Chacon, R. and Ribadeneira, D. (1999, January 22), *Boston Globe*, A1, A10.

Cheers and Jeers (1997, June 21). *TV Guide*, 10.

Cheers and Jeers (1999, June 5). *TV Guide*, 10.

Chronicle News Services (1997, July 18). Road rage found in most fatalities. *San Francisco Chronicle*, A3.

Clark, D. B., Lesnick, L., and Hegedus, A. M. (1997, December). Traumas and other adverse life events in adolescents with alcohol abuse and dependence. *Journal of the American Academy of Child and Adolescent Psychiatry,* vol. 36, no. 12, 1744–58.

Coen, R. J. (1999). Spending spree. *The Advertising Century (Advertising Age* special issue), 126, 136.

Collins, R. (1992). *Dictating content: How advertising pressure can corrupt a free press.* Washington, DC: Center for Science in the Public Interest.

Commission for a Healthy New York (1995). *Women talk to women about smoking: A report of the Women and Tobacco Task Force.*

Commission on Substance Abuse at Colleges and Universities (1994). *Rethinking rites of passage: Substance abuse on America's campuses.* New York: Center on Addiction and Substance Abuse at Columbia University.

Cooper, M. (1999, April 5/12). Postcards from the left. *The Nation*, 21–26.

Cortese, A. (1999). *Provocateur: women and minorities in advertising.* Lanham, MD: Rowman & Littlefield.

Cortissoz, A. (1998, July 25). For young people, swing's the thing. *Boston Globe*, A1, A10.

Cousins, N. (1975, September 20). Dehumanization. *Saturday Review.*

Covington, S. S. and Surrey, J. L. (1994). The relational model of women's psychological development: Implications for substance abuse. In Wilsnack, S. and Wilsnack, R., eds. (1994). *Gender and alcohol.* Piscataway, NJ: Rutgers University.

Crain, R. (1995, October 30). Editorial. *Advertising Age*, 20.

Crain, R. (1997, June 9). Who knows what ads lurk in the hearts of consumers? The inner mind knows. *Advertising Age*, 25.

Crain, R. (1998, November 30). Miller's horrendous mistake example of how little we know. *Advertising Age*, 24.

Crain, R. (1999, January 18). When ads don't produce sales, watch the (phony) excuses fly. *Advertising Age*, 23.

Cuneo, A. Z. (1997, July 28). Levi's unleashing new image ads. *Advertising Age*, 1, 31.

Curtis, J. (1998, May/June). Wait a minute, Mr. Postman. *Applied Arts Magazine*, 49–54.

Daley, B. and Vigue, D. I. (1999, February 4). Sex harassment increasing amid students, officials say. *Boston Globe,* A1, A12.

Davis, W. (1994, August 6). Let's have no more victims of the thinness disease. *Philadelphia Inquirer,* 8.

Dear Karen (1996, December). *Sky* magazine, 226.

Dee, J. (1999, January). But is it advertising? *Harper's,* 61–72.

Defoe, J. and Breed, W. (1979, February). The problem of alcohol advertisements in college newspapers. *The Journal of the American College Health Association,* 195–99.

Delaney, S. (1989). *Women smokers can quit: A different approach.* Evanston, IL: Women's Healthcare Press.

Denby, D. (1996, July 15). Buried alive. *New Yorker,* 48–58.

Derber, C. (1996, April 2). America's corporate 'hit men.' *Boston Globe,* 15.

DeWitt, K. (1996, December 22). Once villainous, now virtuous. *New York Times,* 10.

DiFranza, J. R., Richards, J. W., Jr., Paulman, J. W., Wolf-Gillespie, N., Fletcher, C., Jaffe, R. D., and Murray, D. (1991, December 11). RJR Nabisco's cartoon camel promotes Camel cigarettes to children. *Journal of the American Medical Association,* 3149–53.

Dittmar, H. (1999, Spring). Road to nowhere. *Enough!* Newsletter of the Center for a New American Dream, Takoma Park, MD.

Doherty, E. W. and Doherty, W. J. (1998). Smoke gets in your eyes: Cigarette smoking and divorce in a national sample of American adults. *Family, Systems & Health,* vol. 16, no. 4, 393–400.

Donovan, J. E. (1993). Young adult drinking-driving: Behavioral and psychosocial correlates. *Journal of Studies on Alcohol,* vol. 54, no. 5, 600–13.

Donovan, J. E. and Jessor, R. (1985). Structure of problem behavior in adolescence and young adulthood. *Journal of Consulting and Clinical Psychology,* vol. 53, no. 6, 890–904.

Dooley, C. and Fedele, N. (1999, Spring). A response to the Columbine tragedy. *Connections (Jean Baker Miller Training Institute),* 2.

Douglas, S. J. (1994). *Where the girls are.* New York: Random House.

Duncan, B. (1997, Spring). Television in the 1990's: the quest for marketing and meaning. *Telemedium: The Journal of Media Literacy,* vol. 43, no. 1, 3–4.

Early drinking said to increase alcoholism risk (1998, Spring). *The bottom line on alcohol in society,* vol. 19, no. 1, 46–51.

Ehrenreich, B. (1999, January). Nickel-and-dimed: on (not) getting by in America. *Harper's,* 37–50.

Emert, C. (1998, May 23). Bud critters criticized. *San Francisco Chronicle,* B1, B2.

Endicott, R. C. (1998, November 9). Top 100 megabrands. *Advertising Age,* S-50, S-58.

English, B. (1998, March 16). The girls' movement comes of age. *Boston Globe,* C7, C11.

Enrico, D. (1997, September 15). Absolut vodka's ad spots withstand the test of time. *USA Today,* 4B.

Environmental Protection Agency (1992). Respiratory health effects of passive smoking: lung cancer and other disorders. Washington, DC: Office of Health and Environmental Assessment.

Espen, H. (1999, March 21). Levi's blues. *New York Times Magazine,* 54–59.

Evans, N., Farkas, A., Gilpin, E., Berry, C., and Pierce, J. (1995, October 18). Influence of tobacco marketing and exposure to smokers on adolescent susceptibility to smoking. *Journal of the American Cancer Institute,* vol. 87, 1538–45.

Faludi, S. (1991). *Backlash.* New York: Crown.

Fant, R.V., Everson, D., Dayton, G., Pickworth, H. B., and Henningfield, J. E. (1996, January/April). Nicotine dependence in women. *Journal of the American Medical Women's Association,* vol. 51, nos. 1 and 2, 19–24.

Federal Trade Commission (1998). Report to Congress. Reported by Advocacy Institute (1998, April 17). Issue: FTC reports spending on cigarette advertising and promotion increased in 1996. *Action Alert,* 1.

Feighery, E., Borzekowski, D., Schooler, C., and Flora, J. (1998, Summer). Seeing, wanting, owning: The relationship between receptivity to tobacco marketing and smoking susceptibility in young people. *Tobacco Control,* vol. 7, no. 2, 123–28.

Ferguson, T. (1999, March 8). Impeachment: The sequel. *The Nation,* 11–15.

Field, A. E., Cheung, L., Wolf, A. M., Herzog, D. B., Gortmaker, S. L., and Colditz, G. A. (1999, March). Exposure to the mass media and weight concerns among girls. *Pediatrics,* vol. 103, no. 3, 36–41.

Finkelstein, N. (1996). Using the relational model as a context for treating pregnant and parenting chemically dependent women. In Underhill, B. L. and Finnegan, D. G., eds. (1996). *Chemical dependency: women at risk.* New York: Haworth Press, 23–44.

Fischer, P. M., Schwartz, M. P., Richards, J. W., Jr., Goldstein, A. O., and Rojas, T. H. (1991, December 11). Brand logo recognition by children aged 3 to 6 years. *Journal of the American Medical Association,* 3145–48.

Fitzgerald, K. (1997, September 1). Extreme weirdness. *Advertising Age,* 28.

Fleming, D. (1998, August 15). Total U.S. drinks volumes are flat, but growth is strong in key areas. *Impact International,* vol. 13, nos. 14 and 15, 1–4.

Flint, A. (1997, March 21). Tobacco firm cites danger of smoking. *Boston Globe,* 1.

Foote, E. (1981). Advertising and tobacco. *Journal of the American Medical Association,* vol. 245, no. 16, 1667–68.

Ford, R. (1999, June 2). Pick up lumber, pick up kids. *Boston Globe,* A1, A20.

Ford, R. (1999, May 22). With an SUV (as with all of life), the key is responsibility. *Boston Globe,* D1.

Foreman, J. (1999, March 1). Sugar's 'empty calories' pile up. *Boston Globe,* C1, C4.

Fox, R. F. (1997, Spring). Talking heads. *Stay Free!,* 38–42.

Frankel, M. (1999, June 13). The information tyranny. *New York Times Magazine,* 29.

Fraser, L. (1997, May/June). The diet trap. *Family Therapy Networker,* 45–48.

Frazeur, A. (1997, July). 'Blenders' frozen dessert spikes up adult market. *AG Innovation News,* vol. 6, no. 3, 1–4.

Fredrickson, B. L. (1998, Fall). *Journal of Personality and Social Psychology,* vol. 75, no. 1. Reported in *Media Report to Women,* 5.

French, S. A. and Perry, C. L. (1996, January/April). Smoking among adolescent girls: Prevalence and etiology. *Journal of the American Medical Women's Association,* vol. 51, nos. 1 and 2, 25–28.

Frezza, M., DiPadova, C., Pozzato, G., Terpin, M., Baraona, E., and Lieber, C. (1990, January 11). High blood alcohol levels in women: The role of decreased gastric alcohol dehydrogenase activity and first-pass metabolism. *New England Journal of Medicine,* vol. 322, no. 2, 95–99.

Gaitskill, M. (1997). *Because they wanted to: stories.* New York: Simon & Schuster.

Gallup International Institute (1992, September). Teenage attitudes and behavior concerning tobacco.

Gardenburger hits the spot (1998, September 14). *Advertising Age,* 17.

Garfield, B. (1997, August 11). Levi's heroes vapid, but they wear well. *Advertising Age,* 29.

Garfield, B. (1997, September 29). Lexus shows some new, 'wicked' ways. *Advertising Age,* 61

.Garfield, B. (1997, June 16). Nothing poisonous about Bud's lizards. *Advertising Age,* 59.

Garfield, B. (1997, August 4). Taco Bell fills the bill for teens' tummies. *Advertising Age,* 43.

Garfield, B. (1998, April 20). Fabian turns Denny's meals into side dish. *Advertising Age,* 53.

Garfield, B. (1998, December 7). Levi's teen appeal tied to glamorous, risky acts. *Advertising Age,* 57.

Garfield, B. (1998, July 20). SnackWell's ups fat, but ads are tasteless. *Advertising Age,* 33.

Garfield, B. (1999, February 22). Frosted Flakes adds apropos personality. *Advertising Age,* 77.

Garfield, B. (1999, March 15). Tampax skinnydips into its own ubiquity. *Advertising Age,* 57.

Garfield, B. (1999, March 29). Top 100 advertising campaigns. *Advertising Age (Special Issue: The Advertising Century)*, 18.

'Gay beer' in Australia (1997, January). *The Globe,* 23.

Geggis, A. (1997, August 16). Mainstream soft-core porn at the checkout. *Boston Globe,* C1, C6.

Gerbner, G. (1994, July). Television violence: The art of asking the wrong question. *The World & I,* 395–97.

Getting smarter in the war on drugs (1999, May 2). *Washington Post,* reported in Join Together Online (www.jointogether.org).

Gilligan, C. (1982). *In a different voice.* Cambridge, MA: Harvard University Press.

Gitlin, M. J. and Pasnau, R. O. (1989). Psychiatric syndromes linked to reproductive functions in women: A review of current knowledge. *American Journal of Psychiatry,* vol. 146, 7–15.

Glantz, S. A., Slade, J., Bero, L. A., and Hanauer, P., eds. (1996). *The cigarette papers.* Berkeley, CA: University of California Press.

Glassman, A. H., Helzer, J. E., Covey, L. S., Cottler, L. B., Stetner, F., Jayson, E. T., and Johnson, J. (1990, September 26). Smoking, smoking cessation and major depression. *Journal of the American Medical Association,* vol. 264, no. 12, 1546–49.

Gleason, M. (1997, March 17). Events & promotions. *Advertising Age,* S1.

Gleason, N. A. (1994, May). College women and alcohol: A relational perspective. *Journal of American College Health,* vol. 42, 279–89.

Gleason, N. A. (1994, July). Preventing alcohol abuse by college women: A relational perspective 2. *Journal of American College Health,* vol. 43, 15–24.

Goffman, E. (1978). *Gender advertisements.* Cambridge, MA: Harvard University Press.

Goldner, B. (1998, June 29). Tamagotchi. *Advertising Age,* S43.

Goldsmith, J. (1999, February 10). A $2 billion doll celebrates her 40th without a wrinkle. *Boston Globe,* D3.

Goldstein, A. O., Sobel, R. A., and Newman, G. R. (1999, March 24/31). Tobacco and alcohol use in G-rated children's animated films. *Journal of the American Medical Association,* vol. 281, no. 12, 1131–36.

Goodman, D. W. (1988). *Alcohol and the writer.* New York: Andrews and McNeel.

Goodman, E. (1990, August 23). An American love affair that's too expensive. *Boston Globe,* A23.

Goodman, E. (1999, March 14). Scant progress in working women's fight for equal pay. *Boston Globe,* C7.

Goodman, E. (1999, May 27). The culture of thin bites Fiji teens. *Boston Globe,* A23.

Goodwin, R. N. (1997, February 5). The wreckage of politics. *Boston Globe,* A13.

Gordon, B. (1979). *I'm dancing as fast as I can.* New York: Harper & Row.

Greaves, L. (1990, April). The meaning of smoking to women. A paper presented at the Seventh World Conference on Tobacco & Health, Perth, Australia.

Greaves, L. (1996). *Smoke screen: women's smoking and social control.* Halifax: Fernwood Publishing.

Greenfield, L. A. (1998, April 5). *Alcohol and crime.* Washington, DC: U. S. Department of Justice.

Greenfield, P. M (1996, July 28). The sexes still roles apart. *Boston Globe,* F2.

Greenfield, T. K. and Rogers, J. D. (1999, January). Who drinks most of the alcohol in the U.S.? The policy implications. *Journal of Studies on Alcohol,* 78–89.

Grierson, B. (1998, Winter). Shock's next wave. *Adbusters,* 21.

Grimes, W. (1996, March 10). New! original! nonfat! fat-free! You can sell anything. *New York Times Magazine,* 64–65.

Gritz, E. R., Nielsen, I. R., and Brooks, L. A. (1996, January/April). Smoking cessation and gender: The influence of physiological, psychological, and behavioral factors. *Journal of the American Medical Women's Association,* vol. 51, nos. 1 and 2, 35–42.

Grube, J. (1995). Television alcohol portrayals, alcohol advertising, and alcohol expectancies among children and adolescents, in Martin, S., ed., *The effects of the mass media on the use and abuse of alcohol.* Bethesda, MD: National Institute on Alcohol Abuse and Alcoholism, Research Monograph no. 28.

Grube, J. and Wallack, L. (1994). Television beer advertising and drinking knowledge, beliefs, and intentions among schoolchildren. *American Journal of Public Health,* 84, 254–59.

Grunwald, M. (1997, December 9). Megamall sells stimulation. *Boston Globe,* A1, A26.

Gunderson, E. (1989, November 6). Guitar god comes down to earth. *USA Today,* 1D, 2D.

Haglund, M. (1998, Spring). From the president. *The Net* (International Network of Women Against Tobacco), 1, 3.

Halbfinger, D. M. (1997, July 27). Selling alcohol disguised as punch. *New York Times,* E5.

Halliday, J. (1996, December 2). Cars put new faith in relationships. *Advertising Age,* 24.

Halliday, J. (1998, September 28). Luxury SUVs steal some horsepower from rival car sales. *Advertising Age,* S12.

Hanna, B. (1999, February 12). Man acted alone in fraternity beating death, chief says. *Star-Telegram.* Obtained from the online news service of the Higher Education Center for Alcohol and Other Drug Prevention.

Haran, L. (1996, March 18). Madison Avenue visits dream land. *Advertising Age,* 12.

Harris, R. (1989, November 12). Children who dress for excess: today's youngsters have become fixated with fashion. *Los Angeles Times,* A1.

Hart, J. (1998, June 8). Northampton confronts a crime, cruelty. *Boston Globe,* A1, A12.

Hatherill, J. R. (1999, April 12). Take the gag off food safety issues. *Los Angeles Times* (online).

Hays, C. L. (1999, March 21). Math book salted with brand names raises new alarm. *New York Times,* 1.

Herbert, B. (1998, February 15). Fashion statement. *New York Times,* 13.

Herbert, B. (1999, May 2). America's littlest shooters. *New York Times,* WK 17.

Herman, E. S. and McChesney, R. W. (1997). *The global media: The new missionaries of corporate capitalism.* London: Cassell.

Herman, J. L. and Hirschman, L. (1981). Father-daughter incest. Cambridge, MA: Harvard University Press.

Hewlett, S. A. and West, C. (1998). *The war against parents.* New York: Houghton Mifflin.

Hilts, P. J. (1996). *Smokescreen: The truth behind the tobacco industry cover-up.* Reading, MA: Addison-Wesley.

Hind, J. W. (1975, January 23). Internal memorandum. R.J. Reynolds Tobacco Company.

Hirschberg, L. (1998, September 20). What's a network to do? *New York Times Magazine,* 59–62.

Hirschman, E. (1995, Summer). Letter to the editor. *Tobacco Control,* vol. 4, no. 2, 193.

Holmes, W. C. and Slap, G. B. (1998, December 2). Sexual abuse of male children common, under-recognized, under-treated. *Journal of the American Medical Association,* vol. 280, 1855–62.

Horovitz, B. (1997, May 14). Accounting for taste: Designers tally profits. *USA Today,* B1, B2.

Horton, C. (1996, January 8). Admen lament: If only we could take it back. *Advertising Age,* S28, S30, S48.

Houlahan, J. (1998, May 25). *Advertising Age,* S4.

Howe, P. J. (1999, February 10). Study finds many in U.S. experience sex problems. *Boston Globe,* A1, A18.

Hsu, L. K. (1990). *Eating disorders.* New York: Guilford Press.

Hudes, K. (1998, November 15). Independent film, but with a catch: a corporate logo. *New York Times,* 43.

Hume, S. (1986, April 7). Beer marketers dive into event sponsorship. *Advertising Age,* S6.

Husten, C. G., Chrisman, J. H., and Reddy, M. N. (1996, January/April). Trends and effects of cigarette smoking among girls and women in the United States. *Journal of the American Medical Women's Association,* vol. 51, nos. 1 and 2, 11–18.

Hyde, N. S. (1998, August 1). If the price is right. *Washington Post,* C3.

Iggers, J. (1996). *The garden of eating: food, sex, and the hunger for meaning.* New York: Basic Books.

INFACT Update (1997, Fall), 5.

Inside advertising (1992, July). *American Photo,* 37–38.

Jackson, D. Z. (1996, May 10). Sound of silence in smoking ads. *Boston Globe,* 21.

Jacobson, B. (1982). *The ladykillers: Why smoking is a feminist issue.* New York: Continuum.

Jacobson, M. (1998, November). Liquid candy. *Nutrition Action Healthletter,* 8.

Jacobson, M. F. and Mazur, L. A. (1995). *Marketing madness: A survival guide for a consumer society.* Boulder, CO: Westview Press.

Jessor, R. and Jessor, S. L. (1977). *Problem behavior and psychosocial development: A longitudinal study of youth.* New York: Academic Press.

Jhally, S. (1989). Advertising, gender and sex: What's wrong with a little objectification? In Parmentier, R. and Urban, G., eds. (1989). *Working Papers and Proceedings of the Center for Psychosocial Studies,* no. 29.

Jhally, S. (1998). Advertising and the end of the world (a video). Northampton, MA: Media Education Foundation.

Jobson's Beverage Dynamics (1994, May), 53.

Johnson, G. (1999, March 21). 'And the winner is . . . advertisers.' *Boston Globe,* C5.

Johnson, J. A. (1997, November 10). JonBenet keeps hold on magazines. *Advertising Age,* 42.

Johnson, R. (1998), Advice for the Clinton age. *New York Times Magazine,* 59–61.

Johnston, L. D., O'Malley, P. M., and Bachman, J. G. (1998). *National survey results on drug use from the monitoring the future study, 1975–97.* Rockville, MD: U.S. Department of Health and Human Services.

Jonas, J. M. (1989). Eating disorders and alcohol and other drug abuse. Is there an association? *Alcohol Health & Research World,* vol. 13, no. 3, 267–71.

Kaiser Family Foundation, the Alan Guttmacher Institute, and the National Press Foundation (1996, June 24). *Emerging issues in reproductive health (fact sheet).*

Kakutani, M. (1997, May 18). Adolescence rules! *New York Times Magazine,* 22.

Kakutani, M. (1997, June 8). Taking out the trash. *New York Times Magazine,* 30, 34.

Kakutani, M. (1997, November 9). Bananas for rent. *New York Times Magazine,* 32.

Kane's Beverage Week (1997, January 13), vol. 58, no. 2, 2.

Kauffman, M. (1998, May 15). Ads leave critics sadder but wiser. *Hartford Courant,* D1, D2.

Keller, J. (1998, August 13). The self-centered world of road rage. *Boston Globe,* A19.

Kerwin, A. M. (1997, April 28). 'KidStyle' crafts customized ad opportunities. *Advertising Age,* 46.

Kiefer, M. J. (1997, December 8). A city for people, not cars. *Boston Globe,* A13.

Kilbourne, J. (1977). Images of women in TV commercials. In Fireman, J., ed. (1977). *TV Book.* New York: Workman.

Kilbourne, J. (1986). The child as sex object: images of children in the media. In Nelson, M. and Clark, K. (1986). *The educator's guide to preventing child sexual abuse.* Santa Cruz, CA: Network Publications.

Kilbourne, J. (1994, May 15). 'Gender bender' ads: same old sexism. *New York Times,* F13.

Kindlon, D. J. and Thompson, M. (1999). *Raising Cain: protecting the emotional life of boys.* New York: Ballantine Books.

King, C., Siegel, M., Celebucki, C., and Connolly, G. N. (1998, February 18). Adolescent exposure to cigarette advertising in magazines: an evaluation of brand-specific advertising in relation to youth readership. *Journal of the American Medical Association,* vol. 279, no. 7, 516–20.

Klein, R. (1993). *Cigarettes are sublime.* Durham, NC: Duke University Press.

Kleinke, C. L., Staneski, R. A., and Mason, J. K. (1982). Sex differences in coping with depression. *Sex Roles,* vol. 8, no. 8, 877–89.

Kluger, R. (1996). *Ashes to ashes: America's hundred-year cigarette war, the public health, and the unabashed triumph of Philip Morris.* New York: Knopf.

Kluger, R. (1996, April 7). A peace plan for the cigarette wars. *New York Times Magazine,* 28–30, 35, 48, 54.

Knapp, C. (1996). *Drinking: a love story.* New York: Dial Press.

Knox, R. A. (1998, June 25). Bad gene may temper the desire to light up. *Boston Globe,* A3.

Koch, J. (1999, February 22). Rita Nakashima Brock. *Boston Globe Magazine,* 8.

Kolata, G. (1997, July 13). The fearful price of getting thin. *The New York Times,* E3.

Kolata, G. (1998, June 21). Women and sex: on this topic, science blushes. *New York Times,* 3.

Koranteng, J. (1999, April 12). Sweden presses EU for further ad restrictions. *Advertising Age International,* 2.

Krahn, D. D. (1991). Relationship of eating disorders and substance abuse. *Journal of Substance Abuse,* vol. 3, no. 2, 239–53.

Krol, C. (1998, April 20). Levi's reaches girls as they develop opinions on brands. *Advertising Age,* 29.

Kuczynski, A. (1998, July 19). Between the sexes, it's World War III. *The New York Times,* 1, 8.

Kusserow, R. (1991, June). *Youth and alcohol: a national survey. Drinking habits, access, attitudes, and knowledge.* Rockville, MD: U.S. Department of Health and Human Services.

Labi, N. (1999, April 19). Classrooms for sale. *Time,* 44.

Laing, R. D. (1960). *The divided self.* London: Tavistock Publications. Paperback version (1965). Baltimore, MD: Pelican Books.

Larkin, J., Rice, C., and Russell, V. (1996, Spring). Slipping through the cracks: sexual harassment. *Eating Disorders: The Journal of Treatment and Prevention,* vol. 4, no. 1, 5–26.

Lasch, C. (1979). *The culture of narcissism: American life in an age of diminishing expectations.* New York: W.W. Norton.

Lasn, K. (1999). *Culture jam: The uncooling of America.* New York: William Morrow.

Laumann, E. O., Paik, A., and Rosen, R. C. (1999, February 10). Sexual dysfunction in the United States. *Journal of the American Medical Association,* vol. 281, 537–44.

Lee, L. (1998, May 31). Pass the popcorn (and the khakis). *New York Times,* 2 ST.

Leiber, L. (1996). Commercial and character slogan recall by children aged 9 to 11 years. Berkeley, CA: Center on Alcohol Advertising.

Leigh, J. P., Markowitz, S. B., Fahs, M., Shin, C., and Landrigan, P. J. (1997, July 28). Occupational injury and illness in the United States: Estimates of cost, morbidity and mortality. *Archives of Internal Medicine,* vol. 157, 1557–68.

Leo, J. (1994, June 13). Selling the woman-child. *U.S. News and World Report,* 27.

Leonard, M. (1998, June 25). US suffering from bad case of civic blues, report finds. *Boston Globe,* A1, A12.

Leonhardt, D. (1997, June 30). Hey kid, buy this! *Business Week,* 61–67.

Leshner, A. I. (1998, May). NIDA probes the elusive link between child abuse and later drug abuse. *NIDA Notes,* vol. 13, no. 2, 3–4.

Levin, M. (1994, May 19). Tobacco firm paid $950,000 to place cigarettes in films. *Los Angeles Times,* 1.

Levin, M. (1999, February 14). Big tobacco threatened drug manufacturers with reprisal. *Los Angeles Times* (on-line).

Levingston, S. (1999, March 9). Tests expose SUV's flip side. *Boston Globe,* C4.

Lewis, M. (1997, February 9). Royal scam. *New York Times Magazine,* 22.

Lilenfeld, L. R. and Kaye, W. H. (1996, Spring). The link between alcoholism and eating disorders. *Alcohol Health and Research World,* vol. 20, no. 2, 94–106.

Lipman, J. (1989, October 3). An industry is urged to deal with critics. *Wall Street Journal,* B6.

Liu, E. (1999, March 25). Remember when public space didn't carry brand names? *USA Today,* 15A.

Logan, M. (1998, April 18). A big step for *Baywatch. TV Guide,* 8.

Lowry, M. (1947). *Under the volcano.* Philadelphia and New York: J.P. Lippincott.

Lynch, B. S. and Bonnie, R. J., eds. (1994). *Growing up tobacco free: Preventing nicotine addiction in children and youths.* Washington, DC: Institute of Medicine, National Academy Press.

Lyon, S. Newsbrokers (1997, Summer). *Adbusters,* 15.

Mackler, C. (1998). Memoirs of a (sorta) ex-shaver. In Edut, O., ed. (1998). *Adios, Barbie*. Seattle, WA: Seal Press, 55–61.

Maddox, K. and Jensen, J. (1998, October 5). Online marketers race for tie-ins with *You've Got Mail*. *Advertising Age*, 48.

Mandese, J. (1995, September 25). Star presenter of the year. *Advertising Age*, 1, 6.

Mangione, T. W., Howland, J., Lee, M. (1998, December). *New perspectives for worksite alcohol strategies: Results from a corporate drinking study*. Boston, MA: JSI Research and Training Institute, Inc.

Mannino, D. M., Klevens, R. M., Flanders, W. D. (1994). Cigarette smoking: An independent risk factor for impotence? *American Journal of Epidemiology*, vol. 140, 1003–8.

Martin, G.L. (1998, January). Australian magazine finds fat isn't all 'fab.' *Advertising Age International*, 4.

Martin, K. A. (1998, August). Becoming a gendered body: practices of preschools. *American Sociological Review*, vol. 63, no. 4, 494–511.

Martin, S. (1992). The epidemiology of alcohol-related interpersonal violence. *Alcohol, Health and Research World*, vol. 16, no. 3, 230–37.

Martin-Morris, D. (1998, January). Why smoking is a real drag. *Teen*, 62–64.

Masse, L. C. and Tremblay, R. E. (1997, January). Behavior of boys in kindergarten and the onset of substance abuse during adolescence. *Archives of General Psychiatry*, vol. 54, 62–68.

Massing, M. (1996, July 11). How to win the tobacco war. *New York Review of Books*, 32–36.

Masterman, L. (1990, Fall). New paradigms for media education. *Telemedium*, 1–4.

Maxwell, J. C. (1985, October 7). Wine market rides 'cool' breeze. *Advertising Age*, 45.

Mays, P. J. (1999, April 2). Smoking by youths falls in Fla. *Boston Globe*, A8.

McAneny, L. (1997, June 6). Drinking a cause of family problems for three out of ten Americans. Princeton, NJ: Gallup News Service.

McCarthy, C. (1990, November 11). In thingdom, laying waste our powers. *Washington Post*, F3.

McChesney, R. (1996). The Internet and U.S. communication policy-making in historical and critical perspective. *Journal of Communication*, vol. 46, no. 1, 98–124.

McChesney, R. and Herman, E. (1997). *The global media: The new missionaries of global capitalism*. London: Cassell.

McFarland, B. (1997, May/June). Swords into ploughshares. *Family Therapy Networker*, 36–44.

McLaren, C. (1997, Spring). The babysitter's club. *Stay Free!*, 8–11.

McNamara, E. (1999, February 17). Dartmouth plan relies on myth. *Boston Globe*, B1.

Meltz, B. (1997, January 16). "Mommy, I'm fat!" *Boston Globe*, F1.

Meltz, B. (1997, November 13). Decoding preschoolers' sexualized behavior. *Boston Globe*, F1, F4.

Meredith, R. (1999, May 16). In Detroit, a sex change. *New York Times*, WK3.

Miller, J. B. (1976). *Toward a new psychology of women*. Boston: Beacon Press.

Miller, J. B. and Stiver, I. P. (1997). *The healing connection: how women form relationships in therapy and in life*. Boston: Beacon Press.

Miller, M. C. (1994, March/April). Selling "power" to the powerless. *Extra!*, 22–23.

Mintz, M. (1991, May). Tobacco roads: delivering death to the third world. *The Progressive*, 24–29.

Mohl, B. (1999, January 13). Lend them your ear, and your call is free. *Boston Globe*, A1, A10.

Monday Morning Report (1999, January 25), vol. 23, no. 2, 1–4.

Monet show sets world record (1999, February 2). *Boston Globe*, E2.

Moog, C. (1991, Spring/Summer). The selling of addiction to women. *Media and Values*, 20–22.

Mosher, J. F. (1997). The emergence of an alcohol policy reform agenda in the United States: a Don Cahalan legacy. *Drugs and Society*, vol. 11, 74–91. New York: Haworth Press.

Nathanson-Moog, C. (1984, July 26). Brand personalities undergo psychoanalysis. *Advertising Age*, 18.

National Center on Addiction and Substance Abuse (1996, June). *Substance abuse and the American woman*. New York: Columbia University Press.

National Center on Addiction and Substance Abuse (1998, January). *Behind bars: substance abuse and America's prison population.* New York: Columbia University.

National Household Survey on Drug Abuse (1997). Rockville, MD.: National Institute on Drug Abuse. Reported in *NIDA Notes* (1997, September/October), 14.

National Institute on Drug Abuse (1991). *National household survey on drug abuse: main findings 1990.* DHHS Pub. No. (ADM) 91 1788. Washington, DC: Superintendent of Documents, U.S. Government Printing Office.

National Institute on Drug Abuse (1997). *Monitoring the future study, secondary school students.* Rockville, MD: U. S. Department of Health and Human Services.

National study reveals kids' favorite TV ads (1998, March 24). Yahoo PR Newswire. Online.

Neighborhood convenience stores push lemon drops, butter balls and 30–proof oatmeal cookies (1996, Spring). *The bottom line on alcohol in society,* vol. 17, no. 1, 5–15.

Nelson, J. (1997, July/August). Accepting rage. *Ms.,* 92–95.

Nelson, J. (1997). *Straight, no chaser: How I became a grown-up black woman.* New York: G.P. Putnam Sons.

Nichter, M. Nichter, M., Vuckovic, N., Quintero, G., and Ritenbaugh, C. (1997). Smoking experimentation and initiation among adolescent girls: qualitative and quantitative findings. *Tobacco Control,* vol. 6, 285–95.

Nicklin, J. L. (1999, May 28). Colleges report increases in arrests for drug and alcohol violations. *Chronicle of Higher Education,* 39.

Nike (1997). *30 years of Effie.* New York: American Marketing Association.

Ninth special report to the U.S. Congress on alcohol and health from the Secretary of Health and Human Services (1997, June). Rockville, MD: U.S. Department of Health and Human Services.

Not for Sale! (1997, Spring). Oakland, CA: Center for Commercial-Free Public Education.

Not for sale! (1999, Winter). Oakland, CA: Center for Commercial-Free Public Education.

Novello, A. (1991, October 18). Quoted by Associated Press, AMA to fight wife- beating. *St. Louis Post Dispatch,* 1, 15.

Nyhan, D. (1997, April 16). A capitalist's critique. *Boston Globe,* A15.

Nyhan, D. (1999, April 21). Angry, bored, confused? This book's for you. *Boston Globe,* A23.

O'Connell, D. L., Alexander, H. M. Dobson, A. J., Lloyd, D. M., Hardes, G. R., and Springthorpe, H. J. (1990). Cigarette smoking and drug use in schoolchildren. *International Journal of Epidemiology,* vol. 10, 223–31.

O'Donnell, M. (1995, January 22). From the notebooks of a genius. *New York Times Magazine,* 64.

Orlando, S. (1999, May 19). A material world: Defining ourselves by consumer goods. http://www.sciencedaily.com/releases/1999/05/990518114815.htm.

"Our relationship with 8.1 million teenagers . . ." (1998, June 29). *Advertising Age,* S27.

Overlan, L. (1996, July 2). 'Overweight' girls at risk. *NewtonTab,* 15.

Palmer, L. D. (1999, February 2). Administration unveils new antidrug effort. *Boston Globe,* A9.

Palmer, M. (1998, March 2). Joe Camel goes to Europe. *Washington Post,* A25.

Pareles, J. (1998, February 8). Edging off rock's high road. *New York Times,* D1, D30.

Paris, B. J. (1994). *Karen Horney: A psychoanalyst's search for self-understanding.* New Haven: Yale University Press.

Parker, F. B. (1972). Sex-role adjustment in women alcoholics. *Quarterly Journal of Studies on Alcoholism,* 33, 647–57.

Parking lot pique (1997, May 16). *Boston Globe,* A18.

Peppers, D. and Rogers, M. (1997, June 2). Marketer-customer dialogue comes to fore. *Advertising Age,* 32.

Pérez-Peña, R. (1999, May 30). State efforts to cut smoking leave New York far behind. *New York Times,* 23.

Perkins, H. W. (1992, September). Gender patterns in consequences of collegiate alcohol abuse: A 10-year study of trends in an undergraduate population. *Journal of Studies on Alcohol,* 458–62.

Perkins, H. W., and Berkowitz, A. D. (1986). Perceiving the community norms of alcohol use among students: Some research implications for campus alcohol education programming. *International Journal of the Addictions,* vol. 21, nos. 9 and 10, 961–76.

Petrecca, L. and Arndorfer, J. B. (1998, March 2). Insurer places gay-themed ads in mainstream media. *Advertising Age,* 12.

Philip Morris steps up international influence (1997, Fall). *INFACT Update,* 5.

Phillips, F. (1998, April 9). Steep drop found in Mass. adult smoking; tax is cited. *Boston Globe,* A32.

Pierce, J. P., Choi, W. S., Gilpin, E. A., Farkas, A. J., and Berry, C. C. (1998, February 18). Tobacco industry promotion of cigarettes and adolescent smoking. *Journal of the American Medical Association,* vol. 279, no. 7, 511–15.

Pierce, J. P., Lee, L., and Gilpin, E. A. (1994). Smoking initiation by adolescent girls, 1944 through 1988: An association with targeted advertising. *Journal of the American Medical Association,* vol. 271, 608–11.

Pipher, M. (1994). *Reviving Ophelia: saving the selves of adolescent girls.* New York: G.P. Putnam's Sons.

Pollack, A. (1997, August 17). Overseas, smoking is one of life's small pleasures. *New York Times,* E1, E5.

Pollack, J. (1998, April 13). Kraft takes target-marketing to ground zero via TCI test. *Advertising Age,* S2.

Pollack, J. (1998, July 13). Nabisco doubles ad $ for SnackWell's push. *Advertising Age,* 6.

Pollack, W. (1998). *Real boys: Rescuing our sons from the myths of boyhood.* New York: Random House.

Pollay, R. W. (1986, April). The distorted mirror: reflections on the unintended consequences of advertising. *Journal of Marketing,* vol. 50, 18–36.

Pollay, R. W. (1995, Summer). *Tobacco Control,* vol. 4, no. 2, 188–92.

Pollock, L. (1998, April). *Lusty women.* Paper presented at a symposium at the spring meeting of the Division of Psychoanalysis, Boston, MA.

Popcorn, F. and Hanft, A. (1997, November 10). Relationships key in reaching women. *Advertising Age,* 26.

Presley, C.A., Leichliter, J. S., and Meilman, P.W. (1998). *Alcohol and drugs on American college campuses.* Carbondale, IL: Core Institute.

Pruzan, T. (1996, April 8). Brewing new ties with gay consumers. *Advertising Age,* 13.

Pruzan, T. and Ross, C. (1996, July 8). As liquor ads head toward TV, fear and beer stand in way. *Advertising Age,* 26.

Quindlen, A. (1992, June 28). All of these you are. *New York Times,* E17.

Ragels, L.A. (1996, Summer). Prohibition, alcoholics anonymous, the alcoholism movement, and the alcohol beverage industry. *The bottom line on alcohol in society,* vol. 7, no. 2, 47–53.

Rank, H. (1992, April). Channel One: Misconceptions three. *English Journal,* vol. 81, no. 4, 31–32.

Reading, writing . . . and TV commercials (1999, Spring). *Enough!,* no. 7, 10.

Real, T. (1997). *I don't want to talk about it: Overcoming the secret legacy of male depression.* New York: Scribner.

Reed, B. G. (1991). Linkages: battering, sexual assault, incest, child sexual abuse, teen pregnancy, dropping out of school and the alcohol and drug connection. In Roth, P., ed. *Alcohol and drugs are women's issues.* Metuchen, NJ: Scarecrow Press, 130–49.

Reich, R. B. (1997, July 6). For richer, for poorer. *New York Times Book Review,* 11.

Reidy, C. (1996, June 16). Taking 'mass' out of marketing. *Boston Globe,* 47.

Reidy, C. (1997, September 28). 'This is a car ad?' What else are they selling? *Boston Globe,* D1, D7.

Reidy, C. (1999, January 28). Super Bowl ad campaign goes down to wire. *Boston Globe,* D1, D5.

Reidy, C. (1999, January 30). A super bowl berth. *Boston Globe,* E1, E2.

Rich, F. (1997, June 8). howdydoody.com. *New York Times,* E15.

Richins, M. L. (1991). Social comparison and idealized images of advertising. *Journal of Consumer Research,* 18, 71–83.

Roan, S. (1993, June 8). Painting a bleak picture for teen girls. *Los Angeles Times,* 28.

Rodriguez, C. (1998, November 27). Even in middle school, girls are thinking thin. *Boston Globe,* B1, B9.

Rosenbaum, R. (1995, January 15). The great Ivy League nude posture photo scandal. *New York Times Magazine,* 26, 46, 55–56.

Rosenberg, A. S. (1999, February 1). Ad ideas etched in sand. *Boston Globe,* A3.

Ross, C. (1997, February 3). Jordan brings the heart of a marketer to CBS-TV. *Advertising Age,* 1, 14.

Ross, C. and Teinowitz, I. (1997, January 6). Beer ads had wide underage reach on MTV. *Advertising Age,* 4, 32.

Rothblum, E. D. (1994). "I'll die for the revolution but don't ask me not to diet": feminism and the continuing stigmatization of obesity. In Fallon, P., Katzman, M. A., and Wooley, S. C. (1994). *Feminist perspectives on eating disorders.* New York: The Guilford Press, 53–76.

Rotterdam, S. (1986, January 30). Letter to editor. *Advertising Age,* 21.

Rowe, J. (1996, Winter). Down among the economists. *Adbusters,* 28.

Royce, J. E. (1981). *Alcohol problems and alcoholism.* New York: The Free Press, 105.

Russell, S. A. and Wilsnack, S. C. Adult survivors of childhood sexual abuse. In Roth, P., ed. (1991). *Alcohol and drugs are women's issues.* Metuchen, NJ: Scarecrow Press, 61–70.

Ryan, F. J. (1974, June 10). Relationship between smoking and personality. *Smoker Psychology Monthly Report,* Philip Morris Company. Reported in *Action Alert,* (1998, April 15). Advocacy Institute.

Ryan, S. (1996, December 18). They're not afraid to be labeled. *Boston Globe,* D1, D5.

Ryan, S. (1998, December 8). Meet Calvin Klein's imaginary friends. *Boston Globe,* D1, D8.

Ryan, S. C. (1999, May 26). Fusion is the fashion. *Boston Globe,* F1, F6.

Ryan, S. C. (1999, February 3). Victoria's Secret success at Super Bowl has ad world abuzz. *Boston Globe,* D1, D7.

Sadker, M. and Sadker, D. (1994). *Failing at fairness: how our schools cheat girls.* New York: Simon & Schuster.

Saffer, H. (1996). Studying the effects of alcohol advertising on consumption. *Alcohol Health and Research World,* vol. 20, no. 4, 266–72.

Sandmaier, M. (1980). *The invisible alcoholics: Women and alcohol abuse in America.* New York: McGraw-Hill.

Sandmaier, M. (1997, September/October). Love for the long haul. *Family Therapy Networker,* 23–35.

Savan, L. (1994). *The sponsored life: ads, TV, and American culture.* Philadelphia: Temple University Press.

Schamus, J. (1999, April 5/12). The pursuit of Happiness. *The Nation,* 34–35.

Schneider, K. S. (1996, June 3). Mission impossible. *People,* 65–74.

Schoolgirls as sex toys. *New York Times* (1997, April 16), 2E.

Schultz, R. (1995, Autumn). When men look at women: Sex in an age of theory. *The Hudson Review,* 365–87.

Seid, R. P. (1994). Too "close to the bone": the historical context for women's obsession with slenderness. In Fallon, P., Katzman, M. A., and Wooley, S. C. (1994). *Feminist perspectives on eating disorders.* New York: The Guilford Press, 3–16.

Seiter, E. (1993). Different children, different dreams: racial representation in advertising. *Sold Separately: Aspects of Children's Consumer Culture.* Winchester, MA and London: Unwin Hyman.

Seventh special report to the U.S. Congress on alcohol and health (1990, January). Rockville, MD: U.S. Department of Health and Human Services.

Sharkey, J. (1997, September 28). You're not bad, you're sick. It's in the book. *The New York Times,* 1.

Sharkey, J. (1998, July 5). Beach-blanket babel: Another reason to stay at the pool. *New York Times,* 2.

Sherman, M. (1985). We can share the women, we can share the wine: The regulation of alcohol advertising on television. *Southern California Law Review,* vol. 58, 1107–22.

Shin, A. (1999, April/May). Testing Title IX. *Ms.,* 32.

Skull tapping (1998, November 29). *New York Times Magazine,* 33.

Slater, M. (1996). Male adolescents' reactions to TV beer advertisements: the effects of sports content and programming context. *Journal of Studies on Alcohol,* 57, 425–33.

Sloan, P. (1996, July 8). Underwear ads caught in bind over sex appeal. *Advertising Age,* 27.

Smith, K. A., Fairburn, C. G., and Cowen, P. J. (1999). Symptomatic relapse in bulimia nervosa following acute tryptophan depletion. *Journal of the American Medical Association,* vol. 56, 171–76.

Snell, T. L. (1991). *Women in prison.* Washington, DC: U.S. Department of Justice.

Snitow, A. (1985). Retrenchment versus transformation: The politics of the antipornography movement. In Burstyn, V., ed., *Women against censorship.* Vancouver: Douglas and Mcintrye, 116.

Snook, L. A. (1997, February). Autoeroticism: when his car excites him more than you do. *Cosmopolitan,* 228–30.

Soley, L. (1999, March/April). Corporate censorship and the limits of free speech. *Extra!,* 19–21.

Stark, S. (1990, July 23). Cops are tops cowboys out. *Boston Globe,* 15.

Stein, J. (1986, October 29). Why girls as young as 9 fear fat and go on diets to lose weight. *Los Angeles Times,* 1,10.

Stein, N. (1993). No laughing matter: Sexual harassment in K-12 schools. In Buchwald, E., Fletcher, P. R., and Roth, M. (1993). *Transforming a rape culture.* Minneapolis, MN: Milkweed Editions, 311–31.

Steinem, G. (1990, July/August). Sex, lies and advertising. *Ms.,* 18–28.

Steiner-Adair, C. (1986). The body politic: normal female adolescent development and the development of eating disorders. *Journal of the American Academy of Psychoanalysis,* vol. 14, no. 1, 95–114.

Steiner-Adair, C. (1994). The politics of prevention. In Fallon, P., Katzman, M. A., and Wooley, S. C., eds. (1994). *Feminist perspectives on eating disorders.* New York: Guilford Press, 381–94.

Steiner-Adair, C. (1996). Remarks at the 1996 Leadership Dinner of the Harvard Eating Disorders Center, October 29, 1996.

Steiner-Adair, C. and Purcell, A. (1996, Winter). Approaches to mainstreaming eating disorders prevention. *Eating Disorders,* vol. 4, no. 4, 294–309.

Strasburger, V. C. (1989, June). Adolescent sexuality and the media. *Pediatric Clinics of North America,* vol. 36, no. 3, 747–73.

Sullum, J. (1997, May 23). Victims of everything. *New York Times,* A31.

Supermarket News (1997, January 13), vol. 47, no. 2, 14.

Surrey, J. L. (1984). Eating patterns as a reflection of women's development. Wellesley, MA: Stone Center for Developmental Services and Studies.

Survey finds serious stress on campus (1997, January 13). *Boston Globe,* A5. Report on a survey by the UCLA Higher Education Research Institute.

Sutter, M. (1999, January 25). Marketers boost Pope's visit to Mexico with tie-ins. *Advertising Age,* 14.

Swan, N. (1998, May). Exploring the role of child abuse in later drug abuse. *NIDA Notes,* vol. 13, no. 2, 1, 4–6.

Tagliabue, J. (1997, September 28). Europe offering free calls, but first a word from . . . *New York Times,* 1, 8.

The 10 most serious health problems threatening blacks (1991, November). *Ebony,* 120–24.

Then, D. (1992, August). Women's magazines: Messages they convey about looks, men and careers. Paper presented at the annual convention of the American Psychological Association, Washington, DC.

Thompson, B. W. (1994). *A hunger so wide and so deep.* Minneapolis: University of Minnesota Press.

Tierney, J. (1996, November 24). Virgin territory. *New York Times Magazine,* 50.

Tjaden, R. and Thoennes, N. (1998, November). *Prevalence, incidence, and consequences of violence against women: Findings from the National Violence Against Women Survey.* Washington, DC: U.S. Department of Justice.

Todt, R. (1998, October 23). Suit says menthol cigarettes violate civil rights of blacks. *Boston Globe,* A16.

Top 10 cigarette brands (1997, September 29). *Advertising Age,* S20.

Tracy, B. (1997, September 22). Survey says women want Web sites that build relationships. *Advertising Age,* 32.

Treatment of drug offenders saves money (1999, April 22). Arizona Supreme Court Report, reported in Join Together Online (www.jointogether.org).

Trends in prevalence and patterns of substance use (1997). *Substance use among women in the United States.* Rockville, MD: U.S. Department of Health and Human Services, chapter 2, 2.

Trout, J. (1996, April 22). Ad for Trout and Partners Ltd. *Advertising Age,* 7.

Twitchell, J. B. (1996). *Adcult USA: The triumph of advertising in American culture.* New York: Columbia University Press.

Two men and a baby (1990, July/August). *Ms.* 10.

Tye, J. B., Warner, K. E., and Glantz, S. A. (1987). Tobacco advertising and consumption: evidence of a causal relationship. *Journal of Public Health Policy,* vol. 8, 492–508.

Tye, L. (1997, January 5). For some, it's an Absolut mania. *Boston Globe,* 1, 13.

U.S. Department of Health and Human Services (1994, March 11). *Preventing tobacco use among young people: A report of the Surgeon General, Executive Summary.* Atlanta, GA: Centers for Disease Control and Prevention.

U.S. Department of Health and Human Services (1994, March 11). *Preventing tobacco use among young people: A report of the Surgeon General.* Atlanta, GA: Centers for Disease Control and Prevention.

U.S. Department of Health and Human Services (1995, July 21). Trends in smoking initiation among adolescents and young adults—United States, 1980–1989 (1995, July 21). *Morbidity and Mortality Weekly Report.* Atlanta, GA: Centers for Disease Control and Prevention.

U.S. Department of Transportation (1999). National Highway Traffic Safety Administration (http://www.nhtsa.dot.gov/people/ncsa/FactPreve/alc96.html).

Update: Binge drinking (1998, Fall). *Drug Abuse Update,* 10–12.

Varley, H. (1919, August 14) Dealing in futures: Insuring sales for the years to come by paying the premium of advertising today. *Printer's Ink.* Reprinted in *Stay Free!* (1997, Spring), 23.

Vigue, D. I. and Abraham, Y. (1999, February 7). Harassment a daily course for students. *Boston Globe,* B1, B6.

Vobejda, B. and Perlstein, L. (1998, June 17). Girls closing gap with boys, but not always for the best. *Boston Globe,* A3.

Wallace, D. F. (1996). *Infinite jest.* Boston: Little Brown.

Warburton, D. M. (1988). The puzzle of nicotine use. *The psychopharmacology of addiction* (edited by Malcolm Lader). New York: Oxford University Press, 27–49.

Weber, J. (1997, May 18). Selling to kids: At what price? *Boston Globe,* F4.

Webster, D. (1998, September 21). Will we choke the Web with ad clutter? *Advertising Age,* 26.

Weil, L. (1999, March). Leaps of faith. *Women's Review of Books,* 21.

Welch, C. (1999, February 15). We can do better for abused children. *Boston Globe,* A17.

Wells, M. (1999, March 2). New ways to get into our heads. *USA Today,* B1, B2.

Wentz, L. (1998, May 11). Global village. *Advertising Age International,* 12.

What do they have in common? (1994, Summer). *Tobacco-Free Youth Reporter,* 3–4.

White, D. (1998, June 8). Can marriage survive the wedding? *Boston Globe,* C7.

Wiencke, J., Thurston, S., Kelsey, K., Varkonyi, A., Wain, J., Mark, E., and Christiani, D. (1999, April 7). Early age at smoking initiation and tobacco carcinogen DNA damage in the lung. *Journal of the National Cancer Institute,* vol. 91, no. 7, 614–19.

Wilke, M. (1996, March 4). Subaru adds lesbians to niche marketing drive. *Advertising Age*, 8.

Wilke, M. (1997, August 4). Big advertisers join move to embrace gay market. *Advertising Age*, 1, 10–11.

Wilke, M. (1998, June 22). Ads targeting gays rely on real results, not intuition. *Advertising Age*, 3, 28.

Wilke, M. (1998, June 22). Burgeoning gay web sites spark advertiser interest. *Advertising Age*, 30.

Wilkins, B. (1997, June 2). Moving from blight to blessing. *Advertising Age*, 32.

Williamson, D. A. (1997, May 19). Wanted: info on you and your interests. *Advertising Age*, 60.

Williamson, J. (1986). *Consuming passions: The dynamics of popular culture*. London: Marion Boyars.

Wilsnack, R.W. and Wilsnack, S. C. (1997). *Gender and alcohol: individual and social perspectives*. New Brunswick, NJ: Rutgers Center of Alcohol Studies.

Wilsnack, R. W., Wilsnack, S. C., and Kristjanson, A. F. (1998, Fall). *Ten-year prediction of women's drinking behavior in a nationally representative sample*. Women's Health: Research on Gender, Behavior, and Policy, vol. 4, no. 3, 199–230.

Wilsnack, S. C. and Beckman, L. J. (1984). *Alcohol problems in women*. New York: Guilford Press.

Wilsnack, S. C., Plaud, J. J., Wilsnack, R. W., and Klassen, A. D. (1997). Sexuality, gender, and alcohol use. In Wilsnack, R. W. and Wilsnack, S. C., eds. *Gender and alcohol: Individual and social perspectives*. New Brunswick, N.J.: Rutgers Center of Alcohol Studies, 262.

Wilsnack, S. C., Vogeltanz, N. D., Klassen, A. D., and Harris, T. R. (1997, May). Childhood sexual abuse and women's substance abuse: national survey findings. *Journal of Studies on Alcohol*, vol. 58, no. 3, 264–71.

Winfrey, O. and Greene, B. (1996). *Make the connection: ten steps to a better body and a better life*. New York: Hyperion.

Winski, J. M. (1992, June 15). The ad industry's dirty little secret. *Advertising Age*, 18.

Winters, P. (1987, May 4). Wailin' Willis sets Seagram cooler image. *Advertising Age*, 110.

Wire and Times Staff Reports (1997, May 20). Orange County skate firm's 'destroy all girls' tags won't wash. *Los Angeles Times*, D1.

Women, girls and tobacco: An appeal for global action (1998, Summer). *The Net (International Network of Women Against Tobacco)*, 7–8.

Woodman, M. (1990). *The ravaged bridegroom: masculinity in women*. Toronto: Inner City Books.

Woods, G. B. (1995). *Advertising and marketing to the new majority*. Belmont, CA: Wadsworth.

Wooley, S. C. (1994). Sexual abuse and eating disorders: The concealed debate. In Fallon, P., Katzman, M. A., and Wooley, S. C., eds. (1994). *Feminist perspectives on eating disorders*. New York: Guilford Press, 171–211.

World Health Organization (1997). World No-Tobacco Day Advisory Kit.

World Health Organization (1999). *Making a difference: World health report 1999*. In Nebehay, S. (1999, May 12). UN agency up malaria, tobacco campaigns. Reuters. From Join Together Online (1999, May 15), www.jointogether.org.

World Tobacco File (1994). International Trade Publications Ltd., United Kingdom. Quoted in Advocacy Institute (1998, April 24). Issue: eleventh annual world no-tobacco day, May 31, 1998. *Action Alert*.

Worthington, R. (1992, January 19). 'Cultural psychosis' defense in teen fashion killing. *Chicago Tribune*, 15.

Wren, C. S. (1999, May 31). Bid for alcohol in antidrug ads hits resistance. New York Times, 1.

Wright, R. (1995, September 10). Brutality defines the lives of women around the world. Boston Globe, A2.

Wylie, M. S. (1997, May/June). Our trip to bountiful. *Family Therapy Networker*, 29.

Zernike, K. (1997, February 2). Let's make a deal: Businesses seek classroom access. *Boston Globe*, A1, B6.

Zimmerman, R. (1997). *Social marketing strategies for campus prevention of alcohol and other drug problems*. Washington, DC: U.S. Department of Education.

ACKNOWLEDGMENTS

This book would never have made it from my mind to the page without the vision, emotional support, and incandescent energy of Susan Heath and my agent Jill Kneerim, both of whom have become treasured friends in the process. I am very grateful to my brilliant editor Elizabeth Maguire for her expertise and encouragement, to her indefatigable assistant Chad Conway, and to all my new friends and colleagues at The Free Press. The entire process of doing this book with them has been a joy. I also thank Theresa Burns for her excitement about the book when it was in its early stages, and Marian Sandmaier for her crucial help at two different points in the process.

I am lucky to be affiliated with some wonderful organizations. I thank my friends and colleagues at the Stone Center for Developmental Services and Studies at Wellesley College (especially Jean Baker Miller, Judy Jordan, Irene Stiver, Janet Surrey, and Nancy Gleason), at the Marin Institute for the Prevention of Alcohol and Other Drug Problems (especially Jim Mosher, Eris Weaver, and Robin Wechsler), at Lordly & Dame (especially David LaCamera and Kevin MacRae), and at the Media Education Foundation (especially Tom Gardner and Sut Jhally). I also thank all those I've had the pleasure to work with at the American Academy of Pediatrics, Cambridge Documentary Films, the Center for Media Literacy (especially Elizabeth Thoman), the Center for Science in the Public Interest (especially George Hacker and Michael Jacobson), the National Council on Alcoholism and Drug Dependence (especially Leah Brock, Jeffrey Hon, and Sarah Kayson and, in the past, Susan Galbraith, Christine Lubinski, Paula Roth, and the members of the board), Eating Disorders Awareness and Prevention (especially Jennifer Biely and Michael Levine), the Harvard Eating Disorders Center (especially Anne Becker and Catherine Steiner-Adair), and the Prevention Research Institute (especially Ray Daugherty and Terry O'Bryan).

I am grateful to other friends and colleagues in many different fields for their inspiration, ideas, and encouragement through the years. Some of them probably had no idea they were making a difference in my life and work. A partial list includes Leslie Acoca, Marty Baker, Alan Blum, Jane Delano Brown, Blake Cady, Helen Caldicott, Peggy Charren, Greg Connolly, Stephanie Covington, Bill DeJong, Bob Denniston, Gail Dines, Chris and Greg Dodds, Susan Douglas, Norma Finkelstein, Julie Fiore, David Freudberg, China Galland, George Gerbner, Viveca Greene, Barbara Haber, Jackson Katz, Bob Kubey, Ernie Kurtz, Laurie Leiber, Deborah McLellan, Yonna McShane, Kevin Moore, Rick Pollay, Max Schneider, Connie Seidner, Bob and Linda Shear, Joyce Shui, John Slade, Abigail Stewart, Vic Strasburger, Pat Taylor, Larry Wallack, Ike Williams, and Sharon Wilsnack. My apologies to the many others who have influenced me but who are not listed.

I first explored my interest in advertising images with my students at Norwell High School and Emerson College. Their enthusiastic response was of great importance. I am delighted still to be in touch with so many of them. From the very beginning, I have been encouraged and heartened by my audiences. They helped me overcome my fear of public speaking and spurred me on when I was discouraged. So many people, young and old, have written and sent ads and offered their good wishes. This has meant the world to me.

I am grateful to Marty Connor, whose computer expertise and cheerful support were invaluable, and to my research assistants, especially Nina Huntemann, Dana Everson, and Elizabeth Ablah. Harold Briceno at Copycop and Paul Smith at Newtonville Camera were also very helpful. I want to express my appreciation to all those people who keep my life in order and on track in so many ways, especially Margaret Asailian, Karen Berkley, Glenn Bornstein, Carole DaSilva, Alan Hoffman, Joan Hunt, Van Maksabedian (better known as Max), Siegrid Pedack, Sharon Rich, A. J. Sullivan, Tom Watkins, and Kenneth Wildes.

I am blessed with wonderful friends who encouraged me from the beginning to undertake this project, no matter how terrifying, and who helped me along the way, as well as other friends whom I don't see so often but who were important in my past and thus influence my present: Ben Adams, Susan Arnold, Bonnie Bonbright, Liane Brandon, Dorothy Cahill, Duncan Campbell, Bettie Cartwright and Colin Kennedy, Mary Anne Chew, Della Cyrus, Carmen Dean, Jane and Norma DeNoble, Monika Dorman, Marilee Eaves, Rebecca Faery, Janet

Ferguson, Patricia Blute Fesçi, Judith Emerson Guérard, Julie Hobbs, Janet and Bud Hodgson-White, Connie Lorman Holmes and David Holmes, Mopsy and Duncan Kennedy, Rocco Landesman, Garfield Mahood, Bill and Lucky Marmon, Ann Sonz Matranga, Chuck McVinney and Linda Pollock, Linda Bertocci Nayar, Anne Pitkin, Chris and Carolyn Poll, Ann Cox Porter, Robert Porter, Nancy Roediger, Mary Lou Shields and Ed Fitzgerald, Susan Abell Sinta, Carole Beebe Tarantelli, Yvonne and Peter Waegemann, Dianne Wilson, Linda Wolf, and all those many friends who have shared their experience, strength, and hope over the years.

I very much appreciate the women and girls in our mother-daughter group: Cynthia and Blair Hurley, Joy and Eva Chertow, and Tory and Deborah Cohen. And I am grateful to my wonderful neighbors, Jeanne and Dennis Garro and Brigitte and Terje Korsnes, for being such good friends, ever willing to help (from feeding our dog to occasionally feeding Claudia and me!).

I thank my brothers Rick, Don, and Jim for helping me to understand men a little better than I might have otherwise and for loving me in spite of all our differences. I also love their wives and partner, Kathy, Wanda, and T.J. Wong, and their daughters, Laura, Wendy, Julia, Amy, and April. My stepmother Gil Kilbourne has given all of us love, support, and delicious chocolate cake for many years. I also thank my more extended family, especially my aunt Peggy Brazier, my cousins Doug Brazier and Nancy Michael, and my goddaughter Stephanie Guérard. I am grateful to Thomas Lux for being a loving father to our daughter and to Norman and Elinor Lux for being the world's greatest grandparents.

I don't know how I could have survived the past decade without the help of Tisha Gomes, who entered my life as a nanny for my baby and who has become a dear friend and an important part of our family. And I thank my beloved Claudia for being so patient and willing to put things off until AB (After Book) and for bringing such incredible joy into my life.

In 1968, the same year I saw the ad that changed my life, I met a man who saved my life. His name was Paul L. Russell. He was a brilliant psychiatrist but, more important, he was extraordinarily loving and compassionate, a true healer. Before he died in 1996, I promised him that I would write this book, no matter what, and that, in a very deep sense, it would be for him.

INDEX

Aberlich, Mike, 49-50

Absolut vodka, 47-48, 71-72, 161, 169, 214-15, 221, 227, 241-44, 247-49, 304

Academy Awards ceremony, 34

Acura automobiles, 97

Adbusters magazine, 69, 72, 304

Addiction, 25, 26, 29, 30, 130, 216, 217-33; to alcohol, 119, 156, 179, 191, 219-21, 226-28, 230-33; to consumption, 44; denial and, 228; and diminished capacity for joy, 227; disconnection and, 251-69; to food, 108, 118-19; to nicotine, *see* Cigarettes; normalization of, 230-33; in public health systems approach, 303; recovery from, 313; as relationship, 234-50; treatment of, 293-94; violence and, 288-90

Ad-Free Zones, 304

Adidas, 58

Adolescents, *see* Teenagers

Advertising Age, 34, 36, 37, 39, 40, 43, 48, 54, 55, 58, 59, 62, 67, 70, 72, 96, 120, 160, 162, 183-85, 205, 278, 283

Advertising Age International, 51

Affluent, ads targeting, 36-37

African-Americans, 37, 38, 40, 216, 281, 295, 296; alcohol and, 48, 164-65, 173, 242, 246, 301; children, 142; drug use by, 294; smoking and, 29, 181, 184, 187, 191, 198, 200-202, 301; young women, 130, 140, 144, 150, 152

AIDS, 232, 239, 249, 298

Air France, 59

Aiwa, 60

Akvavit, 172

Alcohol, 20, 24, 26, 29, 30, 73, 135, 155-79, 218; addiction to, 119, 156, 179, 191, 219-21, 226

28, 230-33; college students and, 165-67, 229; disconnection and, 253, 254; freedom linked with, 214-15; gays and, 39; image advertising of, 71-72; minorities and, 164-65; peer pressure and, 40; public health systems approach to, 298-302; rebelliousness and, 168-72, 177-78; relationships and, 86, 235-42; sex and, 242-50; sexual assault and, 274-75; teenagers and, 129, 130, 148, 149, 151, 155-65; women and, 47-48, 166-68, 170-79; *see also* Beer; Liquor; *specific brands*

Alcohol Research Group, 156

Alcoholics Anonymous, 313

Alka-Seltzer, 295

Allen, Woody, 60

Allison, Dorothy, 191

Allure magazine, 55, 161

Alvarez, Everett, 213-14

Amarige perfume, 264

America Online (AOL), 63

American Academy of Pediatrics, 158; Media Matters course of, 304

American Airlines, 61

American Association of University Women, 286

American Automobile Association, 105

American Broadcasting Company (ABC), 35, 61

American Cancer Society, 185

American Express, 39, 60

American Medical Association, 119, 189

American Public Health Association, 158

American Society of Magazine Editors, 50

American Tobacco Company, 187

355